Futurity

**Futurity: Contemporary Literature and
the Quest for the Past**

Amir Eshel

The University of Chicago Press :: Chicago and London

Amir Eshel is the Edward Clark Crossett Professor of Humanistic Studies and director of the Europe Center at the Freeman Spogli Institute for International Studies at Stanford University.

The University of Chicago Press, Chicago 60637
The University of Chicago Press, Ltd., London
© 2013 by The University of Chicago
All rights reserved. Published 2013.
Printed in the United States of America

22 21 20 19 18 17 16 15 14 13   1 2 3 4 5

ISBN-13: 978-0-226-92495-3 (cloth)
ISBN-13: 978-0-226-92496-0 (e-book)
ISBN-10: 0-226-92495-5 (cloth)
ISBN-10: 0-226-92496-3 (e-book)

The University of Chicago Press gratefully acknowledges the generous support of Stanford University toward the publication of this book.

Library of Congress Cataloging-in-Publication Data

Eshel, Amir.
    Futurity : contemporary literature and the quest for the past / Amir Eshel.
        pages. cm.
    Includes bibliographical references and index.
    ISBN-13: 978-0-226-92495-3 (cloth : alk. paper)
    ISBN-10: 0-226-92495-5 (cloth : alk. paper)
    ISBN-13: 978-0-226-92496-0 (e-book)
    ISBN-10: 0-226-92496-3 (e-book)   1. History in literature. 2. German literature—20th century—History and criticism. 3. Hebrew literature—20th century—History and criticism.   I. Title.
    PN50.E84 2013
    809'.93358—dc23   2012019390

Contents

Part Three | Futurity and Action

Acknowledgments

In a meditation on conversation, the poet and anthropologist Zali Gurevitch notes:

> A conversation is limited and endless. Limited since it has its structure, pulse, and core. Endless because it is in constant motion, an inexorable movement from one utterance to the next, from one speaker to the other. It is true that conversations in the family or among friends tend to fixate along predictable structures. One can have the same conversation for decades, without diverting from a set course. In some cases, we may not speak with someone for decades, yet when we finally do, we return to the exact pattern where the conversation left off. Yet even when caught in a firm track, the conversation remains open. It has an edge. All is foreseen, and freedom of choice is granted.[1]

This book originated as an internal conversation: for decades I asked myself, why does the past matter? What is it about some of modernity's most devastating events—the world wars, genocide, and mass expulsion—that draws infinite attention from individuals and nations alike? I wanted to know why these events capture the imagination of historians, thinkers, writers, and artists, even decades after they occurred. When I engaged with colleagues, friends, and family members on these questions, they made my own far more precise and interesting. My inquiry became a collaborative pursuit. This book presents the preliminary responses to this combined effort, yet it remains open—as meaningful conversations ought to—so that it may generate new studies, new conversations.

For the privilege of conversation, I would like to thank those who have given me their time, attention, wisdom, and friendship. Among the many conversations I had while thinking about this book, two early ones were of crucial significance. A discussion with Richard Rorty on the value of retrospection revealed to me that the vocabulary I was using in my attempt to find out why the past matters was too focused on the value of *retro*spection. By asking why retrospection was so important to my pursuit, Rorty led me to consider our interest in the past for the value of what I call in this book prospection: future-oriented thinking and public deliberation. Conversations with Hayden White on the "practical past" (a term he borrowed from the British philosopher Michael Oakeshott) brought me to the recognition that we often turn to even the bleakest of historical moments practically—that is, with an interest in engaging such contemporary concerns as racism or torture. Through these conversations with White I became increasingly aware that telling and retelling historical events is a creative, political, and ethical action. Turning to or avoiding the traumas of modernity can reflect questionable endeavors, such as ideologically justifying injustice. Yet the creative act of writing and rewriting historical narratives of all sorts, these conversations taught me, can also enhance our social sensibilities, expand our political and ethical horizon.

These conversations with Rorty and White resulted in this book's suggestion that the past matters not only because it weighs heavily on the present, as it surely does, but also—and crucially—because the language we forge when we engage our traumatic histories plays a vital role in considering who we would like to become.

Numerous discussions with Klaus Briegleb on German literature before and after the Second World War taught me that the impact of a meaningful literary work, regardless of the writer's intentions and commitments, is endless; that reading is a task one never concludes. Over the years I had the opportunity to place my ideas regarding literature and the past in conversation with more individuals than I can mention here, yet I want to single out and thank my colleagues and friends Leslie A. Adelson, Robert Alter, Ulrich Baer, Mieke Bal, Vincent Barletta, Karol Berger, Russell Berman, Stephan Braese, Michael Brenner, Adrian Daub, Steve Dowden, Arnold M. Eisen, Amy Elias, Sidra DeKoven Ezrahi, Michael Gluzman, Michal Govrin, Hans Ulrich Gumbrecht, Barbara Hahn,

Robert Harrison, Julia Hell, Hannan Hever, Alon Hilu, David Hollo-way, Andreas Huyssen, Maor Katz, Joshua Landy, Nitzan Leibovic, Vivian Liska, Paul Mendes-Flohr, Leslie Morris, David N. Myers, Todd Presner, Karen Remmler, Naama Rokem, Judith Ryan, Gabriella Safran, Eric Santner, Galili Shahar, Vered Shemtov, Thomas Sparr, Sigrid Wei-gel, Yfaat Weiss, Meike Werner, and Steve Zipperstein.

Norman Naimark read the entire manuscript and offered many vi-tal comments, for which I am deeply grateful. Judith Ryan's and Galili Shahar's incisive review of this book for the University of Chicago Press gave me ample opportunities to greatly improve my work. The central ideas that this book presents evolved in seminars I taught at Stanford, and I would like to thank some of the many students I had the privilege to learn from during and after these seminars: Lucy Alford, Lilla Balint, Mike Anthony Benveniste, Joel Burges, Amir Engel, Nir Evron, Harris Feinsod, Idan Gillo, Brian Johnsrud, Renana Keidar, Florian Klinger, Jakov Kuharik, Nathaniel Landry, Gideon Lewis-Kraus, David Marno, and Noam Pines. A work of scholarship by a native speaker of Hebrew for whom German and English remain foreign languages offers unique challenges to those who kindly assist him in making his ideas compre-hensible. For their invaluable help with the editorial work of this book at different stages, I would like to thank Jason Baskin, Bud Bynack, Nir Ev-ron, Ed Finn, Henning Marmulla, Bronwen Tate, Matthew Tiews, Alan G. Thomas, and Pamela J. Bruton.

Special thanks to Sean McIntyre and Webster Younce, who did a fab-ulous job at the crucial concluding phase of my work by helping me turn what has been a gargantuan manuscript into a readable book. Sean and Webster advised me on what could be abridged and, more importantly, offered numerous ways to make the argument clearer and to highlight the poetic value of the literary works this book presents.

For their willingness to talk with me about modernity's darkest mo-ments as they touched their lives, I owe thanks to my parents, Shoshana and Nachman, and my sisters, Hagit and Batik. Conversations about these moments have been a part of my own family's daily life for a de-cade or so. For their endless insights, patience, sense of humor, and love, I'm indebted to my children, Jonathan and Naomi, and my wife, Mar-tina. Looking at you I clearly sense what Futurity is all about. This book is for you.

Introduction: Spelling out Futurity

Writing Points to What Is "Open, Future, Possible"

Franz Kafka's famous parable "Eine kleine Fabel" ("A Little Fable") offers a matchless image of modern consciousness in the era that dawned with the First World War:

> "Alas," said the mouse, "the world is growing smaller every day. At the beginning it was so big that I was afraid, I kept running and running, and I was glad when I saw walls far away to the right and left, but these long walls have narrowed so quickly that I am in the last chamber already, and there in the corner stands the trap that I must run into." "You only need to change your direction," said the cat, and ate it up.[1]

Written in 1920, this little parable captures the predicament of our age: a time overshadowed by a sense that the future, that reliable horizon, might be forever lost. The piece offers a miniature image of the human condition in modern times. "At the beginning," before modernity emerged, along with the sciences, life-improving technologies, and humanism, the world's immensity and natural

forces yielded both great anxieties and—in "walls far away"—mytholo-
gies that kept those forces at bay. These fears subsided as a result of
the economic, political, and cultural changes of the eighteenth and nineteenth centuries. The modern era created a sense of a new time, filled
with immeasurable promise. Yet the era also brought about a sudden
narrowing of the walls: unprecedented violence in the First World War.
Read this way, Kafka's fable suggests that the unparalleled, man-made
destruction of the war shattered the auguries of a new dawn for humanity. There may be no future at all for the human race, whose only choice
lies between different kinds of endings—the trap or the cat's mouth. The
sheer scope of that catastrophe also signaled that any hope of affecting
human history was likely to be but a passing delusion.

The decades following 1920 only intensified the sentiment captured
by Kafka's tale. They have been marked by what Hayden White calls
"modernist events": disasters such as the Second World War, genocide,
the use of weapons of mass destruction in warfare, mass expulsions, ir-
reparable damage to the environment, and seemingly endless regional
conflicts, such as that between Israelis and Arabs.[2] The shocks caused
by the unparalleled use of modern technology in mass killing, the degradation of millions of individuals into means for the creation of superior
nations or ideal societies, and mass dissemination of images from these
events, White argues, exceed what previous ages could have ever imagined. These events function in our collective consciousness in a manner
similar to the working of trauma in the psyche of individuals. The industrial murder of humans in the death camps and the detonation of nuclear
devices over cities cannot be forgotten, nor can they be adequately remembered—"identified as to their meaning and contextualized in the
group memory"—without a significant impact on our ability to engage
with the present or "envision a future free of [these events'] debilitating
effects."[3] Adding to the difficulty of imagining a future free of the after-
effects of these *past* traumas were the development of nuclear weapons
in the twentieth century and the growing consciousness that the next
war might eradicate our habitat and human life. Since the dropping of
"Little Boy" on Hiroshima on August 6, 1945, the name of that Japanese city stands for a global awareness of the human ability to annul in a
coming clash the very notion of humanity's future forever.

Reflecting on this postcatastrophic world and, more specifically, on
the brutal, protracted, and seemingly insoluble Israeli-Palestinian conflict,
the Israeli writer David Grossman noted in his 2007 lecture "Writing
in the Dark" that "Kafka's mouse was right: the world is indeed growing

smaller, growing narrower, every day."[4] Grossman finds himself identifying with Kafka's vulnerable creature. For Grossman, who lost his son,
Uri, during the so-called Second Lebanon War less than a year before
delivering this talk, the merciless realities of the Middle East encompass every aspect of life, creating "a void" between individuals and their
surroundings, a chasm filled with "apathy, cynicism, and above all the
despair . . . that one will never manage to change the situation, never redeem it" (60). As the world grows smaller in light of this reality, one's
"ability and willingness to empathize" with "other people in pain" also
diminish (60).

Facing circumstances one believes oneself powerless to affect, the task
of "thinking and doing and setting moral standards" falls to those who
are presumably "in the know" (60). "Kafka's mouse was right," Grossman says; "when your predator closes in on you, your world gets smaller.
So does the language that describes it" (61). The vocabulary that "the
citizens of the conflict [use] to describe their situation becomes flatter and
flatter as the conflict goes on, gradually evolving into a series of clichés and
slogans" (61). The sense of a world that closes in like a trap, of a language
that diminishes, is a fate shared by countless human beings around the
globe who face threats to their existence, values, and liberty, Grossman
continues (62). This reality informs the literature of novelists and poets
writing in today's Israel, Palestine, Chechnya, Sudan, post-9/11 New
York, and the Congo (62). Facing a recent, traumatic past or imminent
destruction, they struggle with the sense of a world deprived of a future.

Grossman's lecture takes a turn, however, when he says that writers like him engage in "the strange, baseless, wonderful work of creation" (62), weaving a "shapeless web, which nonetheless has immense
power to change a world and create a world, the power to give words to
the mute and to bring about *tikkun*—'repair'—in the deepest, kabalistic
sense of the word" (62–63).[5] Grossman maintains that as "we write, we
feel the world in flux, elastic, full of possibilities—unfrozen" (64).

> I write, and the world does not close in on me. It does not grow
> smaller. It moves in the direction of what is open, future, pos-
> sible. I imagine and the act of imagination revives me. I am not
> fossilized or paralyzed in the face of predators. I invent charac-
> ters. Sometimes I feel as if I am digging people out of ice in which
> reality has encased them. I write. I feel the many possibilities that
> exist in every human situation, and I feel my capacity to choose
> among them. (65)

As contemporary literature engages modernity's man-made catastrophes, it also moves toward the future. That movement is this book's primary concern. All the works I discuss in the following pages were written after 1945—the year that, in the reality of the Nazi concentration camp and Hiroshima, the immense "walls" began to threaten to close in on us and our future. The literature I will discuss invokes our post-1945 age from the perspective of "modernist events" such as the Sino-Japanese War, the Second World War, the Holocaust, the wars of the Middle East, and the political realities that emerged after the end of the Cold War and after 9/11. By addressing modernity's devastations through various combinations of metaphor, theme, plot, character, and textual-visual arrangement, the fiction that I discuss in this book points toward the future to which Grossman alludes.

This poetic movement toward the future is composed of different elements. First, the works I focus on produce the very vocabulary we use to describe ourselves and our realities and thus the very language we draw on as we reshape ourselves—thereby keeping the world "full of possibilities." By producing a "vocabulary" or "language," I mean not just the new words and metaphors but also entire narrative sequences that we may draw on as we form our individual and communal identities. Second, by presenting ethically and politically ambivalent situations, the works here also help to open possibilities for the future by inviting us to debate what may have caused the catastrophe in question and what might make its recurrence unlikely. Third, while these works may express uncertainty and skepticism about our ability to shape our future, they also examine the human action necessary to overcome this doubt. Thus, in an era that has witnessed upheaval on an unprecedented scale and that doubts the very notion that we can affect tomorrow, the works here make available what Grossman calls the "open, future, possible."[6]

Futurity

Contemporary literature creates the "open, future, possible" by expanding our vocabularies, by probing the human ability to act, and by prompting reflection and debate. I call these capacities of contemporary literature "futurity." Throughout this book, I note the various expressions of futurity by describing the ways figurative language—ironies and allegories, stories and characters, a single pictogram or elaborate symbolic arrangements—does not just describe our past catastrophic circumstances but *re*describes them. Svetlana Boym notes that a creative turn to the past "can be retrospective but also prospective." "Fantasies of the past determined by needs of the present have a direct impact on realities of the future," Boym writes. "Consideration of the future makes us take responsibility for our nostalgic tales."[7] The works at the center of my discussion similarly maintain the future as a crucial dimension of their historical tales: by revisiting some of the darkest moments of modernity, they make us aware of our own role in the writing of our lives.

By "futurity," I do not mean the artistic celebration of modernity's technological forward thrust as propagated by the various movements of Futurism. Nor do I mean the promotion of a utopian future in which modern economic, social, and political contingencies are resolved in a conclusive manner. Rather, futurity marks the potential of literature to widen the language and to expand the pool of idioms we employ in making sense of what has occurred while imagining whom we may become. The works I discuss in this book recognize the "modernist events" of our time, those events that cause our world to close in on us with great menace. Futurity is tied to questions of liability and responsibility, to attentiveness to one's own lingering pains and to the sorrows and agonies of others. Futurity marks literature's ability to raise, via engagement with the past, political and ethical dilemmas crucial for the human future. In turning to the past, the works here keep open the prospect of a better tomorrow. Many ponder the human capacity to face hopeless individual or sociopolitical circumstances. Yet precisely by engaging such circumstances, they point to what may prevent our world from closing in on us.

W. G. Sebald's 2001 Austerlitz, for example, remembers the fate of the Jews who were murdered in Theresienstadt, Auschwitz, and elsewhere. Naturally, there is very little that is redeeming or elevating in Sebald's book. Yet on closer examination, Austerlitz is not restricted to the mourning of a modern, man-made catastrophe. Rather, it also signals futurity by presenting fleeting moments of new beginnings. By presenting a powerful image of a Jewish child who was saved in the Kindertransport operation shortly before European Jewry became prey to Nazism,[8] Austerlitz simultaneously recalls the most decisive trauma of the modern age *and* gestures to the constitutive human ability and responsibility to begin, to set off, to engage in action. Similarly, Michal Govrin's novel *Hevzekim* (2002; *Snapshots*) invokes the history of Zionism and the suffering of Palestinians during and after the 1948 Middle East war. As it draws on these historic moments, however, Govrin's work also creates a set of metaphors about land possession and the possibility of land sharing that allows Israelis and Palestinians to view their condition as "unfrozen" in Grossman's sense—to consider relating differently to their disputed land.

The Gigantic Shadows That Futurity Casts upon the Present

In identifying futurity in contemporary literature, this book is within a philosophical-aesthetic tradition that reaches as far back as Aristotle's *Poetics*. Aristotle claimed that the poet's role is higher than that of the historian because the historian aims at accurately describing what occurred in the past, while the poet relates things that "might occur."[9] The poet, in other words, deals with the realm of the possible. According to Aristotle, this distinctive position makes poetry "more philosophical" and more "elevated," granting it greater "ethical import" than history.[10] Unlike history's focus on the particularities of what has occurred, poetry is concerned with the "universal": "the kinds of things which it suits a certain kind of person to say or do in terms of probability or necessity."[11]

The Aristotelian claim found a much later echo in European Romanticism, most prominently in Percy Bysshe Shelley's "A Defence of Poetry" (1821, published 1840). Poetic language offers us utterly new ways to experience the world and all its potential, and thus the possibility to re-create it. "Poets," Shelley declares, "are the unacknowledged legislators of the world."[12] They capture the sense that we human beings have a future to which we may actually relate—that what is to come is not a mystery we cannot try to affect but rather a shade we can move in and out of, a specter whose reach we may actually evade. Poetic works are thus not an expression of what is "moved" by external forces but rather what, potentially, "moves," thereby maintaining the contingency of the "open" realm of the future, to use David Grossman's word. And this view of poetic language, in turn, finds numerous echoes during the late nineteenth and twentieth centuries. The American Pragmatism of John Dewey and Charles Peirce argued that poetic language, in the broadest sense, creates images and symbols that expand our experience of the world rather than simply represent it.[13] In *Experience and Nature* (1925), John Dewey equates "knowledge and propositions which are the products of thinking" with "works of art" such as "statuary and symphonies" because, "like any other work of art," the production of knowledge "confers upon things traits and potentialities which did not *previously* belong to them."[14] Thus, art broadens the vocabulary we use in all aspects of our lives and creates new ways to experience our given circumstances. In *Art as Experience* (1934), Dewey argues that a work of art should be considered through the question of "what the product does with and in experience."[15] He underlines the ability of words to "preserve and report the values of all the varied experiences of the past, and to follow . . . every changing shade of feeling and idea," yet also their "power to create a new experience, oftentimes . . . more poignantly felt than that which comes from things themselves."[16]

Metaphors, Themes, and Plots as Causes

The "futural" aspect of poetic language found recent expression in the Neopragmatism of Richard Rorty—who associates progress with the generation of new, more useful metaphors—as well as in the thinking of Hannah Arendt. For both Rorty and Arendt, poetic language and narrative fiction are capable of reconfiguring our lifeworld by creating new ways to describe how we live and interact with each other.[17] These new modes of expression, in turn, change that lifeworld. Metaphors and creative narratives enable us to reshape habits, feelings, and even social relations. Their imaginative power contributes to the process by which a community can reconstitute itself.

Rorty reaffirms Shelley's definition of the poet, while developing Shelley's perspective considerably, arguing that "the poet does not fit past events together in order to provide lessons for the future, but rather shocks us into turning our back on the past and incites hope that our future will be wonderfully different."[18] In other words, literature does not necessarily offer insights into how our circumstances were or are ("the past") but rather has the capacity to affect our aspirations ("hope") and our future actions.

Rorty thus perceives "imagination" not only as the writer's capacity to depict the world mimetically and induce aesthetic pleasure but also as "the ability to come up with socially useful novelties."[19] Whereas aesthetics in the Kantian tradition strove to outline the distinctiveness of the aesthetic object—its remoteness from all realms of everyday, practical life—the "new story" told by the Romantics, by Nietzsche, and by Pragmatists centers on the notion of the poet and writer as creator of an utterly novel language *for* what Shelley calls the "world."[20] This story was "about how human beings continually strive to overcome the human past in order to create a better human future."[21] Literature is thus the most forward-aiming domain of human language because it is a unique tool "for social interaction," a way "of tying oneself up with other human beings."[22] According to Rorty, "works of imagination, or exercises of imagination, can extend our notion of what might be useful."[23] Rorty's reading of Donald Davidson's concept of metaphor is crucial for understanding his vision of literary language, in all its different manifestations. In this conception, metaphors create new ways to view our natural circumstances and social communication, and thus to consider what we may want to become in the future. By insisting that a metaphorical sentence has no meaning other than the literal one, Rorty notes, "Davidson lets us see metaphors on the model of unfamiliar events in the natural world—*causes* of changing beliefs and desires—rather than on the model of *representations* of unfamiliar worlds, worlds which are 'symbolic' rather than 'natural.'"[24] In other words, "poetic" language, through the entire range of devices subsumed by the term—from a single word, through rhetorical figures, to plot elements and entire stories—is capable of altering "one's sense of what is possible and important," of "pushing" readers to reengage the world and possibly even to change it by inspiring new "patterns of action."[25]

The "new vocabularies" with which we may reshape ourselves include, in my view, not only startling metaphors but also textual sequences—indeed, entire plots. As Paul Ricoeur, Hayden White, and Peter Brooks have convincingly shown, the "emplotment of a sequence of events" transforms what otherwise would be "only a chronicle of events" into a story.[26] By *re*ordering and *re*presenting a certain historical event through innovative modes of emplotment, fictional narrative can cause us to view the past differently and allow us to *re*shape how we conceive ourselves in relation to the past. And such narratives may furthermore enable us to take advantage of this new relation to the past to remake ourselves. Through their overarching modes of emplotment, as well as through structuring poetic figures such as irony, fictional narratives that turn to modernity's catastrophic past produce meanings that are different from what we may find in already-existing chronicles or historical narratives. This new meaning, White explicates through Ricoeur, is "found" in the universal human experience of "recollection," which "promises a future because it finds a 'sense' in every relationship between a past and a present."[27]

Rorty's notion of literature's ability to change our vocabularies has nothing to do with syrupy "value thematics" or with specific political and moral positions.[28] Rather, it is based on viewing what Günter Leypoldt aptly calls the "world-making" capabilities of the literary work.[29] S. Yizhar's (1916–2006) classic novella *Sipur Khirbet Khizah* (1948; *The Story of Khirbet Khizeh*),[30] for example, not only accounts for the expulsion of Palestinians from villages like the fictional Khirbet Khizeh but also redescribes the 1948 war as an event in the course of which Israeli soldiers drove many other Palestinians into forced exile. In its narrative structure and unsettling biblical allusions, the novella casts Jewish soldiers in the role of King Ahab in the story of Naboth's vineyard

(1 Kings 21) and Palestinians as the victim—the deceived Naboth. By using these literary means, the novella "shocks" its readers into reassessing the war that established Israel's independence. Furthermore, Yizhar's work prompts reflection on the future—on what may become of the Jewish state—since in the era following Ahab's reign, the kingdom of Israel was bitterly punished for the king's deeds. The novella thus triggers a consideration of the impact of the actions of Jewish soldiers not only on the lives of Palestinians but also on Israel's future.

Prospection, or the Practical Past

This book's discussion takes up Rorty's view that modern narrative prose expresses the "new story" that emerged in Romanticism. Works such as Günter Grass's *The Tin Drum* mark the shift away from an interest in presenting those "truths" (regarding Nazism, in this case) as something that lies outside human language. Rather, they focus on human contingencies and on the endless array of (often-conflicted) desires, beliefs, fantasies, and actions that make up who we are.[31]

Rorty stresses that while philosophical aesthetics in the tradition of Baumgarten and Kant centers on what is pleasurable for the senses, it neglects the novel's ability to generate "reflection" (55).[32] Aesthetics takes little interest in why some readers believe that experiencing *The Brothers Karamazov*, for example, has changed their lives (55). Yet the novel has been capable of changing a reader's life not by being formally perfect or linguistically sublime but rather by exposing the reader to the needs and views of others—by confronting the self's "egotism" or "self-satisfaction." The novel, Rorty argues, "gives us the most help in grasping the variety of human life and the contingency of our own moral vocabulary" (56–57). Its metaphors, ironies, allegories, and innovative plots both represent realities or enduring moral convictions and acquaint us with the multiplicity of human life and action.

Rorty's idea is that literature can reconfigure "habits of feeling" and social relations; the poet is the creator of new vocabularies rather than a moral apostle. Thus, in this book I examine literary images of the past as they offer us, the readers, new ways to view that past in relation to our present and our possible future—"new" in the sense of allowing us to reconsider our current ethical judgments or political views and thus to evolve or *become*. According to Rorty, writers and readers of literature reconstitute themselves through "redescription," that is, by telling and retelling stories about where they came from and where they are going, making use of ever-changing vocabularies. By consuming new modes of aesthetic expression, readers of literature may reconstitute themselves and their social worlds.[33]

The three parts of this book thus trace the literary invocations of some of the most sinister moments of recent modernity and how the works imaginatively redescribe these moments—that is, how this literature offers the potential for "world-making." I examine how the works create and broaden the language we use in referring to "modernist events" and how, by revisiting a haunting epochal event such as the Second World War, they may affect our future condition.[34]

In his essay "Present, Future and Past," Michael Oakeshott suggests that while in post-Hegelian historiography the main concern is with "historical" inquiry, that is, with what artifacts, documents, or ruins are or what their "provenance" has been, the question for the "practical past" is "what to think, to say or to do" about the past.[35] The issue is not what an object or an utterance meant but rather "what use or meaning [it has] in a current present-future of practical engagement."[36] Many of the works that I discuss here consider, directly or implicitly, what is useful about the past—what it offers us in regard to what Oakeshott calls our "present-future."[37] Put differently, this literature finds in the past the domain of the practical. The works turn to the past with awareness of its potential relevance to contemporary ethical or political concerns.

Limitations

The decision to limit this book to First World literature maintains the focus on how authors who belong to a particular national collective that grapples with guilt, shame, and responsibility engage with these emotions and thus raise future-related ethical and political dilemmas. Given this perspective, in part I of the book I do not discuss post–Second World War literature written by German Jewish authors.[38] Similarly, part II attends to Jewish Israeli writers as they imaginatively redescribe their country's difficult origin—by treating the fate of Palestinians after 1948—with the "present-future" of the Israeli-Palestinian conflict in mind. Since I examine how German and Jewish Israeli writers ponder their respective national, ethical, and political dilemmas by turning to the past, I refrain from examining here the poetry and prose of history's victims and their descendants. Such an examination is much needed; yet undertaking it here would have exhausted the framework of this study.[39]

In part III of the book I examine literature written after the 1989 fall of the Berlin Wall and in light of the debate about the "end of history." Yet another reason for confining my discussion to First World literature is my wish to address the charge that Western culture of recent decades lacks "any thinking of time," as the French philosopher Alain Badiou puts it, and to consider whether we are indeed, as he and others claim, "contemporaries of a period of a-temporality and instantaneity."[40]

Beyond Symptomatic Reading

The charge that Western culture lacks "any thinking of time" flies in the face of numerous works of contemporary fiction. The attention to modern, man-made catastrophes is part and parcel of the broadening concern, in Western and non-Western societies alike, with memory and history. Many scholars have approached works such as W. G. Sebald's *Austerlitz* and S. Yizhar's *The Story of Khirbet Khizeh* by focusing on the past as it haunts the present, asking how such works display trauma, guilt, shame, or their evasion. Countless studies center on fiction's ability to portray the tension between remembrance and forgetting—between a conscious "working through" and an oblivious "acting out" of issues raised by significant events in the past.

Attentive to literature's expansion of our given vocabularies and how it deals "practically" with man-made catastrophes, I wish to broaden the discussion beyond the familiar focus on identifying the symptoms of an authorial or a social condition—most often the ability (or inability) to face up to the past. The study of postwar German literature, for example, is often motivated by the question of the work's or the author's ability to address the crimes of the Nazi regime "adequately." Similarly, the discussion of Hebrew literature's engagement with 1948 is often marked by the effort to find symptoms of the cultural and political repression of the expulsion of Palestinians or to identify the "orientalist" perspective of the writers as mediums of Israeli political discourse. The result in all these cases is the reduction of literature to its ability to display symptoms of the psychological conditions, ethical failings, and ideological commitments of the writers and their communities.

Naturally, the symptomatic reading of literature is part of a highly productive interpretive tradition. Literature's capacity to foster or question ideological convictions or the working of "the political unconscious" plays a fruitful role in the work of such eminent critics as Georg Lukács and Fredric Jameson, gaining considerable momentum with the rise of cultural studies.[41] However productive these symptomatic readings of literature can be, restricting our reading to the symptomatic seriously undermines our ability to grasp the capacity of figurative language to redescribe our circumstances. My emphasis is on literature as it permits—rather than prescribes—thought and debate, emancipation from custom and ritual.[42]

In his pathbreaking study *Multidirectional Memory: Remembering the Holocaust in the Age of Decolonization*, Michael Rothberg discusses how "social actors bring multiple traumatic pasts into a heterogeneous and changing post–Second World War present."[43] Rothberg's discussion moves away from the notion that collective memory shapes hermetic collective identities, that memory is a "zero-sum game" in which a nation or an ethnic group relates to its distinctive past to cement an unchanging identity.[44] Group memories, Rothberg suggests, do not necessarily exclude recognition of "the other's" memory. Memory as such is multidirectional: based in a specific traumatic experience, it is always in dialogue with the memories of others. "When the productive, intercultural dynamic of multidirectional memory is explicitly claimed," Rothberg argues, "it has the potential to create new forms of solidarity and new visions of justice. . . . Memory's anachronistic quality—its bringing together of now and then, here and there—is actually the source of its powerful creativity, its ability to build new worlds out of materials of older ones."[45] Hence, the literary remembrance of Germany's Nazi past in Günter Grass's *The Tin Drum* and Hans-Ulrich Treichel's more recent *Der Verlorene* (1998; *Lost*) does not obscure the suffering of Jews by recounting German history, as some critics have claimed. Rather, these and the other works that I discuss display multidirectional memory, an imaginative engagement with the German collective past and, through it, with the catastrophe of modern Jewish history.

Similarly, eminent works of Hebrew literature of the decades following the 1948 War of Independence negotiate Jewish Israeli memories of the war and the ensuing decades with an awareness of the fate of Palestinians. In both cases—the German and the Israeli—the works examined have played a significant role in shaping a cultural-political discourse that is attentive to the memories and suffering of the respective "other." The imaginative redescription of the past and the working of multidirectional memory imply a futural perspective, examining questions regarding responsibility, ethical and political action, and notions of justice.

After "the Romance of World History"

Part III broadens to a more international framework by turning to the political watershed labeled with the shorthand "1989." My emphasis in this section will be on German, Anglo-American, and Hebrew literature written after the end of the Cold War.[46] Novels discussed in this section focus, too, on recent man-made calamities—on the Sino-Japanese War and the Second World War—yet they also reflect the decisive political changes and broad intellectual debates about the link between past and future that emerged following 1989.

The political order that followed the Second World War changed substantially after 1989: in a matter of months, the Berlin Wall had fallen and the Communist regimes of Eastern Europe were replaced, through (mostly) peaceful revolutions, by democracies. The Cold War came to an end. Postwar Yugoslavia dissolved in a genocidal war into numerous nation-states. The collapse of European Communism was, at the same time, also a defining moment in the ideological and intellectual struggle between liberal democracy and socialism.

For more than a century, the question of the future—of what form sociopolitical organization should take in modern society—was debated along the lines separating these two worldviews. The year 1989 signaled a significant change in this regard. Many observers—most prominently Francis Fukuyama in *The End of History and the Last Man* (1992)—saw in 1989 the end of the decades-long clash over the form sociopolitical organization should take in modern society. Not all share this view. Alain Badiou, Slavoj Žižek, and others remain unwilling to accept the disappearance of a future characterized by a radically different sociopolitical order—a polity based on the abolition of private property, the market, and the Western-style democratic state.[47]

The war in Yugoslavia, the genocide in Rwanda, 9/11, and the wars in Afghanistan and Iraq have proven the hollowness of the notion of "the end of history" in the sense of the disappearance of all forms of political strife. The financial crisis that began in 2008 has revealed that capitalist liberal democracy remains vulnerable to systemic breakdown. Nevertheless, 1989 justifiably marks the exhaustion of speculative thinking about capital-H History—that is, the obsolescence of metahistorical narratives regarding "history's course," "laws," and "trajectory." The year 1989 signaled the demise of what Richard Rorty called "the romance of world history."[48] Since 1989, capital-H History has simply lost its utility as the "object" around which we "weave our fantasies of diminished misery."[49] We no longer need it as an explanatory instrument or a vehicle for debating change. A tradition going back to the writings of Hegel, Marx, Heidegger, Lenin, and Kojève that was saturated with such images as Nietzsche's "last men" and a deep contempt for "bourgeois culture" has lost its utility for promoting social and intellectual conditions that differ from those we inhabit.[50]

A variety of thinkers observe the fading of what the historian Jay

Winter terms the "major utopias" of the twentieth century: those universalist fantasies that called for the uprooting of *all* social and political contingencies, of all "malevolent elements blocking the path to a beneficent future."[51] These eschatological ideologies, Winter notes, produced only "mountains of victims on a scale the world had rarely seen."[52] "The end of the cold war," Mark Lilla observes, "brought to a close the grand historical narrative that had shaped European political consciousness for two centuries by dividing the world into revolutionary and reactionary forces."[53] Discussing global, post-1989, and post-9/11 politics, the political philosopher John N. Gray likewise speaks of the "death" of utopia: the twentieth century is littered with examples of both totalitarian regimes such as Nazism and Bolshevism and right-wing utopianism that strives to spread democracy by any available means. In every case, these "major" utopian fantasies have proven their futility with respect to creating a better future for the human race.[54]

1989 and Contemporary Literature

As Amy Hungerford has noted, 1989 hardly signaled a new chapter in the history of the novel.[55] None of the works I turn to in part III depict 1989 directly or formally signal the dawn of a new literary age. Rather, they consider what the future may mean in view of the political realities and subsequent intellectual discussion that emerged after 1989. Historians such as Russell Jacoby and critics such as Fredric Jameson view the flagging of radical utopian thought as an indication of the "incremental impoverishment of what might be called Western imagination" (Jacoby)[56] and plead for the revival of the "desire called utopia" (Jameson).[57] Yet the works discussed in part III signal just the opposite. Taken together, these novels reflect the demise of the romance of world history while engaging the past imaginatively and raising the question of the future. They ask both "How did we get here?" and "How can we maintain a sense of tomorrow as 'open,' or 'possible'?"

Although these works display interest in the past and its relation to the present and to the possible future, they do not attempt to speculate about History. Rather, by presenting memorable characters contemplating what they may do, by creating dramatic narratives, or by offering metaphors of new beginnings, these works ask if and how we may be able to affect our sociopolitical or ecological conditions by taking political and ethical action. They focus on the choices of their characters, on their wills and actions.[58] Depicting characters that engage in mundane, humble action, they indicate that our time—after the Holocaust and after the demise of the "major utopias"—no longer needs History as a reified object that has "a shape and a movement" of the kind previously reserved for "God" or "Human Nature."[59]

Taken together, the works we will read examine our ability to regard ourselves as capable of acting in our given realities and capable of shaping our future. To put it somewhat differently, confronting the "modernist events" of our era in light of historical occurrences that—given their scope—seem to exclude any notion of meaningful human agency, these works signal futurity by focusing on our ability to address our given conditions in actions small and large. The past serves in these works to explore the human ability to address real social, economic, and political conditions—to hold on to the future by asserting human agency.

On the "Wholesale Liquidation of Futurity"

In recent years, much has been asserted regarding Western "late capitalist," "late modern," or "postmodern" culture as overshadowed by a declining historical consciousness. Alain Badiou, for example, views our culture as lacking "*any* thinking of time."[60] For just about everyone in the West of the late twentieth century, Badiou claims, "the day after tomorrow is abstract and the day before yesterday incomprehensible."[61] Fredric Jameson and others see in the revival of the Hegelian discourse about the "end of history" "an intellectual symptom" of the diminishing factual sense of the "historical past," and with it what Jameson emblematically terms the "wholesale liquidation of futurity."[62]

Yet recent works of literature reveal such fears about the "wholesale liquidation of futurity" to be highly questionable. In the German and Hebrew literature discussed in parts I and II, the past occupies a central role, often serving as a prism through which writers and readers alike reflect on ongoing ethical and political circumstances and thus on their future. The same is true of Anglo-American literature of recent decades, such as Ian McEwan's *Atonement* and Paul Auster's *Oracle Night*, both of which I will discuss. These and other novels display how our capitalist, liberal-democratic culture retains a sense of the future. Close study of our literary culture reveals that anxieties about the vanishing of "thinking of time" should be viewed as symptomatic of a crisis of a utopianism that dwells on the hope of a completely altered social order, one that still views "anticapitalism" as a helpful concept in dealing with the elimination of hunger, the extension of health care to all, and the improvement of education.[63] In fact, the only future we seem to lack is the kind envisioned by the grand social utopias of the nineteenth and twentieth centuries. In all the works discussed in the following pages, it is clear that our time has lost neither a sense of the need to address urgent political issues in South Africa, Israel/Palestine, and elsewhere nor an interest in what the future may look like in Tokyo or New York.

"The Insertion of Man"

In the decades following 1989, numerous critics have turned to Hannah Arendt's analysis of totalitarian rule in their discussions of anti-Semitism, human rights, and statist political terror. In the wake of 9/11, the Italian philosopher Giorgio Agamben, for example, invoked Arendt's treatment of the degradation of humans in the Nazi death camps into mere substance in his development of the concept of "bare life": humans who are deprived of all attributes of humanity by the political sovereign before being eliminated from the face of the earth.[64] More recently, Michael Rothberg has pointed to Arendt's contribution to our understanding of the relationship between anti-Semitism, colonialism, and totalitarian systems of terror.[65]

My own turn to Arendt is driven by her reaction to what she called our "dark times" and by her consideration of the link between the past and the future. In her introduction to *Men in Dark Times*, Arendt notes that our modern "dark times" are certainly not "new" nor a "rarity in history." She goes on to say that "even in the darkest of times we have the right to expect some illumination" and that "such illumination may well come less from theories and concepts than from the uncertain, flickering and often weak light that some men and women, in their lives *and their works*, will kindle under almost all circumstances." [66] Like many of the works I will discuss in this book, Arendt's thought considers both "the past"—modernity's man-made catastrophes—*and* how we may retain a sense of the future as the realm of the possible, even in an age that raises doubts about hopes regarding tomorrow.

Additionally, Arendt proves remarkably fruitful for my discussion when she considers how poetic language, narrative, and thus literature itself open up unfamiliar vistas on our realities and thus "do something" in the world. "Metaphor," Arendt notes, not only displays the "analogy between, say, a sunset and old age" but, as she underlines by referring to Shelley's "Defence of Poetry," "marks the before unapprehended *relations* of things and perpetuates their apprehension."[67] In other words, metaphors allow us to recognize something we have not seen or understood before. Metaphors, she notes in her *Denktagebuch* (Thinking diary), are what uniquely enable us to access our world.[68] In the moment when a metaphor is born, our "reality" is disclosed: we can then better endure our circumstances and gain access to "truth" (*Wahrheit*).[69] Literature is capable not merely of offering an image of the world but also of triggering our ability to do things differently.

These two aspects of Arendt's thought—the exploration of human agency and the consideration of poetic language as a cause—will be constant fixtures of my discussion. For Arendt, events and phenomena such as genocide and totalitarian states cause substantial doubt about the human ability to shape our individual circumstances. Arendt concludes her magisterial *Origins of Totalitarianism* (originally published in 1951) by confronting "the crisis of our time":

> But there remains also the truth that every end in history necessarily contains a new beginning; this beginning is the promise, the only "message" which the end can ever produce. Beginning, before it becomes a historical event, is the supreme capacity of man; politically, it is identical with man's freedom. *Initium ut esset homo creatus est*—"that a beginning be made man was created" said Augustine. This beginning is guaranteed by each new birth; it is indeed every man.[70]

The center of gravity in these sentences, as in Arendt's work as a whole, lies in the gesture "But there remains": it is precisely in the face of such recent end points as the unparalleled terror of the totalitarian state that Arendt emphasizes the constitutive nature of futurity ("there remains" a "new beginning") and human agency.

Throughout her work, Arendt considers how we may hold on to the future in light of modern phenomena such as the "death factories" erected in the heart of Europe, cutting, as she puts it, "the already outworn thread by which we still might have been tied to a historical entity of more than two thousand years."[71] As she reflects on the catastrophes of the modern era, she often turns to Kafka. In *Between Past and Future*, Arendt points to a short prose piece by Kafka titled "ER" ("HE").[72] Kafka's enigmatic protagonist is a metaphor for modern humanity.

> He has two antagonists: the first presses him from behind, from the origin. The second blocks the road ahead. He gives battle to both. To be sure, the first supports him in the fight with the second, for he wants to push him forward and in the same way the

> second supports him in the fight with the first, since he drives
> him back. But it is only theoretically so. For it is not only the two
> antagonists who are there, but he himself as well, and who really
> knows his intentions?[73]

Arendt notes that not only is "the wave of the future" cast here as "a
force," but so is the past.[74] Indeed, Arendt argues, the past is not "as
in nearly all our metaphors . . . a burden man has to shoulder and of
whose dead weight the living can or even must get rid in their march into
the future" (BPF, 10). Rather, as a "force," the past "presses forward"
(BPF, 10); it is a resource where we may discover potentialities. Arendt
in effect rewrites Kafka's short text into an Arendtian story in which she
views the protagonist as "inserted into time": "It is this insertion—the
beginning of beginning, to put it in Augustinian terms—which splits up
the time continuum" (BPF, 10).

Arendt then goes on to emphasize that Kafka presents a unidirectional flow of time to which "he" is subjected—time as a movement
from the past to the future. Thus, according to Arendt, Kafka neglects to
recognize "the insertion of man" (BPF, 11): the fact that this teleological
movement is actually fractured with every birth of a human being.[75]

In Arendt's willful reinterpretation of Kafka's parable, "the insertion of man"—that is, birth—disrupts what often appears to be time's
"continuum" (BPF, 11). For Arendt, time is not something that moves
straightforwardly from the past to an unknown future, with humans
traveling "in time" as we fight the forces of the past and the future.
Rather, the constant "insertion" of humans by birth causes the forces of
the past and the future to "deflect, however lightly, from their original
direction" (BPF, 11). With each and every new birth, a new trajectory,
however insignificant, begins. This means that temporal movement is
multidirectional and infinite, its conclusion never known (BPF, 11–12).

In her 1958 opus, The Human Condition, Arendt introduces the concept
of "natality" as she considers how to think through the future "from the
vantage point of our newest experiences and our most recent fears."[76]
Reacting to the profound impact of totalitarian brutality and of modern
technological innovation, Arendt defines "natality" as the fundamental
human capacity to "insert" oneself into the world:

> With word and deed we insert ourselves into the human world,
> and this insertion is like a second birth, in which we confirm and
> take upon ourselves the naked fact of our original physical ap-
> pearance. This insertion is not forced upon us by necessity . . .

and it is not prompted by utility. . . . It may be stimulated by the presence of others whose company we may wish to join, but it is never conditioned by them; its impulse springs from the beginning which came into the world when we were born and to which we respond by beginning something new on our own initiative. (*HC*, 176–77)

Every birth marks the possibility of "mending" the world (*"eine Garantie des Heilens in der Welt"*), the possibility of salvation (*"Erlösung"*) for those who are no longer a beginning—the living.[77] In an age deeply skeptical of the ability of individual agents to do anything at all, Arendt underscores the capacity of humans to take action that may affect their fates. She rewrites the Judeo-Christian messianic tradition by defining "birth" not as the past or future arrival of a messiah but rather as the fact that each and every human reshapes—to whatever degree—the realities and the circumstances she or he faces. Every human, from birth onward, is part of a network made up of other speaking and acting human beings. The necessity of orienting oneself in this condition brings about action (*HC*, 188–92) and thus the constant evolution of our realities.

Discussing action in *The Human Condition*, Arendt ties natality to futurity: "The miracle that saves the world, the realm of human affairs, from its normal, 'natural' ruin is ultimately the fact of natality, in which the faculty of action is ontologically rooted. . . . Only the full experience of this capacity can bestow on human affairs faith and hope" (*HC*, 247). As she noted in December 1952: "We capture the past through reflection [*Sinnen*], the present by sustaining [*Erleiden*], and the future through action [*Handeln*]."[78]

Arendt often alludes to literature as a prism through which we may consider what constitutes human action and also as a form of "insertion" ("with *word* and *deed*"; *HC*, 176), that is, as a *mode* of natality. For Arendt, the literature of our postcatastrophic age expresses more than the artist's aesthetic genius; it testifies to the human ability to act. In her 1946 essay on Kafka, Arendt ties his work to a modernity in which countless humans have renounced their "freedom and their right of action."[79] She views Joseph K's miserable end in *The Trial*, specifically his adaptation to the rules dominating the world, as displaying to us, modern readers, the predicament of our time: modernity is for Kafka an age that deludes its contemporaries into thinking that they are deprived of any kind of freedom and any "right of action." The character K of *The Castle* is different from K of *The Trial* because he refuses to belong to the submissive villagers and to the omnipotent rulers of the castle. K of *The Castle* displays, in fact, a distinctive path of life in the modern world. His stubbornness, Arendt notes,

> opens the eyes of some of the villagers; his *behavior teaches them* that human rights may be worth fighting for, that the rule of the castle is not divine law and, consequently, can be attacked. He makes them see, as they put it, that "men who suffered our kind of experiences, who are beset by our kind of fear . . . , who tremble at every knock at the door, cannot see things straight." And they add: "how lucky we are that you came to us!"[80]

What K models in *The Castle* for the villagers and what Kafka's novel presents to its readers is both the attraction of conceiving of themselves as utterly submitted to their given conditions *and* the revelation that a different "behavior," what we may call the path of insertion, is possible. K brings to the world the consciousness of the possibility of living a life of resistance to complete submission.[81] Likewise, by exploring what can be done to change our realities through action, the writers considered in this book address what David Grossman calls the "apathy, cynicism, and despair . . . that one will never manage to change the situation, never redeem it" (60).

In Arendt's thought, literature is often presented as a mode of natality. In fact, she chooses Isak Dinesen's statement as a motto for her discussion of action in *The Human Condition* (chapter 5): "All sorrows can be borne if you put them into a story or tell a story about them" (*HC*, 175).[82] Her reference to the Danish writer's aphorism lays a claim for narrative not just as a vehicle for conveying the human condition but also as a means of enabling us to "bear our sorrows" by pointing to the human capacity to affect circumstances. Elsewhere, Arendt approvingly quotes Hermann Broch as saying that the task of the work of art is "the constant recreation of the world."[83] "The modern novel," she suggests, "no longer serves as 'entertainment and instruction.' . . . It rather confronts him [the reader] with problems and perplexities in which the reader must be prepared to engage himself if he is to understand it at all."[84] In sum, Arendt allows us to view the literature of our postcatastrophic age as a mode of "insertion" and as an investigation of what counts as action. Throughout this book, I trace how theme, plot, character, allusion, and symbolic constellations prompt us to contemplate what has occurred in the past and how they assert our capacity to shape our realities. I will furthermore consider those moments when a literary work sets thought, debate, and even action in motion.

A Literary Anthropology of the Contemporary

In assessing recent German, Hebrew, and Anglo-American literature, this book seeks to contribute to what Paul Rabinow terms the "anthropology of the contemporary." "*The contemporary*," Rabinow suggests, "*is a moving ratio of modernity, moving through the recent past and near future in a (nonlinear) space that gauges modernity as an ethos already becoming historical.*"[85] I approach the contemporary through post-1945 literature as it engages "modernist events" that played a crucial role in shaping the "recent past" to which Rabinow alludes: the Second World War, the Holocaust, Hiroshima, the 1948 Israeli-Arab war, and the end of the Cold War, to name only the most important ones. Like Post45—the group of American scholars who examine the work of Don DeLillo, Frank O'Hara, and Toni Morrison, among others, against the backdrop of "specific postwar political-theoretical paradigms and values"—I identify Rabinow's "recent past" as the era that began around 1945.[86] After that year, our global culture (and thus literature) began to absorb the meaning of the world wars, of the implementation of nuclear weapons in warfare, of mass expulsions, and—most distinctly—of the Jewish genocide, the Holocaust.

The Holocaust is the prism through which contemporary literature often considers our recent past.[87] Engagement with the Holocaust, however, is not the theme of this book. Rather, I see 1945 and especially the Holocaust as the historical thread that entangles different narratives across the globe as they shift between past, present, and future. What I mean by the term "historical thread" can be observed in the relationship between the different parts of this book. Portraying pre–Second World War German history, the expulsion of Germans from Eastern Europe at the end of the Second World War, or the air raids on civilian centers, the contemporary German literature we read in part I turns to 1945 and to the Holocaust as central reference points for understanding and debating present-day politics and culture in Germany. Similarly, Hebrew literature's engagement with the flight and expulsion of Palestinians, as I show in part II, often involves the invocation of the Holocaust. As writers revisit Israel's past—specifically, the events of 1948—they often turn to the Holocaust as a potent referent for discussing the ethical and political choices that Israel faces in the present.

In the decades since 1989, as discussed in part III, the political and intellectual backdrop for writers who turn to the past has changed significantly. As they "move through" the catastrophes of the mid-twentieth
century, they also take into consideration the end of the Cold War and
the geopolitical realities that emerged on 9/11. Proceeding in what Rabinow aptly calls "nonlinear" ways, they address the Nazi concentration
camps, British colonialism in China, or the attacks on the World Trade
Center and prompt us to consider what humans *were* and still *are* capable of. It is through the temporal layers of 1945 and 1989 that they challenge us to acknowledge our responsibility to take political and ethical
action and to reflect on the consequences when we fail to do so.

   This book's focus on futurity is a contribution to a broader anthropology of the contemporary, not least because in the coda I point to
possible corollaries between the study of contemporary literature and
the study of the visual arts. The last pages of this study will enlarge on
what futurity offers us as a hermeneutic perspective, that is, as a useful
heuristic in discussing a memorial or a visual work of art. In examining
the Holocaust Memorial in Berlin and an artistic installation in Wadi
Nissnas in Haifa, Israel, I explain how the visual arts create images that
fluctuate between the recent past and the near future. And I show how a
hermeneutic of futurity allows us to discover the often-neglected ability
of contemporary art to go beyond exhibiting ideological commitments
or psychological conditions.

   What emerges thus from the pages of this book is the outline of a cultural and literary criticism that complements David Grossman's view of literature as both looking into modernity's abyssal circumstances *and* keeping the world full of possibilities. As cultural and literary critics, we have
a choice between holding on exclusively to a distanced, analytical position that takes delight in judging works of art for their retrospective merits
(or lack thereof) and, alternatively, recognizing in books, films, memorials,
or paintings their potential for shaping our lives. In other words, we
can remain focused on trying to discover what an artistic creation that
engages the past ostensibly lacks, or we can give up the deliciousness of
detecting the symptoms behind the work in favor of admiring its ability
to help us reinvent our world and ourselves. Reflecting Rorty's observation that literature can shock us into "turning our back on the past" and
incite "hope that our future will be wonderfully different," a hermeneutic of futurity allows us to shift our attention when we study contemporary works of art from poetic retrospection and symptomatic analysis to
understanding art as offering us an opportunity to evolve through ever-

new vocabularies, images, and ideas. The following pages thus respond to Arendt's provocation that we should drop the idea of time's "unidirectional flow" and discover in art's engagement with modernity's recent, deeply troubling past a way to embrace contingency and take up our uncertain future.

**Part One | Coming to Terms with the Future:
German Literature in Search of the Past**

1

Between Retrospection and Prospection

*"It's about Us and Our Future": The 2006 Günter
Grass Affair*

In 2006, in his long-awaited autobiography, *Beim Häuten
der Zwiebel* (*Peeling the Onion*), Nobel laureate Günter
Grass revealed that he did not serve, as he had previously
claimed, in Nazi Germany's air defense forces but rather
in the tank division Jörg von Frundsberg of the Waffen-
Schutzstaffel (SS).[1] The ensuing controversy was characterized by a sense that once again postwar German public
discourse was restricted by a backward-looking approach.
The young and successful writers Eva Menasse and Michael Kumpfmüller criticized the older intellectuals who
flocked to the feuilletons, calling the dispute a "class reunion of old German intellectuals" who seemed to feel
chronically obliged to enlighten "us"—that is, the Germans—on the same topic: "Hitler and me." "Please, no
more confessions!" pleaded Menasse and Kumpfmüller:

> Are there no other topics? Where are the voices on the cur-
> rent political and moral issues? It's time for this country to
> finally liberate itself from the self-reflections of its onion-
> skinned Nazi discourse. . . . It's time for the lessons of his-
> tory, preached a hundred times, to finally be applied to the

politics of the twenty-first century. . . . Let's talk about the terrorist attacks that were prevented in London, let's talk about our relationship to Islam, let's talk about the limits of liberality. It's about us and our future.[2]

This reaction forcefully captured a prevalent agreement in scholarship, intellectual discussions, and public discourse in Germany and elsewhere that post–Second World War German literature and culture are retrospective in nature, that in its struggle with Nazism, the past is "a burden man has to shoulder and of whose dead weight the living can or even must get rid in their march into the future," to point back to our earlier discussion of Hannah Arendt's *Between Past and Future*.[3] More often than not, when discussing National Socialism and the Holocaust, scholarship of postwar German literature is characterized by what Ernestine Schlant labels "absence and silence."[4] In her study of West German literature's depiction of the Holocaust, Schlant maintains that this "absence and silence" has not been "uniform, monolithic emptiness," yet the "great variety of narrative strategies" are "silent about the silence" of postwar German culture when it comes to the Holocaust (1). Schlant builds on Alexander Mitscherlich and Margarete Mitscherlich's well-known psychohistorical diagnosis from the late 1960s that West German society and culture are unable to mourn the loss of the führer. Schlant claims that with the possible exception of Chancellor Willi Brandt's visit to the Warsaw ghetto in 1970, no public ritual "has had an affective impact that would involve the entire personality and thus lead to a genuine expression of mourning" (13).[5] "Germans individually and collectively," Schlant argues, "have been unable to work through and mourn the crimes perpetrated, if working-through demands 'the possibility of judgment' that is 'argumentative, self-questioning, and related in mediated ways to action'" (13).[6] Thus, Schlant follows scholars who claim that authors of the postwar era did no meaningful "labor of mourning," preferring to present isolated historical moments in a highly poeticized manner. According to this view, "repression and silence" regarding the crimes of the regime "structured the literature of *Vergangenheitsbewältigung* [coming to terms with the past] up to 1990" (9).[7]

While such psychoanalytically informed observations contribute to our understanding of the literary engagement with Nazism following 1945, they neglect its futurity and its *prospective* dimension. Challenging the notion that the literary interest in the past is a reflection of the ideological convictions, mental states, and moral standing of the author and his or her community, I trace in the following pages the way in which the fictional evocation of Nazism in German letters brought about a new vocabulary to address that past. The works here do not merely reflect memories, ideologies, perceptions, and the like but also create new ways to address that era. Beyond confronting, admitting, or evading Nazi crimes, these works also perform what I called in the introduction the "world-making" role of imaginatively redescribing the past in ways that open new horizons of thinking and feeling about that past. Taken together, these writings have expanded contemporary cultural and political discourse, an expansion initially involving the integration of the Holocaust as a chapter of German history and then, in the course of the 1990s, a consideration of the role of historical remembrance in the reunited Germany, thus suggesting a different path into what Menasse and Kumpfmüller emblematically call "the future."[8]

Literature, Expansion, and Becoming

Coming of age in the Israel of the 1970s and 1980s, my first encounter with postwar German literature was marked by the expectation that its images, metaphors, and allegories would allow me to grasp better Germany's slide into the Fascist abyss as well as how German culture—in the Federal Republic and the socialist German Democratic Republic (GDR)—made sense of that era once the war was over. When I arrived in the Federal Republic in the late 1980s, I encountered the emergence of a new *Erinnerungskultur* (culture of memory)—an unprecedented wave of interest in testimonies, historiographies, theater productions, and acts of public remembrance recounting the Nazi past.[9]

The 1980s presented a first high point in a process that began in the 1960s with the so-called Frankfurt Auschwitz Trials (1963–65) and the era's student unrest, through which Germans who were (mostly) born after the war began to confront Germany's Nazi past. Yet the budding West German *Erinnerungskultur* of the 1980s was also an expression of a global trend. As in other Western societies, German *Erinnerungskultur* was a manifestation of what Andreas Huyssen labels a "memory boom": the wide-ranging fascination with individual and collective memories and a keen awareness of different modes of historical representation.[10] Huyssen views this development as resulting from a postmodern desire to find some usable pieces of various pasts, since the past seems to offer some grounding in a world where accelerating economic growth and technological and media innovations destabilize our experience of time and lived spaces.[11]

It was also during that era that the Holocaust began to surface as a global signifier for unspeakable atrocities and a central referent in debating human rights.[12] The fascination with memory in the Federal Republic was coupled with a growing sensitivity to the specific nature of Nazism's crimes and to the role of the Holocaust in German self-perception. The detached rhetoric previously used to address the Holocaust gave way to a multifaceted consideration of its origin and course, its effects during the postwar era, and its meaning for the victims and their descendants. The broad public interest in the 1979 screening of the NBC miniseries *Holocaust* and the political reverberations of the 1985 landmark speech of then Federal Republic president Richard von Weizsäcker are two important moments that mark this significant shift.[13] Even though the Holocaust was increasingly regarded in German cultural criticism of the postwar era as a defining moment of German history and of modernity, and despite the central role that Nazi crimes played in the West German youth revolt of the late 1960s, it was not until the 1980s that the Holocaust began to assume a more central role for German identity.[14] This change was also partly in response to some high-profile attempts to revise and contextualize the focus on Germany's Nazi past: the 1985 visit of Chancellor Helmut Kohl and President Ronald Reagan to the Bitburg cemetery (only three days before von Weizsäcker's speech) and the 1986 milestone Historikerstreit (Historians' Debate). The abundant and often ardent discussions surrounding these different attempts at what came to be called "normalization" underscored the extent to which different historical narratives regarding Nazism had direct implications for the West German public sphere.[15]

The disappearance of the most marked trace of the Second World War—the division between East and West Germany—in 1989 provoked fears that Nazism would be relegated to the realm of sufficiently addressed history.[16] As Michael Geyer, Konrad Jarausch, and others observed, some indications of a newly assertive national consciousness did emerge. Soon after the wall fell, a desire for a self-assured German nation arose, an emotion often accompanied by a tendency to universalize the pain of the victims, remembering them together with bystanders and even those who served the Nazi regime.[17] Furthermore, broader sections of the German public began focusing on the suffering of Germans during and after the war: on the Allies' massive air raids on German cities, the plight of ethnic Germans who were expelled (or fled) from Eastern Europe at the end of the war, the fate of German POWs, and the widespread rape of German women by Soviet troops during the Red Army's westward advance.[18] A concern thus arose that a self-assured German national discourse would set a new, disconcerting tone to replace the *juste milieu* of the Federal Republic and the enlightened public sphere of Heinrich Böll, Günter Grass, Jürgen Habermas, and the historian Hans-Ulrich Wehler, among others.[19]

My own reading of contemporary German literature at that point emphasized contending with guilt and shame. The literary depiction of recent German history mattered, I thought, because a reunited Germany was in danger of succumbing to strident nationalism. The wave of xenophobic incidents in the early 1990s and the seemingly endless array of debates regarding the role of the past in the reunited Germany—the dispute surrounding German participation in the "Coalition of the Willing" to drive Iraq out of Kuwait, the row over the exhibition displaying the Wehrmacht's crimes, and the debate surrounding the Holocaust Memorial in Berlin (to name but a few incidents)—strengthened my conviction that the study of literature's engagement with the past was crucial because it could give us an indication of the ability of German discourse to address the past appropriately.[20] Like many of Grass's harshest critics in 2006, I understood the role of the critic to be a moralist and not a reader or thinker focused on unfolding the artwork. What I failed to see, however, was that by reading contemporary German literature exclusively through the lens of its ability to "mourn" or "work through," I became a supervisor of the imagination whose task it was to remind writers and readers alike of the necessity of "confronting the past" and "accounting for the crimes" committed there.

By concentrating on questions of guilt and shame, trauma and its evasion, instead of the figurative language and formal devices employed in German literature about the past, this post-wall discussion failed to recognize the many ways in which postwar German literature (like contemporary literature elsewhere in the First World) displays an awareness of the questions about all historical representations raised by the philosophical "linguistic turn" and the discourse of postmodernity.[21] In this sense many of the difficulties facing German authors as they approached their country's past are shared by writers facing similar challenges in Israel, Britain, South Africa, the United States, and elsewhere. A German writer interested in recent history faces not only the test of meaningfully addressing a deeply disturbing national history but also what troubles many of her peers writing elsewhere: the understanding that "modernist events" amount to a decisive rupture in civilization and thus demand new modes of artistic expression. As we have seen in the introduction, these events function in social consciousness in a similar manner to the working of trauma in the psyche of individuals: they cannot be forgotten without significantly affecting our ability to engage with the present or to "envision a future free of [the events'] debilitating effects."[22] What the literary imagination thus struggles with is precisely the possibility of mobilizing the past in ways that will address its debilitating effects. The literary imagination in Germany and elsewhere does something more significant than display the tension between remembrance and forgetting: it creates new ways of apprehending the world and thereby presents the possibility for new paths into the future.

While I agree with White's view that modernist events challenge our inherited categories for assigning meaning to historical occurrences,[23] I consider less productive his claim that these events escape our efforts to integrate experience into our perception of the realities we inhabit. In West German literature of the postwar era, the poetic exploration of Germany's past was in fact an incorporation of those events into personal and communal narratives. West German literature's engagement with Nazism can thus be read as a constant rethinking of, and dialogue with, postwar cultural and political conditions and thus of Germany's future.

Richard Rorty's reading of Donald Davidson's theory of metaphor inspired this insight. As noted in the introduction, Davidson suggests that rather than symbolically expressing what we already know, metaphors change our beliefs and desires. When a literary work presents the past, it does not express the writer's or her community's knowledge of, or obliviousness to, the past *alone*. Rather, when a work invokes a painful moment of the past, it also offers us the opportunity to know it differently, and thus to rethink our views about its impact on present-day circumstances. In this manner, the literary engagement with the past may enhance our ability, to quote Rorty, "to do lots of other things—e.g., be more sophisticated and interesting people, emancipate ourselves from tradition, transvalue our values, gain or lose religious faith—without having to interpret these latter abilities as functions of increased *cognitive* ability."[24] Works such as Günter Grass's *The Tin Drum* and *Dog Years* introduce new ways to view Germany's Nazi past. When imaginative writers "send shivers down their readers' spines" with their literary innovations, they do not merely indicate what Grass or "the Germans" thought, felt, remembered, or repressed. Rather, they also change the vocabulary, self-perceptions, and ideas of readers, leaving a mark on what Rorty calls their "patterns of action."[25] Thus, I argue that Grass's literary rendition of the Third Reich and its crimes is an *expansion* of the language available to address the past. Metaphors of the past in postwar

German literature can be seen as a source for changes in readers' beliefs and desires, creating possibilities for new ways to see and *become*.

Symptomatic Reading and Moralism

The symptomatic approach to literature—the search for evidence of an individual or a social *condition*—appears in two, often-interrelated modes in the study of German literature's engagement with Nazism: the moralistic and the psychological. "Morality" is defined in the *Oxford English Dictionary*, Wendy Brown reminds us, as "ethical wisdom . . . moral qualities or endowments . . . moral discourse or instruction" motivated by the sentiment of goodness rather than by motivations outside it. Moralism, by contrast, is but a trace of the discourse of morality, "whose heritage and legitimacy it claims while in fact inverting that discourse's sense and sensibility." Moralism is a "posture" and "pose," one "that stands opposed to measured, difficult, and deliberate action that implicates rather than simply enacts the self."[26]

One of the most intriguing questions regarding the 2006 Grass affair is how the indignation at Grass as a hypocritical moralist ostensibly supported self-aware remembrance but was in fact devoid of sense and sensibility. That is, beyond the understandable need to question Grass's silence, his often judgmental language when it comes to others, and his self-assigned role as Germany's conscience, the Grass affair also displayed a deeply questionable impulse to indict Grass from a position of moral superiority.

This moralism obscured what Grass's autobiography actually offers as an imaginative redescription: its ability to suggest a language that can enable the reader to alter the terms used to address the writer's—and his generation's—struggle with a Fascist youth. The stormy debate prevented Grass's readers from measuring the path the writer and others have followed from voluntary conscription into Hitler's army or the SS to writing and speaking in favor of a German culture of memory and a civic public sphere. The rush to the moral high ground kept many from considering what it meant for the writer to tell his life story knowing that it would almost certainly destroy his public persona. Condemning Grass with a language ironically reminiscent of the writer's own moralizing posture, they could not see that the book offers the possibility of overcoming the cycle of guilt, shame, and public accusation with which Grass's name has been almost synonymous since the mid-1960s.[27]

Without defending Grass the person and his individual actions, including his silence about his past and his decades-long stance of public moralizing, it is significant to see that Grass's public confession signaled for his critics merely an opportunity to carry out the same form of moralizing for which many of them had sharply criticized him prior to the Grass affair. Grass's moralism was now ironically echoed in the self-assurance of those who rushed to undo him and his work in the name of a critique of his oblivious silence. But few noted this. Political scientist Claus Leggewie presented Grass's late confession as symbolizing the dilemma of West German intellectuals: their overcompensation for Germany's National Socialist past is paired with an avoidance of personal guilt.[28]

A significant variant of the moralistic, symptomatic reading surrounding the 2006 incident had been offered a decade and a half earlier by Karl Heinz Bohrer. In a variety of articles published before and then with increasing frequency after reunification, Bohrer criticized the didactic thread in the work of such writers as Günter Grass and Christa Wolf, faulting it for its direct or implied subjugation of aesthetics to morals.[29] Writing after the fall of the Berlin Wall, Bohrer maintained that much of postwar German literature was enslaved to *Gesinnungsethik* (the ethics of conviction) and *Gesinnungskitsch* (the kitsch of conviction): ideology in the guise of art.[30] Bohrer and others rightly noted the temptation to see in the poetic engagement with the past a way to uncover history's presumed lessons—lumping arts and morals together. Bohrer's desire to separate all modes of aesthetic production from social discourse, however, turned him, in an ironic twist, into an anti-morality moralist. Fighting any attempt to connect literature and ethics prevented him from acknowledging that a literary work may *allow*, rather than *prescribe*, thought, debate, and emancipation from custom or ritual—in short, provoke consideration of what lies outside the work itself.

The second mode of symptomatic reading is "psychological" in nature. By this I refer to the pathological rhetoric that characterizes some of the psychoanalytically informed scholarship on postwar German literature. The attention in recent decades to trauma in cultural and literary studies has yielded significant contributions to our understanding of engagement with Germany's Nazi past, specifically in how German literature after the war reflected the difficulties of integrating into consciousness the unspeakable crimes of the regime and the nation's devastating defeat.[31] Eric Santner has traced how the avoidance of a "labor of mourning" following Nazi Germany's defeat led to a missed opportunity to mourn the victims of the regime and address the past—a prolonged cycle of guilt and shame seen in the 2006 Grass affair.[32] Furthermore,

Dominick LaCapra has outlined the tension between "acting out" and "working through"—that is, between the behavioral and mental expressions of an unconscious that refuses to recognize a traumatic event and the mental procedure that allows an event to be integrated into consciousness, thus freeing one (at least partly) from the grip of mechanical repetition.[33]

Santner, LaCapra, and others emphasize the *interplay* between "acting out" and "working through": how becoming aware of both may allow the traumatized to become freer by rewriting their life stories and addressing what was initially repressed. In some cases, however, admonitions concerning the failure to integrate National Socialism into consciousness resulted in scholarship that has treated literature merely as proof that Germans individually and collectively have been generally "unable" to work through their past, to engage significantly with their difficult history.[34]

More often than not, the charge of an insufficient "labor of mourning" has left unanswered the question of what a successful "labor" or a viable "working through" might actually look like. Ernestine Schlant, for example, claims "roughly every decade and a half the successor generations developed different strategies and different approaches in their attempts to fashion identity for themselves and come to terms with the legacy of their elders. Yet 'coming to terms' is not equivalent to 'working through,' and it leaves the victims and the crimes as unmourned as they have always been."[35] In Schlant's approach, we find little indication of how remembrance or forgetting evolved over time. Incremental changes and shifting metaphors are overlooked in favor of an ahistorical judgment in which what *has been* simply returns in ever-new shapes.[36]

As Alon Confino has noted, the "myth" of an all-encompassing repression neglects the delicate tension between what is remembered and what is forgotten, as well as between public and private remembrance, thus overlooking what has in fact taken place after all in the vast landscape of Nazism remembrance.[37] If there has indeed been a sweeping, unwavering failure to address the crimes of the Nazi past consciously, it is difficult to account for the increasing number of scholarly studies, novels, films, monuments, speeches, political debates, and international treaties surrounding this presumably unaccounted-for history.

Claiming, as does Ernestine Schlant, that "silence" and "repression" dominated the literary imagination until the 1990s fails to account for many facets of actual literary writing, implicitly comparing it to a model German writer who did not and does not exist.[38] The Mitscherlichs' mixture of psychoanalytic-therapeutic discourse with political and pedagogical attitudes was and remains incisive, I believe, yet it is hardly an exclusive interpretive framework.[39] In invoking historical events, literature is always more than an imprint of the writer's or her community's unconscious.

Toward a Practical Past

The works discussed in these pages are capable of more than merely evading or tackling the traumas of the past.[40] They create what hitherto did not exist: new ways to regard, to experience, and to make sense of the German Nazi past. When we see them exclusively under the sign of trauma, our view of these works is deprived of what is unique to the imagination, namely—in a tradition going back to Immanuel Kant and centered on free play in the aesthetic experience—that while literature and the arts allow us to engage the world outside the work, they cannot be reduced to its reflection.

We should ask, then, in what ways a literary work redescribes the past rather than represents it and consider how forms of literary expression—from irony to the sequencing of plot—change the prevalent vocabulary of a period and allow reflection on social, political, or ethical concerns. These questions will help us avoid the reduction of postwar German literature to the exhibition of ideological commitments or psychological conditions.

Avoiding the temptation of an inclusive, chronologically organized history of German postwar literature as it deals with Nazism, part I of this book presents some of the most significant works by writers of various generations as they address that past. Given the scope and focus of this book, many authors and works of great importance will remain unmentioned.[41]

The next three chapters are dedicated to three writers of the postwar era: Günter Grass, Alexander Kluge, and Martin Walser. Examining their highly divergent work, I will underline how, having experienced National Socialism firsthand, all three used this period as a focal point of the literary imagination. In many of their works, Nazism appears as a central element of individual and communal German self-perception. In distinctive ways, all three offered modes of redescription that together contributed to a discourse of remembrance that went beyond the expression of atonement and the need to "move on" that dominated the first postwar years, helping to establish first West Germany and later a reunited Germany as a progressive liberal democracy.[42]

Since all three authors began publishing in an era still dominated by the presence of many who actively participated in the Nazi "endeavor," it is only natural that their work centered on questions of guilt and shame and that their language often reveals the difficulties of conceiving a future not marked by issues of individual and collective responsibility.[43] With the discussion of Günter Grass's late work and of Martin Walser's polemic against the role of public remembrance in post-wall Germany, we will see how what initially had been a new way to engage German history increasingly became a stale idiom. My aim is not to criticize these writers but rather to trace the process by which once-innovative language becomes stale.

The final chapter of part 1 takes up writers for whom Germany's Nazi past is but *received* history, authors who seek to move beyond exhausted language. In the writing of such relatively younger writers as Hans-Ulrich Treichel, Norbert Gstrein, Bernhard Schlink, Katharina Hacker, and W. G. Sebald, the invocation of the past is less about integrating Nazism into consciousness and more about recasting it as a productive, "practical" past (in Michael Oakeshott's term). The past is invoked less as an unbearable burden and more as a facet of one's own life story. Germany's modern catastrophic history becomes part of German cultural heritage and a chapter of modern human history that prompts us all—Germans and non-Germans alike—to deal with contemporary inhumanities such as torture or racism.

Throughout the discussion, my emphasis remains on the encounter with metaphor as an event, as something that happens to us as we read or recall a remarkable work.[44] I am interested in tracing the ability of literature, by engaging decisive historical moments, to dare its readers to accept the shadow that the future—not the irretrievable past—casts upon the present. I want us to see even a past as difficult as Germany's not merely as the unbearable mark of Cain but also as a prompt for readers to ask what we would like to become. And what might a future look like that is profoundly different from the past?

2

Günter Grass: "Nothing Is Pure"

*"Once Upon a Time" as the Immediate Present:
Günter Grass,* The Tin Drum

How did new vocabularies to describe and address the German past emerge in the postwar era? To what extent did writers introduce novel ways to see what had occurred during and subsequent to the Nazi era that allowed their readers to glimpse the shadow that futurity casts on the German present? How did fiction indicate the possibility of prospection, self-creation, and the formation of a new community? Our point of departure is Günter Grass and his *Danzig Trilogy* (1959–63), one of the most influential works of the postwar era, and the opening words of its first installment, *Die Blechtrommel* (1959; *The Tin Drum*): "Zugegeben: ich bin Insasse einer Heil- und Pflegeanstalt" (granted: I am an inmate in a mental institution).[1] These words come from the mouth of Oskar Matzerath, the thirty-year-old narrator and protagonist of the novel, who will soon offer a panoramic view of German history from the preceding century to Konrad Adenauer's West Germany. As the first sentence indicates, Oskar will tell his story while suggesting that all his images, observations, and judgments should be questioned: how can we count on the historical narrative of a narrator residing in a mental institution?[2] Oskar thus enters the stage as a powerful representative of the significance of doubt: his sumptuous language, his constant shifting from the first to the third person, and his mixing of the ironic and the sentimental determine the novel's perspective on the past and all surrounding realities. Nothing can be taken at face value. All stories are just that: creations of our imagination and as such need to be subjected to scrutiny. At the beginning of the novel, Oskar notes: "You can start a story in the middle then strike out boldly backward and forward to create confusion. You can be modern, delete all reference to time and distance, and then proclaim or let someone else proclaim that at the eleventh hour you've finally solved the space-time problem" (5). As Patrick O'Neill notes, the untrustworthy nature of Oskar's narrative serves as an invitation to the reader to consider "how reliable any narrative . . . can ever be."[3] What the reader calls "reality," as Oskar's picaresque language highlights, is the slippery blend of the mundane and the fantastic, the reasonable and the absurd.[4] Oskar Matzerath is not, however, just another character in modern literature's rich gallery of unreliable narrators. In Oskar, Grass creates a new lexis of substantial doubt, of distrust in social norms and in the ruling ideologies—in short, in the mental and institutional universe that surrounded Oskar while growing up in Nazi Germany.[5] This was a universe that survived the war, at least in part. West Germany of the 1950s was a country focused on reconstruction, on aligning itself with the West in the Cold War. Apart from taking a few significant steps toward recognition of its responsibility for the Nazi crimes—most notably, via the 1952 reparations agreement with Israel—its cultural-political discourse was characterized by silence regarding the crimes of the Nazi past.[6] Robert Moeller has shown how German society of the first decade and a half after the war—contrary to the prevalent notion that the 1950s were characterized by almost complete repression of Nazism—did not simply forget or repress that period but rather selectively remembered it through the prism of German suffering.[7] In a period defined by a selective memory of National Socialism as a German catastrophe, Günter Grass in *The Tin Drum* was among the first young writers to redescribe Nazism in terms other than that of a malaise that infected the Germans. Grass was also among the few who did not resort to the clichés of "unspeakable crimes" committed "in the name of the German people."[8]

With Oskar's brazen language, seditious drumming, and ability to crack glass with his ear-piercing voice, Grass's novel dissolves the prevalent mythical-symbolic rhetoric regarding the "dark past" (*finstere Vergangenheit*) and the vague sense of guilt so common in Adenauer's West Germany of the 1950s.[9] The narrative shifting between different moments proposes a new way to view the past-present relationship. The narrative oscillates between referring to Nazism in the past tense and, in crucial instances, invoking it as an immediate present or even a possible future. Speaking about "November of thirty-eight" (Reichskristallnacht), Oskar moves straightforwardly to "Today," that is, to Adenauer's Germany, in which many present themselves as members of "Resistance circles" or as people who retreated from public life into a quasi-subversive "Inner Emigration" (111). Stating that his former purpose with the drumming was "destruction"—the disruption of the nationalist rhetoric in party rallies—Oskar speaks directly to his contemporary, postwar readers: "and so I ask you, who aren't inmates in a mental institution" (112), prompting them to consider their own stance vis-à-vis the past, their own sociopolitical positions in regard to their state.

Oskar evokes specifically and in the bluntest manner the Nazi rallies and recalls the devastations of Reichskristallnacht (111) and the ensuing war of annihilation against the Jews. In creating a temporal continuity between November 9, 1938, and the immediate present, Grass pries open the Nazi past and lays it like a transparency upon the present. By forcing the reader to view two moments simultaneously, Grass's depiction of the Nazi past is also an assault on the present. This provocation is also evident in the novel's consistent attention to artistic production per se, that is, what it means to communicate with art. Oskar's drumming, for instance, is not merely a means of communication; it is a symbol for the power of art in the face of an inhuman political discourse. At a rally in support of the demand to annex Danzig to the ascending Nazi Reich, Oskar drums playfully against the chauvinistic oom-pa-pa military marches of the Nazi indoctrination machine by beating out jazz rhythms, together with a rendition of the "The Blue Danube" (108), which invokes the relatively peaceful coexistence of many ethnicities and cultures under the Habsburg monarchy.

Oskar's rhythmic disruption of nationalist rhetoric at Danzig Nazi rallies has a parallel in Grass's own disruption of entrenched nationalistic notions of "pure" German ethnicity. Oskar is the legal son of Agnes Koljaiczek, a woman of Kashubian and Polish origin, and Alfred Matzerath, a German. However, because Agnes has had a long-lasting love affair with her cousin, the Pole Jan Bronski, Oskar (and the reader) will never know for certain who his biological father is. Yet another figure with a parent-like role is the Jewish toy merchant Sigismund Markus, who supplies Oskar with his tin drums and thus enables the boy to connect in his unique way with the world of the adults around him. With this elaborate ethnic configuration, Grass forces consideration of one of the central notions behind the war: the purity of *ethnos*, or race. Whether or not Grass intentionally crafted Oskar to undo prevalent notions about ethnic origins, Oskar's complex family history, as a metaphorical constellation, is "world-making" in the sense that it made previous notions regarding purity of origin seem outdated, challenging racial myths that survived the collapse of the Nazi state.

Grass's most distinctive achievement in *The Tin Drum* crystallizes in the concluding chapter of part I, "Faith, Hope, Love" (181–89). Borrowing the temporal trope "once upon a time" from fairy tales, the chapter recounts Reichskristallnacht, a night of attacks on Jewish stores, the burning of the Danzig synagogue, and numerous assaults on Jews.[10] We read of a lethal encounter between Sigismund Markus and members of the Nazi Sturm-Abteilung (SA). The mental world of the latter is displayed in the musician Meyn, a brute who kills his four cats because they spread bad smells. The chapter reaches a crescendo with Sigismund Markus's suicide in the course of the riots and shortly before one of the SA can "pock" him (186).

Grass's achievement here is twofold. First, he forcefully presents the fate of a Jewish victim of Nazi racism—a character Grass develops with clear empathy—and, through this figure, invokes the mental and bodily pain of all the victims.[11] Second, the chapter's linguistic and formal features prevent the terrifying events of Reichskristallnacht from being relegated to the realm of a distant, sufficiently addressed past. What occurred is told in terms of "once upon a time," suggesting that like other fairy tales, this one, too, has an instructive import. Loyal to his role of challenging delivered norms, Oskar refrains, however, from directly pointing to the lessons of his tale. Rather, his fairy tale's message is that what appears to belong to the past is, in fact, a facet of the postwar present.

While most of the narrative surrounding the fateful night of November 9, 1938, is told in the past tense, as the chapter reaches its dramatic climax the narrative shifts between the past and present tense. After portraying Markus's death, Oskar connects Reichskristallnacht to the Nazi genocide and to what is "coming" (187). In the last two pages of the chapter, the narrative moves back and forth between the past, present, and future:

> He's coming! He's coming! And who came? The Christ Child, the Savior? Or was it the heavenly Gasman with the gas meter under his arm, ticking away? And he said: I am the Savior of this world, without me you can't cook. . . . And [he] gave out walnuts

> and almonds in the shell, which were promptly cracked, and they
> too poured forth Spirit and gas, so that the gullible were easily
> gulled, saw all the gasmen in the increasingly thick and bluish air
> outside the department stores as Santa Clauses and Christ Chil-
> dren in all sizes and prices.

The Holocaust—invoked here by the figure of "the Gasman" and the
"bluish air"—does not occur in an earlier, closed period. The era of
the "heavenly Gasman" is not past. On the contrary, he is still "coming," his meter "ticking away." Speaking from the perspective of today,
that is, the perspective of Adenauer's Germany, Oskar notes, "I don't
know . . . who hides behind Santa Claus beards *today* . . . don't know
how to wring the necks of gas cocks, or how to chock them off . . . I
don't know . . . " (188, my emphasis). The puzzling zigzag between temporal realms and the ironic reference in the chapter's title to the Christian virtues of faith, hope, and love (1 Corinthians 13:13) convert the
fate of Sigismund Markus and many others into an open challenge, into
"a stone of stumbling, and a rock of offense" (1 Peter 2:8), a test to all
those who might consider what faith, hope, and love mean in a world
that has experienced the events of November 9, 1938. By asking himself,
rhetorically, "who hides . . . today," Oskar addresses his readers, contemporaries of Adenauer's Germany, prompting them to ask the same
question and consider what kind of West Germany they live in, where
many who hid behind Santa Claus beards in the 1930s and 1940s may
hide behind similar disguises today.

The last two sentences of the chapter further underscore this
question:

> Once upon a time there was a toy merchant named Markus, and
> he took along *all* the toys when he left this world.
>   Once upon a time there was a musician named Meyn, and
> if he's not dead, he's still alive today, playing his trumpet again,
> too beautifully for words. (189, my emphasis)

Reichskristallnacht may be seen as a mythical-distant era by those who,
like Oskar, live in postwar West Germany. Yet even if Meyn and those he
stands for are dead, numerous other ex-members of the SA and other elements of the Nazi machinery are alive and well. The readers of *The Tin
Drum* knew that the Meyns of Adenauer's Germany go about their lives,
playing their instruments—undisturbed. Stating "and he took along all
the toys when he left this world," Oskar asks what a world devoid of

"toys" such as his critical-noisy drum would look like. Grass's narrative implies that Reichskristallnacht and the subsequent Nazi genocide reverberate in the postwar West German present through obliviousness toward the crimes and a willingness to integrate Nazi functionaries and party members into West Germany's political elite.[12] By forging this connection between the recent past and the present, the novel, like Oskar's drumming, agitates readers into a different rhythm of thought.

Moreover, this connection of past and present provides a clear opportunity for what I call prospection. The plot's construction breaks up what Hannah Arendt, in her reading of Kafka, calls the unidirectional flow of time. The past is not just a burden to carry or, as in the case of German cultural-political discourse of the 1950s, to be referred to only through lofty abstractions. Rather, Grass's temporal scheme challenges the reader to begin a new trajectory, breaking out of the cycle to which the narrative alludes: a pattern of violent ethnic and racial politics that brought about the Second World War and the Holocaust.

The Tin Drum's third and final book spells out this continuum of Nazism and postwar West Germany by means of another metaphor that reveals the necessity of a new language to address recent German history. Here postwar Germany of the 1950s is seen through a jazz club called the Onion Cellar (497–511), whose customers belong to West Germany's new elite: businessmen, doctors, lawyers, artists, and journalists—"all those who call themselves intellectuals nowadays" (500). Eager to start up meaningful conversations, "to air things, get things off their chests, talk freely and openly, spill their guts, speak straight from the heart . . . to stop thinking and just let go" (501), they nonetheless bitterly fail. All the visitors to the club remain unable to address their real problems. Despite their best efforts, Oskar notes, they leave the essential, "the past," untouched (501). The only time they can "let go," express their emotions, and cry is while peeling and cutting onions, which they do without any awareness that the source of their weeping is their shared Nazi past.[13]

The metaphor of the Onion Cellar (to which Grass alluded as he was writing his autobiography, *Peeling the Onion*) is the literary manifestation of what the Mitscherlichs describe in *Die Unfähigkeit zu trauern*: that while official discourse in West Germany professed the evil of Nazism, there had not been a genuine individual and societal recognition of guilt and the accompanying acceptance of responsibility.[14] The metaphoric crying in the Onion Cellar exposes the emptiness of the public West German rhetoric regarding the past, leaving no doubt that it is both ineffective and obsolete. As a *poetic* constellation, the Onion

Cellar opens space for a prospective consideration of what may replace this kind of ersatz *Vergangenheitsbewältigung* (coming to terms with the past) in which one cries but hardly speaks in concrete terms about what has taken place, about the prominent role many perpetrators have taken in postwar West Germany, or about one's duty toward the victims and survivors. The novel prompts readers to consider what a more genuine labor of mourning, to use Freud's concept, might be. The metaphor, and thus the novel, allow early postwar readers to see themselves as visitors to the Onion Cellar, able to use artifice (onions or stories) to provoke a creative labor of thoughts, emotions, and memories.[15] Precisely because *The Tin Drum* does not specify the content of what the visitors leave unsaid, the novel prompts its readers to fill in the gaps, to recognize the obsolete language and habits of Adenauer's Germany in regard to the memory of National Socialism.

"But Even Soap Cannot Wash Pure": Günter Grass, Dog Years

In the years immediately following the publication of *The Tin Drum*, Grass took further steps in redescribing Nazism. In "Love Letters," book 2 of *Hundejahre* (1963; *Dog Years*), Harry Liebenau writes to his cousin Tulla Pokriefke in the postwar era, remembering his coming of age during National Socialism in the city of Danzig. He reminds Tulla of their youthful adventures and of her remarkable ability to uncover what the adults tried to hide from. In the key letter of this correspondence, Harry remembers how Tulla's drive to reveal the truth finally led her to discover the true nature of a white mound that she found on the outskirts of Danzig:

> There was once a girl, her name was Tulla, and she had the pure forehead of a child. But nothing is pure. Not even the snow is pure. No virgin is pure. Even a pig isn't pure. The devil never entirely pure. No note rises pure. Every violin knows that. Every star chimes that. Every knife peels it: even a potato isn't pure: it has eyes, they have to be scooped out.
>
> But what about salt? Salt is pure! Nothing, not even salt, is pure. It's only on boxes that it says: Salt is pure. After all, it keeps. What keeps with it? But it's washed. Nothing can be washed clean. But the elements: pure? Even in the beginning not pure. The idea? Isn't it always pure? Even in the beginning not pure. Jesus Christ not pure. Marx Engels not pure. Ashes not pure. And the host not pure. No idea stays pure. Even the flowering

of art isn't pure. And the sun has spots. All geniuses menstruate. On sorrow floats laughter. In the heart of roaring lurks silence. In angles lean compasses.—But the circle, the circle is pure!

No closing of the circle is pure. For if the circle is pure, then the snow is pure, the virgin is, the pigs are, Jesus Christ, Marx and Engels, white ashes, all sorrows, laughter, to the left roaring, to the right silence, ideas immaculate, wafers no longer bleeders and geniuses without efflux, all angles pure angles, piously compasses would describe circles: pure and human, dirty, salty, diabolical, Christian and Marxist, laughing and roaring, ruminant, silent, holy, round pure angular. And the bones, white mounds that were recently heaped up, would grow immaculately without crows: pyramids of glory. But the crows, which are not pure, were creaking unoiled, even yesterday: nothing is pure, no circle, no bone. And piles of bones, heaped up for the sake of purity, will melt cook boil in order that soap, pure and cheap; but even soap cannot wash pure.[16]

With elegiac lyricism, Harry's words evoke the pile of human remains of those who had been incarcerated in Stutthof, the notorious concentration camp in the vicinity of Danzig. The breach of civilization that came about with the industrial killing of humans erupts into the present. Harry's words also evoke the prevailing silence surrounding the world of the camps: "No one talked about the pile of bones. But everybody saw smelled tasted it" (305). His metaphors, however, extend beyond mere historical representation, revealing the emptiness of what lay behind the certificates distributed by the Allies to indicate a person's innocence—documents widely referred to as *Persilscheine* (Persil passes) after the well-known detergent Persil.[17] Furthermore, the mode of reference to the past—tying the whiteness of the pile of bones to the ostensible "purity" of the present—once again breaks the supposed separation between a finished Nazi past and a "normal" postwar Germany. "Nothing *is* pure" transforms what Tulla has seen *there* and *then* into an aspect of the now: "the crows . . . were creaking . . . even yesterday. . . . And piles of bones . . . *will* melt cook boil" (my emphasis). In a world in which "nothing *is* pure," readers are invited to view the events of Stutthof as central elements in their own realities, in their own perceptions and beliefs—including (ironically) what they read: "Even the flowering of art isn't pure."

A dim, negative ontology resonates through these lines: what *is* can never regain a sense of wholesomeness. We can no longer view the sub-

limity of nature ("snow" or "salt"), religion ("Jesus Christ"), social utopias ("Marx Engels"), or other forms of metaphysics ("the idea") as untainted. And if all these are tainted, with what can we orient ourselves?
The strength of Grass's prose results not only from the imagery but also
from the deliberate absence of new systems of values or beliefs to orient
the reader. This labor remains for the reader to undertake; its outcome
is undetermined.

Oskar Matzerath, Harry Liebenau, and Tulla Pokriefke's names are
synonymous with the fate of a generation that grew up during National
Socialism and whose adult lives would be spent coping with this circumstance. They stand for the generation that included Joseph Alois Ratz-
inger, Jürgen Habermas, and Hans-Dietrich Genscher. Through Oskar,
Harry, and Tulla, Grass was one of the main figures to help establish a
meaningful sense of responsibility for the crimes of the Nazi regime in
West German intellectual discourse of the 1950s and early 1960s, a discourse that until then referred to Nazism through abstract markers such
as "catastrophe."[18] By creating an unresolved tension between "was"
and "is" ("There *was* once a girl . . . " and "But nothing *is* pure") and by
bringing into the present historical phenomena like Reichskristallnacht
and the concentration camps, Grass's early work was pivotal in the
changes in West German discourse about the Nazi past. Whereas *Vergangenheitsbewältigung* was used in the first decade and a half after
the war with a strong emphasis on *Bewältigung*—"to manage," "to master," "to overcome"—Grass depicted Nazism as a collective experience
that had yet to be addressed and was thus a task for future decades.[19]
More effectively than any other writer of the postwar era, Grass introduced a new vocabulary and with it helped shape a German democratic
and humanistic public discourse.[20]

The Hereditary Guilt: Günter Grass, My Century *and* Crabwalk

Grass's enormous literary achievements of the late 1950s and the early
1960s were not matched, however, by his later writing. In understanding
this, it is useful to return to Richard Rorty's discussion of figurative language, in which he proposes looking at language and culture as Darwin
taught us to think of the history of a coral reef.[21] Just as a reef is made of
both dead and living corals, and just as living corals are constantly dying
off to be replaced by new ones, old metaphors become dead metaphors
and new ones take their place. Culture, Rorty believes—following Mary
Hesse's view of scientific innovation as "metaphoric redescription"—is
shaped by numerous mutations in how we describe where we came from

and what we will one day resemble. Literature in this case is the site "where old metaphors are constantly dying off into literalness."[22]

Beginning in the 1960s, Grass's consistent references to Auschwitz as an instructive concept in West Germany's political discourse made his previously innovative language literal in Rorty's sense; that is, his metaphors ceased to resonate futurity and instead took their place in a defined set of functions and coordinates within the contemporary political landscape. As Jan Werner Müller has shown, Grass developed the notion of *Vergangenkunft*: a cross between *Vergangenheit* (past) and *Zukunft* (future) indicating that German guilt can never be diminished, and thus the past holds the present and the future in check. Accordingly, if Auschwitz is not remembered in the way Grass finds appropriate, Germany's future is bound to be shadowed by relapse into nationalistic racism.[23] In his 1990 Frankfurt *Poetik-Vorlesung* (Poetics lecture), Grass noted that "we will not get around Auschwitz. We should never attempt such an act of violence, no matter how much we might wish to do so, because Auschwitz belongs to us, it is a permanent scar on our history, and it has—on the positive side! [*als Gewinn*!]—made possible an insight which might run like this: now, finally, we know ourselves."[24] Auschwitz is no longer a challenge that Germany's past poses for the present. Rather, it becomes the prism through which Grass explains what is morally apt when he lectures others about ethical matters. Once an exemplar of thoughtful engagement with moral issues, Grass became another moralist. German guilt appears now in Grass's essays and public addresses as eternal fate—a hereditary weight the Germans will carry forever, regardless of age and personal involvement in the crimes of the Nazi regime.[25]

Much of Grass's post-wall literary work, most notably his *Mein Jahrhundert* (1999; *My Century*) and *Im Krebsgang* (2002; *Crabwalk*), indicate how this more recent writing presents Germans as determined by Auschwitz.[26] Returning to the Nazi era from the vantage point of Germany after reunification, *Crabwalk* revisits the life of the *Danzig Trilogy*'s Tulla Pokriefke. Like millions of Germans who, in the course of the conclusion of the Second World War, fled or were expelled from Eastern Europe, Tulla leaves her native Danzig and embarks on a new life in the German heartland.[27] Her journey begins on board the *Wilhelm Gustloff*. Named after the German leader of the Swiss Nazi Party assassinated in 1936 by the Jewish student David Frankfurter, the *Wilhelm Gustloff* served in the late 1930s as a cruise liner for the Nazi labor organization Kraft durch Freude (Strength through Joy). In 1945, spotted by a Soviet submarine some thirty kilometers offshore, the ship was sunk on

January 30—the date of Hitler's rise to power and Wilhelm Gustloff's birthday—taking with it the lives of some eight thousand wounded soldiers and civilians, including Tulla Pokriefke. It was during that disastrous night that Tulla's only son, Paul, was born.

In *Crabwalk*, Paul assumes the task of telling his mother's story. His account is embedded in the realities of post-wall Germany and reflects the difficulties facing a writer who wants to account for the sufferings of millions of Germans while taking into consideration the possible misuse of German suffering to promote a discourse of German victimhood.[28] Paul is specifically worried about his son, Konrad (Konny), who embodies a new and overtly dangerous approach to the German past. Setting up a nationalistic web page and agitating in chat rooms about the demise of the *Wilhelm Gustloff*, Konny signifies an emerging obliviousness toward German guilt. In *Crabwalk*'s dramatic showdown, Konrad shoots the philo-Semite Wolfgang, who in chat rooms pretends to be a Jew called David. Later, during the police investigation, Konny reasons: "I fired because I am a German."[29]

"I fired because I am a German" echoes all too clearly what, according to *Crabwalk*, David Frankfurter is reported to have said upon shooting Wilhelm Gustloff: "I fired the shots because I am a Jew" (25). Konny's confession also echoes Grass's own essayistic reflection that in confronting Auschwitz, "now, finally, we know ourselves." Konrad's words posit Germanness as characterized by a perpetual guilt.[30] *Crabwalk* accounts for the horrific death that befell German civilians, yet it seems to warn the reader about a reoccurrence of the historical catastrophe because Germans *as such* are prone to relapse into rabid nationalism. Konrad's father, Paul (a figure bearing many similarities to Grass himself), concludes his account with the following ominous words: "It [the German past] doesn't end. Never will it end—'Nie hört es auf'" (234).

Memory as Hide-and-Seek: Günter Grass, Peeling the Onion

Not only did Grass's later work lose its evocative power, but his silence regarding his service in the Waffen-SS, as well as his 2012 poem "What Must Be Said" and the ensuing debate, sheds a disturbing light on some aspects of his significant achievements: "Nothing is pure" might be read now as an implicit attempt to wash oneself clean by suggesting that being human means being culpable.[31] Taken together, however, Grass's works have been central to the broad process by which authors, historians, sociologists, and psychologists spelled out "the German past," turning

"Auschwitz" into an explicit noun in the postwar era, the locus of guilt and shame but also—and here I would put my own emphasis—into a symbolic point of reference for thinking through what it will mean to be German in the future.[32] As Grass's autobiography hints, at the center of this consideration lies the question of the future of Germany's memory culture: thinking through what remembrance should now mean, six decades and more after the war.

Peeling the Onion offers a new perspective on Grass's life and through him an entire generation's difficulties negotiating remembrance and forgetting, caught as they were between the demands of public remembrance and the intricacies of personal memory. "MEMORY" (capitalized in original), Grass writes, "likes to play hide-and-seek, to crawl away."[33] It contradicts what he calls "remembrance" (*Gedächtnis*) (3; translation altered). While remembrance is pedantic in insisting on its truthfulness, memory resembles an onion: it consists of multiple layers that we may "peel," all along knowing that we will never quite reach any core, any conclusive accuracy (3). Looking back in time, Grass is well aware of the follies of individual memory as he notes that the "ignorance" he claims about the crimes of the regime that he willingly served "could not blind me to the fact that I had been incorporated into a system that had planned, organized, and carried out the extermination of millions of people" (111). In *Peeling the Onion*, he is as blunt and honest as his innovative Oskar once was: "What I had accepted with the stupid pride of youth I wanted to conceal after the war out of a recurrent sense of shame. But the burden remained, and no one could alleviate it" (110–11). Telling the story, Grass does not merely represent who he had been but rather—both in writing about his youth and by publishing his late confession—re-creates himself as a character who is finally capable of facing up to what he kept hidden for decades.

Grass's autobiography allows us to consider what the German discourse on National Socialism might *now* become, *following* Grass's confessed inability to admit to his military affiliation. Grass is now the writer who served in the notorious Waffen-SS while for decades claiming to have served as a *Flakhelfer* (the German youth enlisted to assist the Air Force defense against allied bombardments): "It [his silence over his Waffen-SS service] oppressed me," Grass confessed to the *Frankfurter allgemeine Zeitung*. "My silence over all the years ranks among the reasons why I wrote this book. It had to come out. Finally."[34] Now that this "it" is out, Grass offers us the opportunity to reconsider the first five decades of postwar German culture and especially to assess the language of public remembrance.[35]

Contributing to postwar West Germany's democratic culture by imaginatively redescribing Nazism, Grass and other writers of Group 47 nevertheless continued to hold on to some aspects of the "corrupted" Nazi vocabulary they grew up with, as well as promote (consciously or unconsciously) notions rooted in the racist ideology of Nazi Germany. One should, however, evaluate the role of Grass and his peers in Group 47 according to the distance they were able to achieve, in terms of their language and work, from that point of departure, and not according to the critic's notion of where they should have arrived. In other words, I believe that they should be judged in regard to what they were able to write that was different from what writers before them had written and, when applicable, in comparison with their own previous convictions.[36]

As we will see in the following chapters, even a problematic thematic thread or a troubling figurative choice offers us the possibility of thought that exceeds the writer's intention. Ironically, the 2006 and the 2012 Grass affair made this obvious: in continuously redescribing German history (including his own), Grass played a crucial role in the process by which postwar Germany evolved as an open, lively public sphere, even when his literature lost innovative force and a sense of direction. Indeed, even at the moment in which his public posture as his nation's self-proclaimed conscience was diminished to a substantial extent, his vivacious interventions and the reactions they triggered were the best indication of what the literary engagement with Germany's recent history means as redescription and the extent to which contemporary German culture is indebted to this admittedly imperfect writer.

3

Alexander Kluge: Literature as Orientation

"What Can I Count On? How Can I Protect Myself?"

Alexander Kluge, who, like Günter Grass, grew up during
Nazism, has also focused his artistic and intellectual ener-
gies on this past, beginning with his early literary work
through to his extensive cinematic production and theoretical writings. Yet Kluge's crisp, refined prose differs
greatly from Grass's opulent plots and symbolism, and
unlike Grass, Kluge has consistently refrained from a direct involvement in politics and in public debates regarding the role of remembrance in Germany's political culture. Kluge was among the first and, until recently, the
few in postwar German literature to turn to events such as
the battle of Stalingrad or the air raids on German cities,
and his themes and figurative choices thus broaden our
view of German history. With matchless curiosity, Kluge's
literature and his cinematic and television work range far
beyond the confines of his nation's past. With a mixture of
lyricism and distant, Brechtian aesthetics, he turns his gaze
to modernity in all its iterations, be it the 2011 Fukushima
disaster, politically motivated archeological excavations
in Jerusalem, or Eric Kandel's notion of the human brain.
Thus, Kluge's work is not focused on rendering modernist
events intelligible. Rather, Kluge is interested in what he
views as human "orientation" in light of past and possible

future man-made catastrophes: his work asks how a literary and theoretical investigation of modernity may yield different modes of social and
economic organization.

Above all, Kluge's readers are led to engage in this activity of orientation in his magnum opus, the labyrinthine, mammoth *Chronik der Gefühle* (2000; Chronicle of feelings). As we look back in time for a point of
reference that might guide us, the book encourages us—contemporaries
of a world whose political order has changed substantially over the last
decades—to do so with an emphasis on what might prove useful:

> What people need in their lives [*Lebensläufe*] is ORIENTA-
> TION. Like ships navigate. That is the *function* of such an exten-
> sive book: that one compares, feels attracted or appalled, since a
> book functions like a mirror.
>
> No one will read so many pages at once. It is enough if
> one, like in a calendar or indeed in a CHRONICLE, *investi-
> gates* [*nachprüft*] what concerns him. The subjective orienta-
> tion: What can I count on? How can I protect myself? What do I
> need to fear? What holds independent actions together [*was hält
> freiwillige Taten zusammen*]? That is the underlying, unchang-
> ing current that builds the true chronicle.[1]

Kluge's *Chronik der Gefühle*, like much of his prose, echoes the literary tradition of *Kalendergeschichten*, short stories that capture in an-
ecdotal format everyday scenes with the intention of entertainment and
instruction, a genre made popular by Johann Peter Hebel, Bertolt Brecht,
and Walter Benjamin. The two volumes of *Chronik*, which begin with
this succinct readers' manual, are *Basisgeschichten* (Base stories, or Basic stories) and *Lebensläufe* (*Case Histories*; first published as a separate
volume in 1962).[2] Blending fact and fiction, arid realism and feral imagination, they collect Kluge's published work up to 1989 as well as new
pieces written in the post-wall era.[3] *Chronik* thus looks back in time,
often to the disasters of the twentieth century—among them Auschwitz,
Stalingrad, Hiroshima, and Chernobyl. Yet Kluge's focus is on Oakeshott's "practical past," on "what to think, to say or *to do*" about the
past.[4] Kluge views his prose in a similarly "functional" manner. Investigating such decisive moments as an air raid on a city or a mass murder
may help us orient ourselves in regard to our "present-future."

The past, however, is not edifying, for it bears no conclusive lessons.
Furthermore, decisive historical events are never utterly gone. Past events
instead await discovery of their contemporaneity by those facing chal-

lenges in the present. "These two volumes," Kluge continues in the short introduction to *Chronik*,

> tell stories in the reverse order of their creation. That is also how memory functions: from the present backward. One errs if one thinks that the present stops at an earlier point. How many quasi changes and real metamorphoses did we experience since 1945? From the *Spiegel Crisis* of 1962, the changes of 1968, the autumn of 1977, the almost world war of 1981 to 1984, the techno culture, the reunification, to New Year's Eve 2000 (and our feelings, which we possess much longer, bear witness to many other events, from 6000 years ago!) . . . For me, the Alexandria library still burns today. That is what I find worthy of telling. (1:7)

The past is thus a point of departure for thought, which moves freely among past, present, and future. The narrative lays out a map, suggests what might have led to an invoked event, and thus gestures toward the present or the future. The question, however, of what one should think and possibly do remains for the reader to answer. "Orientation" takes place when one moves in multiple, often contradictory directions, when the reader trips, finds herself horrified or fascinated, puzzled or bemused. Rather than absorbing the narrative as a source of knowledge or of aesthetic pleasure, reading is perceived in proximity to prospection: the labor of comparison, consideration, reflection, and—possibly—finding new solutions.[5]

"Worn Out": Alexander Kluge, "The Air Raid on Halberstadt on April 8, 1945"

As a thirteen-year-old boy in 1945, Kluge experienced an Allied attack on his hometown of Halberstadt, during which bombs exploded in his immediate vicinity. Time and again in his writing, Kluge returns to this day—most prominently in one of the unquestionable pinnacles of postwar German literature, "Der Luftangriff auf Halberstadt am 8. April 1945" (The air raid on Halberstadt on April 8, 1945).[6]

When Kluge tells the story of his hometown's destruction, autobiography and fiction, text and image, belong closely together. We read: "[An interrupted matinee screening in *Capitol*, Sunday, April 8, with the movie *Heimkehr* with Paula Wessely and Attila Hörbiger]" (27). And: "The cinema belongs to the Lenz family. The theater's director and cashier is the sister-in-law, Frau Schrader" (27). Before describing

Heft 2
Der Luftangriff auf Halberstadt
am 8. April 1945

I

[Abgebrochene Matinee-
Vorstellung im »Capitol«,
Sonntag, 8. April, Spielfilm
»Heimkehr« mit Paula
Wessely und Attila Hörbi-
ger] Das Kino »Capitol«
gehört der Familie Lenz.
Theater-Leiterin, zugleich
Kassiererin, ist die Schwä-
gerin, Frau Schrader. Die
Holztäfelung der Logen,
des Balkons, das Parkett
sind in Elfenbein gehalten,
rote Samtsitze. Die Lam-
penverkleidungen sind aus
brauner Schweinsleder-
Imitation. Es ist eine Kom-
panie Soldaten aus der
Klus-Kaserne zur Vorstel-
lung herangemarschiert. So-
bald der Gong, pünktlich
10 Uhr, ertönt, wird es im

Kino sehr langsam, den dazwischengeschalteten Spezialwiderstand hat Frau
Schrader gemeinsam mit dem Vorführer gebaut, dunkel. Dieses Kino hat, was
Film betrifft, viel Spannendes gesehen, das durch Gong, Atmosphäre des Hau-
ses, sehr langsames Verlöschen der gelbbraunen Lichter, Einleitungsmusik usf.
vorbereitet worden ist.

Jetzt sah Frau Schrader, die in die Ecke geschleudert wird, dort, wo die Balkon-
reihe rechts an die Decke stößt, ein Stück Rauchhimmel, eine Sprengbombe hat
das Haus geöffnet und ist nach unten, zum Keller, durchgeschlagen. Frau Schrader hat nachsehen wollen, ob Saal und Toiletten nach Vollalarm restlos von Be-

FIGURE 1 Alexander Kluge, *Chronik der Gefühle*, 2:27. Reproduced by permission of Suhrkamp Verlag
GmbH & Co.

how bombs shattered the cinema and the town, Kluge's constellation of text and image compels our gaze to the poster of *Heimkehr* (Homecoming), the film being shown during the attack. In Gustav Ucicky's 1941 *Heimkehr*, a movie commissioned by Goebbels in 1939, the Nazi narrative regarding the fate of ethnic Germans living outside the borders of the Reich presented the viewer with a tale of a beleaguered community whose survival is threatened by Poles. As Johannes von Moltke has shown, the movie inverted the actual historical circumstances in describing the presumed persecution of Germans by Poles, casting "victims as perpetrators." *Heimkehr*'s climax depicts Germans carted away on flatbed trucks "like animals."[7] Those in the cinema during the air raid on Halberstadt might have heard the Nazi film star Paula Wessely fantasize: "Just think, people, what it will be like, just think, when around us there will be lots of Germans—and when you come into a store, people won't talk Yiddish or Polish, but German. And not only the whole village will be German, but all around, everything surrounding us will be German. And we, we will be right in the middle, inside, in the heart of Germany."[8]

This assemblage of text and image disrupts any narrative that may attempt to present Halberstadt's demise as merely a national German catastrophe. It draws the readers' attention to the brutal air raids in relation to a racist ideology and its role in a war Germany initiated to realize its expansionist ambitions, yet also calls attention to the universal questions of targeting civilians in warfare. The collage sets the propaganda of German victimhood in Poland—a crucial component in rationalizing the German invasion of the country in 1939—against the backdrop of the immense human suffering that followed. Avoiding the creation of a singular path through the texts and images that make up the work, the narrative threads, the testimonies, interviews, documents, and photographs all call on the reader to form her own interpretive path. Reading is not merely the intake of words and images.[9] Rather, it is a process demanding an active participant constantly reflecting on ways to relate occurrences to one another, to find orientation in the maze.

While some images, such as the poster of *Heimkehr*, relate directly to the immediate text, others do not. With photo number 2 ("Martiniplan [Martini Plaza]; on the left side [we can see] the southern pillar of the Martinikirche [Martini Church]. In the background the restaurant 'Saure Schnauze [Sour Snout]'"; 2:31), Kluge leaves the reader wondering what the relation might be of image to text, of the restaurant's charming name to the account.

Der Luftangriff auf Halberstadt am 8. April 1945

Abb. Foto Nr. 2: Martiniplan, links Südpfeiler der Martinikirche. Im Hintergrund das Lokal »Saure Schnauze«.

Abb. Foto Nr. 3: Eingang Schmiedestraße.

FIGURE 2 Alexander Kluge, *Chronik der Gefühle*, 2:31, photographs by an unknown photographer. The top photo displays the plaza by Martini Church. The note underneath indicates that on the left we can see the southern pillar of the church and in the background the restaurant Saure Schnauze. The photo at the bottom displays the entry to Schmiedestraße. Both photos were taken during the air raids. Reproduced by permission of Suhrkamp Verlag GmbH & Co.

Attempting to fill in the gaps by thinking about the relation of text to image is but a single mode of the "investigation" Kluge hints at in the introduction to *Chronik*. Another significant vehicle of orientation is Kluge's acidic irony. When Frau Schrader observes the destruction of her town, we read: "the obliteration of the cinema's right elevation cannot be meaningfully related, from a dramaturgical viewpoint, to the film just shown" (2:28). Upon arriving in the cinema's cellar, where Frau Schrader has dutifully appeared to carry out her responsibilities, she discovers the bodies of six matinee guests who were trapped and literally boiled by steam coming out of the heating pipes: "Frau Schrader wanted to restore order at least here and placed the loose, cooked body parts, which came apart either through the heating pipes' explosion or through the bombs, in a laundry basket [*Wasch*kessel] taken from the laundry room [*Wasch*küche]" (2:29, my emphasis).

The absurdity of Frau Schrader's mechanical reaction to the carnage is underlined through the hardly translatable sarcasm inscribed in the alliteration (in the German original) of "*Wasch*kessel der *Wasch*küche."[10] Traumatized or simply too numb to relate emotionally to the sight of horrific death and destruction, she focuses on washing, cleaning, wiping away—on her instrumental function in reestablishing order by trying to "dispose" of the human remains. Echoing Günter Grass's elegiac "nothing is pure," Kluge's prose intimates that nothing can be washed clean here. No effort to wipe out the circumstances that led to this moment (and to the bodies themselves) can ever succeed.

Kluge's irony with regard to the industriousness of the cleanup peaks with the completion of Frau Schrader's tidying frenzy. She joins her friends, the Wilde family, in a bunker, to chew on pepperoni sandwiches and pickled pears while thinking to herself that she was now "worn out" [*zu nichts mehr nütze*], as if what she just experienced is no more exhausting than what she goes through during other days of industrious toil (2:29). In this ironic inscription of distance, Kluge goes beyond what by itself would be a significant account of the immense human misery during the air raid on Halberstadt. The distancing effect challenges the reader to consider the economic, social, political, and cultural circumstances that formed Frau Schrader and led to her essentially detached reaction.

Avoiding any attempt to rationalize the brutality of the carnage and Frau Schrader's industriousness and emotional detachment, the work examines the broad socioeconomic and philosophic-political conditions that made the air raid possible in the first place, conditions that—at least as far as Kluge is concerned—persisted through 1945. Concretely,

Maschinen, würden sie durch Jagdflugzeuge angegriffen, zum Feuerschutz zusammenrückten, würden sie durch Flak beschossen, auseinandergezogen werden könnten.

Die Pionierphase solcher Angriffe mit viermotorigen Fernbombern B 17, jeder eine Werkstatt, aber der kompakte Verband als Fabrik, liegt 3-4 Jahre zurück. Die Komplettierung des Verfahrens hat Faktoren, die in der Pionierphase eine Rolle gespielt haben, wie Gottvertrauen, militärische Formenwelt, Strategie, Binnenwerbung gegenüber den Besatzungen, damit sie angriffswillig sind, Hinweise auf Eigentümlichkeiten des Ziels, Sinn des Angriffs usf. als irrational ausgegliedert.

Diskussion 1976, Nähe Stockholm, OECD-Tagung: *Post-Attack Farm Problems*, gemeinsam mit Sipri-Yearbook, Arbeitskreis VII, der auf einer Terrasse im Lichte des Altweibersommers Platz genommen hat. »Evolutionärer Stellenwert« der Angriffsverfahren »in der Sommerphase des Jahres 1944«:

1. **Professionalisierung:**
Es ist nicht der Einzelkämpfer von Valmy, der bewaffnete Bürger (Proletarier, Lehrer, Kleinunternehmer), der diese Angriffe durchführt, sondern der geschulte Fachbeamte des Luftkriegs: analytische Begrifflichkeit, deduktive Strenge, prinzipieller Begründungszwang in den Gefechtsberichten, Fachverstand usf. Problem des »inneren Auslands« der gelegentlichen persönlichen Wahrnehmung, z. B. Ordentlichkeit der Felder unten, Verwechselung von Häuserzeilen, Karrees, geordneten Stadtvierteln mit heimatlichen Eindrücken, Reflexion über vermutete hochsommerliche Temperaturen unten, wenn Geräteanzeigen oben in den Maschinen doch hierzu keine Veranlassung geben . . .

2. **Konventionalität:**
Die Besatzungen erleben es als »Tages-Geschichte ihrer Betriebe«.

3. **Legalismus:**
Der Angriff unterstellt der Besatzung oder den Stäben außer einem generellen Gehorsam keine sittlichen Motive oder Sinnzwang, bestraft wird nicht böse Gesinnung, sondern normabweichende Handlung, z. B. vorzeitige Umkehr, lasches oder zerfasertes Ausklinken der Würfe. Legalismus insbesondere darin, daß nicht Ziele, die auf den Listen als unterrangig angegeben sind, vor höherrangigen Zielen angeflogen und bombardiert werden. *Gewissermaßen befindet sich eine Justiz im Anflug.*

4. **Universalität:**
Anstelle dessen, was 1942 Thymos (Tapferkeit) oder Disziplin, also *persönliche* und damit, auf das System bezogen, *begrenzte* Eigenschaften

FIGURE 3 Alexander Kluge, *Chronik der Gefühle*, 2:49. Embedded in the description of the attack (at the top of the page), we find (on a gray background) an excerpt from a 1976 Organisation for Economic Co-operation and Development report. Reproduced by permission of Suhrkamp Verlag GmbH & Co.

Kluge's work places the air raids in relation to technological modernity and the kind of reasoning that drives the modern state before and after the Second World War. In the course of "The Air Raid on Halberstadt," we find, for example, embedded in the flow of the text, yet printed against a gray background, the protocol of a 1976 Organisation for Economic Co-operation and Development discussion about a "post-attack farm problem" (2:49).

Referring to problems of the "professionalism" or "legality" of war procedures such as those displayed in the air raid on Halberstadt, the protocol (as well as diagrams of the strike aircrafts' formations [2:52–53]) and references to the history of air raids in modern combat hint at the working of what critical theory in the wake of Theodor Adorno and Max Horkheimer's *Dialectic of Enlightenment* termed "instrumental reason": the employment of technical rationality to address all aspects of human life and social formations, thereby reducing humans to mere matter.[11] Kluge's collage of literary text, embedded protocol, and images thus mobilizes critical theory for orientation: the air raid on Halberstadt is presented in order to examine the economic, social, and political circumstances that made it and similar events possible. In other words, Kluge's text-image constellation is nothing less than an invitation to the reader to ponder the realities of a world in which the targeting of civilian populations is a tool of politics. The author does so without determining the ultimate cause or the meaning of the occurrence. By not establishing his own philosophical or political position on these questions, no limit is placed on the outcome of any "orientation" the work might generate.[12]

On the Meaning of Care in Dark Times: Alexander Kluge,
"Heidegger in the Crimea"

Invoking the German philosophical and literary canon—Leibniz, Kant, Nietzsche, and Goethe's *Faust*—"Heidegger auf der Krim" (Heidegger in the Crimea), one of the newer stories included in *Chronik*, imagines that Martin Heidegger and other leading German scholars were sent off to the recently occupied Crimea on December 4, 1941. Their mission was to secure archeological findings and to represent German scholarship "in a self-conscious" manner (1:420). Probing Heidegger's notion of thinking (*Denken*), the story investigates the place of philosophy in extreme circumstances marked by "case(s) of emergency [*Ernstfall*]" such as the German occupation of the Crimea. Kluge appropriates the word *Ernstfall*, which was a key term for the radical revolutionary Right in the 1920s and 1930s, as a point of departure for thinking about the extremes of morality.[13] His use of the term redescribes it as the consequence of man-made disasters that urgently demand human thought and action.

In placing the fictive Heidegger in a moment of personal and theoretical uncertainty, an *Ernstfall*, Kluge unfolds a fantasy saturated with piercing irony. As in "The Air Raid on Halberstadt," irony is here the rhetorical device that turns the historical event into a goad for reflection and orientation. In the Crimea, for example, Heidegger witnesses mass killings—specifically, the execution of Jews. Yet for him and his fellow "travelers," "intellectual work" (*Gedankenarbeit*) must continue (1:420). Kluge's Heidegger notes in Heideggerian style: "The use of the military for deterrence is ineffective, and, I would like to say, unreal" (1:421). Watching the brutal execution with Heidegger is a historical figure: the SS officer Otto Ohlendorf, responsible for the Einsatzgruppe D, whose task was to follow the Wehrmacht and liquidate Jews.[14] Like Heidegger in Kluge's tale, Ohlendorf is convinced that the military slaughter of Jews is "amateurish" (1:421). The officer thus invites the philosopher to watch an execution that he himself intends to conduct. Heidegger is impressed by the "expertly" (*fachmännisch*) conducted procedure and the calmness of the detainees (1:423).

The story's chilling irony—"intellectual work" during a murderous military campaign, mass executions evaluated as "amateurish" or "expert" acts—reaches a zenith when, in a chaotic moment, a mother who is about to be "transported" to her death manages to get her child close to Heidegger. The child reaches for the hand of the absentminded philosopher, who notices a small hand in his and realizes that he is now holding "destiny" in his hand—here the narrator uses the Heideggerian term *Geschick* (1:424). Feeling obliged to guard or protect the child, Heidegger decides to keep it and perhaps take it with him back to the Reich: "To *hold* [*halten*] means originally to *guard* [*hüten*]" (1:425, emphasis in original). The situation becomes complicated, though, since Heidegger has to face the fact that the child is Jewish. Thus, with the child in his custody, the philosopher is now confronted with an *Ernstfall* (1:427). According to the great philosopher of finitude, leading an authentic life means adhering only to one's own, individual standards. If this means living without submitting oneself to normative demands such as caring for the child out of pity, then the philosopher of authenticity (*Eigentlichkeit*) must consider how he should act now. Does the philosopher of "care" (*Sorge*) remain authentic by staying focused on his own mortal being while he nonetheless cares for the child, or does he act out of sheer pity and thus become inauthentic?

In Kluge's irony-saturated parable, Heidegger hardly has time to worry about these philosophical difficulties. The responsible military officer informs him that the military has "enough concerns" (*genügend Sorgen*) of its own and does not need to add those caused by Heidegger (1:431). Soon thereafter, while Heidegger is out, the child is taken away from his lodging. Now "the philosopher feels dispossessed [*enteignet*]" (1:433). On his way back to the German Reich, he has nothing in his hand "but his small suitcase [*Köfferchen*]" (1:433). The child, he is told, has been transported to the north. Heidegger's last comment—"from the gigantic [*Riesenhaften*] we crash into the tiny [*ins Kleine*]" (1:434)— serves only to underscore further the story's ironic mode. From "amateurish" and "expertly" conducted executions to the many incarnations of "authenticity" and "care," irony turns Kluge's conflation of historical circumstance and fantasy, philosophical inquiry and ethical challenge, into an opportunity for orientation. The story invokes the annihilation of Jews in the course of the Nazi murder campaign, yet it also engenders prospective thought—an opportunity to ask what it means to care. What does this important Heideggerian philosophical category call for in pressing situations, in moments where caring is also a feeling? There is philosophical "care" for oneself, understood as the duty of individuals faced with their finitude in the context of Heideggerian philosophy, but there is also "care" as the emotion one might feel (as the fictional Heidegger does) for others.[15] Kluge's Heidegger is torn between what he views as mutually exclusive notions of "care." His character fails to find orientation. Yet the narrative itself nevertheless poses "care" as a problem for the readers: it prompts us to consider, via the fictive Heidegger, how we may orient ourselves in similar challenging moments—how we may navigate between striving to live an authentic life (in the sense of Heidegger's existential philosophy) and maintaining an awareness of and commitment to those who cannot care for themselves.

Literature and the Capacity for Differentiating

Kluge's approach to his art is best described by his own metaphor—it is a *Baustelle*, a "construction site."[16] In our case, the prose text is a site often infused with images that the reader is invited to enter as an active participant in the labor of constructing meanings, relationships, and distinctions. Much as Kluge never stops revising his work, the reader is also expected to consider, reflect, rethink, and argue, to find direction and then lose it, in an ongoing process of charting a future course of action.

The outcome of this procedure is not the attainment of a finite judgment but rather the advancement of what Kluge, in the tradition of critical theory, calls *Öffentlichkeit*, the public sphere or publicity. When Kluge explains what this public sphere might look like, he avoids any prescription. Kluge instead turns to metaphors. Referring to Adorno and Horkheimer's critique of the Enlightenment, he speaks of the need to enhance the ability to differentiate—*Unterscheidungsvermögen*. Unlike those who, like Habermas, believe in the Enlightenment as "the growth of knowledge," of "moral behavior," and in attempts to dominate these "critically," Kluge hopes to develop (in this case together with his colleague the sociologist Oskar Negt) "massive capacities to differentiate": "The ears are an independent person; the eyes are a further person, much more synthetic than the ears. The nose is a repressed and undeveloped person. The tongue is a cautious man. . . . These are only concrete cases of the capacity to differentiate. . . . Our party is the party of differentiation."[17] In terms of the function of a literary work, this means promoting an ever-evolving ability to ask new questions—a cultural and political discourse that retains the progressive threads of the bourgeois public sphere (*Öffentlichkeit*) while avoiding what Kluge sees as the nineteenth and twentieth centuries' decline into consumption-driven capitalism. Rejecting the Enlightenment tradition of assigning to literature the duty of serving human perfectibility, Kluge notes, "A text is moral when it creates the capability of differentiating [*Unterscheidungsvermögen*]. If it deals with evil, it is not to give an example [*beispielgebend*] but rather to differentiate in this foreign terrain." Critique, he goes on, using his preferred Frankfurt school vocabulary, is "the ability to differentiate, 'difference' in French."[18]

In setting up a tension between the said and the unsaid, Kluge's use of irony invites inference, not only of meaning, but also of attitude and judgment.[19] Unlike postmodern notions of irony that center on its irresolvable ambiguities and its ontological resistance to "mastery," Kluge's ironies count on the ability of readers to actually find orientation.[20] In an interview published shortly after the appearance of *Chronik*, he pointed out: "Nothing of what we produced until now is an adequate weapon against Auschwitz. Thus, we have to rely on unease [*Unruhe*]. Searching, always onward searching [*Suchen, immer weitersuchen*]."[21] "Searching" here indicates looking not just for something that is not yet found, like a set of car keys, but for something that is not yet defined—something that might emerge in the future in a different language, a different mode of action. Reading through Kluge's intricate stories and encountering his unsettling ironies, his readers become an active element of this "searching."

Kluge's pragmatic practice of searching through the past is largely motivated by future-related questions such as "What do I need to fear?"[22] The answers to such questions could indeed be "useful" for changing the conditions that made Auschwitz possible in the first place.[23] His engagement with the past is motivated by the sense that events such as air raids on cities where civilians live or the mass execution of humans have hardly vanished since 1945. These kinds of violent, coordinated actions continue to pose urgent dilemmas, whose answers might involve different forms of social and political organization in the future. "Politics needs a certain type of archeology which looks for volatile junctions in the past," Kluge notes in regard to this very future. Offering his own version of what I call futurity, he goes on to state that we cannot "prognosticate from the perspective past" (Prognosen lassen sich aus ihr [der Geschichte] nicht ableiten). "But," he continues, "we need historical experience when we search for ways out, for solutions [Auswegen]. . . . I have to know the subjunctive, that which I do not wish—war—in order to prevent it." For Kluge it is not enough to strive for a realist representation of man-made catastrophes. This type of realism is, for him (and I agree), often accompanied by the underlying notion that the *factual* catastrophic outcome was somehow *inevitable*. Rejecting an exclusively realist depiction of a disaster such as the Holocaust—that is, accounting for the Holocaust *in the subjunctive* of a literary work such as "Heidegger in the Crimea"—underlines how by excavating the past we use past historical experience to find *Auswegen*: we ponder what could have also happened and thus may, just may, prevent a *coming* disaster. In the words of Kluge, we need to "think in the subjunctive, search for options and possibilities in light of history *and the future*" (my emphasis).[24] With Kluge's "searching, always onward searching," we may ask, for example, how should armies and the international community react to the use of civilians as human shields? What are the moral and political imperatives no military should be allowed to break in warfare? Obviously, Kluge's thinking in the subjunctive and excavating the past for possible *Auswegen* does not mean "learning from the past" as if "the past" were a book just waiting for us to consume its lessons. To think about the past and to tell its stories in the subjunctive means to avert the temptation of regarding it, especially its modern man-made catastrophes, as the unfolding of the inevitable. It means accepting the burden of human agency in history (an issue I will discuss at length in the third part of this book).

Kluge's literary *Guernica*—his collage of words and images dedicated to Halberstadt's destruction—indeed ends on such a "futural" note. The piece concludes with a statement made by an interviewee in a study conducted in May 1945 in Halberstadt by the American military: "As of a certain point of cruelty, it doesn't matter who began it. It should simply stop" (2:82). Without falling back on moralism (the sentence remains a quotation in a collage), Kluge positions the air raid as an event of the present and for the future: "*It* should simply stop" continues to sound even when the last survivor of the air raid has long passed away. The conditions for halting man-made catastrophes such as that of Halberstadt remain outside the work. Thinking about them might be an act generated by literature. Stopping *it*, however, is left to the reader. What is at stake is not the remembrance of racial ideology or of the deadly attack on Halberstadt alone but rather a future for which the central question is how we might reduce the possibility of such moments, if not avoid them altogether.

4 Martin Walser: Imagination and the Culture of Dissensus

Resisting the Norms of Public Remembrance:
Martin Walser, A Gushing Fountain

The story of Martin Walser's work and public persona after the fall of the Berlin Wall is among the most peculiar and telling episodes of German culture in recent decades. Widely celebrated as one of the greatest postwar German novelists and admired by many for his outspoken (and initially criticized) unwillingness to accept the partition of Germany as a permanent fact, Walser seemed poised in the years following German reunification to enjoy an ever-growing public esteem.[1] A decade later, however, Walser found himself at the center of several public debates that threatened to eclipse much of the respect he previously had enjoyed; these controversies made it almost impossible to judge his literary work without reference to his embattled status as a public figure.

Any account of Walser's entanglement in public controversy must begin in the spring of 1998, with the publication of his long-awaited autobiographical novel *Ein springender Brunnen* (A gushing fountain), a work that was compared to Thomas Mann's *Buddenbrooks* and that was named one of the century's greatest books of memory.[2] Read from the perspective of the years that have passed since then, it is not difficult to understand the respect Walser's novel earned. Born in 1927 in the Swabian town of Wasserburg as Martin Johannes Walser, the author recounts with sensitivity and attention to detail his childhood in the southern German province through his alter ego, Johann. Through Johann's penetrating gaze, Walser portrays the years from 1932 to the end of the Second World War and the provincial, petit bourgeois milieu he knew from his parents' humble inn. Beginning with the difficult realities of the economic crisis of the early 1930s, the novel continues through the sunny winter day in January 1933 on which Generalfeldmarschall Hindenburg appointed Adolf Hitler chancellor of the German Reich and on to the end of the war. Walser's novel, however, is focused not on the epochal events of that time but rather on its mundane, quotidian occurrences: the hardly noticeable web of recurring events in the family's life and the cleaning, cooking, patrons' worries, and guests' chitchat that characterized daily life in the inn.

Wasserburg is for Walser the incarnation of *Heimat* (homeland) but also, as Jörg Magenau observes, what Danzig was for Günter Grass: a microcosm of modern German history and, at the same time, of the human condition.[3] *Ein springender Brunnen*'s unique achievement lies in the author's expressed wish to render the past as closely as possible to its imprint in memory. Most writers of Walser's generation viewed their Nazi-era childhood from the vantage point of the postwar period. Grass's *The Tin Drum* and Christa Wolf's *Kindheitsmuster* (1976; *Patterns of Childhood*) account for the past from a retrospective point of view. This allows the narratives to maintain a critical distance from the ideologies and crimes of the Nazis. *Ein springender Brunnen*, however, refrains from such detachment. It seeks what Hans Ulrich Gumbrecht calls "presence": to capture and experience long-gone objects, smells, and colors without judging their historical context (in our case, Nazism) and without musing, retrospectively, on their meaning.[4]

Walser's literary route is, nonetheless, closely entwined with his perspective on the cultural-political discourse of the postwar era. Specifically, he expressed his intention to write differently from what some may have wished and to find a language that would go beyond what other writers of his generation had achieved. In the introductory reflection that begins the third and final part of *Ein springender Brunnen*, Walser juxtaposes his approach to historical narration to that of others, noting:

> Some have learned to reject their past. They develop a past that is now more favorable. They do so because of the present. . . . I saw several times how some have literally shed their past [*aus*

> *ihrer Vergangenheit förmlich herausgeschlüpft sind]. . . .* In
> truth, from decade to decade, dealing with the past becomes in-
> creasingly adherent to norms [*strenger normiert*]. The more ad-
> herent to norms that dealing with the past becomes, the more the
> past itself turns into a product of the present. (282)

Walser's metaliterary notes suggest a growing distance from the progressive tradition of writers and thinkers that placed the Holocaust at the
center of a postnational culture, one that draws the strength of its democratic institutions from a progressive constitution rather than from a national history.[5] Yet in its own way, *Ein springender Brunnen* is written
against forgetting—the kind of forgetting that takes place once memories become subjected to what was established *after the fact* as accept-
able or desired. The past can never be "captured"; it cannot be restricted
to a certain set of forms and expectations.[6] As Walser notes, "Those who
unwaveringly hope to capture the past are at the greatest risk of regarding what they eventually find to also be what they were looking for. We
cannot admit that nothing exists but the present. Since the present itself
hardly exists. And the future is but a grammatical error" (281).

Walser's novel is thus an intriguing case of imaginative redescription: it presents National Socialism as a period that—with all its horrors—still allowed many to experience a serene childhood. The reader
is invited to absorb images as they are engraved in personal recollection
and to consider the possibility that everyday normal life can persist in
proximity to murderous madness such as that of Nazism. Furthermore,
the novel asks to what extent, in adding retrospectively gained knowledge or moral judgments, other available literary accounts of National
Socialism actually produce a somewhat deceptive image. Walser's narrative does not claim any superiority vis-à-vis other literary images of the
same reality—works that include a retrospective moral condemnation
of individuals or groups. Rather, it *expands* the variety of ways German
readers (indeed, readers anywhere) view that era. Walser's narrative also
reminds us that one of the horrific truths about life under totalitarian
regimes is that while some are drawn into the madness as perpetrators
or victims, others can continue to lead an ordinary life. Furthermore, in
noting that "in truth, from decade to decade, dealing with the past becomes increasingly adherent to norms," the writer includes himself and
his own book in the baffling possibility that at least some aspects of the
story he is writing are themselves products of his wish to detach himself
from the expectations of others. *Ein springender Brunnen* is thus both
a poetic account of Walser's childhood *and* a reflection on the longing

for—and impossibility of—revisiting history without adhering to the demands of the present.

On two telling occasions, the stakes of Walser's choice to limit the perspective to what is inscribed in memory become apparent. The first is the crucial scene in which Johann's mother joins the Nazi Party. Before writing the novel, Walser pointed out the significance of that particular event in his own life when he said in an interview that he intended to write the story of his childhood in a novel called "Der Eintritt meiner Mutter in die Partei" (The entrance of my mother into the party). If he could tell this story, Walser noted, he would, in fact, be able to explain why so many in Germany joined the party.[7] Mixing the sacrosanct with matter-of-fact narration, the relevant scene in *Ein springender Brunnen* follows Herr Minn, the local Nazi Party official, as he manages to overcome the mother's last doubts when he gives her a postcard depicting Christ on the cross. In front of the savior, the mother sees two men in brown shirts. While one of them holds the swastika flag, the other holds his arm in a Hitler greeting. The mother asks Johann to read what is written on the card: "God, bless our struggle. Adolf Hitler" (90). Since Walser's poetics dictate that the past should remain unperturbed by retrospective consideration, the literary image of the mother's reaction appears without any comment: "Mother said she wants to join the party" (91).

Before commenting on this key moment, let us turn to another one. Toward the end of the novel, when the war is finally over and Johann returns from his short military service, he meets his friend Wolfgang Landsmann. Johann knew that Wolfgang was viciously expelled from the Hitlerjugend because he came from a *Mischehe*, the Nazi term to describe the fact that Wolfgang's mother was Jewish while his father was Aryan. It is only now that the war is over, however, that Johann discovers through Wolfgang's story what it meant to be Jewish during National Socialism: what it had been like for one of the inn's customers, Frau Haensel, and for Wolfgang and his parents to live in constant fear. He hears of paralyzing terror at the possibility of being deported and of the daily humiliations (397–401). Remaining loyal to the description of what "in reality" went through Johann's head, the narrator observes the protagonist as he considers that Wolfgang told him of his fate because he thought that he, Johann, should know—"weil Johann das wissen müsse" (401). Maybe Wolfgang even thought that Johann ought to be admonished for not noticing the terror nearby (401). Johann, however, for his part, resisted this presumed rebuke. How should he have known that Frau Haensel is Jewish? He was not willing to face any demands. No one should demand any feeling that does not originate from him alone. He wanted to live, not to be fearful. Frau Landsmann [Wolfgang's mother] would infect him with her fear, he sensed. He had to think away [wegdenken] from her and her fear. One fear leads to the next. . . . He was afraid to meet Frau Landsmann. Since he knew how she lived in fear, he did not know how to approach her. How to greet her; how to look at or to look away [wie hin- oder wegschauen]? (401)

Thinking about what he had just heard and reflecting on other moments of his childhood and youth in which he felt subjected to the demands of others, "Johann did not want to be subjected ever again to any power or fear. No one should demand anything of him [Niemand sollte einen Anspruch an ihn haben]. He wanted to be free as no one ever before" (402).

Taken together, these key scenes indicate the difficulties of assimilating the guilt-laden memory of Nazism into consciousness.[8] The mother's decision is based, after all, on a falsified image. A clever hoax is mainly responsible for her political choice and, symbolically, also for Germany's path into unprecedented crime and guilt. The scene with the postcard can be viewed as the symbolic redescription of Nazism as a mass scam that drew numerous individuals—as in a wicked magician's show—into the abyss.[9] Similarly, Johann's inability to relate meaningfully to Wolfgang Landsmann and his experiences could be viewed as unconscious repression or, even worse, as the morally indefensible desire to look the other way ("hin oder wegschauen") when confronted by German history, as the critics Andreas Isenschmid and Marcel Reich-Ranicki noted in their discussion of the novel on Germany's literary television show Das literarische Quartett shortly after the publication of the novel.[10]

These readings are further enhanced when we consider the narrator's sympathetic description of Johann's desire to live his life independently rather than in response to others' demands. In fact, Johann's transformation into an artist (in the tradition of the bildungsroman) seems intimately related to his ability to free himself from the burden of responsibility and socially mediated morality. As we will soon see, much in Walser's public appearances in the months and years following the publication of Ein springender Brunnen points in this direction: Johann's wish to be free is reminiscent of Walser's wish to free post-wall Germany from its omnipresent and, in his opinion, stale *Erinnerungskultur*, its culture of public remembrance. Yet in some significant ways, the novel offers more than a reaction to the German *Erinnerungskultur* of the 1980s and 1990s, more than a mere indication of a desire to look the other way.

Dissensus

In *Memory, History, Forgetting*, Paul Ricoeur considers the historian and the judge, holding that while the latter must make decisions about legal transgressions in a categorical manner, the former cannot claim the role of serving on history's ultimate tribunal.[11] The historian's accounts are submitted to the critique of colleagues and that of "the enlightened public." "The writing of history," Ricoeur notes, is "perpetual rewriting" (320). He then takes up Mark Osiel's study of the juridical prosecution of mass atrocities, specifically his thesis that the trials do not simply reinforce moral consensus but rather generate social *dissensus*: a culture of controversy that both marks liberal societies and serves to enhance one of its core elements: open public deliberation (323).[12] According to Ricoeur, dissensus is the vector for the "civic education of the collective memory" (323). Significantly, he sees in the discussions of the 1986 German Historikerstreit (Historians' Debate) a case of dissensus, whereby the discussion of issues such as the singularity of the Nazi genocide became a vehicle for enhancing a democratic public arena (332).

The effect of Martin Walser's *Ein springender Brunnen* was precisely to stimulate dissensus—to provoke a serious public discussion of the nature of memory, history, and forgetting in the contemporary German context during the fall of 1998. Willingly or not, *Ein springender Brunnen* and the soon-to-erupt Walser-Bubis debate display what I called above, with Richard Rorty, "the gigantic shadow that futurity casts upon the present": Walser's work, one could say with Rorty, does not "fit past events together in order to provide lessons for the future."[13] Rather, it shocks us into considering how we relate to the past and, specifically, what forms Germany's future *Erinnerungskultur* may or should take.

In his previous work Walser used Auschwitz as a metonymy for the importance of facing Nazi crimes. In "Auschwitz und kein Ende" (1979; No end to Auschwitz),[14] for example, Walser noted, "Not a single day has passed since Auschwitz" (25): "We [the Germans] freed ourselves too soon. Every one of us can experience this when confronted with the images of Auschwitz: we must allow the trial to continue. Throughout our life. The trial within our selves" (27). He goes on to confess that he might "prefer to look away" from the images of the Holocaust in the media and elsewhere, but he has to "force" himself to look at them (29). In Ein springender Brunnen, however, Walser generated a vocabulary that allows readers to consider modes of engagement with the past other than those with which they have become accustomed—specifically, to view Nazism without turning, as had become habitual in Germany in the 1980s, to the expression of guilt and shame, indictment, or communal remorse. Through the writer's alter ego, Walser redescribed his generation as the children or young adults he remembered they once were and thus allowed his readers to consider what it meant for them to grow up in that era, and what it must have felt like gradually to become aware, after the war, of the regime's crimes and of the need to address them.

To put it somewhat differently: Walser's novel expanded the German literary imagination and with it the language at the disposal of the country's cultural-political discourse in regard to the Nazi past and the Holocaust. It suggested that some of the dominant metaphors of life under National Socialism had become dull or "literal," to use Rorty's notion of poetic language.[15] The novel both presented a new way to view the past and asked what it means to remember Nazism without the real or assumed demands of a by-now "enlightened" German public discourse. Walser's autobiographical image of the quiet German province under National Socialism hardly undid what we knew regarding the atrocities. Rather, it expanded the scope of our knowledge by asking if one could have grown up in proximity to unthinkable monstrosities without being affected by them. It examined what remains of such a tainted past once one learns more about its broader realities—about what happened outside one's own peaceful confines. Furthermore, it challenged its German readers to consider whether, by displaying images of that historical period or imagining a Jewish character, a writer can avoid being immediately subjected to moral scrutiny.[16]

As a meaningful work of art, Ein springender Brunnen offers no definitive response to these considerations. Intriguing and provocative, the novel illustrates literature's ability to shock its readers into proceeding beyond the dated language of engagement with National Socialism.

"A Clear Conscience Is No Conscience at All": The Walser-Bubis Debate Reconsidered

On October 12, 1998, in Frankfurt's historic Saint Paul's Church, Walser received the distinguished Friedenspreis des deutschen Buchhandels (Peace Prize of the German Book Trade). The conclusion of Walser's controversial acceptance speech is telling for our consideration of futurity. He viewed the present German cultural discourse as either obsessed with German disgrace or manipulated into a fixation on Auschwitz for reasons other than the desire and need to remember, and he also suggested replacing communal with individual remembrance as the standard for commemorating Nazism and its crimes. Memory is and should be restricted to the private realm, Walser argued. Similarly, in issues of conscience, the individual should be her or his own judge. Working from Martin Heidegger's notion of authenticity—"Being guilty is part of being itself"—he appealed to his listeners: "A clear conscience is no conscience at all. Everyone is alone with his or her conscience" (91–92).

Walser's casting of today's Germans as victims and, ironically, as perpetrators of continuous accusations, as well as his confession to want "to look away" and his definition of conscience as a private entity, were together an obvious example of what Jacques Rancière calls "political dissensus." Reflecting on aesthetics and politics, Rancière notes that dissensus is "more than the conflict between a part and another part" (say, between the rich and the poor) and is rather "a supplement to the simple consensual game of domination and rebellion."[17] Dissensus puts "two worlds—two heterogeneous logics—on the same stage, in the same world. It is the commensurability of incommensurables."[18]

According to Rancière, artworks such as Walser's novel or his poetic-polemic speech in Frankfurt "can produce effects of dissensus precisely because they neither give lessons nor have any destination."[19] In other words, even if Walser the writer had a certain sociopolitical agenda as he was writing his memories in a fictional form or as he was drafting his public address on the occasion of receiving the Peace Prize, we should judge both the novel and the speech not only for what they say but also for their *effect*: their ability to serve as "a supplement" to what we may call, with Rancière, the "consensual game" of the German public discourse as of the late 1980s.

Revisiting the debate that followed the speech from the perspective of the passing decade, what strikes one as significant is not so much Walser's indisputable desire to view post-wall Germany as a normal nation-state or his plea against public remembrance and a socially based morality but rather how his novel and subsequent public appearances were able to generate dissensus: an open and at times harsh discussion of the modes of remembrance in contemporary German culture. "We need a new language for remembrance," demanded Walser when on December 13, 1998, he finally met his primary critic in the affair, Ignatz Bubis, for a conversation.[20] A decade and a half after these words were uttered, one can see the Walser-Bubis debate as an admittedly difficult yet necessary step in this direction.

While Walser's polemic against the habitual aspects of Germany's *Erinnerungskultur* helped facilitate a reconsideration of what had become a dated idiom, his literary work in the years following the Walser-Bubis debate, especially his irredeemably dull—and, according to many, anti-Semitic—novel *Tod eines Kritikers* (2002; Death of a critic), suggests that he will probably not be among those developing the new language for which he pleaded. It is not my intention to judge whether the novel is "anti-Semitic" or not. The hundreds of journalistic contributions and the growing number of scholarly works dedicated to this issue will certainly help an interested reader to decide the case.[21] Rather, my point is that Walser's significant literary achievement in *Ein springender Brunnen*, taken together with his Peace Prize speech and the debate generated by *Tod eines Kritikers*, is a telling case of a certain mode of imaginative redescription, one whose effect lies in generating dissensus, an open and at times unforgiving public debate. Notwithstanding the troubling tendencies in Walser's fiction, such as repression of the crimes of Nazism (Johann's looking away), his poetic images nevertheless allow Germans to consider their history and current discourse *prospectively*. At his best, in *Ein springender Brunnen* Walser enriched the German collective historical album with disturbing yet undeniably important images of recent history. The peculiar case of Martin Walser's later writing and his public persona furthermore offered many the possibility of asking, more than a decade after reunification, where Germany was heading. As we will see in the next chapter, his challenge to Bubis in their December 1998 conversation—"We need a new language for remembrance"—became the point of departure for new ways to engage with Germany's Nazi past.

5

The Past as Gift

A New Language for Remembrance

In an essay published a few months after Martin Walser's meeting with Ignatz Bubis, Marcel Beyer (b. 1965) distanced himself from the self-victimizing tone of Walser's Peace Prize speech but nevertheless echoed the older writer's discontent. A *Nachgeborener*, that is, a writer born after the Holocaust, Beyer felt that the main emphasis in addressing Germany's past, especially the Holocaust, could no longer be on questions of personal and collective guilt. The author's task was to write in his or her own "pitch" (*Tonlage*), that is, individual voice, and to avoid "generalizations." One must write out of one's own experiences, practices, and attitudes, and for those born after the Holocaust, these differ from those of writers like Grass and Kluge. Additionally, Beyer's essay reflects a global distrust of philosophies of history and political utopias: "We need to give up the proclamation of worldviews [*Weltentwürfen*]" and cultivate "precision."[1]

Beyer's emphasis on "precision" means first and foremost avoiding the affected rhetoric of public remembrance of the late 1980s. Grass, Kluge, and Walser (and many others, such as Ingeborg Bachman, Uwe Johnson, Thomas Bernhard, Heiner Müller, and Christa Wolf, to name only a few), who experienced Nazism firsthand, moved beyond silence about the crimes of the Nazi regime, departing from such abstractions as "dark times," and thus helped place the memory of the Nazi era at the center of West Germany's and, later, reunited Germany's cultural-political discourse.[2] Yet as Beyer's essay highlighted, this discourse became increasingly marked by platitudes and empty gestures.

In a 1999 public lecture in Vienna, the Austrian writer Norbert Gstrein (b. 1961) observed that the reasons for presenting images of Nazi terror "do not always indicate a wish to remember" but can instead be motivated by habit. Confronted with images of these horrors, viewers are goaded by the fear of saying something wrong and thus quickly resort to a few hollow words that excuse them from further thought.[3] Gstrein identifies this reflexive response as nothing but a form of avoidance.

Marcel Beyer's stress on "pitch" and on the need to avoid generalization about the past and Norbert Gstrein's reservations about habitual public remembrance provide a point of departure in examining some relatively recent works by German and Austrian writers. Novelists such as Beyer and Gstrein avoid the chestnuts of public remembrance by creating characters who weave Germany's past in mediated form into their individual lives, into their own experiences, practices, and attitudes. Like "second-generation" writers, that is, like the children of Holocaust survivors, the writers discussed below "witness" Nazism secondhand. Hence, their literary invocation of the past is an expression of what Marianne Hirsch calls "postmemory." Postmemory is distinguished from memory, Hirsch states, "by generational distance and from history by a deep personal connection." It is distinctive precisely because "its connection to its object or source is mediated not through recollection but through an imaginative investment and creation."[4]

The writers I will discuss—Hans-Ulrich Treichel (b. 1952), Norbert Gstrein, Bernhard Schlink (b. 1944), W. G. Sebald (1944–2001), and Katharina Hacker (b. 1967)—face a public sphere that is no longer marked by ex-Nazis, bystanders to atrocity, or conservative literary critcism, as did the authors of Group 47 and (albeit to a much lesser extent) such authors as Peter Schneider and Hans Christoph Buch, who emerged during and after the youth revolt of the late 1960s.[5] Furthermore, for these younger writers, the very notion of Germany's "recent past" is broader. It includes, besides the Holocaust, aspects of the period stretching from 1933 to 1945 that were relatively neglected in previous decades: the plight of the German civil population during the massive air raids on German cities, the *Vertreibung* (the immense expulsion and flight of Germans from Eastern Europe toward the end of the Sec-

ond World War), and Germany's partition and the forty years of socialist dictatorship.[6] Addressing Nazism in the decades following 1989 has
meant, then, also engaging with the more immediate past, with events
following the Cold War such as the 1991 Gulf War and the aftermath
of 9/11.[7]

"No More Past!": Hans-Ulrich Treichel, Lost and Human Flight

As Klaus Briegleb observed, a new "poetics of remembrance" began to
emerge in German literature of the 1980s with the work of such writers as Anne Duden (b. 1944) and Birgit Pausch (b. 1942).[8] These and
other writers invoked the crimes of the Nazi regime and their aftermath
while exposing the lingering suffering of the survivors and the effects of
growing up in the *Täter* culture (the culture of the perpetrator) of postwar Germany. This new "poetics" has been further transformed in the
last two decades in works containing narratives of gift giving and receiving, as well as metaphors of exchange. In this most recent literature,
the German past is increasingly examined for its "productive" import,
as the historical and mental material one inherits, receives, or may take
on in the creation of individual and societal identity. As characters exchange stories and objects, Germany's Nazi past emerges in these works
as an offering or gift that demands engagement and even action. In other
words, these works are futural in recasting twentieth-century German
history as a taxing, yet also useful, endowment—the source of deep personal misery (how should one deal with such an inheritance?) but also a
catalyst for personal and communal growth.

In considering exchange and gift giving, I regard the gift as something
other than a gesture of selfless generosity. As Marcel Mauss has shown,
a gift is but the material element of a choreography that involves three
acts: giving the object, pondering whether to accept it, and, finally, reciprocating with a gift of one's own.[9] By accepting a gift, the recipient
acknowledges the giving person, and by returning the gesture with one's
own bequest, social bonds are created, enhanced, or renegotiated. Gift
giving is thus inherently social: a complex maneuvering that involves not
only norms, customs, and a given set of conventions but also—in the
process of giving and receiving a gift—the reformulation of social relations and structures.

Casting the German past, especially the Holocaust, in metaphors
of exchange and gift giving is hardly imaginable if one remains within
the confines of Marcel Mauss's discussion, however. Indeed, we need to
draw on Jacques Derrida's notion of the gift to perceive how writers such

as Gstrein and others refer to the past not only as an unbearable burden but also as a figure of the unattainable—a given with which one grapples without attempting to master it, overcome it, or put it behind. Derrida maintained that a gift lies outside the logic of economic calculation.[10] A gift is a figure for the impossible, since it is weighted with requirements from the moment it is given. In other words, like a difficult history we inherit from our ancestors, a gift marks the difficulty of becoming the owner of an item or a heritage never requested.

Writers such as Hans-Ulrich Treichel ponder what to do with the impossible gift of the German past: how to react, in narrative form, to what their predecessors handed them as their individual and communal identity. Treichel's interconnected novels *Der Verlorene* (1998; *Lost*) and *Menschenflug* (2005; Human flight) trace the legacy of the Second World War in the life of a family that is in some crucial respects his own.[11] In *Der Verlorene*, Stephan, a young adult born after the war, recounts his childhood in the West Germany of the 1950s. The narrator's family was among the millions of Germans who fled Eastern Europe in the course of the massive flight and exile that accompanied the Red Army's advance westward. As a young child, Stephan knew that his older brother, Arnold, starved in his mother's arms during that trek. Years after those dreadful days and well into Stephan's childhood, his mother asks him to join her for "something she called a 'discussion'" (6). In a well-choreographed scene of telling, listening, and pondering what to do with what one just heard, with the past one inherited, the mother tells Stephan that he is now "old enough to know the truth" and then presents him with what had actually happened during the hurried retreat:

> The Russians were suddenly there. . . . They [the parents] realized at once that something dreadful was going to happen, and as one of the Russians had already put his gun to my father's chest, my mother just had time to put her child in the arms of a passing woman, who luckily wasn't detained by any of the Russians. . . . "But something dreadful happened after all," she said. She started crying again when she said this, and I was sure that she was crying about Arnold, so to comfort her I told her that she'd really saved Arnold's life and she didn't have to cry, to which my mother said that Arnold's life had never been in danger. Neither had my father's, and neither had hers. Something dreadful had apparently been done to her by the Russians, but they'd no intention of taking her life or those of her family. (9–10, translation modified)

Treichel's figurative choices are telling: while the book is narrated in the first person, much of this scene is in indirect speech. The narrative thus indicates the difficulties of the relationship: Stephan's mother passes on to her son her life's painful truth and is then given Stephan's attention in return. He attempts to reciprocate thoughtfully with some comforting words. His mother, however, proves incapable of relating to what he has to offer. Stephan nevertheless is now forced to deal with his inheritance, with truths that affect his life considerably. His reaction to his mother's bequest, his solution for this "impossible" gift, is decisive: he writes her story, her past, and, by extension, the national history through the prism of his own voice. The result is a distant, ironic tale of a childhood in Adenauer's oblivious Germany.[12] Yet Stephan becomes himself in this process, narrating his way into creating a life story with which he can live.

Growing up in a West Germany that is consumed by the reconstruction efforts of the 1950s, Stephan presents himself in *his* story as the real lost son: the son who was never noticed, because his parents were absorbed in their traumas. Since both his father and his mother are incapable of dealing with their trauma, Stephan fills in the gaps. He mercilessly recounts the realities of his childhood and the afterlife of the racial language and culture of Nazism. While trying to find Arnold, the parents contact the German authorities, who are then able to locate an ostensibly matching child. Yet before reuniting him with his presumed parents, "foundling 2307," as he is called, needs to be "confirmed"—proved to be biologically related to the family. Stephan's part in the choreography of giving—pondering what to do with the inheritance of the past and reciprocating with one's own story—is developed through the narrator's ironic perspective. A highly revered Professor Liebstedt, an expert in a racist version of forensic anthropology and reminiscent of scientists in the service of the Nazi state, measures and compares the shoulders, chest, stomach, and feet of the "foundling" (71–72). Stephan's irony borders on sarcasm when he describes how Professor Liebstedt reaches for forceps and vise, noting the "relative width of the angle of the jaw" (88), only to deliver in his final report the bad news that, due to marked differences in the "lower part of the nose" and the "flare of the nostrils" (114), "foundling 2307" is "reasonably unlikely" to be the lost Arnold (118).

Not only racism is invoked here. While the family awaits Professor Liebstedt's judgment, little Stephan talks to a hearse driver who is full of admiration for the new crematorium in the city of Heidelberg: "Everything stands or falls by the ovens. If the ovens were no good, the whole crematorium would be no good [*Taugten die Öfen nichts, taugte das ganze Krematorium nichts*]. The new ovens were absolutely fantastic" (80). The talkative driver goes on to elaborate on a conversation he recently had with the director of the crematorium. To convince the hearse driver "how perfectly clean and hygienic" the ovens are, the director had reached into one of the ovens, taken one of the small bones into his mouth, chewed on it, then had asked the hearse driver whether he might also like to try it (80). Thanking him, the hearse driver had declined and had said that "everything had its limits" (81). Dealing thus with received history, Stephan recasts his mother's fractional account of her past, and, by extension, Nazism, with what he has observed and heard, including what she has chosen to ignore—the reality of the genocide that recently took place in "efficiently" run concentration camps. That past is now inscribed in the form of the effective "new crematorium."

Avoiding the omnipresent synecdoche "Auschwitz," Treichel's prose pursues the proximity between the racism of the forensic anthropologist, the industrial killings of the death camps (the "crematorium"), and the fate of his own family. The novel engages the past through what Michael Rothberg calls "multidirectional memory" as it brings together multiple traumatic pasts into a heterogeneous textual present.[13] Treichel's memory of a childhood in the shadow of German loss is not a "zero-sum game" in which a German writer relates to his distinctive past to explore his identity. Rather, through the invocation of the "new crematorium," his narrator's memories include recognition of "the other," of Jewish memory. "Memory's anachronistic quality—its bringing together of now and then, here and there," Rothberg considers, "is actually the source of its powerful creativity, its ability to build new worlds out of materials of older ones."[14] Indeed, *Lost* bears no trace of the hollow rhetoric of the German *Erinnerungskultur*, of such dated phrases as the need to "confront the past" or the "duty to remember." Rather, it explores how different remnants of the Nazi era—idioms, memories, material objects, and much more—are woven together in the life stories of those born in its aftermath. *Lost*'s question is not so much about what one should remember but rather about how to negotiate different memories of a past that continues to affect the present.

In his follow-up novel, *Menschenflug* (2005), Treichel returns to his protagonist from a more contemporary perspective. Stephan is now the acknowledged author of a book that dealt with a brother who went missing during the *Vertreibung*. He lives in reunited Berlin with the psychoanalyst Helen, earns a good living, and apparently has every reason to be content. Yet Stephan cannot find peace. He takes a sabbatical from his work and from his family in the hope of discovering more about the family's past. Digging up dusty documents and taking a journey that leads him across Germany and even to Egypt, he finally believes he has discovered his lost brother in the northern German city of Celle. Once in Celle, however, Stephan is shocked to admit to himself that his presumed brother is a grumpy, sick old man (217).[15] Because his expedition into the past has provided none of the fulfillment for which he had longed, Stephan wanders into the annual gathering of ethnic Volhynia Germans—like his parents, expellees from Eastern Europe. Their nostalgic obsession with the lost homeland shakes Stephan to his core. On the express train back to Berlin, he finds solace in the rumblings of passengers with their cell phones: "Ten minutes and this whole history and ghost of the past was wiped out" (229; Zehn Minuten und der ganze Geschichts- und Vergangenheitsspuk war wie ausgelöscht). When he finally arrives in Berlin, Stephan feels strong, and an inner voice repeats time and again: "No more past!" (229; Keine Vergangenheit!).

Stephan's journey ends with his breaking away from a certain compulsive approach to his own and German history.[16] Journeys in quest of the family's history do not necessarily grant the possibility of living one's life to its fullest. As the text ironically notes, Stephan had previously mastered the technique suggested by his wife, a psychoanalyst, for overcoming his crisis through the famous Freudian formula of "remembering, repeating, and working through" (43).[17] This recipe, Stephan realizes now, has its limitations. In fact, in order to live, he needs to break away from the past altogether—to move on from retrospective excavations—and write his own life.

The Gift of Geschichte: Norbert Gstrein, The English Years

Norbert Gstrein's Die englischen Jahre (1999; The English Years) engages both Nazism and the culture of denial that characterized post–Second World War Austria, yet it does so without resorting to what Gstrein clearly views as ritualized remembrance.[18] Gstrein's narrator is a young Viennese doctor focused on reconstructing the life and work of Gabriel Hirschfelder, a celebrated exiled Austrian writer of Jewish descent who after the war lived in Southend-on-Sea in Great Britain, supposedly working on a masterpiece entitled The English Years. Gathering information from Hirschfelder's wives and lovers, she travels from Vienna to London and to the Isle of Man, where he had been interned during the war by the British, together with other German Jews and Nazi sympathizers, because he was a citizen of Austria and thus a potential security hazard.

Step by step, the young woman uncovers the fact that Hirschfelder was never the person he claimed to be. The real Hirschfelder died in 1940 when a ship carrying refugees from England to Newfoundland was torpedoed; the imposter was an Austrian by the name of Harrasser who had fled Austria because of his involvement in the death of a Jewish girl. Harrasser met Hirschfelder in the British internment camp on the Isle of Man. The latter's death presented him with the opportunity to adopt the untainted and (*after* the war) distinguished identity of the Jew. Harrasser was then able to achieve respectability by spreading rumors about his soon-to-be-published masterpiece and thus to be celebrated by a media frenzy that sent Austrian journalists to Britain on *Judenschauen* (view the Jew) trips, during which they met the writer and added to the ever-growing heap of praises that were being piled on the brilliant Jewish émigré.[19]

Even before the climactic revelation, we gradually find out that the search for Hirschfelder is not the narrator's motivation. One of the main reasons for embarking on her journey is, in fact, her difficult relationship with Max, her ex-partner. A failed Viennese writer, Max adores the little he knows of Hirschfelder's work. It is this admiration and her puzzlement over her ill-fated relationship with Max that trigger the young doctor's pursuit of the truth regarding the alleged Jewish writer (280). The dispassionate tone of Hirschfelder's writing about exile now strikes her, after she has found out who he actually was, as echoing the placidity of Max's own writing (279–80). The ways in which truth and lie, authenticity and empty posturing, became indistinguishable in Hirschfelder remind her of Max's barren speech: how, in admiring the imagined Jewish genius, he characterizes his own traveling elsewhere to write as "disappearing into exile" (279), as going to the desert, when, in fact, he simply travels to Paris (280).

Gstrein's novel gives a clear sense of the artificiality of the culture of memory in the late 1980s, yet it refrains from the moralist conceits that it mimics.[20] Deeply troubled by what she has discovered, the narrator confronts Max in a Viennese cafe. When she reveals her findings about Hirschfelder, Max remarks: "Now you can write a novel about that" (294). Puzzled, she replies that that is the last thing she would do: there are already so many versions of this story, she does not see why she should add her own. Max replies, "if you were to make me a present of your story maybe I could start over again. . . . I feel sure something different would come of it this time" (294, translation modified; "wenn du mir die Geschichte schenkst, könnte ich vielleicht noch einmal von vorn anfangen. . . . Ich zweifle nicht, daβ dass dann etwas anderes herauskommen *würde*").

Astonished, she begins to leave the café, wishing him "the best of luck with [his] new novel" (294), which Max then says he will write from *her* perspective (295). Thus, we are invited to consider the possibility that the entire narrative might actually be written by Max. Accepting her gift, Max gives the narrator her distinctive, uncompromisingly truthful voice. Furthermore, he is able to find out how complex his relationship with the Austrian past actually is and how flawed the current culture of memory, to which the neologism *Judenschauen* is central, has become. Writing the narrative—pondering what to do with the bequest and how to reciprocate with a gift of his own—Max peels away the layers of narcissistic fascination that determined his relation to Hirschfelder and becomes the artist he always wanted to be. Invoking the impossible, Nazism, through the figures of those who remain almost invisible in the novel—the real Hirschfelder and the imposter, Harrasser—the narrative turns what is increasingly distant in time into a central thread in the lives of younger Austrians.

Endowing the Past with New Meanings: Bernhard Schlink,
The Reader

While Treichel's and Gstrein's novels recast the past within the confines of German and Austrian internal discourse, in the concluding scene of Bernhard Schlink's eloquent and controversial *Der Vorleser* (1995; *The Reader*), a taxing gift comes to signify the relationship between second-generation Germans and Jews.[21] The narrator, Michael Berg, travels to New York, where he is to deliver to an elderly Jewish woman an unusual bequest—money accumulated in a bank account and in a little lavender tea tin that had belonged to a woman called Hanna Schmitz.[22] In 1958, when Michael was fifteen years old, he had a stormy affair with Hanna Schmitz—then a thirty-six-year-old tram conductor. Eight years after their affair, while Michael is attending law school, he finds out that Hanna is a defendant in a trial of concentration camp personnel. When he later encounters the woman to whom Hanna left her gift, he finds out that she barely survived internment in one of the satellite camps of Auschwitz where Hanna Schmitz had served as a guard.[23]

By the time Michael travels to New York, Hanna is already dead. She took her own life a few hours before she was to be released from a German jail after serving her sentence for crimes she committed during the war. During her imprisonment, the formerly illiterate Hanna had learned to read, following "word for word and sentence by sentence" (206) printed versions of audio books that Michael sent her in jail. She then eagerly studied all the literature of the Holocaust she could put her hands on: Primo Levi, Elie Wiesel, Jean Améry, and others (205). The fact that Schlink's novel does not attempt to explain why Hanna committed suicide after her "conversion," that is, after she actively engaged with the fate of Nazism's victims, underlines its symbolic thrust: rather than accounting for (or avoiding) Hanna's and her generation's crimes, *The Reader* is centered on Michael's attempt to integrate the truth about Hanna into his own life story, to accept the fact that he could love a perpetrator. Hence, important as this might be, the novel's symbolism is not confined to Hanna's illiteracy and thus to what might be seen as the narrator's (or, worse, the author's) attempt either to exonerate her and through her the so-called *Tätergeneration* (generation of perpetrators) or to Michael's "inability to mourn," as some critics claim.[24] Rather, we should pay attention here to Schlink's choice of first-person singular narrative. The narrative is thus less a historical account of the past—be it Nazism, the Holocaust, or West Germany of the 1960s—and more a creation that explores a young German's attempt to become. The unquestionable and at times disturbing force of Schlink's novel comes from the intimacy of many sentences such as "I wanted simultaneously to understand Hanna's crime and to condemn it. . . . But it was impossible to do both" (157). Rather than indicating Michael's (or Schlink's) psychological or moral culpability, Schlink's narrative traces how dealing with the inheritance of German history becomes the condition of an evolving personality and leads to the creation of new human bonds.[25]

The difficulties of creating such bonds are, in fact, at the center of the scene we began with. In a short testimonial note she wrote before committing suicide, Hanna Schmitz asks Michael to deliver her modest savings and the lavender tea tin to the Jewish woman who survived the concentration camp: "She should decide what to do with it." Having given him the task of dealing with the impossible, with her unbearable life story, Hanna wants to "give" her years of imprisonment, as Michael puts it, "her own meaning, and she wanted this giving to be recognized" (212). Yet it is Michael, not Hanna Schmitz, who endows this gesture with meaning. He uses this gift as an opportunity to tackle what is more difficult than finding words to condemn his former lover: the chance to develop his own relationship with the past. Once he meets the now elderly woman face-to-face, we read:

> I told her about Hanna's death and her last wishes.
> "Why me?"
> "I suppose because you are the only survivor."
> "And how am I supposed to deal with it?"
> "However you think fit."
> "And grant Frau Schmitz her absolution?" (212)

The Jewish woman's reluctance to grant forgiveness does not prevent her from a rapport with Michael, difficult as it may be. Indeed, seeing the lavender tea tin where Hanna kept some of her savings, the survivor tells him that as a child, she, too, possessed a similar chest—a little girl's treasure box that she had managed to take with her to the concentration camp (214). It is that tea tin that gives the woman an idea about how to deal with Hanna's inheritance: Michael is to take Hanna Schmitz's bequest and pass it on, create with it a new trajectory by donating the money to a Jewish organization that deals with illiteracy. The book thus ends with her laughing and saying, " 'If the recognition is so important, you can do it in the name of Hanna Schmitz.' She picked up the tin again. 'I'll keep the tin' " (215).

In presenting the survivor with her humble savings, it might be that Hanna aimed at closing the abyss separating perpetrator from survivor with an act of reparation similar to the projections associated with the *Wiedergutmachung* (the payment of reparations) of West German politics and culture as of the 1950s.[26] Yet there is little that would support such an interpretation. The narrator approaches the survivor with noticeable distance and refrains from stylizing her as an archetypal Jewish character. The plot underlines that the two remain alien. There is no indication that Michael will ever see the woman again or that the past will be undone. Nevertheless, the conversation they have and the woman's decision to hold on to the tin—the choreography of gift giving and the pondering of what to do with it—signal the emergence, humble as it may be, of a social bond. Nothing can change the past. Recasting it as a difficult endowment, however, makes it possible that the illiterate may learn to read and allow Michael, after he has met with the survivor, to become a different person—not redeemed or cured but evolved as a human being.

While the encounter between Michael and the survivor could be seen as signifying a "fantasy of reverse restitution" by which "the successor generation" of the perpetrators (Michael) is "validated by a Holocaust victim," I agree with Ernestine Schlant that this scene hardly gestures toward reconciliation but is instead "the beginning of a dialogue—albeit a tenuous and a painful one."[27] Imagining what a conversation between Germans born after the war and Holocaust survivors or their descendants might be like, Schlink wishes (much like Marcel Beyer and Norbert Gstrein) to move beyond the "sort of banality" of the *Erinnerungskultur* in the late 1980s.[28] Both in his literary writing and in his essays he suggests avoiding the "moral pathos" that characterized (and partly still does characterize) much of that culture of memory and engaging the Nazi past with awareness of contemporary concerns such as what might prevent "civilized nations," such as Germany prior to 1933, from falling into a barbaric state (29). "Moral courage," Schlink notes, can hardly be taught in a "didactic way" (31): "I think it is learned mostly by living example, experience and repeated practice" (31).

On Giving: Katharina Hacker, A Kind of Love, *and* W. G. Sebald, Austerlitz

Whereas in *The Reader* the regretful perpetrator is the one to initiate an encounter between Germans and Jews, in Katharina Hacker's novel *Eine Art Liebe* (2003; A kind of love) it is the Jewish survivor. Set in Israel and Germany in the 1990s, *Eine Art Liebe* tells the story of distinctive friendships.[29] The first is between the Israeli lawyer Moshe Fein and the narrator, the thirty-something German, Sophie. Like Hacker, who studied history and Jewish studies at the Hebrew University, Sophie arrives in Jerusalem in the 1990s. There she experiences the 1991 Gulf War, the peace negotiations between Israelis and Palestinians, and the 1995 assassination of Yitzhak Rabin. *Eine Art Liebe* also portrays the decades-long difficult camaraderie between Moshe Fein, a Jew born in Berlin in the 1930s, and Jean, a Trappist monk. They met when Moshe was taken into hiding in a Catholic boarding school in Vichy France.

At the beginning of the novel, Sophie returns to Israel three weeks after Jean was found dead in a Berlin bar. Visiting Moshe in Jerusalem, her older friend tells her: "I give you Jean's story as a gift. Write it down" (11; Ich schenke Dir Jeans Geschichte. Schreib sie auf). *Eine Art Liebe* thus recounts Sophie's quest for the past. She seeks facts, but also insights into the intricate bond between a Catholic French boy and a young German Jew—and through it into the relationship between Christians and Jews in light of the Catholic Church's role during the Holocaust. Sophie's task is not easy, because Moshe has forgotten or repressed much of his past. She tackles it by bringing the lives of Moshe and his Catholic friend to bear on her own. She notes: "His [Moshe's] story, Jean's story, and my own are constantly mixed now. . . . There are fragments of the memory, and there is the memory that one remembers [Es gibt Bruchstücke der Erinnerung, und es gibt die Erinnerung, an die man sich erinnert]. One tells [a story], and only for as long as one speaks, the parts are joined together" (16).

In imagining and inventing Moshe's *Geschichte*, his story, and the German-Jewish shared past of the Holocaust, Hacker recasts *Geschichte* along the lines of Michael Oakeshott's "practical past." The past Moshe gives Sophie as a gift is not a point in time to which one can actually return or a reservoir of coherent data waiting to be channeled directly into the present and put to use. Rather, it is a fragmentary set of ephemeral texts, verbal memories, testimonies, and remnants that are waiting to be made useful in narrative form. As we enter the time in which no survivors or witnesses are left, what we cannot imagine and utilize might indeed be forgotten. We need to explore new ways to engage the past, Hacker's novel suggests; we need to examine new forms of telling its horrors as they relate to our lives. "Using" the past imaginatively to construct our identities and reflecting on this use itself may be a way to avoid the disappearance of the Holocaust from our personal and public life.

As Sophie approaches the end of her account, she acknowledges to Moshe that her account of his life "is not what [he] expected" (265). Reiterating his preliminary gesture, Moshe for his part replies, "I didn't expect anything. . . . It is your story. I gave it to you as a present [*es ist deine Geschichte, ich habe es dir geschenkt*]" (265). Echoing Norbert Gstrein's and Bernard Schlink's metaphorics of the gift, of giving and receiving the tasking inheritance of the German past, Hacker makes use of the alliteration of *Geschichte* and *Geschenk*. In a time when the victims, perpetrators, collaborators, and bystanders are almost gone, in an era characterized by a sense that the past has become a mere "sublime desire," as Amy Elias has aptly observed, *Geschichte* is not the ruin, the blemish alone.[30] Rather, it is also a heritage offered to the *Nachgeborene* (successor generations), a gift that calls on them to accept it as a facet of their own lives, be it in Berlin, in Jerusalem, or elsewhere.

While the gift of history enabled Max of Gstrein's *The English Years* to write without resorting to the platitudes that paralyzed him before, in Hacker's novel, as in Schlink's *The Reader*, it is the ground for establishing new kinds of human bonds, be they between Sophie and Moshe or between her and her Israeli Jewish boyfriend, Shai (115). Once her relationship with Shai is established, Sophie is confronted with his parents—Holocaust survivors and Orthodox Jews who now face the fact that their only child has fallen for a German Gentile. As Shai's parents are "forced" to react to Sophie's presence, she, in turn, changes their lives. Once having received the past and having reciprocated that gift, Sophie has woven a new web of human relations that, while leaving the traumas unchanged, nevertheless constitutes something that was not there before.

Sophie never discovers any ultimate truths about Moshe's life. Rather, she makes his life story useful in redefining herself. She notes, "A story [*eine Geschichte*] is not an answer to a question; sometimes a story [*Geschichte*] is not even a question" (264). Significantly, once the novel is concluded, the reader finds a note written by the author. It is here that Katharina Hacker discloses what many might have sensed all along: that the story of Moshe Fein is closely related to Saul Friedländer's (Friedlander) memoir *When Memory Comes*.[31] *Eine Art Liebe*, Hacker writes, "deals with the question of how it is possible to understand with the help of the imagination, there, where one has no memory. . . . Regardless of what time will bring, there always exists the unrelenting attempt to understand, and the imagination" (267). Sophie's attempt to piece together Moshe Fein's life now emerges as the result of the desire to arrive at an instructive image of times past. However, understanding does not mean calling on the faculty of comprehension to yield epistemological judgments about vanished realities. Rather, the novel uses the imagination to make the past useful for those born after the events involved.

The question that Hacker so eloquently poses, "how it is possible to understand with the help of the imagination, there, where one has no memory," drives what is perhaps the most impressive work of recent German literature that explores the past as a "useful" inheritance and medium of growth: W. G. Sebald's masterful *Austerlitz* (2001).[32] Born in 1944 and thus without conscious experience of Nazism, Sebald's narrator in *Austerlitz* is a German man living in the United Kingdom in the late 1990s who tells the story of his intricate friendship with Jacques Austerlitz. Austerlitz is an art historian who survived the war as a Jewish child only because his parents sent him to Great Britain in the so-called Kindertransport, the rescue operation that brought some ten thousand Jewish children from Nazi Germany to Great Britain before the beginning of the Second World War.

Although Sebald's narrator does not say much about it, we can assume from the intermittent nature of this friendship that it has not been an easy one. At one point, the acquaintances even lose contact for almost twenty years, since the narrator decided to return to his homeland in 1975, and, as he understood only in retrospect, "Austerlitz did not like writing to Germany" (34). Having grown up in Adenauer's West

Germany, the narrator understands his older friend's reservations: his professors were, after all, those "who had built their careers in the 1930s and 1940s and still nurtured delusions of power" (33). Like Sebald himself, who had left Germany because of his sense that his homeland evades its Nazi past, the narrator of *Austerlitz* thus drew a line between himself and the discourse of forgetting that characterized West Germany in the first decades after the war. It is, in fact, precisely the haunting German past that draws him to the Jewish survivor and that ultimately creates their bond. Upon returning to the United Kingdom in the 1990s, the narrator meets Austerlitz again, and their relationship intensifies. In the course of that period—the bulk of the novel—the narrator will "receive" Austerlitz's past: he will gradually find out from him much about his forced separation from his parents and a subsequent life determined by the attempt to repress the traumas of a Jewish childhood during the Holocaust. Austerlitz will also share with his German friend one of the most difficult chapters in his life, his mental collapse. Finally, he will unveil the events that had led him out of the mental abyss: the biographical stations that led him to embrace his repressed past.

During their last encounter, in Paris in the late 1990s, before bidding farewell to his German friend for the last time, Austerlitz hands over the key to his house in London's Alderney Street. The narrator realizes that this gesture is not simply an invitation to "stay there whenever [he] liked" but also—and here lies the crux—a challenge to "study the black and white photographs which, one day, would be all that was left" of Austerlitz's life (293). The house key indicates the confidence the friends have come to share through traveling and discussing the past. At the same time, it marks a test presented by the giver, the survivor, to his German friend to put together the threads of Austerlitz's life according to the narrator's *own* design. The book we hold in our hands is, in fact, the result of this bequest. In accepting the key, putting the photographs in order, and writing up Austerlitz's story—indeed, all the latter's memories and reflections are given in indirect speech—the novel is the narrator's reaction, his countergift to his friend's generous and tasking gesture.

From the moment he is given the key, the narrator embarks on his own path of discovery. On his way back to London, the narrator stops in Antwerp and from there travels to a place he had visited in 1967, at the beginning of the novel: the Belgian fortress Breendonk, a structure used during the war by the SS. In 1967, in a casemate, one of the fortified gun emplacements at Breendonk, a scent sends a wave of revulsion through his body:

a nauseating smell of soft soap rose to my nostrils . . . linked
to the bizarre German word for scrubbing brush, *Wurzelbürste*,
which was a favorite of my father's and which I had always disliked. Black striations began to quiver before my eyes, and I had
to rest my forehead against the wall. . . . It was not that as the
nausea rose in me I guessed at the kind of third-degree interro-
gations which were being conducted here around the time I was
born, since it was only a few years later that I read Jean Améry's
descriptions of the . . . tortures he himself suffered in Breendonk
when he was hoisted aloft by his hands, tied behind his back,
so that with a crack and a splintering sound, which, as he says,
he had not yet forgotten when he came to write his account,
his arms dislocated from the sockets in his shoulder joints and
he was left dangling as they were wrenched up behind him and
twisted together above his head. (26)

Much in *Austerlitz*'s cyclical structure leads away from and back to this
early scene in Breendonk. Here the past is made present through what
Hans Ulrich Gumbrecht calls "presence effects"—techniques that produce the illusion that worlds of the past "are tangible again."[33] Jean
Améry's torture is not simply *re*presented but rather made present
through a distressing bodily imposition into the narrator's lifeworld—
that narrator being a German, who like Sebald himself, was born during the time Améry and others were subjected to Nazi torture. Like the
Proustian madeleine, Sebald's soft soap turns what is long gone into a
contemporaneous sensation, thus turning the tortures experienced in
Breendonk into a constant of the present.

While evoking the traumatic pains that Améry experienced in Breendonk, Sebald's novel confronts what the narrator explicitly fears: that
"the world is . . . draining itself, in that the history of countless places
and objects which themselves have no power of memory is never heard"
(24). The novel confronts these fears in order to allow the reader to view
past torture—through the prism of nausea—as a condition that never
completely ends. The novel's smells and sounds (the soap, the "splintering sound") redescribe the inhumanity of Nazism, as pain that remains
as immediate an experience as one occurring in the preceding moment.

Austerlitz's key thus allows the narrator to write a story that ensures
remembrance of the perpetrated crimes. Yet at the same time the key is
also an invitation to engage the past and consider the pains of political
torture as such. As Eric Santner has shown, Sebald's work explores modern liminal situations such as torture under Nazism, in which humans

are rendered "creaturely" and turned into mere subjects of political or "biopolitical" order, using a term from Giorgio Agamben.[34] In other words, by invoking the torture at Breendonk, the narrative becomes a meditation on torture beyond the confines of the Belgian fortress. Sebald's work thus enables us to engage with what Santner calls "the creaturely dimension of our neighbor."[35]

The Paradoxical Achievement

In *The Ethics of Memory*, Avishai Margalit notes that "even the project of remembering the gloomiest of memories is a hopeful project. It ultimately rejects the pessimist thought that all will be forgotten."[36] The anxiety one registers in *Austerlitz* about what might be lost to oblivion signals hope in the novel, because the narrative makes it difficult to relegate historical inhumanity to the realm of pastness. This becomes evident in the novel's move from the past to the present, from the suffering of those who were tortured to the narrator's own memory of the *Wurzelbürste*—"I do remember . . . I had always disliked . . . the nausea rose in me . . . I guessed . . . I was . . . I read . . ."—thus making the horrific past into an unsettling aspect of the narrator's lifeworld. And as in the case of Alexander Kluge's "it should simply stop,"[37] the invocation of the longgone serves as the departure point in considering what might prevent those conditions from reoccurring.

As in Bernhard Schlink's *The Reader* and Katharina Hacker's *Eine Art Liebe*, one could understand Austerlitz's gift to his German friend as the fantasy of reconciliation or, even worse, as an attempt to take on the role of the victim.[38] One does so, however, only by assuming a hermeneutics of suspicion, which is mainly interested in tearing away textual masks and in uncovering unconscious intentions and false consciousnesses—in short, a symptomatic reading.[39] Reconsidering the relationship between the past and the present as an intricate procedure of exchange seems to me a much richer approach to Sebald's metaphors. The house key and the narrator's recurrent visits to Breendonk are indications of an ongoing process whose outcome remains open. Every time the narrator travels to Breendonk, he does so as a different person. His story is hardly a finite account of what he takes interest in, but rather an invitation to engage with that story in different, ever-evolving ways—an invitation for one to reflect on the meaning of torture for those who endured such pain in twentieth-century European history *but also* to reflect on present-day cases of politically, ethnically, or racially motivated torture. Reconfiguring the past in this manner does not undermine the severity of what was done by the SS in Breendonk, nor does it signal a forgetting of concrete historical circumstances. It does mean, however, viewing the events of Austerlitz's life from a broader perspective than that of the recent German and Jewish past.

Stephan in Treichel's *Lost*, Michael Berg in Schlink's *The Reader*, Sophie in Hacker's novel, and Sebald's German narrator all receive the thorny endowment of the German past as gift. They ponder what to do with it, how to live with that inheritance, and what role it may play in their futures. The outcome of their consideration, however, becomes a gift to the reader. These novels' metaphors of exchange and symbols-imbued stories of giving and receiving offer the very new cultural lexis of memory for which Walser, Beyer, and Gstrein in their distinctive ways pleaded.

The literary works we discussed in this chapter are thus "events" or "acts" in Derek Attridge's sense: we bring them "into being, differently each time."[40] Engaging the past, we make it meaningful for ourselves in our own lifeworlds. Presented with history as gift, as both a burdening *and* potent heritage, readers are bound to reciprocate with their own associations, narratives, considerations, discomfort, and possible actions, thus generating a new chain of giving and taking. Considered for its "practical" significance in literature, the past thus offers us more than knowledge regarding guilt and punishment, shame and repentance, pain and mourning.

Reading and rereading the works discussed thus far, one can hardly escape the impression that literary engagement with Germany's Nazi past across the significant divides of age, aesthetics, political convictions, and philosophical inclinations reveals the ability of literature to help readers revisit their histories prospectively and reconceive themselves and their communal realities. Via theme, plot, metaphor, or irony, the writers considered here participated in the process of creating first a West German and then a German "culture of civility."[41] As Timothy Garton Ash noted (not without puzzlement and irony),

> the Germany of the early years of the twenty-first century is one of the most free and civilized countries on earth. . . . In this good land, the professionalism of its historians, the investigative skills of its journalists, the seriousness of its parliamentarians, the generosity of its funders, the idealism of its priests and moralists, the creative genius of its writers, and, yes, the brilliance of its filmmakers have all combined to cement in the world's imagination the most indelible association of Germany with evil. Yet without

these efforts, Germany would never have become such a good land. In all the annals of human culture, has there ever been a more paradoxical achievement?[42]

The works we have read in the previous pages accounted for that evil and reminded us of what Germans and, one could argue, humans were and are capable of doing. Yet they have provided a "shock," to use Richard Rorty's term, and caused many to turn their back on that history and create a future that is indeed, as Rorty puts it, "wonderfully different."[43]

**Part Two | Writing the Unsaid:
Hebrew Literature and the Question of
Palestinian Flight and Expulsion**

6 The Unsaid

Zeitschichten

The stretch of land covered by modern Israel is saturated with history. Numerous ruins, archeological sites, and memorials make the country a vast open-air museum of world history: antiquity and the Crusades, the Mamluk and the Ottoman eras, the rise of Zionism, as well as the ongoing conflict between Israelis and Palestinians, are ever present. Moreover, many of the country's most evocative places—Acre, Masada, the Temple Mount in Jerusalem—remind us of more than one event or period. They display the complexity of Israel's *Zeitschichten*, in Reinhart Koselleck's metaphor: the layering of different historical times in a single space, in turn containing a simultaneity of diverse, often-conflicting memories.[1]

Israel's landscape thus speaks to and is spoken of by many, often mutually exclusive narratives. It is, in W. J. T. Mitchell's words, "both a representation and presented space . . . both a frame and what a frame contains, both a real place and its simulacrum, both a package and the commodity inside the package."[2] For example, while some view Israel's many pine forests, a product of early reforestation efforts, as proof of Zionism's success in rejuvenating the land, others regard them as a projection of

European aesthetics and evidence of the colonialist, orientalist sensibilities of the Zionist movement.[3]

In recent decades, the contested meanings of Israel's landscape have been a crucial issue in the debates surrounding 1948. For the majority of Israeli Jews, this year marks the War of Independence and the beginning of national sovereignty. For most Palestinians, however, 1948 represents al-Nakba, "the Disaster," in which seven to eight hundred thousand men, women, and children either fled or were forced into exile by the armed might of the young Jewish state.[4] Indeed, 1948 is the most decisive "modernist event" of Israel/Palestine's history. It is the war that began all wars of the Arab-Israeli conflict, and its outcome—the dispute over the border and the future of the Palestinian refugees—remains the crux of the ongoing conflict between Israelis and Palestinians, as well as between Israel and the larger Arab world.[5]

It is not my aim here to offer a comprehensive account of the debates surrounding 1948, nor do I wish to present any judgment as to who is ultimately responsible for the plight of the Palestinian people.[6] Rather, I wish to examine a variety of significant works, written by Jewish Israeli writers over six decades, that redescribe the flight and expulsion of Palestinians from their homeland and thus prompt their readers to consider the implications for Israel's present and future.[7]

The Unsaid

From its beginnings in the late nineteenth century, as Yael Zerubavel has shown, Zionist culture has relied on the projection of meanings onto the land for the creation of the modern Jewish national narrative.[8] Building on elements from the archive of Jewish cultural memory—the Bible, Mishnah, Talmud, Jewish liturgy and literature—and on European Romanticism, with its fascination for the Orient, Zionism rejected Judaism's millennia-long exilic condition and imagined in Palestine/Eretz Yisrael a modern Jewish national renaissance.[9] Creating spatial images and metaphors surrounding Jerusalem and the first modern Jewish city, Tel Aviv, Hebrew literature was part and parcel of what Gershon Shaked and Yigal Schwartz describe as the Zionist "metanarrative," according to which modern Jews were returning to their ancestral homeland, to an empty land waiting to be redeemed.[10] As Michael Gluzman has suggested, this metanarrative of redemption sought, furthermore, to transform what was perceived as an anachronistic, deformed national body into a Nietzschean, modern, and healthy one.[11]

Only around the turn of the century and then more decisively after the violent clashes of 1929 was the fantasy of empty land waiting to be redeemed by Zionism finally put to rest. It was then that the conflict over Palestine/Eretz Yisrael began to emerge as an important concern of Hebrew literature.[12] Soon after 1929, writers and intellectuals of both the Left and the Right, such as Uri Zvi Greenberg (1896–1981), Shin Shalom (Shalom Joseph Shapira, 1904–90), and Berl Katznelson (1887–1944), expressed serious resentment toward what they saw as a feral Arab insurgency.[13]

The bitter conflict that flamed after the November 1947 United Nations resolution to divide Palestine into a Jewish and an Arab state and the ensuing 1948 war endowed the relationship between Jews and Arabs and thus Hebrew literature's relation to the Israeli-Palestinian conflict with an entirely new, catastrophic dimension. From this point onward, two dramatically opposed narratives came to occupy the geographic and human landscape of Israel/Palestine. For the majority of Jewish Israelis, 1948 signaled the hard-won *komemiyut* (independence), a sign of hope for Jews all over the world, coming only three years after the extent of their national catastrophe during the Holocaust became evident. Many citizens of the young Jewish state believed, for a variety of reasons, that the Palestinian exodus in the course of the war was the result of voluntary flight: Palestinians went into exile hoping that they would soon return with the victorious Arab militaries to evict the Jewish population and enjoy the fruits of its toil. For Palestinians, however, 1948 signaled an incomprehensible disaster by which they were forced out of their homes and villages, abruptly losing their livelihood, sites of cultural heritage, and sense of belonging.[14] Many of them experienced the war not as a military defeat but rather as the brutal expulsion of helpless citizens, an eviction that involved plundering, rape, and humiliation.

After the 1948 war and al-Nakba, we find major Israeli Jewish writers turning to the war, to the flight and expulsion of Palestinians, to the bitter conflict over the land and its moral ramifications. In fact, immediately after 1948, both prose and lyrical works begin to appear that give serious consideration to the complexities of 1948 and to the existence of multiple, conflicting memories surrounding the events of that year. Many of these works also reflect the pressing political and ethical dilemmas stemming from the fate of Palestinians.[15] Thus, the subject of expulsion, which many Israelis preferred to see passed over in silence, came to the fore through literary representations. Indeed, novels and poems written by Jewish Israeli writers played a crucial role in addressing "the unsaid" and, in this way, broadened and deepened the moral vocabulary with which Israelis consider 1948—and thus who they are and who they would like to become.

I use the term "unsaid" in two interrelated ways. The first is to mark a specific series of historical events referred to only implicitly (if at all) in Israeli political discourse during the first decades following 1948: the forceful expulsion of Palestinians from their homes that occurred during the war; the prevention of refugees from returning to their homes; and, finally, the erasure of Palestinian villages emptied in 1948, either leveled to the ground or turned into Jewish Israeli communities.[16] Thus, for Israeli writers, writing the unsaid meant recognizing, first, that winning Jewish national sovereignty was experienced as a catastrophe by the land's Palestinian population and, second, that the 1948 exodus of Palestinians involved expulsion, as well as flight.

The second meaning of "the unsaid" is more structural and refers to what the literary works in question *do* rather than *say*—to the ethical and political reactions prompted by their choice of characters, themes, plots, and symbolic constellations. In other words, "the unsaid" points to the pragmatic consequences of Hebrew literature: to its capacity to inspire reflection, debate, and possible action—that is, to inspire "practical engagement," in Michael Oakeshott's words.[17]

At times, the literature I present has generated dissensus, which here means bearing in mind the moral identity and political realities of the Jewish state and pondering this enterprise's past, present, and future. Operating in many of these works is a tension characteristic of the entire Zionist movement, between particularistic national Jewish tendencies and universalistic notions of justice, as proclaimed by the biblical prophets and by Enlightenment humanism. The writers in question do not resolve this probably irreconcilable tension in any satisfying manner. However, their works do offer an opportunity for readers to consider how they may negotiate between the vectors of nationalism and justice that effectively polarize Israeli public discourse to this day.[18]

This latter meaning of "the unsaid"—its ability to point to issues such as the tension between particularism and universal humanism without overtly expressing it—owes much to Hannah Arendt's concept of the *Unausgesprochene*, what is not spoken. Arendt explores this term in her *Denktagebuch*, her "thinking diary," in reference to Martin Heidegger's idea that literary works encompass more than what they explicitly utter.[19] Arendt notes that Heidegger's "interpretations" go beyond the hermeneutic assumption that the meaning of the literary work lies in its overt "said" to reveal its "unsaid" (*ihm spezifisch Unausgesprochenes*) as its actual kernel (*seinen eigentlichen Kern*). Psychologically speaking, Arendt notes, this kernel is the reason the work arises in the first place (*der Grund seines Entstehens*): because one thing is inexpressible, all the rest is written. This metaphoric kernel is the vacant, yet central, space around which the written and said revolves, organizing everything else. Hence, the unsaid marks what remains concealed for psychological reasons, or what is latent in a work. Yet it also points to what literature creates regardless of what is articulated: its unique capacity to generate reflection, in the processes of reading and public reception, on what it cannot or would not specifically utter. In Arendt's view, the unsaid is the place where the author is no longer present, creating a place for the reader, the listener: "from here the work transforms itself back from finite, frozen-printed speech into a vital speech. The result is a dialogue in which the reader no longer comes from the outside but rather participates from within."[20]

As we will see, the unsaid figures in both its senses—the invocation of al-Nakba and the hinting at what the work does not directly utter—in literary creations such as S. Yizhar's *The Story of Khirbet Khizeh* and A. B. Yehoshua's *Mul hayearot* (Facing the forests).[21] To begin with, these works refer explicitly to the concrete historical fact of the expulsion (*Story of Khirbet Khizeh*) or to its human and moral consequences (*Mul hayearot*). They present lasting images of Palestinians going into exile or Palestinians whose bodies bear the traces of 1948. Furthermore, works like these deploy a variety of literary devices that provoke their readers to consider what the works themselves never specifically express: the challenge of navigating between the demands of the Zionist national creed and possibly conflicting ethical standards. As the public debates surrounding S. Yizhar's *The Story of Khirbet Khizeh* and other works demonstrate, this provocation creates a text-reader dialogue in Arendt's sense. Reading and discussing this literature, the Jewish Israeli reader cannot remain *outside* the work but is rather prompted to engage with its questions *from within*. Ultimately, what unites all the works discussed here is their ability to prompt a future-oriented self-examination on the part of their readers, inviting them to consider their personal and collective "patterns of action" (as Richard Rorty phrased it), as well as the broad moral consequences of those patterns.[22]

Loyalist Literature?

My emphasis on Hebrew literature's ability to write the unsaid departs from several recent discussions of representations of the Israeli-Palestinian conflict in Hebrew poetry and prose. Examining al-Nakba in Hebrew literature, the poet and critic Yitzhak Laor (b. 1948), for instance, has claimed that the work of major Israeli writers such as Amos Oz, A. B. Yehoshua, and Yehoshua Kenaz participated in the political silencing of the forced Palestinian exile and played a crucial role in establishing a hegemonic, oblivious Israeli narrative regarding 1948. The calculated silence of Israel's political discourse—from Israel's first premier, David Ben-Gurion, onward—regarding the expulsion of Palestinians has been echoed, Laor claims, in the silence of "the academy, the historians," and, significantly, Israel's "loyalist literature" (*sifrut mitaam*). Laor views different generations of writers as accepting "almost completely" the "Zionist narrative" regarding the genesis of the Israeli-Palestinian conflict and, "foremost, the forced forgetting."[23]

Yochai Oppenheimer has recently offered a much more nuanced assessment of al-Nakba in Israeli narrative prose. Following the theoretical premises of postcolonial discourse, Oppenheimer claims that Hebrew literature's image of the Arab over the last hundred years reflects "political, cultural, and literary interests" rather than an attention to its presumable object. From the beginning of Zionist migration to Palestine, the Arab has been the object of the orientalist gaze, described as culturally different and usually less worthy than their Jewish counterparts. Oppenheimer concludes that al-Nakba was never a major theme of Hebrew prose, just as the civil life of Arabs never became a meaningful concern for Jewish Israeli writers.[24] In fact, the cover of Oppenheimer's extensive study states categorically: "Hebrew literature managed to evade, if not erase, Palestinian history and especially al-Nakba. To do so required much imagination and considerable effort."[25]

"Apart from a few exceptions, Hebrew poets did not display sensitivity to the human evil that occurred in their immediate vicinity and time," echoes Hannan Hever in an introduction to an anthology of Hebrew poetry from 1948 to 1958.[26] According to Hever, dominant literary figures such as Nathan Alterman (1910–70) and others remained, even as they were writing on the expulsion of Palestinians, essentially numb to the Palestinian suffering and reluctant to acknowledge their own personal responsibility as Israelis.

While Hever's readings are responsive to Hebrew literature's grappling with the past, Laor and Oppenheimer tend to read it symptomatically, uncovering cultural ills by tracing a text's omissions and misrepresentations. From their readings, Hebrew literature engaging 1948 and al-Nakba emerges *solely* as a condensed expression of public or political, semiconscious or unconscious, attitudes. Laor's and Oppenheimer's work thus has much in common structurally with the symptomatic readings of postwar German literature by Ernestine Schlant and others.

This mode of symptomatic reading, the negative thrust of which is usually focused on what writers *could* or *should* have written, often misses what the works actually have accomplished. It overlooks the novelty of their images and metaphors and, most significantly, the power of certain works of literature to expand their culture's moral and political vocabularies.

Works discussed in the following pages integrate elements of the Palestinian "other's" experience into the vocabulary of Hebrew prose and, ultimately, into an Israeli discourse generally oblivious to the suffering of Palestinians. Their themes and symbolic arrangements generate public deliberation about what the literary works themselves never explicitly state: that Israel needs to address the pain it inflicted and inflicts on Palestinians in the course of the ongoing conflict, and furthermore, that it cannot navigate between its national interests and its own idea of justice by claiming that the exiled Palestinians of 1948 simply fled their land.

Sentinel for the House of Israel

One can always argue that the writers discussed here could have written more about al-Nakba or done so differently or been more attentive to the suffering of Palestinians. Yet at its best, this literature presents readers in Israel and elsewhere with a range of imaginative redescriptions of 1948 and has had a noticeable and cumulative effect on Israeli public discourse that—alongside historical and sociological studies—has helped turn the attention of many Israelis to that recent past as well as to the ethical and political challenges it poses to Israel's present and future.[27] Indeed, as Hannan Hever and Haggai Rogani have shown in their extensive studies of Hebrew poetry and al-Nakba, as early as 1949 a number of Israeli poets expressed critical perspectives about the 1948 war and the excesses of Jewish nationalism. In fact, these writers proved more attentive to these issues than their counterparts in the history departments of the Israeli academy.[28] With this in view, my discussion emphasizes the innovative metaphorics employed by A. B. Yehoshua and others rather than considers the writers as *sifrut-mitaam*—loyalists merely voicing Jewish Israeli national-ideological convictions.

One can trace, in fact, a visible thematic thread that leads from a novella such as S. Yizhar's 1949 *The Story of Khirbet Khizeh*, to Alon Hilu's 2008 novel *Achuzat Dajani* (translated into English as *The House of Rajani*),[29] to Yoram Kaniuk's 2010 memoir *Tashach* (1948).[30] Together with the critical work of historians, sociologists, anthropologists, and many others, these works bring the unsaid of 1948, along with its ethical-political implications, to the consciousness of their Israeli readers. As suggested by the ongoing and heated debates around the proposal made by Yuli Tamir, Israel's minister of education (2006–7), to include references to al-Nakba in schoolbooks, these literary works were instrumental in the process through which Israelis came to accept the existence of multiple, conflicting narratives regarding 1948 and to acknowledge the human and ethical challenges that the forced exile of Palestinians continues to pose more than six decades after that fateful year.[31] Even if the term "al-Nakba" remains highly contentious in present-day Israel, it is impossible to imagine that this new awareness regarding 1948 will ever disappear from public discourse.[32]

With regard to their position in Israel's public sphere, the writers we will discuss below all played a distinctive social role, one that in the tradition of Hebrew literature is referred to as *hatsofe leveit Yisrael*, "the sentinel for the house of Israel" (Ezekiel 3:17, 33:7).[33] This cultural figure is, as Todd Hasak-Lowy puts it, "a type of prophet, whose task is to show the straight path, to identify the 'generation's sin,' to exhort its rehabilitation, and to chart the nation's path toward a better future."[34] As Hasak-Lowy notes, the historical model of the Hebrew writer as "the sentinel for the House of Israel" suggests a creative individual who is capable of admonishing the people as well as of providing them with a normative perspective on the conditions and challenges facing the nation. In this capacity, the writer-prophet also plays a role in shaping history "in a double sense," because such sentinels "both narrate a past and shape the future."[35]

In essays, newspaper commentaries, and public statements, writers such as A. B. Yehoshua, Amos Oz, and David Grossman clearly display their commitment to this tradition, while others, such as Yehoshua Kenaz, maintain a much more distant relation to it.[36] Regardless of their personal identification with the role of "sentinel," however, the works by these writers also display an interest in shaping the country's future as they narrate Israel's past, and it is precisely this "double sense" that guides my subsequent discussion.

To be sure, recent literature in Hebrew that invokes 1948 also includes works by prominent Palestinian or Arab Israeli writers who focus primarily on the impact of 1948 on Palestinian consciousness, such as Emile Habibi (1922–96), Anton Shammas (b. 1950), Naim Araidi (b. 1950), Salman Masalha (b. 1953), and Sayed Kashua (b. 1975). My interest here, however, is on the effect of 1948 on the Jewish Israeli side of the conflict. As in the discussion of postwar German literature in part I, I focus on how authors who belong to a national collective that grapples with guilt, shame, and a sense of liability engage with these emotions. My decision not to include these Palestinian authors' works in the analyses below is thus a result of the constraints of my topic and not a reflection on their importance or quality.

Another qualification regarding the choice of material has to do with the inevitable sacrifice of scope in favor of manageability, focus, and cohesiveness. My choice of works reflects both the judgment of relative literary value and the degree of cultural significance and moral weight that their reception by readers and critics has accumulated (in some cases over five or more decades). I touch on this reception in my discussion, because it is partly my intention to challenge some of the theoretical presuppositions that have informed much of that critical attention. In brief, I examine literature for its potential to challenge political reality by keeping our view of this reality "unfrozen," as David Grossman puts it, by remembering the power of certain books to point their reader's gaze toward what is still "open, future, possible."[37]

7

The Silence of the Villages: S. Yizhar's Early War Writing

The Great Jewish Soul: S. Yizhar, The Story of Khirbet Khizeh

Soon after his service as an intelligence officer in the 1948 War of Independence, S. Yizhar (Yizhar Smilansky, 1916–2006) published two novellas that deal with that chapter of his life, *Sipur Khirbet Khizah* (*The Story of Khirbet Khizeh*) and *Hashavui* (The captive).[1] The war was a recurrent theme among Yizhar's peers—Haim Gouri, Moshe Shamir, Hanoch Bartov, Aharon Megged, and Nathan Shaham—in the Dor Hapalmach (Palmach Generation).[2] However, Yizhar's distinctive and richly embellished language and his sensitivity to the moral consequences of the triumph in 1948 quickly distinguished him from his generation's predilections for the realist style and its largely unquestioned commitment to the political discourse of the young Jewish state.[3] Unlike his contemporaries, who tended to concentrate on native-born, able-bodied, secular figures of the "new Jew" and to describe the conflict over Palestine as the just struggle to bring the land out of its premodern state (represented by the "native" Arab adversary), Yizhar's early post-1948 works focused on conflicted individuals—on soldiers who struggle to find a way to cope with some of the more questionable aspects of Israel's War of Independence.

Furthermore, Yizhar's work diverged from the uncontested conflation of death and the nation typical of Zionist culture during that era. The formative poem "Magash hakesef" (The silver salver), by Nathan Alterman (1910–70), published in December 1947, turns this ideal into its central metaphor: soldiers presenting the Jewish state to the people on the silver salver of their bodies. Through imagery such as this, Israel's cultural discourse played a significant role in turning the mourning of dead soldiers into a facet of a nationalist vocabulary that combined individual death with the birth of the Jewish nation.[4] Conversely, Yizhar's early postwar novellas—like his later magnum opus *Yemei Ziklag* (1958; The days of Ziklag)—depicted the horrors of the war with all their brutal implications for individuals, as well as for the Jewish and Palestinian collectives.

It is precisely the question of the war's effects, specifically the pain of expulsion and its implications for the moral identity of the young Jewish state, that drives the more unsettling of the two novellas, *The Story of Khirbet Khizeh*.[5] From the very first lines, Yizhar's emplotment highlights the injustice of driving Palestinians from their villages. When we first encounter the group of Israeli soldiers at the center of the work, they are leaving camp and are reported to be "showered, well fed, and smartly turned out." As the narrative progresses, we learn that these men are not ordered to fight an equal enemy that threatens them but rather to "burn-blow-up-imprison-load-convey"—to deport the Palestinians of Khirbet Khizeh and eradicate the village from the face of the earth.[6] The ill-fated villagers are described by Moishe, the commander, as a "band of ruffians" (10–11). However, when the soldiers look at the scattered houses in front of them, they recognize no visible "problem" (11). Against this background, it is with piercing irony that Yizhar's narrative asks what following such an order might mean for "the Jewish soul, the great Jewish soul" (9), thus giving the first indication of the tension between the drives of the emerging modern Jewish state and the notions of justice as proclaimed by the Jewish prophets.

The Idealist Motivation

From the outset the novella's realistic portrayal of events is inflected by distinctive figurative choices: first, the ironic abbreviation of the order's actual language ("burn-blow-up-imprison-load-convey"); second, the narrator's indication of the discrepancy between what the commander says and what the soldiers actually see; and third, the sarcasm-tinged reference to the high standards of Jewish ethics. Yizhar's narrator, in fact, early on halts the flow of the plot to deconstruct each and every phrase in the "operational order" (8). By quoting pieces of army jargon and then ironically commenting on them (e.g., "in a wonderful turn of phrase"; 8), Yizhar's narrator criticizes the very language that is partially responsible for the events about to unfold. The narrative use of these poetic devices questions the logic behind the new order, as well as the new order's ignorance of its human "objects." It is through the employment of such poetic effects that the novella allows its reader to consider the unsaid in both senses noted earlier. In other words, the novella raises questions about how the recently established state of Israel can negotiate between its loyalties to the ethos of universal values—partly rooted in the Jewish tradition itself, to which Yizhar ironically appeals ("the great Jewish soul")—and the actions that many believe are called for by national aspirations (9).

In his reflection on the potential of fictional narratives to represent complex ethical or political realities, the Israeli critic Menachem Brinker discusses *The Story of Khirbet Khizeh* and, specifically, what he calls its "idealist motivation."[7] Brinker fittingly reads Yizhar's reduction of the order to "burn-blow-up-imprison-load-convey" as modeling a historical reality and historical characters yet also as a way to "force the reader consciously and specifically to relate to his or her views and beliefs, as well as to those of the writer, regarding the [relevant] reality."[8]

I would add another facet to Brinker's convincing argument, namely, the gradual way in which the novella's "idealist motivation" is introduced in a manner that enhances its critical import. The plot first takes its reader through the attack on the village, followed by the summoning of its inhabitants for an as-yet-unclear purpose. In this way, it is only gradually that we are made aware of the emerging conflict between the soldiers: "What . . . what have we done today and what have the others done today?" asks Gaby, one of the members of the army unit (81). Moishe, the commander, responds with a laconic "That's it" (82). Referring to what seems now likely (the expulsion of the villagers), the narrator then challenges Moishe: "Do we really have to expel them? What more can these people do? Who can they hurt? . . . What's the point?" Moishe's answer is striking: "That's what it says in the operational orders." The narrator counters, "But it's not right. . . . It really isn't right," only to hear, "So what do you want?" (83). When he answers: "I just don't know anymore," another soldier, Yehuda, snaps, "If you don't know—then shut up" (84).

The realist mode of the narrative then shifts to a symbolic register in which historical fact, allusion, metaphor, and allegory quickly follow one another. Here, the conflicted narrator recounts the moment in which he suddenly became fully aware of what he and his friends were actually doing as they were carrying out their orders. He says to Moishe, "this is a filthy war" (107). His angry comrade responds by rearticulating the Zionist vision of creating a refuge for Jews persecuted in Europe, a colonial endeavor to beautify the land: "Immigrants of ours will come to this Khirbet what's-its-name . . . and they'll take this land and work it and it'll be beautiful here!" (107).

Note that Yizhar's Moishe is not talking about the events in the Palestinian village as a "necessary evil," as a result of the need to fight for a shelter for the Holocaust survivors. Rather, his words allude to the fantasy of re-creating, beautifying the land. The novella as a whole acknowledges, however, the more complex historical realities of the 1948 war—specifically, the need to ensure at least some relief to the survivors of the Holocaust in Israel/Palestine. To this end, the new state placed Jewish refugees in homes that were occupied only recently by Palestinians.[9] The narrator's ironic tone in his reply to Moishe's vision underlines the injustice of the expulsion: "Of course. Absolutely. Why hadn't I realized it from the outset? Our very own Khirbet Khizeh. . . . We'd open a cooperative store, establish a school, maybe even a synagogue. . . . They would plow fields, and sow, and reap. . . . Long live Hebrew Khizeh!" (108).

Yizhar's narrative thus redescribes as thievery the actions that Moishe regards as a natural process, where some are made to leave their homes and others come to inhabit the land. The narrative suggests, moreover, that the crimes committed against Jews hardly justify offending the rights of Palestinians:

> My guts cried out. Colonizers, they shouted. Lies, my guts shouted. Khirbet Khizeh is not ours. The Spandau gun never gave us any rights. . . . What hadn't they told us about [Jewish] refugees? Everything, everything was for the refugees, their welfare, their rescue. . . . Our refugees, naturally. Those we were driving out—that was a totally different matter. Wait: two thousand years of exile. The whole story. Jews being killed. Europe. We were the masters now.
>
> The people who would live in this village—wouldn't the walls cry out in their ears? Those sights, screams that were screamed and that were not screamed, the confused innocence of dazed sheep, the submissiveness of the weak, and their heroism, that unique heroism of the weak who didn't know what to do? (109, translation modified)

The reference to the German Spandau gun (the MG 42), the metonymic invocation of "Europe," the sarcastic quotation of slogans such as "everything for the refugees," and the cynicism of "our refugees, naturally," bring into controversial proximity the expulsion of Palestinians and the deportation of Jews during the Holocaust. The metaphor "dazed sheep" (*tson hamum*) is particularly striking in this regard, because the idiom "like lambs to slaughter" (*katson latevach*) (the Hebrew word *tson* [sheep, cattle] being used in both cases) had by then become a prevalent image for the helplessness of Jews.[10]

Yet Yizhar's allusions do not equate the soldiers' actions with atrocities committed against Jews during the Holocaust. Rather, the narrative raises the question of whether what had been done to Jews in Europe, especially the Holocaust, has driven the national collective to which the victims belong to acts they themselves cannot justify. It asks whether what the Jews had experienced in Europe did not actually command a different moral standard than the one employed in cases such as that of (the fictional) Khirbet Khizeh. Whatever the answers to these questions may be, Yizhar's novella brought the frequently silenced events of 1948 to the fore and presented them as a fateful moral crossroads in the history of the young state and of the Zionist movement. Moreover, as David N. Myers notes, *The Story of Khirbet Khizeh* helped expand the pool of images used by Israelis to describe what had occurred during the War of Independence.[11] It questioned the stylized icon of the Sabra, the Israeli as the morally upright warrior, and cast a previously inconceivable doubt on the prevalent story line that Palestinians simply fled their homes out of fear or because they were called to do so by the leaders of the Arab nations that invaded Palestine in 1948.

The Trucks of Exile

Yizhar's literary work soon after the 1948 war comes directly out of what the writer himself witnessed during the war. When debate erupted in 1978 over the airing of a television production based on *The Story of Khirbet Khizeh*, Yizhar emphasized that he wrote the story as someone who had been hurt by events to which he was completely unable to reconcile himself: "Inside me was nothing but a sense of outrage. . . . The act of expelling the residents and blowing up the houses of the village shook me to the very core. There was something here that went against my whole outlook on life." He went on to describe his protagonist's psyche in the novella as the site of a conflict between "his conception of Zionism—that always said the Arabs would not be evicted, that the goal was to live together with them in peace"—and the realities that Yizhar's novella depicts.[12]

Yizhar's novella confronts the topic of Jewish antiquity in Palestine, a constitutive element in the Zionist metanarrative. Yizhar makes use of biblical allusions—the rhetorical linking of Zionist aspirations with ancient Jewish sovereignty over the land—to emphasize that the renaissance of Jewish life in the Promised Land also meant the end of a significant portion of Palestinian existence.[13] The novella's implicit questioning of the Zionist metanarrative, which spoke only of the Jews' return to their ancestral homeland (without considering the land's non-Jewish population), is most evident when the narrator compares the Palestinians waiting for their imminent expulsion to those biblical Jews on the verge of their Babylonian exile. The Palestinian villagers are portrayed as wondering whether some fiery Jeremiah may not be sitting among their tired, hungry, and frightened number; if this Jeremiah might be silently calling on a God who watches from "atop the trucks of exile" (*kronot hagolah*) (105). This allusion casts a Palestinian in the role of a modern Jeremiah and the young protagonist and his comrades in that of Nebuchadnezzar's soldiers.

This inversion of historical roles is further intensified as the narrator's thoughts gradually turn to anger and moral outrage: "What in God's name are we doing in this place!" and then "we expelled and took possession" (*gerashnu vegam yarashnu*) (108). The latter declaration, an allusion to the prophet Elijah's bitter condemnation of Ahab, king of Israel (1 Kings 21:19),[14] portrays the actions in the Palestinian village as a grave betrayal of the ideal of justice and, moreover, as a reincarnation of another biblical drama, with the part of Ahab played by the Zionist soldiers and that of Naboth by the Palestinians.

The allusion to biblical narrative eventually becomes a vehicle for future-oriented reflection on the course of the Jewish national endeavor and the politics of the young state. The ear-piercing "desolate abandoned silence" (26) of a village that has now fallen into ruin becomes an ominous sign of what is to come:

> Everything was suddenly so open. So big, so very big. And we had all become so small and insignificant. . . . All around silence was falling, and very soon it would close upon the last circle. And when silence had closed in on everything and no man disturbed the stillness, which yearned noiselessly for what was beyond silence—then God would come forth and descend to roam

the valley, and see whether all was according to the cry [*haket-saakata*] that had reached him. (113)

While the narrative does not disclose what happens next in Khirbet Khizeh, the grammatical figure of *haketsaakata* (whether all was according to the cry) ends the novella on a futural and interrogative note. The trope is taken from Genesis (18:20–21), where God addresses Abraham, telling him that the outrage of Sodom and Gomorrah is reputedly so grave that he will come down and see whether the Sodomites have indeed acted as unlawfully as the outcry from the city suggests (Hebrew's compactness enables the complex act of ascertaining "whether all was according to the cry" to be expressed by the single word *haketsaakata*). Ending the novella on this pregnant note suggests several readings. It may inspire the notion that God—as a cipher for moral authority, for the idea of justice—will harshly judge those who carried out the expulsion and leveled the village. Yet the question of whether the acts are as horrific as the cry indicates may also be understood as asking for the reader's own judgment. Finally, *haketsaakata* raises the possibility that the soldiers and the Jewish state might have acted in ways that would lead to an apocalyptic end similar to what took place in Sodom.[15]

The dramatic, futural conclusion of *The Story of Khirbet Khizeh* avoids the traps of moralistic tragedies. While agonizing over the act of expulsion itself and its moral consequences, Yizhar keeps open the answer to the question that he raises. His poetic choices, irony and allusion, aim to produce debate over the acts carried out in the name of Zionism. In this way, the novella becomes a textual space in which readers can weigh Zionism as a national endeavor versus the demands of the humanist ethos.

A Recurrent Light of Terror on the Bare Facts of Our Existence

In July 1949, before the publication of his work, Yizhar wrote a letter to his editor asking him to consider adding an introduction he had drafted to the novella.[16] In the introduction, which for unknown reasons remained unpublished, Yizhar ponders the future that his story leaves open. He first notes that he wrote *The Story of Khirbet Khizeh* to testify truthfully to what he had seen and to "not remain silent" (*lo lehacharish*). However, he adds that another reason for writing was that, "as it seems today," "we [i.e., Israeli Jews] will return to the same issues"—to the dark aspects of the 1948 war. This past, Yizhar warns, will continue to haunt the present and the future.

Yizhar's refusal to stay silent led both to the creation of a work of art and to a series of robust and fruitful public debates in Israel. The novella's question, "*haketsaakata*," continued to occupy Israeli public discourse for decades. The work has been included in the Ministry of Education's official literary syllabus since 1964, and in the late 1970s, a dispute over a TV film adaptation raged in all the major daily newspapers, involving many leading politicians and intellectuals and persisting for more than a year.[17] The ethical and political questions raised by the novella in 1949 became a prism through which Israelis could consider their past and present—specifically, the ongoing occupation of the territories Israel conquered in 1967 and the meaning of successive governments' (more or less direct) support of the emergent settler movement.[18]

To be sure, the inclusion of Yizhar's work in official reading lists and its adaptation for television may indicate that Yizhar's novella was subsumed by the cultural discourse it originally scandalized. Moreover, Yizhar's novella may reflect the dubious tendency that journalist Nahum Barnea and others have called the *yorim huvochim* syndrome (they shoot and they cry): the pattern of first committing questionable acts (usually in a military context) and then seeking repentance by engaging in public, overtly emotional, and ultimately self-affirming bouts of self-recrimination.[19] Critic Hannan Hever has suggested that Yizhar's novella should be seen as an example of an "allegorical technique" typical of Hebrew literature in the first decades after 1948, a procedure that Hever regards as ultimately serving the needs of the national narrative. By equating the personal with the collective and recasting the political violence of the expulsion as an abstract allegory about the universal human condition of war, works such as *The Story of Khirbet Khizeh* fail to address the full brutality and moral significance of the violence inflicted on Palestinians.[20] Yet Yizhar's novella did help to change Israeli public discourse from 1949 onward, and the impact of Yizhar's work did not diminish over the years, as the public debate around the TV production revealed. Yizhar's work propelled an ongoing, evolving process of public deliberation on al-Nakba and its implications, even if, as Anita Shapira notes, this civic discussion often lacked the necessary focus and political edge.[21]

Regardless of the merit of these points of view, what unites them is their approach to their artistic object as a cultural symptom rather than as an imaginative engagement of the past in its practical dimensions. More specifically, criticism in this vein ignores the novella's seminal redescription of the Palestinian exile as the forceful expulsion that, in large measure, it was. "As a writer," notes Raja Shehadeh, the Palestinian lawyer and intellectual, "Yizhar presented the situation as it happened: armed soldiers moving against an unarmed village . . . went ahead with their orders to force the villagers out, bomb their homes, and eradicate the village. He thus revealed what the state was trying to conceal."[22] Furthermore, culturally symptomatic readings disregard the work's ability to generate the reflection and debate on political and ethical issues crucial to the conflict over the land, which, as we have just seen, it quite forcefully did. Finally, the symptomatic reading fails to recognize the way Yizhar's novella represents the Palestinians as human beings with human faces, thus enabling readers to identify with the perspective of the other in the Israeli-Palestinian conflict. This accomplishment is especially evident in one of the work's concluding and most telling scenes. As the soldiers view the destruction of the village, they notice a woman with a young child. The woman is described as "stern, self-controlled, austere in her sorrow. Tears, which hardly seemed to be her own, rolled down her cheeks. And the child too was sobbing a kind of stiff-lipped 'what have you done to us?'" (103, translation modified). The image enacts a shift of perspective from the soldier-narrator's own interiority to his attempt to address the experience of the other. Likewise, the focus on the woman enables another reversal as the virtues of proud resilience and dignity are transferred from their conventional bearer, the young Jewish soldier, to the Palestinian woman, his victim. Indeed, the narrator exalts the woman's bearing in the midst of her tragedy: "We understood that she was a lioness, and we saw that the lines of her face had hardened with furrows of self-restraint and a determination to endure her suffering with courage" (104). Moreover, the future implications of what the woman and child are made to endure are not lost on Yizhar's narrator, who prophetically notes: "Exalted in their pain and sorrow about our wicked existence they went on their way and we could also see how something was happening in the heart of the boy, something that, when he grew up, could only become a viper inside him, that same thing that was now the weeping of a helpless child" (104, translation modified).

Falcons over New Villages: S. Yizhar, "A Story That Did Not Yet Begin"

In the decades following the publication of *The Story of Khirbet Khizeh*, S. Yizhar continued linking contemporary issues of the Israeli-Palestinian conflict back to the defining moments of 1948.[23] His 1963 prose piece

"Sipur shelo hitchil" (A story that did not yet begin) includes a section titled "Shtikat hakfarim" (The silence of the villages), thus merging a deep personal loss with the pain inflicted on Palestinians. "A Story That Did Not Yet Begin" mourns Yizhar's brother, Yisrael, who died with a Palestinian friend in a motorcycle accident at a train crossing, and the loss of the beloved, prestate Palestine, a land in which Jews and Arabs lived side by side.[24]

Initially covered only by dust, the deserted Palestinian villages started vanishing completely from sight during the 1950s as pine forests were planted across the country. The narrator's gaze excavates a seemingly insignificant hill to discover there Israel's *Zeitschichten*, ranging from antiquity and "the age of the fathers" to the recent past: "less than twelve years ago a lively village was here, a bustling human place of dwelling. This might appear now an incredible fairytale."[25]

The ensuing pages invoke the memory of this lost village while resurrecting the political discourse that had contributed to its disappearance in the first place. It quotes the references made to destroyed Palestinian villages as "the murderers' village" and a "wasps'," "ravens'," and "eagles' nest" (147), thus invoking the question of whether one can view the expulsion of Palestinians and the prevention of their return as a justifiable act of war. Organized as a set of polyphonic statements, the work voices a thread within Israeli discourse of the 1950s and early 1960s that refused to acknowledge the pain of Palestinian refugees and employed dismissive language, such as "Deserted villages? Where don't you find such?" (147).

To its implicit criticism of pre-1948 and post-1948 political discourse, "The Silence of the Villages" adds the suggestion that the motivating force behind the expulsion of Palestinian villages was the desire for purity. The process of taking over the lands of villages, driving out their inhabitants, and settling Jewish refugees in their stead is depicted as an expression of the wish to create an utterly new and sanitized space and social order: now that the villages are gone, the narrator ironically states, "order is in place" (*yesh seder*) (148). Likewise, the Jewish villages that replace the Palestinian ones boast "more scientifically processed . . . better planned" agricultural fields (157). In the new world being created over the ruins of the old, even the names of these villages are changed to "more cultivated" (*tarbutiyim yoter*) Hebrew ones.

At the same time, however, falcons hover over these well-organized new villages (157), signaling the looming presence of the recent past, of death. In the engineered world of post-1948 Israel, rodents and pests are subjected to a "deadly extermination storm," and while this fate is

"well-deserved," the birds that feed on them die, as do the larger preda-
tors that feed on them in their turn (159). What remains in this purified
world, in which the chain of life leads to death, is the untainted white
cotton grown "for export" (159). What appeared at first as a manifestation of progress is revealed as the product of lethal rationalism, coupled with a nationalistic mythology. Additionally, Yizhar plays with the
sounds of the new names and their meanings to suggest that the attempt
to reinscribe space with a new, purified purpose does not fully succeed in
obliterating the past. The new name given to the Palestinian settlement
Kastina, for instance, is the Hebrew Keshet Teenah (Fig's Arc), which
also brings to mind *"kaas vetina"* (anger and hatred) (157). Likewise,
the biblical allusion implied by the fig, whose leaves Adam and Eve had
used to cover up their nakedness after committing the original sin, ties
the notion of shame to the act of concealment.

"The Silence of the Villages" thus points to what was not yet evident
in *The Story of Khirbet Khizeh*, namely, that the eradicated Palestinian
village—"its death is also its totality, its wholeness [*moto shlemuto*]"
(148)—persists in a kind of terrifying afterlife that haunts its destroyers
like "a wailing voice [that] surrounds [them]" (148). Against the drive
to forget and suppress the unsaid—"let's go, you lot, let's forget this
place. . . . Why should we carry this hump on our back?" (155)—other
voices continue to speak through the medium of the narrator:

> There were houses there and alleys and men and women and
> children who didn't know. And animals were there. . . . Right
> here used to stand the olive press, heavy on its pillars and
> studs . . . all erased and obliterated [*nitmachek venimchak*]. And
> the shop with its heavy candy jars full of colorful, dusty sweets,
> and the sleepy shopkeeper . . . all became dust . . . the oven out-
> side . . . the fields . . . the olives and the summer . . . and the sing-
> ing while grinding the wheat, and the new oil engine and the
> hose that someone planned on and saved for and finally bought
> (or borrowed from another farm) . . . and the tricks to get better
> yields and the conversations and the fables . . . and the smell of
> golden straw, its powder blowing during sunset. (155–56)

Yizhar's prose testifies to the former existence of the village and, as Yochai Oppenheimer maintains, to the erasure of that life by dust and pine
forests.[26] Yet it also parodies Zionism's orientalist discourse and thus
creates a distanced perspective on its claims regarding the "backward-
ness" of the culture of the Palestinian "natives." The tone of "The Silence

of the Villages" is elegiac: the narrative bemoans and makes visible what is physically gone, using a highly disquieting idiom to describe what happened during the war as continuing to haunt the Jewish state and thus demanding ethical responsibility and political solution. Moreover, as we will see in the following chapters, the trope of dust-covered ruins will resurface in the Hebrew literature of the following decades. Yizhar himself never stopped emphasizing the lingering presence of 1948. As Hannan Hever reminds us, as late as 1992, Yizhar described the prestate life of Palestinians in the disputed land as a reality that never fades. From the perspective of the intifada (an event to which we will later turn), Yizhar engaged the questions that Israelis never quite dared to ask: "What do you do with these people? They did not vanish into thin air. They did not simply disappear at the end of the path leading to the fields. The expulsion did not solve anything. No expulsion solves a thing. Here they are and so are we, the expelled and the expellers."[27]

8   "Then, Suddenly—Fire": A. B. Yehoshua's *Facing the Forests*

Exploring the Dark Matter

S. Yizhar's "The Silence of the Villages" first appeared in the 1963 summer issue of the literary journal *Keshet*. In the same volume, A. B. Yehoshua (b. 1936) published his novella *Facing the Forests*, a work likewise centered on the trope of the destroyed Palestinian village.[1] However, whereas "The Silence of the Villages" evokes the life of a Palestinian village that is now haunted, dust-covered remains, Yehoshua's work focuses on characters, Israeli and Palestinian, touched by the war. It answers the question that ends *The Story of Khirbet Khizeh*, "whether all was according to the cry" (*haketsaakata*), by spelling out some of the traumatic human consequences of 1948. Yet Yehoshua's novella also provides its readers with a powerful allegorical depiction of the devastation that the conflict over the land will bring about if ignored. The novella reveals, in fact, how the wrongs committed by Israel's founding generation against the Palestinian population in 1948 became, fifteen years after the fact, the liability of their descendants—a responsibility they need to tackle head-on or face dire consequences.

Yehoshua's choice to render the conflict through an allegorical structure reflects his aesthetics, especially his attraction at the time to modernist symbolism. Yehoshua's poetics would undergo changes in the course of his long career, yet the emphasis placed in the novella on the depiction of psychological processes has remained a constant. This focus on the individual psyche, moreover, marks the young Yehoshua as a member of the generation of writers, Dor Hamedinah (the Statehood Generation), who were coming into their own during the early 1960s and included figures such as Amos Oz (b. 1939), Amalia Kahana-Carmon (b. 1926), Aharon Appelfeld (b. 1932), and Yehoshua Kenaz (b. 1937). For these writers, in contrast with their literary forerunners, the existence of the Jewish state was an established fact and a self-evident reality rather than a hoped-for and fought-for prospect. This difference provides as good an explanation as any for the common thematic threads running through the works of these writers.[2]

Yehoshua's protagonist in *Facing the Forests* is a young, disoriented student of history who is both a peculiar outsider and, as Hannan Hever observes, an emblematic figure of Dor Hamedinah.[3] In lieu of roaming the streets of Jerusalem, the young student decides to follow the advice of his friends and accept a position as a forest ranger, a fire warden in one of the newly planted pine forests south of Jerusalem. In the 1950s, many such groves were planted to provide work for the country's unemployed. Seen from the perspective of its symbolic function, however, the forest is emblematic of the projection of European aesthetics onto Palestine's landscape or, worse, an attempt to conceal the flight and expulsion of Palestinians in the course of 1948.[4] Like the trees of S. Yizhar's "The Silence of the Villages," Yehoshua's forest is thus a metaphor for Israel's conflicted *Zeitschichten*.

Taking the job of watching over the forest, the young historian hopes to use the peaceful setting to concentrate on his study of the Crusades. This topic is, of course, symbolically charged and highly polemical: since the late nineteenth century, the Zionists were often regarded by their adversaries as a modern reincarnation of the Christian crusaders.[5] Correlatively, sensing the precariousness of their national situation, many early Israelis worried that their presence in the land would turn out to be as transient as that of the medieval Christians.[6] Thus, this single detail conveys Yehoshua's *engagée* stance and the work's role in warning "the house of Israel." This is evident in the symbolic features of its protagonist. Charged with guarding the budding forest—and, by extension, the young Zionist project—the young man is himself a "sentinel for the house of Israel." Moreover, he watches not only over a spatial landscape but also over its unseen historical dimensions, via his academic pursuits.

Ultimately, Yehoshua's protagonist prompts readers to consider whether they are a modern reincarnation of the crusaders and, if so, what implications this may have for their future in the land.[7]

These political and historical dimensions of *Facing the Forests* are evident in the way it depicts the generational breach—through the protagonist's break with his father—that emerged soon after the establishment of the Jewish state. For the father, the Crusades are a fascinating topic of study because of the massive loss of Jewish life during that era. Indeed, this catastrophe is "a wonderful and terrible thing [*davar nifla venora*]" (213). The father's words thus echo the political language of the time. His pairing of *nifla venora* (wonderful and terrible/awful) clearly invokes the stock phrases of contemporary Zionist rhetoric—for example, *Shoah vegvurah* (Holocaust and heroism) and *Shoah utkuma* (Holocaust and resurgence).[8] The political function of this rhetoric was to redescribe the catastrophe of the Holocaust as a chapter in a metahistorical trajectory of disaster and resurrection that finally leads to the establishment of Israel. By parroting this rhetoric, Yehoshua's narrative strikes an ironic chord, bringing to the reader's attention that rhetoric's mechanical and bombastic aspects. Moreover, the father's words also refer to the historical moment in which Yehoshua was writing *Facing the Forests*, the period preceding and immediately following the Eichmann trial in Jerusalem (1961). As Idith Zertal and others have shown, during and after the Eichmann trial, the Holocaust became a crucial point of reference in attempts to redescribe Jewish history teleologically, that is, as the necessary progression of the nation from exile and persecution (culminating in the catastrophe of the Shoah) to national renewal and resurrection in an independent Jewish state.[9]

The son's academic interests, however, reveal a different orientation toward history from the father's. The young scholar is interested in the "dark matter" (*inyan afel*) (211, translation modified) at the core of the Christian Crusades, which he would like to examine "from a universal, that is to say ecclesiastical aspect" (*beaspect klal enoshi, klomar knesiyati*) (211). This important difference in interpretive stances toward historical "darkness" touches directly on one of the key tensions underlying the fledgling Zionist project and also informs the emerging generational rift between the father and his son. The protagonist's desire to examine history from an "ecclesiastical aspect" betrays the clash (seen in Yizhar's work) between the particularistic aspects of Zionism (and the historical narrative that would justify them) and the universal humanist ethos. For the father and his generation, renewed Jewish sovereignty over the land is the logical outcome of a historical trajectory and therefore justified a priori. The son, however, is unconvinced by this logic. A "dark matter" that does not let him rest subconsciously drives his discontent.

Unlike Yizhar's protagonist, who is vocal about his views but remains passive, Yehoshua's historian will eventually turn from static observation to action. After arriving at his new post, he becomes increasingly obsessed with the recent, rather than the medieval, past. Sensing that the stillness of the trees conceals an ominous secret, he begins to take an interest in his assistant, an old Palestinian man whose tongue had been cut out in the course of the 1948 war—"by one of them or one of us? Does it matter?" (210). Through his troubled interaction with this figure, as well as his daughter, the disoriented young Israeli both discovers the truth about the forest (namely, that it is planted over a demolished Palestinian village) and evolves as a character by wrestling with leaden passivity. At the end of the novella, we see him helping the Palestinian literally to unearth the past, thus allowing the mute man to express what his mutilation had up until then prevented him from voicing.

The powerful metaphor of the voiceless Palestinian highlights the extent to which *Facing the Forests* further expands the vocabulary of Yizhar's *The Story of Khirbet Khizeh* and "The Silence of the Villages" to include what is indeed a symbolic, but poignantly evocative, expression of Palestinian pain. Whereas Yizhar's work had focused (daringly for its time) on 1948 as a war that had brought about national sovereignty at the steep moral price of expulsions, and while it had questioned the moral justification of the means used to this end, it did not depict any fleshed-out Palestinian character who might try to reclaim his or her rights by words or actions. In *Facing the Forests*, however, we encounter precisely such a character. Moreover, what the figure of the old Palestinian's daughter suggests is that the terrible reckoning initiated by the father will persist for generations. The Palestinian characters in *Facing the Forests* are hardly silenced; on the contrary, by their very depiction as isolated and uprooted in the selfsame space that used to be their and their community's home, they clearly evoke the catastrophic implications of 1948, as well as challenge them.

To Remember One's Own Name

Another facet of Yehoshua's poetic polemic against the rhetoric of Israel's founding generation is seen in his protagonist's arc of development. Through his disillusionment with the ideological principles of his father and his conflicted empathy for the plight of the Palestinian, the fire warden finally manages partially to overcome his chronic passivity. As he gradually penetrates "the dark empire" of the forest, this "cemetery" (211, 214), he slowly comes to regard it as a political reality rather than a neutral, tranquil setting for his studies; he recognizes it as a reinscription of space in the service of a definite political agenda. The plaques placed there to honor foreign donors—one "Louis Schwartz from Chicago," as well as "the King of Burundi and his people" (215)—leave a "vacuous smile" on the fire warden's face. Upon an encounter with a group of enthusiastic hikers, he describes the young forest as simulated nature: "everything is still artificial here. There is nothing here, not even some archeology for amateurs" (217). From his increasingly distant political perspective, the hikers, whose oblivious cheeriness he wants to deflate, come to appear as another aspect of the strategy of repression and silencing; he regards them as "still dwelling in a world that lives between sleep and sleep [*olam shechai bein tardema letardema*]."[10]

Facing the Forests reaches a crucial junction in its quest for the past when the visitors inquire about the village covered by the forest. The protagonist's preliminary answer, "there is no village here," is definitively contradicted by his Palestinian assistant's revelation of the area's past. Shortly afterward, a ministry official responsible for the forest arrives, and the student begins asking questions and wondering about what he is told. At his suggestion that the Palestinian is "a local" (222), from the "small village . . . our forest is growing over" (222), the ministry official admits that "there used to be some sort of a farmstead here. But that is a thing of the past" (222).

The narrator's sarcastic retort—"Of the past, yes, certainly. What else . . . ?" (222)—represents a direct challenge to the Zionist rhetoric of the 1950s. Moreover, the exchange causes the young Israeli to reconfigure his perspective of this space. He begins to draw his own map of the area, thus resignifying the forest (and, symbolically, Israel's map) by reinserting what had been eradicated: "What interests him in particular is the village buried beneath the trees" (222).[11] Indeed, the young historian's act points toward the future. He signs his name on the map, not only so that those who follow him will remember, but also so that he himself will not "forget his own name" (*kedei shelo yishkach et shmo*) (223, translation modified). This odd detail in the narrative—that of a signature not solely marking the origin of the work *for others* but also so one does not forget one's own name—is key. It implies that by failing to recognize, or, indeed, by actively forgetting the past, one is in danger of losing both personal integrity and moral grounding, as these are in-scribed in one's "name."[12]

The young historian's process of coming to terms with the history and pain of his Palestinian assistant represents, to a large extent, the course of his own maturation, which had hitherto been obviously stunted. In the symbolic universe of Yehoshua's novella, individual maturation en-tails responding to the ethical and political dimensions of 1948 and ad-dressing them in a manner diametrically opposed to the strategies of con-cealment and silencing typical of Israeli discourse in the 1950s. In fact, the centrality accorded by the novella to what is covered over and obfus-cated corresponds to what Hannah Arendt called "the kernel" in her dis-cussion of the unsaid. Indeed, everything in *Facing the Forests*—the plot, the characters, the symbols, and so on—points precisely to the need to *voice* what has been silenced. The novella urges its readers to acknowl-edge that actions taken in 1948, as well as their long-term consequences, have been passed over in silence and are now the realities of the descen-dants of Palestinians and Israelis who fought during that war. Arendt's concept of the unsaid, the vacant hub around which what is written and said revolves, is therefore very useful in this context. Indeed, what the Palestinian cannot utter—what happened to him (and, by extension, to his people)—becomes the center of the young historian's quest and of the novella as a whole. As its readers, we participate alongside the protago-nist in the excavation of the recent past and engage in the moral delibera-tion that accompanies it. We are given the opportunity to grasp 1948 as an ongoing moral and political challenge.

Following Arendt's notion of "the kernel," we can say that the no-vella implicitly raises a set of questions about actions taken in 1948 but leaves them open: What did, in fact, happen to the man, to his daughter, and to their community during the war? Who is responsible for his mu-tilation? Who is responsible for their fate? These historical questions, moreover, are accompanied by a set of moral challenges: How should the fire warden deal with the Palestinian's plan to uncover the forest's se-cret? What is the young Jewish Israeli's responsibility toward the Pales-tinian's daughter and, by extension, toward the descendants of the Pales-tinian refugees? What is the future of the forest as a space now shared by Jewish Israelis and those Palestinians who remained on their land after 1948? Many of these questions are reflected in the symbol of the map. Charting his map, signing his name so he would not forget it, the fire warden suggests that readers should consider what their map looks like, what they may need to do so they will not forget their names.

The Day of Judgment

The map, then, has several functions. Symbolically, it warns against the danger of Israel's losing its moral orientation. It also reveals Hebrew literature's increasing awareness, in the early 1960s, of the interdependency of addressing the fate of the Palestinians after 1948 and the moral identity of the Jewish state. Finally, the map plays a role in the story of the protagonist's growth. Indeed, after uncovering what the forest has hidden since 1948, the fire warden is finally able to discover the "chiseled stones . . . outlines of buildings, ruins and relics" of the destroyed village beneath (224).

The fire warden's evolution does not lead to a complete transformation, nor does he become a moral paragon. His inability, for instance, to recognize the cultural distinctiveness of the Palestinian persists, intimated through small details, as when he addresses the Arab with the Hebrew *shalom* (224). Nevertheless, the fire warden does undergo a noticeable change. When he finds cans of kerosene—"liquid treasure" (*ha-otzar hanozli*) (224, translation modified)—concealed by an old dress that used to belong to the Palestinian's daughter, he does not report his finding to the authorities, nor does he confront the old man. Here, not doing anything at all is a mode of action, a sign of his development from inert student of a distant past and a mere observer of recent history into a voluntary player in the eventual burning down of the forest.

Yehoshua's novella is not a story of redemption. The student's willingness to keep silent regarding his assistant's plan to ignite the forest is not offered as a symbolic act of reconciliation. At the end of the narrative, the Israeli and the Palestinian remain as distant as ever. When the protagonist tells the old Palestinian about the Jews who committed mass suicide during the Crusades, the man "listens with mounting tension and is filled with hate" (229). He counters with his own story of the recent Palestinian past, a history he can only hint at with "confused gestures, squirming his severed tongue" (229). Yet the fire warden believes the old man struggling to tell his story is performing an act of "pantomime" (229). Unable to understand what the Palestinian is trying to convey, he interprets him wrongly and "his heart fills with joy" (229) as he fails to grasp what stirs up the Arab. The only answer he comes up with is telling: "Apparently his [the Palestinian's] wives have been murdered here as well. A dark matter [*inyan afel*], no doubt" (229, translation modified).[13]

Indeed, these moments in which the Israeli and Palestinian narratives collide prevent *Facing the Forests* from becoming didactic or moralistic.

The novella is not *about* doing justice to Palestinians, nor does it deliver moral relief to the progressive Israeli reader or serve as a literary expression of Yehoshua's essayistic work and his oft-expressed plea for reconciliation between Israelis and Palestinians.[14] Rather, its strength lies in creating metaphors that undermine prevalent idioms of an Israeli political discourse in which "trees have taken the place of words, forests the place of books" (227). It uses the language of concealment to move beyond merely *facing* the forests.

As the plot reaches its zenith, the shift from compliant passivity to action leads to the actual destruction of the forest. At this point, *Facing the Forests* also unfolds a futural, warning scenario. Rather than attempting to call for help in putting out the fire, the protagonist is elated: "Then, suddenly—fire. . . . A long, graceful flame. One tree is burning, a tree wrapped [*mitatef*] in prayer. For a long moment one tree is going through its day of judgment [*yom hadin*] until it breathes its last breath (231, translation modified).

In this passage, the novella's symbolism draws on Jewish history, on the Jewish calendar, and on Jewish liturgy. The Hebrew verb used to describe the burning tree—*mitatef*—is the same verb used to refer to the Jew wearing the tallit, the Jewish prayer shawl. The day of the fire is, in fact, Yom Hadin and Yom Kippur—the Day of Judgment and Day of Atonement—the day in which Jews reflect on their transgressions of the recent past and ask for forgiveness.[15] Yom Kippur is traditionally seen as the day on which God decides who will live and who will die during the new Jewish year. For the young student grown hostile to the political rhetoric of the state, the Day of Judgment is associated with the physical elimination of the trees used to conceal the land's recent past, to veil the memory of al-Nakba. For him, the burning of the forest resembles divine rage, and the fire is the "most wonderful of moments [*beshaah niflaah zo*]" (231). However, it is not divine intervention but rather the actions of the Palestinian and the fire warden that put the decisive event into motion.

As Hannan Hever argues, the fire symbolizes the land rising up against those who would control it, an act of aggressive deterritorialization, a metaphoric contestation of the power and authority claimed by the majority culture when it planted the forests.[16] Yet the fire signifies more than the mere literary empowerment of victims and an embarrassment for the Jewish claim on the land.[17] The Jewish return to the Promised Land is recast as not only an act of creation and renewal but also a Palestinian "catastrophe" that may very well have dire consequences. By referring to the scene of the burning of the forest as Yom Hadin, the

Day of Judgment, *Facing the Forests* warns of similar and perhaps worse days to come. Thus, if Yizhar's *The Story of Khirbet Khizeh* ended by questioning whether 1948 was as horrific as "*haketsaakata*" suggests, the symbolic fire indicates that it was terrible indeed and that it may lead to even worse things in the future.

Although the protagonist's growth is limited, the development he does undergo demonstrates the *potential* for a different course of action, for the possibility of a different mode of coexistence.[18] Although during the investigation the fire warden does point out the old Palestinian as the likely culprit, he is also capable of "suddenly" walking over to the official, after the fire, to "demand a solution for the child" (235), the Palestinian's daughter. Yehoshua's protagonist remains, in other words, not fully evolved. He is conflicted and ambiguous about his agency and about what he should do, reflecting the problems facing Israeli cultural discourse of that time.

The novella offers Israeli readers a new outlook on their discursive sphere, on how they might perceive and discuss their contested homeland. The new map is, significantly, the only object that survives the fire. Through the smoke and haze of the fire's aftermath, the reader, like the protagonist, comes face-to-face with the small village, previously only imagined, as it is "born anew in its basic outlines as an abstract drawing, as all things past and buried" (233). While the novella does not end on a redemptive note, the protagonist's new vision includes the knowledge that the struggle over the meanings of the Israeli/Palestinian landscape is bound to continue. Hence, his homecoming lacks all elements of closure. Trying to sleep, "green forests will spring up before his troubled eyes" (236), just as the vanished village reemerged in the destruction of the fire. What remains is the significant potential of memory: although the student's notes have been burned, "if anyone thinks that he does not remember—he does" (236). The memory of the ruins in the forest, the memory of the burning trees, ensure that the past will resurface as long as Israelis attempt to conceal it and as long as they neglect to consider the descendants of the vanished village.[19]

The Afterlife of the Burnt Forest

Yehoshua's positions in public debates regarding the conflict between Israelis and Palestinians did not always reflect a sensitivity to the rights and sensibilities of Palestinians living within and outside Israel's borders. In a stormy 1985 debate with Anton Shammas—then one of the most prominent contemporary Palestinian writers living in Israel—Yehoshua went so far as to suggest to Shammas that he could find full expression of his Palestinian national identity only in a future Palestinian state, one that would be created one day *outside* Israel's borders.[20] In his acclaimed novel *Arabeskot* (1986; Arabesques) Shammas presents Yehoshua with a literary response to this absurd suggestion: in the satirical character of Yosh (Yehoshua) Bar On, Shammas brilliantly ridicules the inability of many liberal Israeli intellectuals such as A. B. Yehoshua himself to acknowledge the Palestinians living in their midst as capable of possessing a particular, Palestinian national identity within the Jewish nation-state.[21] However, in numerous essays, interviews, and newspaper articles, Yehoshua continued to expand upon his imaginative redescription of 1948 in *Facing the Forests*, demanding a peaceful resolution of the Israeli-Palestinian conflict by dividing the land among the people who claim it. In telling cases, his public statements as well as his literary works found their way into the writings of younger authors. Some of the key metaphors of *Facing the Forests* found echoes, for example, in Alon Hilu's 2008 *Achuzat Dajani* (*The House of Rajani*, a work discussed in chapter 10) and even more explicitly in Amir Gutfreund's 2002 novella *Yaaran* (The forester).[22] Gutfreund was born in the same year that Yehoshua's *Facing the Forests* was published, and his *Yaaran* also features a forester as protagonist. In an ironic reference to the early Yehoshua's penchant for symbolism, Gutfreund's forester sees nothing marvelous in the forest trees (143). Forestry itself is for him without any purpose at all (146). In a further ironic gesture toward Yehoshua's novella, his only goal, apparently, is to warn those who still wish to become foresters of the hidden pitfalls of the job—to put them on notice that they can no longer expect even to burn down the Keren Kayemeth LeYisrael (Jewish National Fund) groves of thin pine.

The forester himself is thus the ghost of Yehoshua's humanist: a contemporary, postmodern—indeed, postnational—Israeli who can speak a light, "happy" version of Arabic (148) and whose colleagues learn the art of forestry in Germany, in woods so thick that the sun never penetrates their inner darkness (144). Yet even for Gutfreund's forester, the forest retains some ominous mystery and contains "clearings that one cannot see, even caution would not help" (148). Even if the police today can forensically uncover an arsonist, the danger of a devastating fire—the gaping chasm of the Israeli-Palestinian conflict—persists. Written some five decades after 1948 and three decades after the 1967 war, Gutfreund's words indicate how the Hebrew literary imagination continues to trace the inability of large segments of Israel's political discourse to face up to what occurred where today grown trees stand. If we follow Gutfreund's metaphor of the forest's holes, we must note that just because one cannot see the chasms in the forest, this does not mean that one would not fall into them. Through figures such as the forester, and more directly in interviews, Gutfreund expresses anxiety regarding the prospects of the Jewish state should it continue to shun the consequences of the dark matter hidden in the metaphoric national forest and feign obliviousness to the lingering effects of the historical circumstance that Yehoshua's *Facing the Forests* so forcefully explores.[23]

9 "A Land That Devours Its Inhabitants. Its Lovers Devour Its Lovers"

A New Generation

During 1960–62, Israeli Jews experienced the immensely charged capture and subsequent trial of Adolph Eichmann. The stirring testimonies of Holocaust survivors and the extensive media coverage brought the repressed memory of the Holocaust into the center of Israeli consciousness.[1] Eichmann's prosecution also served to help justify Israel's self-appointed role as the protector of the Jewish people. However, by revisiting the trauma of the Holocaust, the trial also triggered existential fears of a similar future catastrophe. Five years later, these anxieties peaked during Tkufat Hahamtana, the "Waiting Period," immediately prior to the outbreak of the 1967 Six-Day War. Moreover, their resurgence seemed to unravel the prevailing confidence that the creation of an independent state would finally turn the Jewish diasporic experience of persecution and annihilation into a thing of the past.[2]

Following Israel's momentous victory in 1967, fears were swiftly replaced by a wave of national exuberance. The same military triumph, however, also made Israel ruler over territories that were home to hundreds of thousands of Palestinians, many of whom were refugees of the 1948 war. Yet instead of trying to resolve the conflict over the land by using the conquered territories as a bargaining chip, Israel preferred to hold on to what was now often described as "liberated land."

The 1969–70 War of Attrition and the 1973 Yom Kippur War hardly changed this approach. In fact, the shock many Israelis felt in the course of the fierce fighting of the Yom Kippur War was accompanied by the rise of the settler movement.[3] What had begun in 1968 as a small Jewish outpost on the outskirts of Hebron became, by 1974, a significant political movement, Gush Emunim (Bloc of the Faithful), whose outspoken aim was to maintain Israeli control over the West Bank and the Gaza Strip even at the cost of oppressively controlling their large Palestinian population.[4]

Looking back at the period stretching from the 1963 publication of S. Yizhar's "The Silence of the Villages" and A. B. Yehoshua's *Facing the Forests* to the 1982 Lebanon War, it is striking to see how little attention Hebrew literature paid to the Israeli-Palestinian conflict and to the occupation of the territories.[5] This, however, changed considerably after the Lebanon War, the results of which were devastating. While the Palestinian Liberation Organization (PLO) was forced out of Lebanon, Israel found itself implicated in the horrific massacres of Sabra and Shatila and engaged in a protracted occupation of southern Lebanon that did not ensure peaceful cohabitation in the region.

The decades from 1960 to 1982 were an era of missed opportunities. Instead of facing 1948 and the post-1967 occupation, Israeli politics and public discourse opted to indulge in the fantasy that the past might simply go away, as if by a wave of a magic wand. Written in the 1980s, all the works I discuss in this chapter—David Schütz's *Shoshan lavan, shoshan adom* (1988; White rose, red rose), Yehoshua Kenaz's *Hitganvut yehidim* (1986; *Infiltration*), and David Grossman's *Ayen erech ahava* (1986; *See Under: Love*)—make it clear, however, that the unsaid of 1948 had not disappeared. On the contrary, these works suggest in various ways how, if left unresolved, the problems stemming from the 1948 exodus of Palestinians and from the occupation of the West Bank and Gaza were bound to lead to ever more violent outbursts. Yet through their metaphors, allusions to different historical layers—1948, 1967, 1982—and well-crafted plots, the works also pushed readers to engage with the past practically, with its "use or meaning" for the ongoing Israeli-Palestinian conflict. While each work provides different answers to this question, they all suggest that keeping 1948 on the outskirts of public consciousness means surrendering ever more lives to the quicksand of the conflict. Ignoring the pain of the Palestinians, they furthermore imply, may also affect Israel's very chances of survival.

"Something Horrible Happened There": David Schütz, White Rose, Red Rose

Three acclaimed novels that appeared in the second half of the decade— David Schütz's *White Rose, Red Rose*, Yehoshua Kenaz's *Infiltration*, and David Grossman's opus *See Under: Love*—signal, in different ways, to what extent the 1982 Lebanon War had refocused the attention of Jewish Israeli writers on the Palestinian exile of 1948, on the plight of those living in the Occupied Territories, and, thus, on the core issues of the ongoing Israeli-Palestinian conflict. In *White Rose, Red Rose*, a lyrical-psychological novel, David Schütz (b. 1941) manages to weave together several key moments in Israel's history.[6] The story is narrated by the protagonist Judith Wind, who, with her husband, Simon, immigrates to Palestine in the late 1930s, where they live through the 1948 war. With the years in which Europe was "torn into pieces" on her mind (211), Judith Wind recounts how, soon after the 1948 war, on one of her husband's hikes with their adopted son, Felix, himself an orphaned Holocaust survivor, Simon Wind discovers that the neighboring Bedouin tribe, the Halibna, are gone, with only the tip of their small mosque left lying in the field "like a cut finger" (214). Schütz's metaphor of bodily mutilation, which stands for the brutal removal of Palestinians from the land, is reminiscent of the severed tongue in Yehoshua's *Facing the Forests*. As in Yehoshua's work, the defaced landscape reflects the brutalities of 1948 and the way the memory of that past persists as a painful presence. When Judith tries to claim that the Halibnas "fled because of the war" (215) and that they will "soon be back," he replies angrily, in a phrase reminiscent of Ychoshua's "dark matter" (*inyan afel*): "No, no . . . they will not return. . . . Judith, something horrible [*mashehu nora*] happened there and we, here, did not hear a thing" (215). Simon can hardly suppress the moral weight of the event and of his passivity. He now understands the conversations about the expulsion of the Halibnas he had overheard in the village's grocery—sounds he had avoided out of what he claimed then to be politeness (215)—and these torment him.

A bystander to the fate of the Halibnas, Simon becomes a figure of spectatorship. Simon sarcastically snaps at his wife, for example, for "talking about guilt. . . . I am not guilty and no one is guilty. Even the boys who set the explosives [that blew up the village] are not guilty, and not even those who gave them the command" (215). The narrative thus gestures toward the individual and collective avoidance of responsibility for the expulsion. In fact, Simon makes an explicit connection to what Jews experienced in Europe and the indifference of non-Jews to their condition: "the newspapers would remain silent while the radio would sound patriotic music" (215). The "good of the state," he tells Judith, is not a plausible excuse for what has been done: "the Halibnas are gone. Their homes ruined, their orchards deserted, here and there a dog or a donkey wanders over ruins" (215).

Simon Wind's claim that no statist interest can justify the uprooting of the Palestinians refers to 1948. However, his words also allude to the deepening of the conflict after 1967 as well as to the 1980s, when *White Rose, Red Rose* was written. The reference to newspapers that remain silent when injustice is done, to the radio that sounds "patriotic music," and to a national discourse that glorifies the "good of the state" hints at the first weeks of the 1982 Lebanon War, when most of the Israeli media supported the invasion of Lebanon. Schütz's novel reiterates Yehoshua's insight that without dealing with the "horrible matter" (*mashehu nora*), with 1948 and its consequences, Israelis will find themselves repeating the questionable actions of their predecessors.

On Being Awfully Strong: Yehoshua Kenaz, Infiltration

The question of how 1948 affects the present (the 1980s) and may determine the future similarly haunts Yehoshua Kenaz's much broader social-historical opus *Infiltration*.[7] Kenaz (b. 1937) focuses on a group of young Israeli conscripts in the early 1950s who, due to various medical impairments, are drafted into a less strenuous course of basic training. In the novel, Israel's formative years (the 1950s) are depicted through the country's weak and unfit.[8] These "invalids" represent a microcosm of the Israeli society of that era: immigrants, Sabras (Israelis born in the country), young men from Sephardic (Middle Eastern and North African) families, and those of Ashkenazi (European) backgrounds (28–29).[9]

As Michael Gluzman notes, the novel depicts the army camp as a "penal colony."[10] Moreover, via the perspective of the narrator, the young recruit Melabes, the training camp emerges as a metonym for a national culture characterized by a siege mentality and an unrelenting sense of threat. Yet Kenaz's complex work hardly presents Israel as a one-dimensional, beleaguered ogre. Rather, through the use of polyphony, the novel gives voice to a variety of (uniformly male) figures, each with his own sensibilities, views, and positions. It thus presents a spectrum of views regarding Israel's recent past (i.e., 1948) and what such views imply for the future.

Infiltration's polyphonic structure comes into play in handling the exile of Palestinians from their homes in 1948. In a crucial scene, the young soldiers arrive at a sand hill during one of their training exercises. Behind it, they discover a "wide, shallow pit . . . the remains of a hedge with only a few bits of green to testify to the remnants of life still surviving in it" (468). The bushes, the trees, and the shifting sands barely cover the remains of a Palestinian village. While some of the soldiers remain unmoved by the sight, others attend to the plight of the Palestinians while simultaneously voicing the communal convictions of Israeli discourse of the 1950s. One of the soldiers, Alon, explains that "anyone who didn't flee was expelled. Because there wasn't any choice. There was no room for them here. Today they're over there in refugee camps in Gaza. And you can feel sorry for them. . . . But you should know that most of them are still hoping, dreaming, they haven't given up hope of returning to their homes one day" (470). Like Simon Wind, Alon spells out the relation between the nationalist logic, based on the principle of the "good of the state," and the fate of the expelled. Employing the spatial metonymy of "room" (or lack thereof) to justify the removal of Palestinians from their land, his words come disturbingly close to the Nazi concept of *Lebensraum*. Yet even in the midst of these troubling connotations, Alon's language is ambivalent about the fate of the expelled. While justifying the expulsion, he acknowledges their pain and displays understanding, even sympathy, about their hope of returning to their homes.

Alon's words realistically present the language of a young, idealistic Israeli of the early 1950s without (unlike A. B. Yehoshua's fire warden) developing a critical stance toward the founding generation. Yet his short speech also points to other historical moments. Readers in the late 1980s were aware of the refugees living in the Gaza Strip, and by referring to "hope," Alon hints at the Palestinian attempt to reverse history's course through the PLO. Furthermore, contemporary readers could hardly fail to draw the connection between Alon's words and the 1982 Lebanon War. Weaving together these historical moments into a densely associative fabric, the scene ties together the past and the future in a manner similar to what we observed in Schütz's work. Alon states: "we have to be awfully strong [*chazakim nora*]. . . . Only the strong would last here. Only those who believe in what they are doing here, those who are prepared to sacrifice everything for it—only they have a chance of prevailing and surviving here" (470).

While his words suggest the importance of believing in the Zionist cause, what he actually expresses is an ideology that celebrates uninhibited power (*nora* implies both "immense" and "awful"). The same ideology also demands that the individual remain willing to "sacrifice everything," even basic human values, for what is presented as sheer survival.

A throwback to the mind-set of the founding generation, Alon is thus a tragic and pathetic figure; born too late to be a part of the political movement that realized the dream of a Jewish national entity in Israel/Palestine, his ideal self is outdated, already a cliché.[11] Written in the 1980s, Alon's words also expose the Israeli political rhetoric of the period shortly before and during the 1982 Lebanon War for its obliviousness to the consequences of the state's actions and to the impact of its policies.

This obliviousness is complicated by Alon's response to what follows. The young soldiers, "as in obedience to some secret, inner command," approach the edge of the pit, "unbutton their flies, and urinate into it" (470). Although they assume their act settled their accounts with the place and the unsaid of 1948, the narrator knows it has not. As he returns to base camp, he imagines encountering ancient mounds and the remains of orchards buried in the sand "like evil omens, traps set for us by time" (471), knowing that what lies visible on the surface is "like a kind of camouflage . . . over the ancient life that went on stirring underneath it" (471). Like Simon Wind, he knows this "real ground" will resurface, forcing those who are unwilling to face the ruins and the pain to repeat the mistakes of their predecessors.

Struggling with the Nazi Beast: David Grossman, See Under: Love

Much of the work of David Grossman (b. 1954)—which includes fiction, journalism, and essays—is an exploration of Kenaz's "real ground." Beginning with his 1983 novel *Chiyuch hagdi* (*The Smile of the Lamb*), a work about Palestinian-Israeli relations after 1967, Grossman's writing turns, time and again, to the particulars of life in what he calls the "disaster zone."[12]

This "disaster zone" has spatial, temporal, and psychological dimensions. First, it marks the disputed land itself—its groves and ruins, its new cities alongside its ancient ones. Second, it denotes the brutal conflict between Jews and Arabs, Israelis and Palestinians, as it unfolds in recurring cycles. Finally, the "disaster zone" signifies the mental landscape of Israeli Jews and Palestinians, where all are "ready for flight or fight" and where "one's entire being anticipates imminent pain, imminent humiliation."[13] For Israelis, life in the "disaster zone" is shaped by anxieties born during the Holocaust, by angst that gives rise to "passivity . . . self-erasure," and, most importantly, by "the talent for being a victim."[14]

In Grossman's *See Under: Love*, the "talent for being a victim" precludes one from evolving beyond the fight-or-flight mentality.[15] The first part of the novel, "Momik," takes place in the Israel of the 1950s and is written in what Dan Miron aptly calls a "metonymical" mode. On one level, the novel depicts the lives of Holocaust survivors and their children through the perspective of the nine-year-old Momik.[16] On another level, however, the novel clearly sets up the character of Momik as a stand-in for the condition of the entire "second generation," those sons and daughters of the traumatized survivors who grew up in the oppressive shadows of their parents' horrific and oftentimes repressed memories.

Following Momik's struggles to make sense of his parents' anxieties, the story focuses on the child's flight into a fantastic world of heroes and villains.[17] These fantasies serve as powerful symbolic devices, the most telling of which is Momik's literal interpretation of an exhausted figure of speech of the time, "the Nazi Beast." According to Bella, a family friend and a Holocaust survivor who introduces the concept to Momik, the Nazi Beast's most distinctive feature is its ability to break out of "any kind of animal if it got the right care and nourishment" (13). The dreamy and imaginative child gives Bella's words a literal interpretation and begins to engage in experiments designed to lure out the beast so that he can finally face and vanquish it, avenging the pain inflicted on his parents. To this end, he locks ravens, hedgehogs, turtles, and cats in the shed by his house, hoping to force the beast to come out and be destroyed.[18]

In Momik's hands, the Nazi Beast becomes a universal, ever-present menace threatening to emerge at any moment, from anyone. Indeed, Momik even wonders if Bella herself "might have the beast in her too" (40). Momik's revitalization of the metaphor is a commentary on the way existential anxieties originating in the Holocaust continued to shape the Jewish Israeli psyche and political landscape in the 1980s. The novel suggests that alongside the external threats to their state, Jewish Israelis face an internal peril that feeds upon the personal and cultural memory of persecution. This is the threat of psychological defense mechanisms degenerating into moral numbness, callousness, and even sadism, seen in Momik's decline. At the height of the boy's attempts to lure out the Nazi Beast, the narrator reveals that

> Momik has also been kind of enjoying it lately when he does something really bad, it happens mostly after dark, when he starts being more afraid and hating the Beast more than ever and hating the whole world. . . . and he almost explodes with power

and cruelty, and that's when he could almost . . . just to smash it and bash it and kick it and stomp on it and torture it and blow it to its bits, and you could even throw an atom bomb in its face now because that article finally came out about our atomic reactor which is huge and awesome rising out of the golden sand dunes of Nahal Rubin near Rishon Le-Zion, towering proudly over the shore and the roaring blue waves . . . and the name of the first Israeli nuclear reactor will be "Kivshan" [furnace, crematorium], which is an acronym standing for, as its director explained, Reactor–Swimming Pool–Nahal Rubin, and even though the newspaper says that the reactor was built "for peaceful purposes," Momik can read between the lines and he catches the meaning behind those smiles of Bella's, whose son is a very high-ranking major in the army, peaceful purposes, yeah sure, sure, let them blast the Arabs away. (70, translation modified)

Momik's desire to destroy the Beast becomes a blind rage, as the Beast becomes both a concrete threat and a kind of timeless being, lifted from its association with "Over There"—the marker for Nazi-occupied Europe—and identified with the contemporary Arab threat. Echoing the soldier's claim in Kenaz's *Infiltration* that "we have to be awfully strong" (*chazakim nora*), Momik concludes that confronting the Beast requires vanquishing "the Arabs" with every available means, including nuclear weapons. Grossman's metaphor thus becomes a commentary on how ingrained fear and hatred toward the Nazi victimizers of the past are transferred to today's Arab adversary.

The reference to the nuclear reactor, "Kivshan," is especially significant in this regard.[19] The semantic scope of the word *kivshan* evokes the ancient cult of animal sacrifice and, much more immediately, the memory of the Nazi crematoriums, the *kivshanim*.[20] In this way, Grossman creates a volatile link between one of the ultimate signifiers of the Holocaust and the contemporary, even cultish, Israeli reverence of military might. The cyclical quality of life in the "disaster zone" is played out again as the traumatic aftershock of the German *kivshanim*, yielding the creation of an Israeli Kivshan that is seen as serving to preserve the nation. Yet this means of self-protection has the potential to turn into a tool for new forms of annihilation.

Grossman's novel also reveals a palimpsest of temporal layers in Israeli consciousness. Shortly before Bella introduces the Nazi Beast for the first time, the narrative refers to "Moroccan construction workers from the new housing developments at Beit Mazmil" (12). In July 1948,

Khirbet Beit Mazmil was taken by Israeli soldiers during "Operation Dani." As Benny Morris notes, the soldiers were ordered to prevent the return of Palestinian inhabitants to their homes after the fighting, if necessary by force.[21] Later, in the 1950s—the time of Grossman's narrative—the Jewish neighborhood of Kiryat Yovel was built on this very site. Thus, as the novel turns to the suffering of Holocaust survivors and their descendants, it also implicitly asks to what extent that pain has led some Jews to ignore the plight of the Palestinians whose fates have become entangled, not least because of the Holocaust, with theirs.

The narrator of *See Under: Love* is the 1980s-era adult Momik, who in "Momik" revisits his childhood in the third-person.[22] Thus, Momik's urge to "explode with power and cruelty" and to do "something really bad" hints at the 1982 Lebanon War, when the memory of the Holocaust was mobilized in a highly contested manner. On the eve of Israel's invasion, Menachem Begin told his cabinet, "Believe me, the alternative is Treblinka, and we have decided that there will be no more Treblinka."[23] Begin also justified the war by referring to Yasser Arafat as a "two-legged beast," a phrase he had used years earlier to describe Adolf Hitler.[24] Faced with criticism regarding Israel's role in massacres in the Palestinian refugee camps of Sabra and Shatila, near Beirut, Begin invoked the necessity of Israeli Jews to defend themselves, arguing that they could not rely on the Western powers—who had, after all, surrendered to Hitler in Munich.[25] To justify Israel's presence in Beirut, Begin likened Yasser Arafat's enclave in the city to Hitler's bunker in Berlin.[26]

Whereas Begin's political rhetoric made practical use of the past with the aim of harnessing fears to drive a political agenda, Grossman's novel presents the possible outcome of such rhetoric. Indeed, Grossman's use of the Nazi Beast metaphor should be understood in this historical-political context. It is not that Momik and, by extension, his generation of Israelis—those born after the Holocaust—hold the Nazi Beast captive. Rather, they themselves are to a large extent captives of the beast, enslaved by their fear of an outside danger.

Grossman's metaphor of the Beast reveals Begin's rhetoric to be hollow and irresponsible, while stressing the need to overcome fears whose origins lie in the past. The novel thus argues that the use of historical traumas as justification for present actions can lead those victimized by their fears into becoming victimizers of others.

This critical dimension, implicit in the first parts of the novel, becomes explicit in the fourth and concluding section, "The Complete Encyclopedia of Kazik's Life." Here the narrator, now an adult, reflects on the narrative of the first three parts. He distills many of the novel's overarching themes into concise theses presented as encyclopedia entries, which continue the novel's plot while underlining the ethical and political issues at stake in the work. This is accomplished by the content of the entries and their cross-referencing. For instance, the entry *koach* (force) (362) is cross-referenced with what the narrator offers as its synonym, *zedek* (justice) (409). The irony here is unmistakable and is clearly geared toward involving the reader in a conscious examination of the relationship between the two concepts *as such*, and thus not least in the context of contemporary (1980s) Israel. Current Israeli political culture, Grossman obliquely states, only pays lips service to the demands of justice, all the while speaking the language of *koach*.

Other entries similarly expand the concerns of the story into the realm of broad aesthetic and moral concerns by linking Nazism and the Holocaust to the present and possible future. Grossman's unique approach to the past in its "practical" dimensions is here further underscored in his definitions of art and artists. *Omanut* (art), for example, is defined in this encyclopedia as "the expression of human creativity in the pursuit of aesthetics and functional objectives" (307). Hence, *omanim* (artists) are "persons who express the creativity of mankind, in pursuit of aesthetic and functional objectives" (307). Likewise, *yetzira* (creation) is both what the artist-genius has formed as an expression of his or her capacities *and* "the act of creating the world. The formation of something new" (361).

In *See Under: Love*, Grossman opens a space for literature to form "something new" by uncovering and reviving the metaphors that defined the founding decade of Israel. In presenting the consequences, both intended and unintended, of the rhetoric of the 1950s, the novel reveals the dangers of remaining subjected to the repressed nightmares of the past. "I may occasionally like to write an entertaining book," he noted in a 2007 interview, "but I take literature seriously. You're dealing with explosives. You can change a reader's life, and you can change—you should change, I think—your own life."[27] Describing his thoughts on the origins of *See Under: Love*, Grossman points to such questions as "how an ordinary, normal person . . . becomes part of a mass-murder apparatus. . . . What is the thing that *I* must suspend within myself . . . so that *I* can ultimately collaborate with a mechanism of murder?"[28] Writing in quest of the past, trying to portray characters who had perpetrated unspeakable crimes (especially in the third part of the novel, "Wasserman"), Grossman is motivated by the wish to comprehend historical circumstances such as Nazi Germany better. Yet he also conducts a poetic-practical self-examination of an "I" that belongs in the different, though not utterly removed, "disaster zone" of his own time.

To Enter the Shared Space, to Begin: David Grossman, The Yellow Wind *and* Sleeping on a Wire

Following his treatment of the ways the memory of the Holocaust is at once a haunting source of existential anxiety, a tableau of personal and collective psychosis, a powerful tool of political manipulation, and a prism through which the "I" may examine himself or herself, Grossman turns in his essayistic work to the Israeli-Palestinian conflict and to the plight of Palestinians. In his travelogues on the territories Israel occupied in 1967 (*Hazman hatzahov* [*The Yellow Wind*], 1987) and his conversations with Palestinians living as Israeli citizens on the border between 1948 and 1967 (*Nochechim nifkadim* [*Sleeping on a Wire*], 1992), Grossman directly ties his poetic reflections on key words in *See Under: Love* to the lives of the people he meets on his way: he ponders how *bechira* (choice), as the "voluntary selection of one possibility out of many," relates to "decision" (*See Under: Love*, 312), and to what extent *hachlata*, "the process of arriving at a conclusion after study and consideration," is linked to "responsibility" and to "choice" (ibid., 331).

The travelogues make explicit the exploration of questions of human agency and reflection that are implicit in the novel. In *The Yellow Wind*, Grossman examines both the conditions to which Palestinians in the West Bank are exposed under the Israeli occupation and the role of the occupier. His account is also a document of self-examination. He admits that, like many Israelis, he, too, was intoxicated in his youth by the victory of 1967, only to find out later that "an enlightened nation, by all accounts, is able to train itself to live as a conqueror without making its own life wretched."[29]

Grossman presents a powerful consequence of the conqueror's bifurcated life by recounting his encounter with an old woman named Hadija in the Dheisheh refugee camp. With her stories about Ain Azrab, the village from which she was expelled in 1948, she reminds him ("with some bafflement," he admits) of his own grandmother, who had been expelled from Poland during the Holocaust: "Time has marked both their faces with the same lines, of wisdom, of irony, of great skepticism toward all people, both relatives and strangers."[30]

Grossman's imaginative merging of the two women in a single frame illustrates that remembering his grandmother's pain does not mean he cannot relate to the pain of Hadija. This intentional dialogue with memory is both "multidirectional" in Michael Rothberg's sense and suggestive that it is possible for Israelis haunted by memories of the Holocaust to relate to the memories and pain of people like Hadija. The author does not efface Palestinian suffering by evoking Jewish pain. On the contrary, Grossman would like to see Israeli Jews include the suffering of Palestinians in their own, Holocaust-oriented understanding of victimhood. *The Yellow Wind* repeatedly invokes the flight and expulsion of Palestinians in 1948 and presents their fate during the following decades in the starkest terms. Indeed, what was novel and daring when *The Yellow Wind* was first published in 1987 has since increasingly infiltrated Israeli public discourse. In May 2004, for example, then Israeli justice minister Yosef "Tommy" Lapid—a Holocaust survivor and leader of the centrist Shinui Party—went on record saying that a picture of an elderly Palestinian woman searching through the rubble of her house, destroyed by the Israeli military, reminded him of his grandmother who was murdered in Auschwitz.[31]

In *Sleeping on a Wire*, Grossman specifically pleads for a new conversation about 1948, a plea that one should take as closely interlinked with his public call to Jews and Arabs, Israelis and Palestinians, finally to take the political actions that are needed to end the conflict. Returning to 1948 by telling the story of villages such as Majd al-Krum and Ein Hud, Grossman invokes the plight of exile, indicating how the expulsions remain for many Palestinians living in Israel a feared future possibility. In the final scene of this book, Grossman refers to a conversation he had with a hospital surgeon who tells him of his constant fear of a future expulsion from Palestine: "It's always on my mind. Either they'll press us to the wall and I'll have nothing to do here, or they'll do it physically: bring me to the border on foot, in a truck, and say, Go!"[32]

After his initial, angry rejection of this anxiety as a wild exaggeration, Grossman comes to understand that many Palestinian citizens of Israel do in fact live in "the terror of that nightmare" (325). Grossman comprehends his work as the result of a desire to create a space in which the Palestinian side of history could be heard. The author suggests that by presenting the voices of Palestinians as they account for their past experiences and future-related fears, *Sleeping on a Wire* offers

> the opposite of the idea of transfer; that this is the attempt to
> internalize, finally, the Arabs in Israel, into Israeli life. To bring
> you [his Arab counterparts] to the place set aside for you with
> us, the Jews in Israel, the place imposed on all of us forty-four

years ago and which has remained since then hard and twisted, like scar tissues on a bone that was broken and badly set and every careless movement threatens to break it again. . . . The place in which, only when we reside there together, we will be able to have our first conversation about all we have distorted and hidden for more than forty years. (325–26)

Sleeping on a Wire thus strives to create a new kind of Jewish Israeli textual space in which Israelis (Grossman's primary addressees) can finally engage with the unsaid—and in which Palestinians are invited "to enter [this space] and begin" a conversation between often hostile, yet inseparable neighbors (326).

At no point in his work does Grossman display the naïve belief that this new beginning can be easily achieved. On the contrary, in many of his reflections on the "disaster zone" that Israelis and Palestinians inhabit, he remains painfully aware of the fact that Israel has yet to successfully align its aspiration to serve as an Or Lagoyim—a light to the nations (Isaiah 42:6), a universal moral beacon—with its self-perception as a national Jewish state. In his speech given at the Yitzhak Rabin memorial ceremony in Tel Aviv on November 4, 2006, soon after the so-called Second Lebanon War of 2006—a war in which Grossman lost his son, Uri—he noted that so far, Israel has wasted not only the lives of many of its sons and daughters but also "the great and rare opportunity that history granted it, the opportunity to create an enlightened, properly functioning democratic state that would act in accordance with Jewish and universal values." Grossman then went on to observe that at the beginning of the twenty-first century Israel finds itself, much like Momik in *See Under: Love*, "precisely when it enjoys its greatest military power ever—in such a feeble, helpless state. . . . A state in which it is again a victim, but now a victim of itself, of its fears and despair, of its own shortsightedness."[33]

In a provocative poem written in the late 1970s and published in 1982, "Targilim beivrit shimushit" (Exercises in practical/everyday Hebrew), the poet Dan Pagis (1930–86) reflects on the lost opportunities to break the seemingly endless cycle of violence between Palestinians and Israelis by alluding to Numbers 13:32:

A land that devours its inhabitants.
Its lovers devour its lovers.
Turn all sentences into future mode.[34]

The imperative "Turn all sentences into future mode" is one of the most startling lines in Hebrew literature. A literal reading of these lines would suggest that they express a deterministic view in which the past is bound to repeat itself in the future in inevitable bouts of violence. More than twenty years after Pagis issued this warning that Israel/Palestine may continue to consume its inhabitants, that its lovers will always "devour its lovers," Grossman notes:

> We, the citizens of that conflict, were born into a war, we were educated within it, and in a sense we were educated for it. Perhaps for that reason we sometimes think that this madness that we've been living in for a century now is the only true thing, that it is the life we are destined for, and that we have no way, even no right, to aspire to a different kind of life. We will live and die by the sword, and the sword shall devour forever.[35]

Yet even as he observes with horror the conditions in the Middle East at one of its most desolate hours, and even as he mourns his own devastating loss, Grossman's viewpoint remains futural. He ends this address by turning to what Israelis and Palestinians as individuals and as political agents can do:

> From where I stand at this moment, I request, call out to all those listening—to young people who came back from the war, who know that they are the ones who will have to pay the price of the next war; to Jewish and Arab citizens; to the people of the right and the people of the left: stop for a moment. Look over the edge of the abyss, and consider how close we are to losing what we have created here. Ask yourselves if the time has not arrived for us to come to our senses, to break out of our paralysis, to demand for ourselves, finally, the lives that we deserve to live.[36]

For Grossman, no reconciliation seems conceivable until several things begin: an open dialogue about what occurred in 1948 and after; acceptance of the multitude of narratives regarding the past; and recognition that these narratives can and do coexist in the same geographic space. Literature offers an example, demonstrating how conflicting narratives about the past may become threads of a single fabric, as in Grossman's novel, where the memories of Momik emerge side by side with the memories of Palestinians.

   The works that I discuss in the next chapter, the final chapter of part II, reveal how literature can acknowledge the diversity of contradictory memories in the space that is Israel/Palestine. Recent Hebrew prose, in evoking 1948 and its lingering effects, imagines what it would take to create a physical reality of coexistence—a land that no longer consumes its lovers. First and foremost, it entails paying attention to each other's painful histories and integrating them into literary wholes without effacing their distinctiveness. Evoking Jewish pain does not efface Palestinian suffering; memory is not a zero-sum game. On the contrary, when Israeli Jews include the suffering of Palestinians in their understanding of victimhood, the memories of the Holocaust can include the memories and pain of their Palestinian neighbors. This integration of memories has the potential for a new beginning in Hannah Arendt's sense: a future based on the possibility of sharing not only a literary landscape but also the physical land that both people claim.

10   The Threads of Our Story: The Unsaid in Recent Israeli Prose

A Gate or an Abyss? Amos Oz, A Tale of Love and Darkness *and* Scenes from Village Life

In the past two decades, a variety of works in Hebrew have sought to create David Grossman's textual space that gives voice to the fate of Palestinians since 1948 and thus creates a basis for future reconciliation. These works invoke in the clearest terms to date the Palestinian experience of 1948. Imagining Palestinian characters and their experiences, they acknowledge, in Hebrew and from a Jewish Israeli perspective, the individual and collective predicament of the exiled and their descendants.

The short stories and novels discussed below were all written during a period of bitter debates regarding 1948 and al-Nakba. These debates, begun in the 1980s, reflected the gradual recognition by broad parts of Israel's cultural and intellectual elite of the deficiencies of the official Zionist discourse about 1948.[1] Yet the works also take into account a further series of traumatic events in the Israeli-Palestinian conflict: the massive settlement of a Jewish population in the West Bank, often conducted with blind brutality; the first intifada (1987–93); the collapse of the 1993 Oslo Accords; and the second, unprecedentedly violent al-Aqsa intifada (2000–2005). Perhaps precisely because of the despair that developed in the wake of the events, works by Amos Oz (b. 1939), Yitzhak Laor (b. 1948), Eshkol Nevo (b. 1971), Alon Hilu (b. 1972), and Michal Govrin (b. 1950) consider Palestinian exile not as the fate of distant others but as a chapter of Jewish Israeli history that demands utterly new forms of engagement. At a moment when a resolution seems more distant than ever, these narratives imagine what remains feasible in the years to come.

The path traveled by Israeli literature from the 1960s to the present with regard to al-Nakba and to the deadly conflict over the land is, perhaps, most visible in the long career of Amos Oz. Amid the al-Aqsa intifada, which shattered hopes for a near-term resolution of the conflict, Oz acknowledged that Palestinians were "kicked out of Palestine."[2] And in both his 2003 autobiographical opus, *Sipur al ahava vechoshech* (*A Tale of Love and Darkness*), and his 2009 work *Tmunot michayey kfar* (2009; Scenes from village life), Oz turns to 1948.[3] His earlier novella *Navadim vazefa* (1965; Nomads and viper) and novel *Michael sheli* (1968; My Michael) revealed how Israelis view the Palestinian as the exotic, eroticized, and threatening other. *A Tale of Love and Darkness* and *Scenes from Village Life* trace the impact of these orientalist projections that Israeli public discourse for decades failed to address.[4]

A panoramic memoir that deals primarily with his childhood in Jerusalem under the British Mandate, Oz's *A Tale of Love and Darkness* also recounts, implicitly, the trajectory of the Israeli-Palestinian conflict. In a key scene, Oz describes a visit just prior to the 1948 war to the house of a distinguished Palestinian family, the al Silwani, in the Sheikh Jarrah neighborhood of Jerusalem. Recounting the visit, Oz merges his first-person narrative with a distinctly Palestinian perspective. He remembers the charged encounter with the family's young children, Aisha al Silwani and her little brother, Awaad, in the garden of the al Silwani mansion. The writer, conscious of the years separating him from this childhood self, recalls with irony how he sought to approach the beautiful Aisha while mindlessly spouting the Zionist rhetoric he had adopted from "neighbors, . . . teachers, from my uncles and aunts" (324): how determined he was "to explain" to her the "pure" intentions of the Zionist movement, to "enlighten this oblivious girl" with the aim of getting her "to understand once and for all the rightness of the Jewish return to Zion" (324), and to teach her about the "abhorrent . . . British plot" to "stir up conflict between our two peoples" (324).

Very quickly, however, young Oz's self-righteousness leads to disaster. When Aisha asks him if besides speaking he can also climb a tree, the boy transforms himself "into Tarzan" (327). Filled with "national representativity" (327), he leaps to the top of the tree where he finds a rusty chain tied to a heavy iron ball. At the peak of his exuberance, he waves the chain and whirls the iron ball in quick circles, his mind filled with the rhetoric of his Zionist "revisionist" (i.e., right-wing) upbringing:

> For sixty generations, so we had learned, they [the Gentiles and now the Arabs] had considered us a miserable nation of huddled yeshiva students, flimsy moths who start in a panic at every shadow, *awlad al-mawt*, children of death, and now at last here was muscular Judaism taking the stage, the resplendent new Hebrew youth at the height of his power, making everyone who sees him tremble at his roar: like a lion among lions. (327)

Precisely at this moment, catastrophe strikes. As young Amos Oz stages the powers of the New Jew for Aisha, her younger brother, Awaad, playing nearby, repeatedly utters one of the few expressions he knows in Hebrew, "Jest a minutes! Rest a minute!" The older Oz reflects that the "awesome tree lion," intoxicated with his own grandeur, had no time to stop and listen and so was "blind, deaf, [and] foolish" (327). He could not hear Awaad, and by extension could not comprehend that other voices, other perspectives, existed. Even though "everything was ready for the horror to come" (327), he—the young nationalist—will not stop for a second, will not end his perilous waving of the chain with the iron ball. A moment before the iron ball breaks away and plummets down to crush Awaad's foot, he and Aisha face each other with no sign of common ground: "the delicate, thoughtful girl with the thick black eyebrows" looks up at him with a pitying smile, "as if to say, that's nothing, all those efforts of yours . . . we've seen much more than that already, you can't impress us with that" (328). Unable to stop for a second, incapable of recognizing any external viewpoint, the boy is locked in his own "arrogance. His folly. The prison of his rising virility. The intoxication of vainglorious chauvinism" (328).[5]

Oz never learns the consequences of the accident. The events of that day remain unspoken in his family; a "dense veil" (331, translation modified) of silence shrouds the memory. Afterward, he continues to think of Aisha and her brother while playing in the yard (337). He wonders what they are doing as he and his parents consider the prospects of a Jewish state (347–48). When the Jewish inhabitants of Old Jerusalem were expelled from the city or taken hostage by the Trans-Jordanian Arab Legion during the 1948 war, Oz does not remember thinking of the al Silwani children (369). Sitting frightened, thirsty, and hungry in the foul-smelling basement of his Jerusalem house during the Arab blockade of

West Jerusalem (385), however, he regards the al Silwanis as much better off than he is. Yet he also longs to "go to them at the head of a deputation for peace and reconciliation, to prove to them that we were in the right, to apologize and receive their apology . . . and maybe also to convince Aisha and her brother and all the Silwani family that the accident had not been entirely my fault, or not only my fault" (385).

The question of Oz's responsibility and, by extension, that of the Zionist movement for the plight of Palestinians is a driving force of this book's future-oriented self-interrogation. Shortly before the establishment of the Jewish state, Oz recalls, his father describes Herzl's position in the First Zionist Congress in 1897 as a prophetic revelation: "fifty years have passed, and the state is literally standing at the gate" (337). His mother, however, had replied to the irritated father: "It's not standing. There is no gate. There's an abyss" (337). Oz is reminded at this exact point of how he would "freeze with a stab of terror" when remembering Aisha carrying her wounded brother, looking like Mary holding Christ's body (337). The words that accompany his memory of his mother's forecast are the words uttered by little Awaad: "Jest a minute rest a minute jest a rest a jesta resta," juxtaposing his own youthful obliviousness with that of the Zionist nationalist project (337).

A Tale of Love and Darkness revolves around the author's struggle with the memory of that inauspicious day: "suppose I found Aisha, somewhere in the world . . . how would I introduce myself? What could I say? What could I really explain? What could I offer?" (369). Repeating the child's attempt to talk himself out of responsibility—"It wasn't all my fault. Not all of it"—he knows that his action "can't be undone" (370). Yet Oz's narrative itself, by returning to Awaad al Silwani's utterance, transforms his deafness into a narrative about the dangers of hermetic nationalism. Oz's telling of his inability to listen enlarges his and his readers' perspective by expressing remorse. His ironic, distanced presentation of his childhood self creates a critical distance from the arrogant nationalism that obscures the human consequences of 1948. The narrative cannot undo the ridiculous "awesome tree lion's" words and deeds, but it can give voice to the fate of those affected by them. It can note the two equally valid, if conflicted, views of the 1948 war: one that stresses the fight of Israeli Jews for survival in the parts of the land they inhabited (such as in the western section of Jerusalem) and another that stresses the pain of the Palestinians who have lost their homeland.

Oz's narrative thus displays, with considerable success, a complex situation in which both Israelis and Palestinians are trapped with their "backs to the wall," as the writer once put it.[6] Moving out of this position, which is strikingly reminiscent of the narrowing of alternatives for a livable future in Franz Kafka's "Eine kleine Fabel" ("A Little Fable"), surely depends on finding a political solution to the Israeli-Palestinian conflict that would allow the likes of Amos Oz and Aisha and Awaad al Silwani to inhabit the land together. Although Oz was often attacked for not doing enough to promote such a solution, indeed, for being a part of "the myth of liberal Zionism," I view works such as *A Tale of Love and Darkness* and his numerous essays and political statements on the issue as a clear refutation of such reductive criticism, indeed, as an indication of his commitment to face the threat of a brutal reality that threatens to "close in" on Israelis and Palestinians alike.[7]

"To Remind Us of What Used to Be Here. To Amend the Wrong": Yitzchak Laor, Ecce Homo; *Daniella Carmi,* To Free an Elephant; Eshkol Nevo, Homesick; *and Alon Hilu,* The House of Rajani

A variety of recent Israeli novels have defined 1948 as a central component of Israel's landscape. Unveiling the repressed, forgotten, and neglected expulsions that took place during Israel's War of Independence, these works both acknowledge the historical wrongs and participate in the public debate on the trajectory of the Jewish state. Yitzchak Laor's *Hineh adam* (2002; Ecce Homo) invokes 1948 as a manifestation of what Laor views as Zionism's colonial enterprise.[8] The novel satirizes Israel's contemporary intellectual elite as they dine at Tel Aviv University's clubhouse—a venue built over the remains of a Palestinian village now buried "like a soundless scream under the university" (12).[9] The muted screams from the past eventually destabilize the mind of the novel's protagonist, ex–major general Adam Lotem. Yet prior to this mental collapse, the novel takes Lotem on a road trip through Israel with the alluring Shulamit. It is through her gaze, and its virulent critique of Zionist ideology as it is reflected in Israel's landscape, that Lotem perceives how Jewish villages resemble a "junk heap" (48) as they obscure the ruins of Palestinian life of the pre-1948 era.

Daniella Carmi's 2001 experimental novella *Leshachrer pil: Massa bricha mizichronot yaldut mefukpakim* (To free an elephant: A journey of escape from doubtful childhood memories) likewise exposes what lies beneath—haunting collective memories many Israelis try to escape.[10] Carmi's lyrical prose presents the whimsical mental life of patients treated in an Israeli psychiatric institution near Jerusalem, and the book

FIGURE 4 Mel Brikman's photograph of the psychiatric hospital in Givat Shaul, Jerusalem, formerly a house in the Palestinian village Deir Yassin. From Daniella Carmi, *Le 'schachrer Pil* (Tel Aviv–Jaffa: Am Oved Publishing, 2001), 141.

includes a variety of photographs. The last eight pages show various psychiatric institutions in Jerusalem, all of them converted from Palestinian dwellings after 1948, as Carmi notes (135).

One of the photographs shows the psychiatric clinic in Givat Shaul, a house formerly in the Palestinian village Deir Yassin, where on April 9, 1948, the paramilitary Jewish groups Lehi and the Irgun (Etzel) killed dozens of Palestinian civilians.[11] In Carmi's textual-photographic constellation, 1948 haunts the dwelling and its inhabitants in present-day Israel. The houses Palestinians used to occupy now lodge Israelis who struggle with mental diseases—and thus the ghosts of the past return to trouble the Jewish Israeli national house. In its use of photographs

Carmi's narrative has a material quality: the reader is confronted visually with what a house built on the ruins of Palestinian existence actually looks like. Furthermore, the novella suggests a link between the current mental condition of Israel's Jewish inhabitants and the past, in a kind of Freudian return of the repressed. While the authorities wanted to give the remains of Deir Yassin a new purpose after 1948, Carmi's work reverses this process: what has been occluded and repurposed regains its previous connections.

Eshkol Nevo (b. 1971) and Alon Hilu (b. 1972), in their less experimental but highly popular *Arbaa batim vegaagua* (2004; *Homesick*) and *Achuzat Dajani* (2008; *The House of Rajani*), similarly reveal the hidden. Yet what makes the novels significant here is their overt theme and market success: that combination suggests that numerous Israelis are now willing to consider the conventional view of their collective history as obsolete.

Written with the horrific suicide bombings of the al-Aqsa intifada in the background, Nevo's *Homesick* is a polyphonic work containing the voices of Israelis and Palestinians, immigrants and native-born, young and old.[12] It focuses, however, on a young student couple, Amir and Noa, who rent a new apartment in the Jerusalem suburb of Maoz Zion built on the foundation of a formerly Palestinian house. The village in which the Palestinian house stood was until the 1948 war called Al Qastal, replaced in 1951 by the Hebrew name Maoz Zion, literally "Zion's Fort."

This fort seems symbolically to protect not only its new inhabitants but also the buried Palestinian past. Thus, Maoz Zion effectively shelters its Jewish inhabitants from their complex history. Yet Nevo gives voice to a Palestinian character, Saddiq, thus revealing the cracks in the fortification. Saddiq is a construction worker in a Palestinian refugee camp in the West Bank. Nevo's narrative imagines the pain and the anger Palestinians felt upon discovering that Al Qastal's Palestinian past has been eradicated: the Jews "built ugly buildings that didn't fit in the mountains, and . . . they gave all the streets the names of wars, Independence Street, Victory Street, Six Days Street" (71).

Saddiq returns to his former home in the hope of reclaiming the golden necklace his mother had hidden in the wall shortly before the family was uprooted. The narrative suggests the possibility of a symbolic restitution: if Saddiq claims the jewelry, he might be content and the conflict resolved. Yet state authorities, in the figure of the policeman who arrives at the scene, refuse the claims of memory. *Homesick* thus rejects any notion of atonement: there can be no simple restitution for 1948.

Yet what one may and should do is acknowledge the existence of multiple memories—both Israeli and Palestinian—in one and the same space.

Noa's path to the recognition that Israeli and Palestinian longings are not mutually exclusive is reflected in Eshkol Nevo's own encounter with the past. While he originally intended his book to deal with the Israeli longing for a home, for a stable place, he finally realized that he "couldn't write about longing for a home without writing about the longing of the original owner for his home." "It's hard to reconcile [the Palestinians'] narrative with ours," Nevo goes on to say. While meeting with Palestinians in writing *Homesick*, he felt the extent to which "the myth of return"—the idea that the refugees of 1948 could resettle in the homes, villages, and towns they left or from which they were expelled—"is still alive among them, and I said to myself: If they haven't given up, then how is it at all possible to reach an agreement with them?" Like David Grossman, Nevo took what he considers the first step in a possible reconciliation: acknowledging the Palestinian suffering and pain, making space within his own narrative for the story of the Palestinian others. Born in 1971, Nevo notes that, for his generation, "the question of whether or not Israel would survive did not exist. We grew up with confidence in our place, confidence that there is a state. Therefore I can hear another story. I don't adopt it, but I listen to it. I can give room to the Palestinian story without fear that it will burn me, as is the case with A. B. Yehoshua [in his *Facing the Forests*]."[13]

The market success of Nevo's *Homesick* mirrors that of Alon Hilu's 2008 postcolonial historical novel *Achuzat Dajani* (*The House of Rajani*).[14] Instead of pointing to 1948 as the root of the conflict, Hilu's novel returns to the year 1895 and to the first Aliya, the initial wave of Zionist migration to Palestine, seeing the expulsions of 1948 as part of the colonial thread in Zionism extending to the movement's very beginning. Undermining the Zionist metanarrative, *The House of Rajani* presents two conflicting narratives side by side as they both regard the same territory, the Dajani estate near Jaffa. The two stories appear in the form of personal journals: one written by Haim Margaliyot Kalvaryski (1868–1947), an agronomist employed by the Palestine Jewish Colonization Association and a historical figure, and the other by Salah Dajani, a fictional Palestinian child whose family owns the Dajani estate.

Salah Dajani's journal parallels and simultaneously undercuts Kalvaryski's account by representing the Palestinian perspective of the events the Zionist agronomist describes. His notes present the charming young man as a Zionist version of Claudius in *Hamlet*, who, by tempting the mother, stands to inherit the kingdom, the Dajani estate.[15] The journal entries further describe prophetic hallucinations in which the realities of the next hundred years are foretold: the decline of Arab Palestine and the rise of the Jewish state in its place, bringing skyscrapers and "blond children" who "stomp" with their feet the uprooted citrus orchards of Jaffa (178). By presenting an image of 1895, the novel also gestures toward 1948 and 1967. Through the prism of Hilu's postcolonial narrative, the zealous nationalists' settlement of the territories Israel occupied in 1967 assumes familiar overtones. Their desire to return to the biblical Promised Land is viewed as part of a colonialist thread within Zionism that runs from the late nineteenth century through 1948 to the present.

With its 1895 setting, *The House of Rajani* prompts debate about the course of the Jewish state. The historical Kalvaryski was both a shrewd power broker of Zionist land and someone who sensed the devastation that the conflict over that land would bring. A member of Brit Shalom (1925–30), a group of Jewish intellectuals dedicated to promoting a peaceful cohabitation between Jews and Arabs, Kalvaryski openly admitted the morally questionable nature of his actions, saying "during the 25 years of my colonizing work, I dispossessed many Arabs of their land, and you understand that this work—to dispossess people of land that they, and perhaps their ancestors, were born on—is not at all an easy thing, especially when the dispossessor does not view the dispossessed as a flock of sheep, but rather as people, with a heart and a soul."[16] He also warned his fellow Zionists that "we must not ignore the needs of our neighbors. Because we must not build our national home over the destruction of others."[17] Hilu's novel raises the question of what might have followed 1895 had the work of Brit Shalom continued.

At least in one respect, the novel suggests an answer to this question. It redraws Israel's map in a way that echoes the map in A. B. Ychoshua's *Facing the Forests*. Before the narrative begins, Hilu's novel presents readers with a map (11) that questions their notions regarding familiar spaces. On the right-hand side, readers find a sketch of the square and walled historical Dajani estate as the author imagines it. Superimposed over this space (represented by the dark bubble with its dark, penetrating arrow) stand today the Azrieli Towers, a series of three skyscrapers that make up part of Tel Aviv's modern skyline.

For Hilu, the insertion of the land's Palestinian past back into the map of contemporary Israel does not imply a plea for a removal of the Azrieli Towers. "I am not in favor of dismantling everything," Hilu noted in an interview published after the novel appeared in print.[18] Rather, "I am trying to tell the story as it should have been told—to remind us of what used to be here. To amend the wrong [*letaken et haavel*]." Hilu's

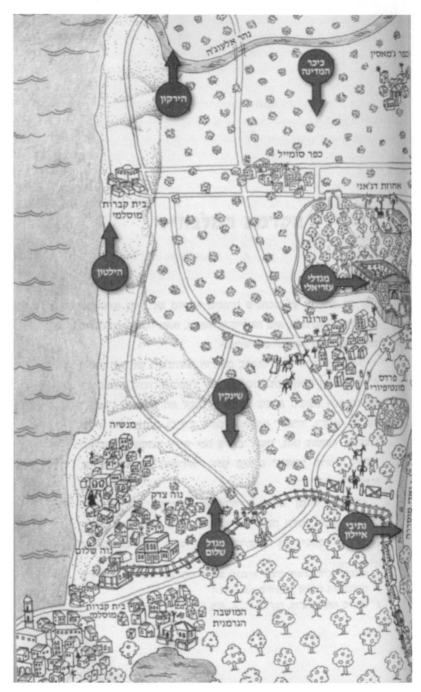

FIGURE 5 Alon Hilu, *Achuzat Dajani*, 11. Alon Hilu mentions (10) that the drawing by Julia Filipone Erez is based on historical documents, maps, and data taken from the Zochrot group's databases, as well as the Web site www.palestineremembered.com. He also states that the map only assumes the exact location of the Dajani estate. Reproduced by permission of Alon Hilu, La Maison Dajani, Yedioth Books, Israel, 2008. Illustrated by Julia Filipone Erez.

use of the infinitive *letaken* echoes David Grossman's notion of literary writing in "the dark" of the Israeli-Palestinian conflict as an act of *tikkun* (repair), as I mentioned in the introduction to this book. His web of narratives, characters both real and imagined, and a telling image (the map) creates what Grossman aptly labels a "shapeless web, which nonetheless has immense power to change a world and create a world, the power to give words to the mute and to bring about *tikkun*—'repair'—in the deepest, kabalistic sense of the word."[19] Hilu does not believe that Israel should return the property that was in fact purchased from the Dajani family, some of the members of which, according to his sources, live today in utter poverty in the refugee camp of Khan Yunis. One cannot undo the pains of the distant past by inflicting new suffering of forced displacement. "But," he goes on to stress, "we should recognize their pain."

Hilu's presentation of the Palestinian and the Zionist narratives side by side generated clear dissensus. The novel has become the subject of a legal dispute between Hilu and Kalvaryski's family, which claims that the writer has besmirched the pioneer's legacy.[20] It was this dispute that led him to change the name Kalvaryski to Luminksy and the name Dajani to Rajani in the translation of the novel into other languages.[21] From the left, the critic Oren Kakun accused Hilu of writing an "aestheticized," "kitschy" drama that merely helps Israelis forget the occupation of the West Bank: in *The House of Rajani*, Kakun notes, "aesthetic pleasure trumps any genuine moral imperative."[22] From the mainstream (perhaps conservative) end of the spectrum, the writer Aharon Megged (b. 1920)—a towering figure of Dor Hapalmach (the Palmach Generation)—wrote a letter accusing Hilu of writing a distinctly "anti-Zionist" work. In his response to Megged, Hilu emphasized (not without irony) that he simply wanted to be "a good Zionist," that is, an Israeli Jew recognizing the right of Jews for self-determination, yet also their need to revise the "misleading Zionist narrative" according to which Tel Aviv, and by extension Israel, simply rose "out of the sands" without inflicting any pain or suffering on the Palestinians. Revising the story Israelis tell themselves about the origins of this conflict, Hilu continued, may be "the first step in the desired reconciliation between the two peoples, a compromise that is necessary for the continuation of Israel's existence as a Zionist state in a hundred or two hundred years."[23] Writing is thus an act of self-making and, potentially, world-making. Incorporating the Palestinian story into one's own ultimately enlarges the self: one becomes capable of listening, of absorbing, of empathizing without feeling immediately helpless or worrying that the "other's" narrative will come at the price of one's own.

Revising the Zionist narrative as a modest act of *tikkun* meant for Alon Hilu choosing the specific name Dajani to represent the Palestinian family and, by extension, Palestinian history in the nineteenth and twentieth centuries. It was in the hospital that Dr. Fouad Dajani (1890–1940) founded in Palestinian Jaffa in 1933 that Alon Hilu was born in 1972.[24] Hilu came into the world in the Dajani Hospital thirty-two years after Dr. Dajani's sudden death, and twenty-four years after the Dajani family fled Jaffa to Cairo for fear of its fate at the hands of the Israeli army. Hilu's literary *tikkun* is mirrored in a humble political act. In 2000, the Israeli architect Samuel Giler learned of Dr. Fouad Dajani and his family through a televised documentary that featured the doctor's daughters. The daughters lamented in this film that their father's memory, like the memory of countless other Palestinians, was eradicated from his own city, Jaffa, and that even his grave did not have a tombstone to mark his final resting place. Giler then contacted the municipality of Tel Aviv with the request to arrange for a tombstone to be placed atop the grave. His request was fulfilled. A Palestinian member of the Tel Aviv municipality, Ahmed Mashrawi, later moved that a square in front of the old building that used to house the Dajani Hospital and currently serves as a geriatric institution be named after Dr. Fouad Dajani. In February 2012 the square was named after the Palestinian doctor in the presence of his extended family, whose members live around the world. At the ceremony, Dr. Dajani's sole surviving son, Omar, said that he hoped that the day's event would be "an example to the two peoples, descendants of Abraham, Isaac and Ishmael, to whom God promised this land, that like the healer we are honoring, we will heal the wounds of our differences and find a way to live in peace and harmony in this holy land."[25]

A Rickety Place of Hope: Michal Govrin, Snapshots

Combining text, image, and philosophical-theological reflection on the meaning of land ownership, Michal Govrin (b. 1950) goes significantly beyond "listening" to the Palestinian narrative in her novel *Hevzekim* (2002; *Snapshots*). Central to her ambitious work is a focus on the multifaceted symbolism of Jerusalem—the city whose ruins and places of worship are arguably the most emotionally charged sites of the Israeli-Palestinian conflict. *Snapshots* unveils the temporal layers of the city that endow it with its unique attraction, while also pointing to those *Zeitschichten* that seem to make any resolution of the conflict over its future impossible. Following the 1967 Six-Day War, Jerusalem lost the interior border that had divided it since 1948, a "reunification" (*ichud yerusha-*

layim, in official Israeli rhetoric) that became an emblem for the Israeli occupation of the territories gained during that war. Jerusalem's Palestinians and much of the Arab world regard Israel's claim—based on biblical accounts—to exclusive rule over the city, including the Muslim shrines in the Old Quarter, as illegitimate and offensive. Many Israelis, however, view the "reunited" city as a symbol for the rightful return of Jews to the land of their ancestors after two millennia of exile. For left-leaning Israelis such as the literary critic Dan Miron, Jerusalem after 1967 represents the atavistic, intolerant, and domineering side of the modern Jewish state, "the driving away of the other from his land, the fulfillment of your rights as if these were the only rights, eternal, transcendentally valid."[26]

Alluding to these conflicted narratives and their violent impact, Govrin's *Snapshots* seeks to use Jerusalem's past as a means of escape from the seemingly irresolvable struggle between mutually exclusive rights.[27] As the title suggests, *Snapshots* defies the very notion of a cohesive, "true" Israeli "being" that draws on the holy and the timeless, and the novel imagines how language could be used to alter the course of the conflict over rights, over national and religious predominance.

Told through the distinctive voice of its protagonist, Ilana Zuriel, *Snapshots* explores the various conflicting Jewish Israeli notions regarding the inhabitance of space.[28] An Israeli architect and leftist activist living in Paris, Zuriel conveys these ideas in frantically jotted "snapshots," journal entries she directs at her recently deceased father, Aaron. A Zionist of the third Aliya (the third wave of Zionist migration to Palestine, 1919–23), Aaron Zuriel came to fulfill the dream of Jewish self-determination, in which modern Jews were "returning" to their ancestral homeland, to an empty land waiting to be "redeemed."[29] More than half a century and a series of traumatic wars later, Ilana Zuriel reconsiders this vision as she tries to hold together "the fragments of our torn story" (15), a story that includes Aaron Zuriel's Zionism, Ilana Zuriel's turbulent marriage to Alain Greenberg, a French Jewish historian and survivor of the Holocaust, and her affair with Sayyid Ashabi, a Palestinian dramatist from East Jerusalem.

Zuriel's interest in the settlement of "Displaced Persons"—Jewish survivors of the Holocaust who arrived in Israel during the 1950s (39)—leads her to become aware of Palestinian suffering, to notice that as Jewish Displaced Persons came to Israel, Palestinian refugee camps emerged across the border (40). Her attentiveness to the entanglement of Israeli and Palestinian histories grows substantially during the 1988 intifada, when she participates in a UNESCO competition to create an

Israeli-Palestinian "site of peace" in Jerusalem (46). Zuriel then meets her Palestinian counterpart in this endeavor, Sayyid Ashabi, through whom she intimately encounters the fate of Palestinians during the last century.

Govrin's characters thus represent the working of divergent memories in Israeli consciousness, tracing how in recent decades al-Nakba has become an explicit element of the Israeli-Palestinian encounter. Zuriel's Palestinian lover describes his emotions during a bus ride to Tel Aviv. Watching Israel's landscape as it passes by, Sayyid sees merely "a map that's erased. I pass Lod, Ramle, Beit Lid, and my heart is cut with pain" (48). As Zuriel recounts Sayyid's emotions, she also notes her own association, the words of her husband, the Holocaust survivor, who told her while pointing at a different map that he is dealing with an "architecture of the past," with places such as Belz, Bratslav, and Berdichev—centers of Jewish life that were erased during the Holocaust (48). The invocation of the Holocaust in *Snapshots* hardly serves as a maneuver to avoid confronting Sayyid's pain. On the contrary, Palestinian memory is prevalent in Zuriel's narrative, invoked both by Sayyid and by her uncle's recollection of the Palestinian "expulsion" during 1948: "Children, old people, pregnant women, we [Israeli soldiers] took them out of their houses and put them on trucks. Took them in the dark across the Jordan" (260). The novel thus reflects the working of multidirectional memory. The Jewish memory of the Holocaust and the Palestinian memory of 1948 are not mutually exclusive; in fact, they must coexist in one and the same space for any dialogue or cohabitation to emerge.

Govrin's novel also offers a set of concepts—based on Jewish tradition—that may help both sides move beyond their violent history and even beyond simple acceptance of conflicting memories. Zuriel's proposal for the competition envisions the creation of an "anti-monument" (75), a "Settlement of Huts" on what she calls "Mount Sabbatical" (59). Rather than using the past to enhance tradition and identity, Zuriel's creation is "a projection into the future . . . an anti-monument to the evanescent, perhaps unrealizable hope for peace," as Shlomit Rimmon-Kenan argues.[30] Zuriel's futural projection is based, however, on an ancient Judaic tradition: on the biblical command of *shmita*, literally "letting go," "dropping"—the imperative to let the land lie fallow every seven years.[31] In the theological discussion of *shmita*, Zuriel finds a way to address her "uneasiness with the Zionist story, with all the love of the Land steeped in paganism or German Romanticism" (73–74).

In her sketches for the project display, Zuriel seeks to insert into Jerusalem's landscape a different kind of settlement, a "rickety place, not

FIGURE 6 Michal Govrin's photograph/collage from his novel *Hevzekim* (Tel Aviv–Jaffa: Am Oved Publishing, 2002), published in English as *Snapshots* (New York: Riverhead Books, 2007), 193. By permission of Michal Govrin. Zuriel's proposal for the creation of an "anti-monument" (75).

monumental" (75), in which Israelis do not drive away Palestinians but rather engage with them in artistic performance, in learning and debate in sukkot (tabernacles) (107).[32] The project aims to create a space based on a discourse of exchange, of giving and receiving hospitality, and thus on cohabitation and peace. She hopes to settle the tension between the contingencies of national interest and justice by creating an altogether different approach to space.

Zuriel proposes new, transient structures amid Jerusalem's "consecrated stone fortresses": interstitial buildings signaling the possibility of cohabiting—or at least of inhabiting—the city without seeking to possess it exclusively (95). To use Hannah Arendt's notion in *Between Past and Future*, with this "insertion," Zuriel breaks the "continuum" of time, envisioning instead what Arendt calls "the beginning of beginning."[33] By inserting her structure into the physical site of the conflict and by creating a symbolic space of encounter, Zuriel hopes to disrupt this continuum of eternal brutal war, to deflect the current trajectory determined by the Zionist dream of return, by the messianic zeal of the settler movement, and by the Palestinian ideology of *tsumud* (or *sumud*) (136), the steadfast clinging to the land.

Introducing a metaphorics of dwelling free of permanent rights, Zuriel's project also promotes an ethics that is not based on metaphysical imperatives. She wants to build her settlement of huts on Jerusalem's Hill of Evil Counsel, where, according to Jewish tradition, Abraham paused on his way to Mount Moriah, where God instructed him to sacrifice his son Isaac (Genesis 22:4). There Abraham learned that human sacrifice is not essential to devotion; humans can express fidelity to belief through a symbolic, substitutive act. By placing her huts there, Zuriel underlines the possibility of a religious attachment to the land that "let[s] go of the knife" (59).

Moreover, the New Testament views the same hill as the location of the high priest Caiaphas's residence, where the Jewish Sanhedrin conspired against Jesus. Later, the symbolism of domination continued when the British Mandate authority built an octagonal structure there to serve the ruling high commissioner, a dwelling that embodied colonial rule. In 1948, the Palestinian village Abu Tor, located nearby, was taken over by Israelis, its empty houses resettled by Jews to create the neighborhood of Givat Hananya. Although between 1948 and 1967 Abu Tor/ Givat Hananya was a mixed neighborhood of Palestinians and Israelis, after the 1967 Six-Day War Israel annexed the area and began to add Jewish neighborhoods, a policy that caused continual conflict between Israelis and Palestinians.[34]

In placing the settlement of sukkot on this site, Zuriel's vision and Govrin's narrative suggest how one might rewrite the legacy of oppressive domination. The novel's UNESCO project and the key terms sukkot and *shmita* introduce a creative notion of dwelling and governance that could actually enable a future. The premise is that Israelis should not consider themselves as holding the land by divine sanction, sealed by an act of sacrifice—a crucial element in the ideology of the settler movement after 1967. Rather, Govrin argues that Israelis and Palestinians should consider relating to the land via the symbolism of substitution rather than of continuous human sacrifice. One can be mindful of the Jewish connection to the Promised Land, Zuriel's plan suggests, by assuming ceremonial practices that do not depend on exclusive possession and on occupation. The way Govrin draws on Jewish cultural memory acknowledges the significance of scripture and myth for Zionism while at the same time emphasizing that those archives also offer the idea of consensual division of the land as a way out of the conflict.[35]

Written in clear dialogue with deconstructive philosophy (Govrin sets the book's origin in conversations with Jacques Derrida; 321), *Snapshots* is hardly a naïve fantasy about the future. Zuriel is aware that the very idea of a monument for peace in Jerusalem may reek of "kitsch" (74) and that her "selection of fundamentalist quotations from holy books" (276) may be an escapist hallucination.

After leaving Israel and returning to France once it becomes clear that her project will not be realized, Zuriel is killed in a car accident. The child she carries in her womb—either Sayyid's or Alain's—will never be born. In *Snapshots*' symbolic net, this death is especially ominous. The dead child hints that failing to realize the vision of sharing the land may bring about the disappearance of a futural dimension altogether. The book we hold in our hands remains incomplete: fragments of thought and threads of lives brutally ended. Yet precisely in its fragmented form and in its consciousness of the limited validity of utopia—an awareness of the devastations brought about by modern eschatology—*Snapshots* calls on its readers to fill in the gaps, to consider what they can do to alter the realities the book describes.

In an interview, Govrin said, "I've been living with a feeling that our existence here [in Israel] cannot be taken for granted. Jerusalem is the heart of the conflict and if we succeed in softening this place with water flowing over stone, as described in *Snapshots*, that is hope. . . . This city demands a new invention of sovereignty and then there will be an end to the conflict."[36] In presenting seemingly nonnegotiable Israeli and Palestinian narratives in the same textual space, the novel itself alludes to what such inventive governance may look like. In fact, it becomes the metaphorical sukkah (booth) that Zuriel sketches: a place in which the conflicting Israeli and Palestinian narratives coexist in debate, discussion, and mutual respect.

Without any politics of utopia, any actions forcefully attempting to end the conflict once and for all, the novel nevertheless disrupts, through character, biblical allusion, and imagery, what appears to be an unchangeable reality. According to Fredric Jameson, the literary break with the past that utopian fantasies such as Ilana Zuriel's execute is not an expression of an escapist imagination but rather "the answer to the universal ideological conviction that no alternative is possible."[37] Michal Govrin's seemingly strange decision to include in the book an "appendix" of Zuriel's drawings of her planned architectural work at Mount Sabbatical makes sense if we regard the drawings as the disruption of that ostensibly unchangeable reality. The sketches imply how feasible the fantasy may be, right down to the level of fine-lined detail. Reflecting on her role as a writer in the desperate time following the 2000–2005 al-Aqsa intifada, Govrin noted in an interview her wish "to imagine another architecture, beyond the walls of hate and the walls of separation, beyond the violence and the extreme intolerance, to believe and to imagine how this region can one day find a way to live in peace."[38] Although Zuriel's child remains unborn, it also signals, Govrin adds, "an audacious gesture of hope."

Snapshots reveals the ability of literature to voice the unsaid and create a space for reflection on contemporary ethical and political concerns. In crossing the lines separating past, present, and future, works such as Govrin's provoke readers to rethink previously held "judgments" and—to again use Richard Rorty's words—to go back in time prospectively. If literature can help us grasp the contingencies of our lives and "our own moral vocabulary," as Rorty thinks, *Snapshots* allows its Israeli readers and readers elsewhere both to accept the multiplicity of memories surrounding their homeland and to imagine inhabiting space in a different manner than they do today.[39] With its metaphors and visual images, the novel supplements diplomacy's efforts to imagine an Israeli-Palestinian future with less humiliation and less suffering on both sides of the divide.

Part Three | Futurity and Action

11 The Past after the "End of History"

Mendacious Time

On a cold day, not long before Christmas of 1996, the narrator of W. G. Sebald's *Austerlitz* and the protagonist, elderly historian of architecture Jacques Austerlitz, arrive in Greenwich, England. After climbing up through the park, they finally reach the Royal Observatory. There, while viewing various measuring devices, regulators, and chronometers, Austerlitz bursts into a passionate monologue, declaring that "time" is "by far the most artificial of all our inventions."[1] He continues,

> A clock has always struck me as something ridiculous, a thoroughly mendacious object, perhaps because I have always resisted the power of time out of some internal compulsion which I myself have never understood, keeping myself apart from so-called current events in the hope . . . that time will not pass away, has not passed away, that I can turn back and go behind it, and there I shall find everything as it once was, or more precisely I shall find that all moments of time have co-existed simultaneously, in which case none of what history tells us would be true, past events have not yet occurred but are waiting to do so at the moment

when we think of them, although that, of course, opens up the bleak prospect of everlasting misery and neverending anguish. (101)

Austerlitz's words echo the ageless desire to counter the transience of existence. In the context of the novel, they also reflect upon the man-made catastrophes of the mid-twentieth century, specifically the Holocaust. Yet Austerlitz's polemic here voices primarily a pointed aversion to a certain modern view of time. He rejects the concept of time as a natural procession of regular units, of past, present, and future, in which humans are carried forward by a powerful thrust—the Hegelian view of history as a story that "tells us," the passive addressees, of unfolding events that "have not yet occurred but are waiting to do so."

Rather than submit to the allegedly external forces of "time" and "history"—prominent figures in post-Hegelian thought—Austerlitz ventures to "go behind" them. His quest raises the question of what having a future means in light of modernity's catastrophes *and* in view of the events occurring less than a decade before 1996—the "modernist event" labeled "1989." Indeed, in resisting "the power of time," Sebald's novel reflects its immediate historical horizon and expresses our changing perspective on the very concept of the future.

Beginning with *Austerlitz*, this final part of my study turns to a broad range of works that were written after the fall of the Berlin Wall and that grapple with intellectual, cultural, and political realities after 1989. In a direct or an implicit manner, through plot, character, narrative technique, and a variety of symbolic arrangements, these works ponder the "power of time" in our immediate age. They ask what "history" may tell us, what the notion of "future" may mean now, in light of the past Fascist totalitarian state *and* in light of the recent demise of the totalitarian Soviet empire and with it the ideological wall that separated East and West.

Why 1989? Although history hardly ended in 1989, the year signals in my view a noticeable shift in our cultural and intellectual discussion of the past as it relates to the future, a change reflected in the contemporary novel. For more than a century, ideological wars were fought and questions of sociopolitical organization were debated in the context of Hegelian thinking about capital-H History, in which the past was a reservoir for formulating History's "lessons," "laws," "course," and "trajectory," giving direction and guidance to hopes for the future. Linking the past to a possible future was at the core of utopian socialist and Marxist ideas. The transience of former socioeconomic orders (say, from feudalism to capitalism) was seen as a clear indication that, like former modes of economic production, capitalism was bound to make way for a new, *possibly* more just, socioeconomic order. The events of 1989 changed this, ending—as noted in the introduction—"the romance of world history," that metaphysical tradition of thought that saw capital-H History in a manner previously reserved for "God" or "Human Nature."[2] *Austerlitz*, with its protagonist's polemic against time, among other things, marks a much broader departure from speculative thinking about capital-H History in our culture and intellectual life, away from ideas about the future that are based on claims about the nature of time, the transience of any socioeconomic order, or History's "inevitable" direction.

As I mentioned in the introduction, I agree with Amy Hungerford and others that 1989 hardly brought about a cultural or an aesthetic watershed.[3] Rather, novels such as Ian McEwan's *Black Dogs* contemplate what the future may mean now, following the downfall of what Jay Winter aptly calls the "major utopias" of the nineteenth and twentieth centuries.[4] Unlike the works I discussed in parts I and II, novels such as *Black Dogs* do not consider a specific set of historical events in the delimited context of a national history. Rather, they contemplate our personal circumstances and political lives as these have changed following the momentous collapse of Soviet Bolshevism—together with Nazism, the movement "that consumed so many in their fires," as Ian McEwan puts it in an interview. They take measure of these blazes, as the smoke emerging from them "still hangs in the air."[5]

McEwan is especially poignant in reflecting on his work and thus on contemporary literature as it engages our post-utopian realities. "I'm not a utopian writer," he says in an another interview.[6] "Once they start to act politically, utopianists are people to be feared, with all their talk of breaking eggs to make omelettes" (135).[7] Yet for McEwan this move away from utopianism does not mean an escape from the world. Rather, issues such as "climate change" and "poverty" preclude him from a pessimistic worldview, an outlook he sees as "intellectually delicious," but little more (135). "I'm with [Peter] Medawar," he concludes, "total pessimism is one more luxury of the over-fattened West" (135).

McEwan's turn to poverty and climate change—issues he dealt with in novels such as *Saturday* (2005) and *Solar* (2010)—is telling. It suggests that contemporary literature continues to engage our past, present, and future circumstances, albeit without ruminating about the "laws" and "trajectory" that characterize "history's" or "time's" presumable course. Abjuring such speculations as well as utopian fantasies, the works examined here explore such present and future concerns as genocidal violence and political terrorism by investigating *avenues of human action*. These novels are not concerned with what time or history *is*. Here are no attempts to grasp the quintessence of these concepts, as in Leo Tolstoy's *War and Peace* or Thomas Mann's *The Magic Mountain*. Nor can we discover the same utopian desires that haunt Mathieu in Jean-Paul Sartre's *Les chemins de la liberté* (*The Roads to Freedom*; 1945–49). Rather, Kazuo Ishiguro's *When We Were Orphans*, Philip Roth's *The Plot against America*, and Cormac McCarthy's *The Road* explore what having a future may mean today by examining the possibilities for ethical or political action. Turning to the past without hoping to find indications of a future society where all the contingencies of capitalism will be resolved, these novels contemplate the questions that J. M. Coetzee raised in 2008 in an address at the Kosmopolis literary festival in Barcelona, Spain. For Coetzee, in the face of global warming, rising food prices, famine, and so forth:

> The sole question that remains is whether we at the individual level and at the social and political level are prepared to put into practice what our reason tells us; whether we are prepared to act. Whether we are prepared to act is a real question, and a substantially philosophical one. For we have been asked to change the way of living, a way of living that we enjoy very much, in the name of the future, of the planet, and more specifically in the name of as yet unborn generations. And the philosophical question is what duty if any do we have to as yet unborn generations? What duty if any do we owe the planet? In another form, the question is, who is this "we" in whose name we should act? Who are we?[8]

Coetzee's and Sebald's "we" (in the monologue we began with) are one and the same: contemporaries of our post-utopian modernity living in relatively affluent societies and facing the prospect of future man-made disasters that make the very prospect of a human tomorrow uncertain. They ask, "Who are we?" by considering what constitutes meaningful human action, especially in an age that has witnessed "fires," to use McEwan's idiom, of a scale that seems to exclude human agency, indeed the future of humanity, altogether. In view of such past and possible future calamities as world wars, genocide, devastating acts of terror, and an ecological Armageddon, the works I turn to now ponder what humans as individuals may effectively *do*. Like Sebald's *Austerlitz*, they turn to "modernist events"—from the Sino-Japanese War of the late 1930s to 9/11—without offering any conclusions about the shape of time or the ultimate lessons of history. What they do investigate, however, is our capacity to affect our circumstances and hold on to the future as a viable prospect through individual, ethical, or political action.

The novels we discuss here largely refrain from suggesting what the exact nature or the explicit content of those ethical or political actions should be. Even if their characters—for example, June Tremaine of McEwan's *Black Dogs* or JC of Coetzee's *Diary of a Bad Year*—express unequivocal views about post-1945 politics or what the statist reactions to 9/11 command "us" to do, the novels avoid prescribing any specific course of action, any definitive ideological point of view. This may be an expression of the retreat from the political certainties of the twentieth century such as Jean-Paul Sartre's Maoism. Yet taken together, these works go to great length to defeat what Jonathan Lear in his discussion of Coetzee's *Diary of a Bad Year* calls "ersatz ethical thought"—substituting thinking and deliberation about ethical and political issues with the moralism of *litterature engagée*.[9] These works investigate our ability (restricted as it may be) to tackle our social, economic, ecological, and political circumstances through action, rejecting the view that we are powerless objects before forces over which we have no control. Ultimately, these works leave to readers the task of giving concrete content to ethical or political "action" (e.g, what to do to ensure the future of our planet). They give us crucial clues about how Austerlitz's "we"— contemporaries of the decades following 1989—relate to our future. If time and history—the "mise-en-scène of modernity"—are no longer useful in imagining our future, these works display how "we" nevertheless maintain a sense of what the future holds as a challenge and a promise.

None of these works reflects a trivial optimistic faith in the future or suggests that a better future is promised if we engage in political and ethical action; none of them revels in what Slavoj Žižek views as the post-1989 "great utopia of liberal capitalism," a utopia that together with "global capitalism," according to Žižek, rapidly approaches its due death.[10] On the contrary, many of the works exhibit a profound fear that we face the prospect of the complete destruction of life on earth. At the same time, however, they also indicate the possibility, via human agency, of ensuring a future worthy of its name. The future here entails no less than maintaining the prospect of humanity's survival, and to achieve this goal, we—Austerlitz's "we"—must acknowledge our ability and responsibility to act. Through stories about what "we" could have done but did not, about what we should or must be doing, the literature here retains a sense of what is possible, and a notion of hope.[11]

The Road Ahead

Once again, the works in this part of the book share crucial concerns with Hannah Arendt's thought discussed in the introduction. Arendt maintained a critical approach to modernity, to the modern state, and to the politics of her time, yet she never indulged in speculative thinking about capital-H History or fell prey to utopianism of the kind that led to the Bolshevik state. "The breaking of eggs in action never leads to anything more interesting than the breaking of eggs," Arendt notes. "The result is identical with the activity itself: it is a breaking, not an omelet."[12] Arendt viewed the Hegelian notion of *Weltgeschichte* (world history) as crucially informing those political philosophies that consider humans as a mass or an object.[13] "Radical evil," she states, "always emerges when we desire the radical good [*radikal Gutes*]."[14] In grappling with modernist events and their implications, she focuses on the capacity of individual humans to act, and thus upon action's futural implications.

As we saw in part I, Sebald's *Austerlitz* portrays the fate of a Jewish child who survived the Holocaust via the Kindertransport operation, yet the novel also alludes to the human capacity to set off, to begin anew, a central element in Arendt's thought on action. Attempts at new beginnings are also a central theme in Kazuo Ishiguro's *When We Were Orphans* and Ian McEwan's *Black Dogs* and *Atonement*, yet they focus on highly peculiar actions: Ishiguro's protagonist Christopher Banks, for example, believes he can simply rescue his long-absent parents from captivity, as if the decades since their disappearance were but a few days. McEwan's Briony Tallis repeatedly rewrites her account of a childhood crime she committed in the hope of somehow undoing the deed. This wish to bend the past, to make intervening years not count, is clearly reflected in Austerlitz's desire to view time as a fluid entity. Moreover, McEwan's and Ishiguro's protagonists' wish to do the improbable displays an affinity with Arendt's consideration of what constitutes action: according to Arendt, nothing changes the fact that "the unexpected can be expected" of humans. We can never release ourselves from our ability "to perform what is infinitely improbable."[15] In these novels, futurity comes down to the ability of individuals to perform the "improbable," to take action in situations that may seem (or in fact are) hopeless.

Philip Roth's *The Plot against America* (2004) ties futurity and action together by invoking some aspects of the past as we know it from history books *and* by imagining events that could have, but in fact did not, take place. Through its alternate history, Roth's novel also deflates the idea of historical inevitability: what Arendt in her consideration of action referred to as the "mental perplexity," the idea of an "invisible actor behind the scene" (*HC*, 185).[16] By imagining what other decisions and actions *could have* transpired, the novel emphasizes that a choice has, in fact, been made, thus affirming the capacity of humans to be agents of their fate, shapers of their history.

Finally, we will consider how after 9/11 the trope of the threatened or dead child mirrors an anxiety about the prospects of natality and of the future of mankind itself. Paul Auster's *Oracle Night* and Cormac McCarthy's *The Road* echo Arendt's concern that we live in an age that is facing the possibility of complete and ultimate destruction. Both Arendt's writings and these novels underscore the prospect that natality as such might come to an end when some deem other humans to be mere matter, nothing more than means to realize radical ideological goals. Placing the figure of the threatened child at the center of the literary imagination, these works draw the link between past modern brutality—the Holocaust or Hiroshima—and a looming future in which children do not live to see the light of day. By imagining the possible end of natality, however, they also underscore the possibility of human agency as a way to ensure the future of humankind. In imagining the possible end point as also a beginning, they gesture toward what could ensure a human tomorrow.

Hannah Arendt: Narrative and Action

As noted in the introduction, Arendt postulated that we gain a sense of human agency through narratives. Modernity's man-made catastrophes left traumatic marks on the individual and the collective psyche while unsettling our confidence in the human ability to affect any given political condition. Yet because of what she calls "insertion" and "natality," we can speak of a human history, one distinct from natural history and its subordination to the forces of nature. For Arendt, literature is both a mode of natality and a prism through which we may consider what constitutes action. Narratives, she believes, examine what represents action in the first place. In *The Human Condition*, she argues that "although everybody started his life by inserting himself into the human world through action and speech, nobody is the author or producer of his own life story" (*HC*, 184). Action emerges through narrative, and it is only "stories, the result of speech and action," that "reveal an agent" (*HC*, 184).[17] In stories, therefore, mere doing gains its full distinctiveness as human action. Narratives about humans acting thus underline our agency, and the works discussed below indicate futurity by pondering that agency. Through diverse historical and fictional settings, the novels consider the effect of human action under the conditions of modernity and thus the validity of action itself in our time.[18] By struggling with the pragmatic and ethical questions par excellence (What should I do? What should we do?), they also underline our capacity to address whatever historical conditions we may face.

The Specter of a Limbo World

Literature's probing of human agency after 1989 has gone mostly unnoticed by cultural critics in recent years. Indeed, many critics view our era as lacking a sense of human agency and as deprived of futurity altogether. This view stems from specific positions about historical consciousness in the First World. According to Andreas Huyssen, the global move to restore old urban centers, the avalanche of films that invoke cataclysmic historical events, controversies about history, and psychoanalytical literature about trauma all suggest that the "world is being musealized" with "total recall" as its trajectory.[19] Huyssen links this turn to memory with the rapid technological change, proliferation of mass media, and new modes of consumption, work, and global mobility that emerged after the Second World War. Furthermore, he claims these trends display a "displaced fear of the future" (21), in that the faster we are pushed into "a global future that does not inspire confidence, the stronger we feel the desire to slow down, the more we turn to memory for comfort" (25). The interest in the past is thus the result of a need for refuge in our turbulent, postmodern age—for a "transformation of temporality in our lives" (21)—and not a symptom of an oblivious present.

Other philosophers and critics fail, however, to acknowledge a genuine historical consciousness in Western "late capitalist," "late modern," or "postmodern" culture. They view the culture of the First World after the 1960s as "presentist": shadowed by a disconnect between the local and the distant, the present and the past. Conservative scholars such as the historian Jonathan C. D. Clark regard postmodernism, with its emphasis on identity, the questioning of traditional institutions, and its tendency toward secularism, as "a rejection of the historical": postmodern culture dehistoricizes, "since it involves the foreshortening and even discarding of the historical dimension." Privileging the present, it erases "symbols or institutions that are designated 'old'" and tends "to say little or nothing about the new social forms that are intended to flourish once some undergrowth of prejudice has been cleared."[20]

Similarly, thinkers on the left such as the historian Harry Harootunian claim that the end of the Cold War, the collapse of European Communism, and 9/11 have been accompanied by the "removal of the conception of the future, or at least its indefinite deferral."[21] What we were left with is "presentism."[22] Alain Badiou likewise views our (post-1980s) present by what it lacks: "No revolution, no political invention, no creation of anything at all. . . . We are now in a limbo world, suspended between an old, inactive dialectical figure (war and/or revolution) and a false commercial and military present that seeks to protect its future by dispensing with the present, and by erasing everything of the past that was, in the past, in the present."[23] We, citizens of the First World, claims Badiou emblematically, have lost our ability to draw meaningfully on the past in debating ideology and politics. Our culture is practically "bereft of any thinking of time."[24] The "end of ideologies" that came with the demise of Communism in Eastern Europe represents for him "nothing less than the forsaking of any novelty that could be ascribed to man," marking "a total transformation of humanity" according to the objects of global capital—or, as Slavoj Žižek puts it, the "'naturalization' of capitalism."[25]

Fredric Jameson similarly sees contemporary literature and culture as "dominated by categories of space," resulting in an inability to conceive of time with past and future as its relevant coordinates.[26] Terry Eagleton echoes that during the "dreary decades of post-1970s conservatism," our "historical sense" has grown "increasingly blunted, as it suited those in power that we should be able to imagine no alternative to the present." Nowadays, "it is not anarchists for whom anything goes, but starlets, newspaper editors, stockbrokers and corporation executives. The norm now is money; but since money has absolutely no principles or identity of its own, it is no kind of norm at all." Whereas during previous decades (especially the 1960s), "utopia lay just beneath the cobblestones of Paris," the 1980s and 1990s have witnessed "a rejection of the very idea of global politics."[27]

Badiou, Žižek, Jameson, Eagleton, and other critics in the Neo-Marxist tradition thus see a diminishing sense of the "historical past" and with it what Jameson views as the "wholesale liquidation of futurity."[28] According to Jameson only a few periods previous to ours have proven "as incapable of framing immediate alternatives for themselves let alone of imagining utopian alternatives to the status quo." The "end of temporality" or the "crisis of historicity" is the "virtual effacement of that past and future that can alone define a present in the first place."[29]

Like Jameson, Walter Benn Michaels views our era as a "posthistoricist," oblivious age. In *The Shape of the Signifier: 1967 to the End of History*, he argues that works such as Toni Morrison's *Beloved* (1987), Art Spiegelman's *Maus* (1986), and Leslie Marmon Silko's *Almanac of the Dead* (1991) indicate that our age has become victim to the illusion that fundamental "disagreement" about the ideal form of social organization and of political institutions has all but vanished.[30] Lacking historical consciousness, specifically the recognition that all given forms of economic and social organization are transient, our culture is thus "posthistoricist." For Michaels, "posthistoricist" ideology implies that 1989 marked the demise not only of the socialist superstate but also of the idea that given sociopolitical conditions should be debated, that 1989 ended our obligation to argue about the distribution of resources, the organization of labor, and the division of wealth. Our contemporary posthistoricist age is thus, according to Michaels, effectively postpolitical (20–21). Those who speak of our "postideological era," he notes (quoting Slavoj Žižek), are not interested in creating new realities but rather are busy with changing themselves, "replacing the devotion to a 'Cause' with the commitment to 'new forms of (sexual, spiritual, aesthetic . . .) subjective practice.' "[31]

As history, ideology, and politics appear to fade away, so does literature's futural dimension, claims Michaels. In Morrison's *Beloved* and Spiegelman's *Maus* he discovers a tendency to turn the past into a mere resource for the enhancement of individual and group identity. Rather than seeking ways to overcome economic and social inequality in the history of slavery or in the Holocaust (Michaels's main concern), these and similar works turn a traumatic past into a constitutive of identity (133), with the factual result that "history" becomes "memory" (136).[32] Through "talking with the dead," reenacting the past, "facing horror" (142), and similar motifs of "posthistoricist" culture, these and similar novels do not expect the reader to understand a historical event (144) but rather to become "co-owner" of it (145): they thus enhance who one is and, ultimately, the given cultural-political conditions. Michaels concludes that in these works, "history" becomes irrelevant for "making our society more just," that is, for promoting "equal opportunity" (167) and the redistribution of wealth (168): "What we owe the victims of injustice," he proclaims, "is justice, not a causal account of how they came to be victimized" (167). Our concern should be with inequality, material ownership, and "inherited property" (168) and not with history as the constitutive narrative of our identities.[33]

Just as Jameson, and Eagleton before him, could see no more in post-modern literature than depthless, trivial kitsch, Michaels sees in novels by Morrison, Spiegelman, and Silko the evasion of any political engagement.[34] Like Jameson, he dismisses the possibility that novels such as *Beloved*, in presenting protagonists who "go behind time," can challenge the epistemological and ontological locus of the past as something completed. And thus he rejects the possibility that they also question the stability of given economic and social circumstances. Yet as Linda Hutcheon in *A Poetics of Postmodernism* convincingly shows, toying with realist and modernist temporal structures in postmodern literature is, in effect, a "re-evaluation of and a dialogue with the past in light of the present" rather than the mere acceptance of the given.[35]

To Start at Ground Level

Questioning Walter Benn Michaels's diagnosis, I see novels such as Toni Morrison's *Beloved*, Art Spiegelman's *Maus*, and the works discussed below as actually tying together the past and the future, as thoughtfully engaging social, political, and ethical circumstances and thus as signaling futurity. They do so not through speculative thinking about the "essence" or "course" of capital-H History, nor by imagining the elimination of social injustice in the spirit of nineteenth- and twentieth-century leftist-utopian thought. Rather, they investigate the human capacity to reduce social and political unfairness by taking concrete, often mundane action, thus affecting tangible political conditions.

Here I follow Arendt and, to some extent, critics such as Hans Ulrich Gumbrecht, Eelco Runia, and Amy Elias, who in their recent work address issues of time, history, and the role of the past in contemporary literature and culture. Gumbrecht, for example, sees the birth of a new "presence culture," which aims at experiencing the past by capturing the tangible materiality of objects, smells, and colors without suggesting what history's trajectory might be.[36]

The historian and psychologist Eelco Runia argues that "presence" reveals how the past can enable us "to *rewrite* our stories about ourselves."[37] The contemporary shift to dealing with time and history through creative modes of commemoration, Runia suggests, does not reveal a postmodern cultural desire to find refuge from unpleasant social conditions in a stylized past. Rather, our engagement with the past is an expression of the "creative" human faculty to "become what we as yet do not know."[38]

What is significantly absent in both Gumbrecht's and Runia's emphasis on "presence," however, is an acknowledgment of the role of a future-related, ethically or politically motivated interest in the past. In their desire to move away from the theoretical commitments and aesthetic preferences of Marxist criticism, Gumbrecht and Runia discount contemporary longing to engage the past as a means of advancing human causes. In our case, while the literary turn to the past can be seen to express a wish to experience what Fascism may have felt like for those caught in its brutal thrust, a novel like *Austerlitz* is hardly confined to the wish to relive the history it invokes. Rather, this and other contemporary historical fiction undeniably include the drive to keep our own circumstances "unfrozen"—in David Grossman's term—by way of revisiting the past, and thus to be open for ethical or political engagement.[39]

Amy Elias emphasizes precisely this point in her discussion of the "metahistorical romance," contemporary literature that self-consciously engages the past.[40] Elias regards fragmented narratives such as *Beloved* and *Maus* as works marked by modernity's cataclysms and by changes in our conception of history following the philosophical "linguistic turn."[41] As I mentioned in the introduction, Elias views novels such as Thomas Pynchon's *Gravity's Rainbow* (1973) and D. M. Thomas's *The White Hotel* (1981) as articulating a posttraumatic imaginary—a literary world that "bears striking similarities to those produced by traumatized consciousness."[42] According to Elias, portraying the past as "terrifying" by imposing literary images and innovative metaphors (think of Grossman's "Nazi Beast"; see chapter 9) reflects a significant aspect of futurity: these are works that might lead the reader to "contemplation and enactment of ethical action," to thought and deliberation with others regarding social, economic, and political conditions.[43]

Elias's suggestion that historical narratives can affect how we relate to our given conditions points squarely to Arendt's notion (quoting Isak Dinesen) that "all sorrows can be borne if you put them into a story or tell a story about them." Indeed, novels such as *Beloved, Maus*, and J. M. Coetzee's *Disgrace* (1999) ponder the possibility of bearing pain—the capacity of humans, inscribed at birth, "to set something into motion" (*HC*, 177), to begin anew.

Portraying worlds marked by troubled genealogies, *Beloved*, *Maus*, *Disgrace*, and the novels I discuss below offer images of past horrors *as well as* metaphors, plots, and symbolic constellations that signal the possibility of a new beginning in Arendt's sense. A novel about a mother struggling to live with the memory of a daughter she has killed to spare her the destiny of slavery, *Beloved*, for example, also traces how Sethe,

Denver, and Paul D. try to proceed beyond the abyss: Paul D. tells the mourning mother at the end of their journey back in time, "me and you, we got more yesterday than anybody. We need some kind of tomorrow."[44] While *Beloved* is "an act of memory and love for the child who could not live for her story to be told," as Timothy Parrish has noted, and "a defiant . . . expression of the belief that history cannot be destroyed—cannot be written away," Paul D.'s emphasis on "some kind of tomorrow" signals the work's underlying futural dimension.[45]

If making this "tomorrow" tangible in Morrison's *Beloved* means turning to the story of a dead child, in J. M. Coetzee's *Disgrace* it comes about through the acceptance of a new life.[46] Robbed and brutally raped by three men on her ranch in South Africa's East Cape, Lucy Lurie is unwilling to separate that act of violence from the decades of racial oppression in her country. Pregnant with the child of one of her assailants, Lucy nevertheless decides not to have an abortion. To her bewildered father, David, who cannot believe she will become the mother of a child conceived in rape, she says: "Should I choose against the child because of who its father is?"[47] Lucy agrees with David that staying on her farm and learning to cope with the incalculable reality of postapartheid South Africa mean enduring humiliation, but she decides that carrying the child in her womb and raising it on that land also mean bearing a human who will signal the country's painful new beginning. From the position of the cruelty she suffered, she opts to see what remains possible, even promising, despite her immense pain: "But perhaps that is a good point to start from again. Perhaps that is what I must learn to accept. To start at ground level."[48]

Thus, some of the most notable works of literature after 1989 explore futurity through metaphors of new beginnings (*Austerlitz*), of action (*When We Were Orphans*), and of natality (*Disgrace*). They consider the human capacity to affect the present and shape the future by beginning anew, by attempting to carry out the improbable, or simply by taking concrete, mundane actions. Other works employ alternate histories to make us aware of the role of choice in shaping historical events, suggesting that we should not lose sight of our role in forming our fates.

Significantly, the literature here does not explore the effects of any suprapersonal power or principle behind the scene. Rather, it focuses on the respective "contributions" of character and circumstance in shaping the present, on what we can and perhaps should do in light of modernity's recent catastrophes and those possibly to come. This literature makes it difficult to ignore our capacity to form our circumstances and thereby "produce the future." Without invoking the Cartesian "I" or returning to the Kantian notion of an autonomous human subject, the novels here discover, even in the face of the darkest past, what humans are capable of: both the complete devastation of lives and habitats and the capacity to sustain them or create new ones.

12 Arresting Time: W. G. Sebald's *Austerlitz*

Probing the Spectacle of History

W. G. Sebald's masterful novel *Austerlitz* displays almost the entire formal and thematic assemblage of contemporary literature after 1989 as it engages modernity's manmade catastrophes. Borrowing from such diverse sources as *The Odyssey* and Wittgenstein's philosophy and employing the dense syntax of the interior monologue, *Austerlitz* reads like a medley of novelistic forms—it is realist, psychological, historical, modernist, and postmodernist all at the same time. Invoking by turns the rapid economic growth of the nineteenth century, colonialism, the Second World War, the Holocaust, and the Cold War, the novel offers a critical commentary on two hundred years of European history.[1] Fascinated with the ghosts that haunt today's Europe, *Austerlitz* is a poetic reflection on both the afterlife of the past and the human condition at the beginning of the twenty-first century.[2]

Earlier in this book, we observed that *Austerlitz* derives its unique force not only from Sebald's historical themes but also from grappling with modernity's idea of time: the novel struggles with the notion of "time" and "history" as external forces to which "we" humans are simply subjected. Yet Sebald's work also challenges "the power of time" in several distinctive, interlinked ways through the life stories of Jacques Austerlitz and his younger acquaintance, the German narrator. *Austerlitz* tells a story of a past that cannot be relegated to oblivion; it examines the relationship between rationalist modernity and the Nazi genocide; and, finally, with its use of visual images and distended syntax, it produces its very own sense of time, one that does not proceed in a linear manner or divide easily into the distinct realms of past, present, and future. Written in the 1990s, the novel turns to modernity's abyss and asks how "we," contemporaries of the era following the man-made catastrophes and the major utopias of the twentieth century, may hold on to a notion of tomorrow as the realm of the possible. *Austerlitz* approaches this question by exploring the human capacity to begin anew.

Austerlitz's polemic against the ontology of a separable past, present, and future points back to Sebald's interest in questions of historical remembrance in postwar Germany.[3] Throughout his writing, resisting "time" meant for Sebald moving beyond the historical forgetting that characterized Konrad Adenauer's West Germany as well as the vocabulary of established writers such as Grass and Walser and the thematic and formal choices of his own generation. In *Austerlitz*, Sebald does this by telling the emblematic story of a Jewish survivor of the Holocaust. Born in 1934 in Prague, his protagonist is a middle-aged historian who, as noted earlier, was one of the children of the Kindertransport.[4] Thus, in *Austerlitz*, survival and disaster, end points and beginnings, all remain inseparably connected. In one of the most moving scenes of the novel, the narrator imagines the moment in which Austerlitz, like many other Jewish children, was forced to bid his mother farewell in Prague's Wilsonova Station (173–74). The traumatic end of Austerlitz's quiet childhood is also his rescue. Unlike so many Jewish children of that age, he will survive. Yet his is a rebirth under a dark star: when he arrives in the small town of Bala, Wales, he is adopted by a Calvinist priest and his wife. Wanting to save his soul, "innocent as it was of the Christian faith" (138), the couple force him to give up all his belongings and erase his entire previous existence, including his own name.

Growing up as Dafydd Elias, Austerlitz will spend most of his adult life trying to recover the story behind his actual name, his origin. His tale thus details the fate of countless survivors of the Holocaust, whose lives were ruined first by Nazism and then by forgetting or by repression: "As far as I was concerned," Austerlitz reflects back on his initial approach to the past, "the world ended in the late nineteenth century" (139). As a scholar, he chooses early on to avoid the twentieth century and thus to suppress his childhood traumas: "I dared go no further than [the nine-

teenth century]," he admits, "although in fact the whole history of architecture and civilization of the bourgeois age, the subject of my research,
pointed in the direction of the catastrophic events already casting their
shadows before them at the time" (140). The result of Austerlitz's repression is his complete mental breakdown in the summer of 1992 (140).

Although *Austerlitz* documents with painful precision the end
points—Nazism, the traumas that came with survival, and their debilitating effects on one person's psyche—the novel also presents distinct
images of new beginnings, with the past offering points of departure.
The Kindertransport is one such instance of what Arendt discusses as
the human capacity to begin. The interplay between end points and new
beginnings also runs through the novel's attention to Austerlitz's unique
name. Austerlitz reclaims his own name—Jacques Austerlitz—through
an encounter with a charismatic history teacher, André Hilary (68–74).
It is Hilary who encourages him to think about the past in ways beyond
those that historiography offers: "We try to reproduce the reality" of
the past, Hilary tells his students. "Our concern with history. . . is a
concern with preformed images already imprinted on our brains, images at which we keep staring while the truth lies elsewhere, away from
it all, somewhere as yet undiscovered" (71–72). In other words, the past
should compel us to go beyond existing "images," that is, beyond existing knowledge and given historical narratives. Turning to the past and
making it meaningful, searching for "the truth" that lies "elsewhere," demands active engagement, a process in the course of which one evolves.
The encounter with the past is not only an opportunity to face its traumas but also a chance to be personally changed in the process. Indeed,
Austerlitz notes, the more often Hilary mentioned the word "Austerlitz"
as he taught his students of the December 1805 battle of Austerlitz, "the
more it really did become my own name, and the more clearly I thought
I saw that what had at first seemed like an ignominious flaw was changing into a bright light always hovering before me, as promising as the
sun of Austerlitz itself when it rose above the December mists" (72). The
battle of Austerlitz, like all modern man-made disasters, is not only a tale
from history's book of calamities but also an opportunity to consider the
past's value for one's own life. Austerlitz's interest in the event and its
surrounding historical narratives allows him to discover in the landscape
of the battlefield both the bodies left behind and "the sun."

Another crucial new beginning is Austerlitz's visit to Penelope Peacefull's antiquarian bookstore right after he is released from the hospital
following his mental collapse. There he overhears voices of women in a
radio broadcast that, he says, "cast such a spell over me that I entirely

forgot the engravings lying before me, and stood there as still as if on no account must I let a single syllable emerging from the rather scratchy radio set escape me" (141). The voices of the women describing their experiences in the Kindertransport trigger Austerlitz's turn to his origin, signaling the beginning of a growing awareness of the events that brought about his breakdown. As he bids farewell to Penelope Peacefull, who, like Homer's Penelope, might have waited for him to return from his long journey all along, he sits for an hour on a bench, watching as, on this "sunny day," starlings march up and down the grass (142).[5] In this spring moment of natural regeneration, where the darkness of his past is followed by an encounter with the sun, Austerlitz begins his journey back in time.

His quest leads him back to Prague, where, much like Ulysses, he encounters his childhood in the figure of his nursemaid, Vera Ryšanová. Through her he learns what happened before he was sent to Wales, of the persecution of Prague's Jews, and of his mother's later deportation to Theresienstadt and then to the death camps in the East. Visiting Theresienstadt, Austerlitz will have arrived at the place for which he had set off from Penelope Peacefull's store. Walking through the streets of the Czech fortress city, visiting the ghetto museum, it seems to him now as if he has entered the timeless kingdom of the dead. He senses, even though only for a while, that the sixty thousand Jews who were crammed into the walls of the ghetto "had never been taken away after all . . . that they were incessantly going up and down the stairs . . . filling the entire space occupied by the air" (200).

As in Toni Morrison's *Beloved*, Austerlitz's encounter with the ghosts of the past hardly signals a "posthistoricist" escape from the present.[6] Rather, his encounter with both real (Vera's) and imagined voices from the past indicates the capacity to find a way to reengage with life. This means that Austerlitz must both uncover his lost history and turn his attention to broader political conditions. Indeed, as much as Austerlitz's mind is given to the fate of Jews during the Holocaust, it is also given to the sufferings of some of modernity's other victims—to the pain inflicted on the Congolese by Belgian colonial rule and thus to colonialism as such (9). Invoking the Holocaust, the novel furthermore accounts for the terror of life under totalitarian rule. Austerlitz's recollection of his visit to Marienbad as a child before the Second World War is entwined with a recollection of the Czechoslovak Socialist Republic (SSR) in 1972, only four years after the brutal crushing of the Prague Spring. The palimpsest-like narrative refers to the "two uniformed motorcyclists" wearing "leather crash helmets and black goggles," their "carbines . . .

slung at an angle over their right shoulders" (207) and how they made Austerlitz deeply "uneasy." Austerlitz also recalls his "abysmal sense of distress" (211) when he woke up on the second day of this visit. Soon after, Austerlitz literally escapes the SSR (217). His visit to the post-Communist Czech Republic in the 1990s thus gestures toward the new beginning that came in 1989.

The dual role of remembrance as both an assumption of burdens *and* a sign of new beginnings is most evident at Austerlitz's and the narrator's final parting, when Austerlitz entrusts the narrator with the keys to his London house on Alderney Street. "I could stay there," the narrator says, "and study the black and white photographs which, one day, would be all that was left of his life" (293). Since the narrator is writing *after* this and all other events, we may read the entire plot as the outcome of this gesture; the novel is not only a recounting of Austerlitz's quest for his past but also the product of the narrator's own ability to set off. The narrator crafts a text out of what he only heard from his Jewish friend, creating a work that also includes the events of his own life after his encounter with Austerlitz. *Austerlitz* is simultaneously the protagonist's story of unearthing the past and the narrator's story of becoming.[7] As if following the advice of André Hilary, the narrator does not attempt to "reproduce the reality" of the past, to participate in "the *spectacle of history*." Rather, he seeks—through the novel we hold in our hands—his own "truth," what he himself needs to discover.

What Lies Underneath

Aware of the pitfalls of the spectacle of history, *Austerlitz* draws a line connecting rationalist-empiricist notions of time, capitalist modernity, and "instrumental reason." "Time," against which Austerlitz polemicizes so vehemently, becomes a central tool of capitalist modernity, an expression of the brutal forces that exterminated humans in the death camps. Sebald's sermon against time is delivered in Greenwich, the ultimate signifier of the economic, scientific, and technological changes of post-Enlightenment Europe. The need to regulate railway transportation in the 1840s brought about the standardization of all local times in England, and in 1884, Greenwich Time became World Time, with Greenwich as the world's prime meridian—the topographic marker of a modern universe based on the brisk transportation of goods and individuals.[8] Austerlitz's Greenwich monologue refers to the novel's first scene, the 1967 meeting of the narrator and Austerlitz in the Antwerp railway station (7). Here, Austerlitz takes his German acquaintance through the

Centraal Station and remarks how entering passengers are "seized by a sense of being beyond the profane, in a cathedral consecrated to international traffic and trade" (10).

Austerlitz underlines the crushing force of modern time, noting that the station's clock is placed "even above the royal coat of arms," becoming the "governor of a new omnipotence" (12). This time—what Elizabeth Deeds Ermarth calls "the time of project, the time of Newton and Kant, the time of clocks and capital"—obliges all to adjust their activities to its demands.[9] Austerlitz sees this as the decisive mark of the modern era: not until the clocks were standardized did "time truly reign supreme," allowing us to "hasten through gigantic spaces separating us from each other" (12).

The narrator views Austerlitz's lecture as "a kind of historical metaphysics" (13), the core of which involves railway transportation and train stations—spaces of "blissful happiness and profound misfortune" (34) that hold Austerlitz "in the grip of dangerous and entirely incomprehensible currents of emotion" (33–34) and lead him to "thoughts of the agony of leave-taking and the fear of foreign places" (14). Train stations are for Austerlitz the signifier of his personal fate, marking his leave-taking from his mother in Prague's Wilsonova Station in 1939. Yet in his "historical metaphysics," the entire railway system embodies "the idea of a network" based on what Wittgenstein called "family resemblances," by which extensions of a certain concept word may be united in a system of similarities (33).[10]

This system is first seen in London's Liverpool Street Station. Covered by smoky darkness caused by diesel oil and locomotive steam, the station lures and appalls both narrator and protagonist. In their descriptions, this place emerges as the crypt of the modern age, "a kind of entrance to the underworld" (127–28). The grounds of the station served in the past to house the Order of Saint Mary of Bethlehem and the Bedlam hospital for "the insane and other destitute persons" (129). When, during demolition work in 1984 at Broad Street Station, the skeletons of over four hundred people are found "underneath a taxi rank" (130), Austerlitz is drawn to the site to unearth their story, in turn invoking the network organizing this marked space. The modern consciousness of temporality, the destruction of space and time brought about by railway transportation, is set in relation to the disregard for human life and human remains: before work on the construction of the two northeast terminals began, "poverty-stricken quarters were forcibly cleared" (132). "Vast quantities" of soil mixed with human bones were removed from the site to enable the placement of railway lines, which "on the engineers'

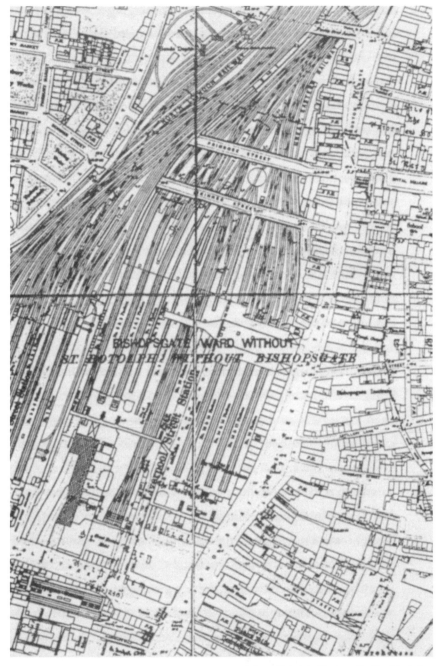

FIGURE 7 A nineteenth-century map of Bishopsgate Ward. From W. G. Sebald's *Austerlitz* (Munich: Carl Hanser Verlag, 2001), 191.

plan looked like muscles and sinews in an anatomical atlas" (132). The burial site is now nothing more than a "gray-brown morass, a no-man's land where not a living soul stirred," and the symbols of a once-verdant nature—the little river, the ditches and ponds, the elms and the mulberry tree—are all but gone (132). The symbolism could not be clearer: humans and human remains are removed from their "natural" place, while nature itself is crushed by the nonhuman, indeed inhuman, body of modernity—a body whose threatening muscle, as the image inserted in the narrative suggests (133), is that of railway transportation.[11] Only railway tracks are left, spaces of transition where trains carrying their material and human loads rush back and forth.

The consequences of modernity are thus unveiled during Austerlitz's visit to Theresienstadt. Here the "star-shaped" fortification of Breendonk from the seventeenth century (15), the octagonal observation room of Greenwich (98), the star-shaped flower at the entrance of his childhood house (151), and the star-shaped form of Theresienstadt itself come together. Theresienstadt is thus "the model of a world made by reason and regulated in all conceivable respects" (199), a world enabled by standardized time and the modern temporal consciousness reflected in railway transportation. In Theresienstadt, time and the railroad achieve their unity as two elements in the nexus of modernity and barbarism. They participate in and perpetuate the cycle of ruthless rationalism embodied in the reference to Newton's idea that time is a river like the Thames (100)—in the ever-growing demand for more production, more consumption, and more movement.

Austerlitz's polemic against time is thus connected to his study of "the architectural style of the capitalist era" (34) and of "the compulsive sense of order and the tendency toward monumentalism evident in law courts and penal institutions, railway stations and stock exchanges, opera houses and lunatic asylums and the dwellings built to rectangular grid patterns for the labor force" (33)—a "sense" that culminated in Theresienstadt. Modernity's culture of time signals freedom from the boundaries of nature, but it also signals an all-encompassing drive to subjugate all aspects of human life to the demands of capitalist modernity, including, eventually, the transformation of humans into "material" in the death camps.

It is here that Austerlitz, the literary figure, and Sebald, the author, seem to be speaking the same language: a critique of the enlightened, capitalist world in the tradition of the Frankfurt school, with a strong emphasis on the alienation of humans from nature—"the context" in which they "originally" belonged.[12] Although Sebald is careful not to identify either the narrator or the protagonist with himself, Austerlitz's "historical metaphysics," his *Kulturkritik* lament echoing the rhetoric of Marx, Adorno, and Foucault, unquestionably results in a dark allegorical philosophy of history, in what Andreas Huyssen has described as Sebald's "conceptual framework": writing that is indeed "too closely tied to metaphysics and to the apocalyptic philosophy of history so prominent in the German tradition."[13] To be sure, on more than one occasion, Sebald himself voiced concerns regarding "the liberal dreams" of the nineteenth century, in which humanity was to consist of "emancipated, autonomous individuals."[14] Humanity, however, Sebald maintained, became instead "a mass" that, once brought to a boil through pressure from outside, "becomes fluid, and then gaslike [*gasförmig*]." Although mobility may have seemed "from an economical standpoint" a positive development, in Germany it was nevertheless the subject of a "dialectics" that led to catastrophe.[15]

Sebald's affinity with Benjaminian metaphysics and his pessimistic view of modernity combine a lament over the decline of nature, of educational institutions, and of culture with more general discontent over the fact that many in his sleepy German hometown now drive BMWs.[16] He is convinced that most subjects of the modern culture of consumption suffer under "the conditions of the present" and that the mountains of painkillers used in a country such as Germany deliver the proof of collective mental anguish—anguish whose cause lies ultimately in the beliefs and practices of the "enlightened" capitalist world.[17] His literary archeologies trace the "aberration" of the human species[18] via an investigation into the genealogy of historical phenomena: how the individual psyche is determined by family history, how family history in Germany was determined by the realities of the German middle class in the 1920s and 1930s, how these conditions were fixed by the history of industrialization in Europe and in the end by the natural history of the human species.[19] Sebald's *kulturkritische* notions amount at times to a questionable teleology in which modernity is all too clearly configured as necessarily leading to Theresienstadt. As J. J. Long and Mark Anderson noted, for Sebald, Theresienstadt is only a manifestation of the *longue durée* of European modernity.[20] Indeed, the reader is expected to find inscribed in Austerlitz's name the modern, Napoleonic "historical paradigm,"[21] the idea of a forcefully united Europe under one economic, political, and symbolic hegemony.

It is precisely this "paradigm" of organizing, aggressive rationality that is echoed in Austerlitz's Greenwich monologue, especially in the ironic invocation of Newton's view of time as a neutral entity. Modernity's deification of standardized time is challenged in the monologue in Greenwich by the voice of the one speaking, a figure longing for a different, fundamentally Romantic "paradigm," a temporal consciousness that can, he argues, still be found "in many parts of the earth governed to this day less by time than by the weather" (101). Read in this light, Austerlitz's polemic is not only a poetic challenge to the temporal consciousness of the modern age, the practices of accelerated production, consumption, and movement. It is also a challenge to the "ultimate" logic of modernity, a logic that removes humans from the "natural," "true," and "authentic" and is as much reflected in mechanized mass agriculture as in the Fascist cataclysms.[22]

"Things One Would Never Have Anticipated"

More than simply a critique of time as a deity in the kingdom of rationalist, capitalist modernity, *Austerlitz* is a work that poetically creates a different sense of time by maintaining a tension between the flow of the plot and moments that shatter linear time. To put it differently, *Austerlitz* alternates between what Frank Kermode calls *chronos*, the successive repetition of the same, and *kairos*, events of "intemporal significance."[23] Clocks tell time, but Sebald's prose uses "time effects" to allow readers to experience time in ways different from "the time of project, the time of Newton and Kant, the time of clocks and capital."[24]

Austerlitz signals, in fact, a way to move beyond the end point of modernity, with its oppressive culture of time, by poetically disrupting modern temporality—its speed, its obedience to forward movement, and its logic of production and consumption. In the novel's longest sentence (236–44), for example, the imprisonment of humans in Theresienstadt under unimaginable conditions—enacted with "crazed administrative zeal" (241) and with the help of clocks that keep the "system" running (241)—is countered by the sentence's near-limitless elasticity. Creating its own temporality, one diametrically opposed to the demands of a rationalized culture driven by the need to "move on," this sentence allows no rest, no quick absorption of its referent into our conceptual systems. No clear pattern is discernible in the sentence's labyrinthine sequences—moving from the absurdity of the Red Cross delegation's visit (242–44) to the Nazi propaganda film made in the ghetto (244)—which offer us bits and pieces of an unimaginable reality.

Sebald's masterful employment of time effects is also evident in the description of Austerlitz's journey from Prague through Pilsen in western Bohemia to the West:

All I remember of Pilsen, where we stopped for some time, said Austerlitz, is that I went out on the platform to photograph the capital of a cast-iron column which had touched some chord of recognition in me. What made me uneasy at the sight of it, however, was not the question whether the complex form of the capital, now covered with a puce-tinged encrustation, had really impressed itself on my mind when I passed through Pilsen with the children's transport in the summer of 1939, but the idea, ridiculous in itself, that this cast-iron column, which with its scaly surface seemed almost to approach the nature of a living being, might remember me and was, if I may so put it, said Austerlitz, a witness to what I could no longer recollect myself. (221)

Here we are not just reading *about* time but also *experiencing* time, and in a way that does not adhere to a standardized, unified, linear form. Sebald's verbosity, the stretchy syntax, the shifting from one tense to another within the paragraph ("I remember" and "we stopped"), his zigzagging between an anthropomorphized object's being "a witness" and the "I" that can no longer "recollect," the irritating diversions of such gestures as "ridiculous in itself," "seemed almost to," "if I may so put it," and the muddled rhythm created by the repetitive "said Austerlitz" all extend the duration of time. The placement of a visual image— a photo of a steel-and-glass construction, taken in a train station—in proximity to the scene (220) further denies easy progression: we stop, try to interpret a blurry image with an unclear potential relation to Austerlitz's narrative, to detect its details and link it to other images in the book.[25] Rather than conventionally enhancing and reinforcing the narrative, Sebald's images are multilayered and opaque, as with the photo of the porcelain statue of a hero on horseback (197). They demand attention, concentration, and indeed considerable time. As Sebald himself noted, the images in his works have not only the purpose of "verification" but also the "function" of "arresting time." While fiction is an art form that moves forward in time and thus is hardly capable of halting "the passage of time," Sebald claims, visual art takes us "out of time" and "is in a sense a form of redemption" (41). Photographs "act like barriers or weirs which stem the flow" (42).[26] While dwelling on these images, modernity's efficiency-driven temporality is suspended. Thus, the time of reading itself becomes an element of the book's temporal fabric. Continuing the modernist tradition of Proust's *À la recherche du temps perdu* and Thomas Mann's *The Magic Mountain*, *Austerlitz* both thematizes time and creates his own sense of it, with deceleration, the reversal of modern time's gallop, at its core.

As we have seen, the life that led to Austerlitz's mental collapse in 1992 does not end in melancholy or renunciation. In the same paragraph in which he tells the narrator of his descent into the mental void, Austerlitz also reveals what brought him to new life the following spring (140): remembrance, which, like Sebald's entire work, is a reflection on life after catastrophe, an affirmation of life in the face of destruction, rather than a fixation on the past's disasters and the dead themselves. "Melancholy," Sebald noted, "is something different from depression. While depression makes it impossible to conceive or to mediate, melancholy . . . allows one to be reflective . . . to develop things one would never have anticipated."[27] Melancholy is thus an integral part of finding in a grim past a sense of beginning, of something that may well come to be. Melancholy, Sebald elaborates, has nothing to do with the will to die (*Todessucht*). It is rather "a form of resistance" (*Widerstand*). The function of melancholy in art is not reactive: "The depiction of calamity encompasses *the possibility* of its overcoming."[28] Disaster allows us to view circumstances we faced in the past or face today as indicating a prospect, an ability to react to what is and to develop an active position vis-à-vis what might come. Sebald's notion of melancholy as "resistance" is the unwillingness simply to accept any catastrophe as an inevitable event or as a past occurrence to be left behind. On the contrary: telling and retelling the story of destruction not only testifies to history's traumas but also investigates the role humans actively play—and can continue to play—in their own histories.

Sebald's antiquarian manner, his uncompromising, deliberate slowness, allows us—through the act of reading, through reflecting on and debating what we read—to experience time as always open to human defiance. *Austerlitz* thus indicates how significant works of contemporary literature (and thus of our culture of time) are marked, not by a radical retreat from historical consciousness or the disappearance of historicity, but rather by the pursuit of a different way to approach both: by searching in the telling moments of modernity for a way to advance, not least through what Sebald labels "resistance." Well aware of the void left by the demise of the grand ideologies of the twentieth century and highly skeptical of the desirability of any new redemptive scenarios, *Austerlitz* holds on to a notion of a future in the form of such humble abilities as seeing the starlings in spring. Without "History" to tell us what was and what should be in a commanding manner, the capacity to begin suffices.

13 To Do Something, to Begin

The Fatal Quality Called Utopia: Ian McEwan,
Black Dogs

Twenty years after the fall of the Berlin Wall and the end
of the Cold War, contemporary Anglo-American literature has begun to assess the magnitude of the events labeled "1989."[1] Works such as Ian McEwan's 1992 *Black
Dogs* and J. M. Coetzee's 2007 *Diary of a Bad Year* invoke 1989 thematically and in a direct manner, while others—Kazuo Ishiguro's 2000 *When We Were Orphans* and
Ian McEwan's 2001 *Atonement*, for example—reflect it
only implicitly. Yet all consider the link between past and
future and in particular examine what a sense of the future implies after the end of the ideological debate between capitalist democracy and state socialism.

Ian McEwan's 1992 *Black Dogs* is organized as a pru-
dent memoir, with a "preface" (xiii–xxiv) and four distinctive historical sections that convey critical distance,
while the entirety of the novel itself is tied both to the
catastrophes of the mid-twentieth century and to the historic events of 1989. It was, in fact, the collapse of Communism in Europe, McEwan has noted, that allowed him
to focus as a writer on the Second World War as a defining event in his personal life and in our era.[2] Following
his 1990 psychological spy thriller *The Innocent*, which

revisits Cold War Berlin, *Black Dogs* uses a symbolically charged relationship to examine the intellectual-political debates that determined European intellectual life from the rise of Communism up to 1989 and asks what the future might mean after the collapse of Communist utopianism in Europe.[3]

The novel's plot is driven by the news coming from Berlin in November 1989, news that has finally moved the narrator, forty-year-old Jeremy, to complete a literary project he long had in mind. The owner of a small publishing company, Jeremy wanted for years to write a memoir of his in-laws' turbulent relationship. In 1988 he had actually begun to interview his ailing mother-in-law, June Tremaine, yet it is only as the Berlin Wall comes down that Jeremy sets his mind on completing this task. Because the struggle between June and her husband, Bernard Tremaine, revolved around utopian-Marxist politics—its sources, course, and prospects—Jeremy's quest to make sense of their lives also involves reflecting on what future-oriented politics may mean after 1989.

Immediately after the border between East and West Berlin opens, Jeremy visits Berlin with his father-in-law. During these momentous days, Jeremy discovers the explanation for the lifelong conflict that defined the marriage of June and Bernard Tremaine, the same clash that shaped the lives of many progressive European intellectuals after the Second World War. Like many other young intellectuals of their time, June and Bernard joined the British Communist Party after the war. They did so with the hope that the ideology that helped defeat Fascism would now bring about "a sane, just world free of war and class oppression."[4] They wanted to be associated with what was "youthful, lively, intelligent and daring" (5). As the young couple talked about their plans for the future, June tells Jeremy, they decided to "forgive the [Communist] party its stupidity at the beginning of the [Second World] war, and to join [the party] as soon as there was peace. . . . Marx, Lenin, Stalin, the way forward—we agreed on everything. . . . We'd founded a private utopia, and it was only a matter of time before the nations of the world followed our example" (35).

Yet soon after their marriage in 1946, as the young couple goes on a hiking tour through Languedoc, their shared vision of realizing utopia in our time dissolves. When Bernard, the gifted young entomologist, decides to add a magnificent ruddy darter to his collection, placing the precious insect into "the killing bottle," as June puts it, she snaps and accuses him of being "cold, theoretical, arrogant" (54). She charges that Bernard's ideology comes, not from a genuine love of "creation," but simply from his need "to control it, label it, arrange it in rows" (55). It is less "injustice" that motivates Bernard's politics "so much as untidiness"; not "the brotherhood of man" so much as "the efficient organization of man . . . a society as neat as a barracks, justified by scientific theories" (55). June senses that by joining the Communist Party, she and her husband did not engage the present political circumstances in any ethically meaningful way but rather "used" the "wretchedness" of others to "mask" their own (20).

By juxtaposing June and Bernard, *Black Dogs* engages both European intellectual and political life from the postwar era to 1989 and the question of what the future means after the fall of the Berlin Wall and the utopian ideology that sustained it. As Bernard finally understands from the perspective of November 1989, his political path began with what Isaiah Berlin described as "the fatal quality of utopias" (66). Bernard explains to Jeremy his state of mind during the decade he was a party member: "If I know for certain how to bring humanity to peace, justice, happiness, boundless creativity, what price would be too high? To make this omelet, there can be no limit on the eggs I might need to break. Knowing what I know, I wouldn't be doing my duty if I couldn't accept that thousands may have to die now so that millions can be happy forever" (66). Bernard goes on to justify his willingness to sacrifice human lives so in the future more would live in perfect harmony, as well as his unwillingness to face the facts about the Communist regimes of Eastern Europe as they emerged during the decade of his party membership: "If you ignored or reshaped a few uncomfortable facts for the cause of party unity, what was that to the torrent of lies from what we used to call the capitalist propaganda machine? So, you press on with the good work" (66).[5]

On that fateful, sizzling day in Languedoc, while walking slightly ahead of her husband on the hiking trail, June comes across two black dogs of "an unnatural size" (119)—creatures that resemble "mythical beasts" (120). Having walked for a while behind her, Bernard is busy sketching in his notebook "two dozen brown caterpillars" that aroused his "scientific curiosity" (122). Bernard does not register June's distress, leaving her utterly vulnerable. Oblivious to the person with him and, by extension, to the human world, Bernard wants only to know where the caterpillar procession is going "and what would happen when it arrived" (122), thus recapitulating June's earlier accusation against him.

Frozen by fear and not knowing what to do in a situation that seems to exclude any effective reaction, June watches the dogs draw near. The frightened woman tries to hold off the ravenous beasts by giving them food, whispering "please go away" (125), then tries to discourage them by throwing stones. In desperation, she reaches for her bag and finds a knife the couple has used for their picnic meals. McEwan's portrayal of the triangle—composed of the oblivious Bernard, the terrified young woman, and the diabolical black dogs (122–27)—reaches its peak when one of the dogs springs at June, who is able, shockingly, to drive the knife into it. At a moment of utter despair, faced with the prospect of terrible injury, if not certain death, June does the unexpected—she uses the "good little knife" (127) against the creature that threatens her.

The symbolic dimension of June's deed and thus of the novel as a whole is closely tied to the nature of the creatures she fights and to the transformative effect of her act. It is both the experience of horror that these colossal dogs inspire as well as June's discovered ability to cope with them that constitute the crux of the scene and give the novel its symbolic import. To recognize this, we must consider this incident in the context of its historical time, the summer of 1946. Both June and other characters in the novel view these deadly creatures as a symbol for the modern, man-made catastrophes that Nazism exemplified. Brought to the area by the Gestapo to hunt down the French Resistance (133), the huge dogs were left behind when the defeated Germans left France. Out on their own, the dogs run wild (137), preying on sheep and occasionally attacking humans. June regards the black dogs she encounters as the incarnation of "evil" (36), as a "malign principle, a force in human affairs that periodically advances to dominate and destroy the lives of individuals or nations, then retreats to await the next occasion" (xxiii).

Like June, her daughter, Jenny (the narrator's wife), is convinced that the black dogs symbolize the presence of evil in modernity. On a visit to Communist Poland in 1981, for example, Jenny invokes the black dogs at the entrance to the concentration camp Majdanek when she notices that the Polish authorities have chosen to ignore the fact that Jews and not just "Poles, Lithuanians, Russians, French and British [prisoners]" (87) were murdered in the camp. This obliviousness is for her an indication of the afterlife of "the black dogs"—that what these monsters stand for "goes on" (87) in the form of willful forgetting.[6] Even Bernard, who always rejected the supposedly mythical nature of the black dogs and who thought that June's description of her struggle with them as an encounter with evil was "religious cant" (82), refers to the black dogs to make sense of a decisive moment in November 1989 near Checkpoint Charlie in Berlin, when he and Jeremy witness half a dozen neo-Nazi skinheads attacking a Turkish man (72–73).

For the other characters in *Black Dogs*, the diabolical creatures embody the need to do something in the face of a historical circumstance that appears to exclude human action. Action in the face of "black dogs" is, in fact, positioned in the novel as an alternative to utopian politics. Indeed, it is immediately after June's experience with the black dogs in 1946 that she abandons "the materialism of her politics" (xxiii) and leaves the Communist Party. June's act in the face of paralyzing fear allows her to begin savoring the present (144)—to engage what life brings at any given moment. Acting to fend off the black dogs drives her apart from "committed intellectuals" who wish, as she puts it, "to engineer social change" (146). All she believes in after that fateful day of 1946, she tells her daughter, are "short term, practical, realizable goals. Everyone has to take responsibility for his own life and attempt to improve it, spiritually in the first instance, materially if need be" (146).

June's experience has a significant effect on the lives of those around her. In 1989, for example, Jeremy is inspired by June's courage as he faces a violent father who attacks his son (101–8). And, during the incident at Checkpoint Charlie, Bernard acts decisively: " 'Now off you go,' he said brightly, shooing them [the skinheads] with the backs of his hands" (74). Jeremy also moves to help the Turkish man. For a moment, it seems as if Bernard and Jeremy will themselves become victims of the horde. Yet their ability to do what is obviously dangerous, their capacity to act, finally causes others to step in and save the man (75).

McEwan remains aware, however, of the danger of simplistic symbolism in which mundane individual acts are juxtaposed with progressive politics. In the "preface" that precedes this "memoir," Jeremy cautions: "Whether June's black dogs should be regarded as a potent symbol, a handy catch phrase . . . or a manifestation of a power that really exists, I cannot say" (xxiii). Jeremy encourages the reader by implied gestures to remain "skeptical" of the "inventions of storytellers and dramatists" (27). He also warns against focusing too much on "turning points" in plots, "when a morality must be distilled from a sequence of actions, when an audience must be sent home with something unforgettable to mark a character's growth" (27). He himself finds June's "almost nonexistent animals too comforting" (27). What *Black Dogs* thus investigates is not only modern, human evil but the condition of intellectual life after 1989. The issue for McEwan's novel is not simply the ability to recognize evil but also acknowledgment of the human capacity to address it when it appears—to engage in action without reflexively resorting to grand ideas about a new dawn for humankind, the very ideas that began to fade after the political purges in the Soviet Union of the 1930s and that lost the last traces of their viability around 1989. It is this ability to step in and face the "black dogs" that ensures the viability of the future itself.

The book ends with words warning of the possibility that the black dogs of the twentieth century will "return to haunt us, somewhere in Europe, in another time" (149). In addition to expressing this fear, however, McEwan's novel hints at what may be our best defense against the dogs: our ability, as Hannah Arendt would put it, to insert ourselves into the world with words and with deeds.

Strong and Soft Opinions: J. M. Coetzee, Diary of a Bad Year

With a mixture of philosophical eloquence and elegant irony, J. M. Coetzee's 2007 *Diary of a Bad Year* presents the views and troubled psyche of an elderly, left-leaning writer after 1989 and, more specifically, in light of the political realities that followed 9/11.[7] Beginning on September 12, 2005, the novel's narrator and protagonist, JC, scrutinizes state reactions to the attacks on New York and Washington, DC, the detention facilities in Guantánamo Bay, and the wars in Afghanistan and Iraq. A South African author now living in Australia, JC should remind us, the readers, of Coetzee himself. Yet as Jonathan Lear cautions, we should not collapse the distinction between the two.[8] At the beginning, we find out that JC, or C (as the narrator/protagonist is often referred to), was asked by a German publisher to participate in a volume of collected essays that display "Strong Opinions" regarding "what is wrong with today's world" (21). The idea is that these statements by authors who live in various countries and on different continents might serve as some sort of moral compass for the perplexed of our era.

Armed with his pen, C ventures to produce, in the first section of Coetzee's book, "Strong Opinions" (1–154)—sturdy views about the contemporary condition in the German tradition of critical thinking. He rethinks the "origins of the state" and how it relates to the notion of "spreading democracy" in the Middle East (9); he muses on "terrorism" in the context of the fall of the Berlin Wall (22); and he considers the (presumed) relationship between "guidance systems" and suicide bombers in the Israeli-Palestinian conflict (29). We tend to think of the Cold War, C notes, as a period in which capitalism competed with socialism. But, he wonders,

> would the hundreds of thousands of men and women of the
> idealist Left, perhaps millions, who were imprisoned and tor-

tured and executed during those years for their political beliefs and public actions concur with that account of the times? Was there not a hot war going on all the time during the cold war, a war waged in cellars and prison cells . . . around the world, into whose conduct billions of dollars were poured, until it was finally won, until the battered ship of socialist idealism gave up and sank? (124)

While C's rhetorical questions indicate his political stance, the narrative itself displays an awareness of what C seems to forget in this reflection: that the "hot" war was also fought with billions of rubles that were poured into the struggle to keep Communism afloat until that vessel of global revolution was sent to its final resting place.

Indeed, Coetzee creates a complex narrative structure to examine the views of C. Coetzee's plot and formal choices serve to prevent any reflexive acceptance of the opinions C presents and, as Jonathan Lear puts it, to "defeat ersatz ethical posturing and promote genuine ethical thought in his reader."[9] Soon after C begins producing his "strong opinions," he runs into Anya, a young, attractive "Filipina" living with her lover, a dull investment consultant named Alan, in the same apartment building. Gripped by Anya's exotic beauty and lost in his desire, C manages to convince Anya to prepare his cultural-political musings for publication—to type up his thoughts and make occasional corrections and stylistic suggestions.

Anya, however, is hardly the obedient puppet that C thinks he has allured. She is exceptionally attractive, but she also asks troubling questions while fulfilling her secretarial duties, such as "what is so wrong with today's world?" (22). Anya does not accept C's quick and all-too-emblematic intellectual's reply that our world is characterized by "an unfair dispensation, an unfair state of affairs" (22). She wonders, "*Is this all?*" (22, emphasis in original) he and his fellow writer-intellectuals ask themselves when they look at today's world. And: "*Was it worth all that sweat?*" (22, emphasis in original). Anya does not answer these questions in the way the worried, enlightened man with "great thoughts" (29) would expect. She is hardly moved by his "know-it-all tone" where "everything is cut and dried: *I am the one with the answers, here is how it is, don't argue, it won't get you anywhere*" (70, emphasis in original). Rather, she examines her surrounding realities with a fresh and curious gaze. Indeed, very soon, Anya begins to "deconstruct" C's strong opinions with modest, yet piercing remarks.

Anya's role as a probing voice in the narrative is underlined in Coetzee's formal choices. Most of the pages of *Diary of a Bad Year* are divided into three parts. On the top, we find C's leftist, enlightened, critical, and all-too-expected considerations regarding post-1989 politics. The middle section presents C's internal monologue: his confession about the desire that drives him in his relationship with Anya, his ironic stance toward his own convictions ("grumbling in public"; 23), or his view of the comic situation of the writer and the muse. Finally, the lower section of the page is dedicated to Anya's perspective, to her nagging doubt vis-à-vis C's "strong" opinions: "All he writes is about politics. . . . It makes me yawn" (26). "He dictates great thoughts into his machine. . . . I take away the tapes. . . . Fix them up where they lack a certain something, a certain oomph, though he is supposed to be the big writer and I just the little Filipina" (29). While the sheltered sage, C, has an "insuperable distaste" for typing up his thoughts about Australia's prime minister, John Howard, and "the Liberals" (he views them as pro-Bush authoritarians) (33), she, the "Segreteria," as she calls herself, expresses cautious yet explicit doubts about C's position on the different parties in the so-called War on Terror. She suspects C has never come across "a real Muslim fundamentalist" (73): "You are wasting your pity on the fundamentalists Mister C" (75), she tells him in her thoughts. "They don't believe in talking, in reasoning."

It is not that Coetzee, or the narrative, gives Anya the final word in regard to politics post-1989. Rather, it brings the "strong opinions" of the progressive intellectual into a dialogue with "the people"—the same "people" who were often regarded in leftist lingo as victims of their "false consciousness." C himself senses the effect of Anya's independent, if not scholarly, perspective: he notes that since he moved into Anya's orbit, his sense of his opinions has changed (136). Coetzee's book thus reveals that there is no simple going back to clear-cut separations between "Left" and "Right" as we knew them before 1989 (in fact, one of the sections of "Strong Opinions" is titled "On Left and Right"; 121). Rather, the work invites readers to think about how to hope for the future after the decline of the redemptive fantasies about *Weltgeschichte* and the inevitable coming revolution, prompting new ways to understand politics and political action. C's views as expressed in "On Machiavelli" (17), "On Guantanamo Bay" (37), and "On National Shame" (39) are first steps, yet nothing but first steps in this regard.

To further relativize the "Strong Opinions" of the first part of Coetzee's *Diary of a Bad Year*, the second part is simply titled "Second

Diary" (155–228). It reads like a poetic, prospective labor of mourning for the lost utopias of the progressive Left. C writes:

> If I were pressed to give my brand of political thought a label, I
> would call it pessimistic anarchistic quietism, or anarchist qui-
> etistic pessimism, or pessimistic quietistic anarchism: anarchism
> because experience tells me that what is wrong with politics is
> power itself; quietism because I have my doubts about the will
> to set about changing the world, a will inflected with the drive
> to power; and pessimism because I am sceptical that, in a funda-
> mental way, things can be changed. (203)

Echoing Nietzsche or Foucault in their more hazy moments ("what is wrong with politics is power itself"), C here voices positions that many intellectuals on the left have resorted to since 1989 ("quietism," "pessimism"). Following this farewell to the revolutionary tradition, he then goes on to write with unmatched beauty the following entries: "On J. S. Bach" (221) and "On Dostoevsky" (223). Once the possibility of "changing the world" in a radical manner seems utterly gone, we are left with subjects such as "On the Birds of the Air" (207) and "On Children": "I approve of children, in the abstract. Children are our future" (213). Children as related to the future also figure prominently in C's entry on the South African writer Antjie Krog. Krog's theme, C notes, is "historical experience in South Africa of her lifetime" (199). Whereas C approves of children, he admires Krog deeply for her call to others to take specific action in regard to them: "Her [Krog's] answer to the ter-rible cruelties she had witnessed, to the anguish and despair they evoke: turn to the children, to the human future, to ever-self-renewing life" (199).

These digressions are accompanied, however, by a significant twist in the plot that is the centerpiece of Coetzee's *Diary*. In the course of the narrative, Anya discovers that her partner, Alan—the incarnation of our capitalist-greedy "Western" way of life—is about to swindle the writer C out of his little fortune. Alan's scheme is hardly ideologically motivated. Like C, Alan believes that after 1989, politics as a substantial struggle between the leading worldviews is over: "There are no big issues in any modern state, not any more," Alan says (99). "The big issues, the issues that count, have been settled. . . . Politics is no longer where the ac-tion is" (99). Squeezed between these two men and their essentially iden-tical narcissism, Anya is in fact the only character in Coetzee's *Diary of a Bad Year* who embraces the ability to begin, to take meaningful action. By simply asking Alan, "Is this your true face, Alan?" (149)—that is, by inserting herself with these words into the situation (in Arendt's sense) and confronting him—she prevents her partner from badly harming the writer. She makes it clear to Alan that by taking the path he is on, he is exposing his real, despicable character.

Coetzee's narrative does not stylize Anya and turn her into a heroic figure. On the contrary, with her little rebellion against Alan's greed, she simply sticks to her conviction that one should not harm another human being. Inventing Anya and placing her between C and Alan, the narrative hints at what political action can mean now that capital-H History, utopias, and politics of the kind to which C and Alan refer are over. Politics in today's "First World," Anya's character suggests, may mean focusing on reducing human pain and humiliation wherever one can. The kind of politics and ethics that Anya's character outlines has very little to do with what these terms meant in the era that ended around 1989. Coetzee's book as a whole suggests that there is much that we can still do politically and ethically, and that politics in our age is not restricted to the kinds of choices the Left considered the most important after 1945 and especially in the late 1960s.[10] What if we were to define politics along the lines of reducing human pain and humiliation? Would politics really vanish?

Here Coetzee's Anya seems to offer us some strong words: "What [C] says about politics sends me to sleep. Politics is all around us, it's like the air, it's like pollution. You can't fight pollution. Best to ignore it, or just get used to it, adapt" (35). Adapting means for Anya refusing to retreat into *inaction*. Adapting means understanding that only a certain kind of approach to politics became obsolete in 1989: the view that meaningful political action necessarily means revolutionizing society. C himself seems to sense what remains possible now that utopian-revolutionary politics has lost its sway. He notes with a clear tone of defiance vis-à-vis Hegelian thought: "But surely God did not make the market—God or the spirit of History. And if we human beings *made* it, can we not unmake it and remake it in a kinder form? Why does the world have to be a kill-or-be-killed gladiatorial amphitheatre rather than, say, a busily collaborative beehive or anthill?" (119). The issue is not to fashion an utterly new human tomorrow using any means necessary but rather to remake, through concrete acts, our modes of production and exchange so they will become "kinder," to embrace our ability to reduce human pain caused by injustice rather than strive for a radical revision of the way we live.

On the Intricacies of "Doing Good in This World": Kazuo Ishiguro,
When We Were Orphans

In recent years, Kazuo Ishiguro has commented several times on his
evolving interest in modernity's calamitous past, noting that he moved
from viewing history as "almost . . . another kind of technical device,"
similar to the choice of "a location" in a movie, to seeing its wide-
ranging significance. For one thing, he became more sensitive to the fact
that the "older generation" that lived through the Second World War
is dying out, giving "added responsibility" to his generation of British
writers. The death of the generation that experienced Auschwitz firsthand has brought to the fore the question of how "to keep the lesson of
this rather awful century," how to make sense of it for "people who are
voting for the first time this or next year."[11] For Ishiguro, then, considerations of the past compel us to consider how we are to act.

Hardly any literary character of the past decade or so wrestles with
the difficulties and possibilities of taking action more than Christopher
Banks, the protagonist of Ishiguro's *When We Were Orphans* (2007).
Against the backdrop of British colonialism in Asia and the opium trade,
Banks tells a story that bears striking resemblances to Sebald's *Austerlitz*. Like Jacques Austerlitz, Banks loses his parents abruptly as a child
and grows up trying to cope both with that loss and with what he discovers are the circumstances of their disappearance in Shanghai in the late
1910s. As in *Austerlitz*, the parents' disappearance marks a traumatic
rupture in the family's genealogy while simultaneously connecting the
event to immense political upheaval: the fallout from British rule in Asia,
the Second World War, and the rise of Communism.[12] Banks remains
throughout his life an orphan in a world marked by a universal sense of
orphanhood: his formative years are the time in which prevalent norms,
ideologies, and the sociopolitical structures of the fin de siècle crum-
ble. Although it is never stated clearly, the mysterious disappearance of
Banks's parents clearly expresses this systemic chaos.[13]

Brought up by his aunt in England, Banks becomes a successful detective, a figure reminiscent of Sherlock Holmes in his intention to deci-
pher the world through rationality.[14] Yet his desire to comprehend the
world is accompanied by a drive to engage its circumstances through
peculiar, if not utterly absurd, actions. This is most clearly seen when
he is about to change his life with his lover, the flamboyant Sarah Hemmings. Orphaned during her childhood, Sarah Hemmings offers Banks
the chance to create with her and with Jennifer, an orphan he adopted
earlier in the story, "a little family, just like any other family."[15] Banks is

at a crossroads: his conversation with Hemmings takes place in Shanghai in 1937, where he arrived a month earlier to try to solve the mystery of his parents' disappearance. As the conversation with Hemmings takes place, the Sino-Japanese War transforms Shanghai into a hellish chaos. Banks is uncertain how he should react to her offer. Were he to accept it, he would travel into safety and cope with his family's destruction by giving birth to a new one. Yet Banks refuses to follow through. Although Hemmings seems to convince him to forget about finding his parents and set off with her into matrimonial bliss, he suddenly moves in a different direction. As they are about to leave Shanghai for Macao, he receives word about a certain house that might lead him, or so he believes, to the exact location of his parents. A determined Banks begs the befuddled Hemmings, "let me just go and do something." To her puzzlement ("Do something?"), he replies, "Just . . . just something. Look really, I won't be gone long, just a few minutes. You see, I just have to ask someone something" (238–39).

Although Banks could reverse his fate by creating a new family with Sarah Hemmings, he senses that leaving Shanghai would mean accepting the finality of his parents' disappearance. Rather than break away from the condition of inner loss, Banks opts for trying to resolve the mystery with acts he himself initiates. He also believes—implausible as it may seem—that trying to find his parents in Shanghai will somehow affect the course of the Sino-Japanese War and even help avert the impending world war.[16] Early on in *When We Were Orphans*, we read that civilization is a "haystack at which lighted matches are being hurled" (154), that the advent of Mussolini signals an impending disaster even worse than the First World War (152), and that Nazism might pose "a threat to Christianity" (145). With the world "on the brink of catastrophe" (227), Banks is bewilderingly sure of his role as a possible savior.

While Banks's wish to do "just something" may be a mere expression of a hallucinating psyche, I suggest it is both a realistic rendition of a traumatized adult and a symbolic figure through which the narrative probes the ability of modern humans to act in the face of ostensibly or plainly impossible situations.[17] Indeed, Banks's seemingly confused plea to Sarah Hemmings—"let me just go and do something"—expresses quite literally what, according to Arendt, defines the human capacity to act. Banks could have accepted Hemmings's challenge to begin a new life with her, yet this would mean following a path she, not he, initiated.

When Banks leaves Hemmings on October 20, 1937, Japanese and Chinese forces are engaged in fierce fighting in Shanghai's Chapei—the very quarter in which he will search for his parents. Oblivious to the immediate danger that the omnipresent bullets slicing through the thick air pose to his life, Banks opts "to perform what is infinitely improbable," to act under circumstances that make this acting ludicrous. Going into Chapei in search of his parents, Banks expresses his freedom in Arendt's sense. Indeed, in her thought, freedom hardly means the limitless ability of an autonomous monad to choose unreservedly from a variety of options; rather, it designates the facility to maneuver, in a restricted way, within the web of the given natural, historical, and social contingencies—to act, even if this seems, like Banks's movement into the battered Chapei, "infinitely improbable." It is precisely this ability to carry out what is utterly far-fetched that Ishiguro's novel investigates. Our bewilderment at the rational detective's decision to enter the war zone is compounded by a promise he makes to a wounded child whom he discovers in the same house where his parents are ostensibly held, that "whoever did this ghastly thing, they would not escape justice" (291). Even though it is obvious that no power in the world can find out who "did this" or bring them to justice, Banks will not accept what *is*.

Banks's rejection of the given mirrors the words and deeds of his mother, Diana Banks. Named after the "forever untamed" goddess of the hunt and defender of slaves, Diana Banks is, until her abrupt disappearance, a defiant opponent of the opium trade—the business in which her husband's company, Morganbrook and Byatt, is engaged. Together with other British dissidents in Shanghai of the 1910s—most importantly the shady "Uncle Philip"—she launches a quixotic campaign against those involved in getting Indian opium into China and in turning a profit from the misery of millions.

As a defiant social activist, Diana Banks inserts herself into this reality with words and with deeds. When one of Morganbrook and Byatt's employees arrives at the Banks's residence to ask her to fire her Chinese workers, arguing that the massive opium addiction has given rise to bad hygiene and rampant dishonesty (61), she explodes, "Are you not ashamed, sir? As a Christian, as an Englishman, as a man with scruples? Are you not ashamed to be in the service of such a company?" (62–63). Reversing the moral condemnation with which the man came to her into a frontal attack on the ethical norms that characterize the colonial universe he serves, she counters "our company's actions" (64) with her own (admittedly also determined by colonial norms). Diana Banks is willing to oppose what she regards as appalling—even if her actions mean, as soon becomes apparent, the demise of her own family. Like Christopher Banks, who in moving into Chapei declines the possibility of personal rebirth in the form of creating a new family, Diana opts for a course of action that may entail giving up other expressions of natality, such as protecting her son, and, even worse, may entail inflicting pain on him. Ishiguro's narrative sets her up as a person who must choose between mutually exclusive forms of action: a person ultimately committed more to combating the brutality of the opium trade than to maintaining the quiet life of her family.

When We Were Orphans is thus hardly a literary manifesto in favor of activism; instead, it is a careful reflection on what is involved in choosing to act in the philosophical sense, scrutinizing the uncertainties, risks, costs, and failures of human action. As Banks himself will realize upon the failure of his mission in Chapei, those who choose to act do so without knowing the outcome of their actions. In fact, at times, the consequences of what humans do in the face of an inhuman reality are as horrendous as the catastrophe they hoped to address. Banks confronts this truth at the end of the narrative, when he faces the person he knew as "Uncle Philip." Banks learns from Philip that his mother's idealistic efforts to stop the opium trade involved collaborating with a Chinese warlord (309)—the very man who eventually turned her into his slave and thus brought about Banks's orphanhood. Diana's disappearance and his own ensuing loss, Banks now realizes, were directly related to her willingness to take action. The desire to do the improbable was also what dragged Philip down morally: it was Philip who arranged Diana's enslavement to the warlord (311), believing that this was the only way to avert her death and that of her son. Committed to fighting the opium trade, Philip continued to collaborate with the warlord until drug trafficking was abolished by Chiang Kai-shek's government. Yet instead of celebrating the success of his and others' actions, Philip saw firsthand that Chiang Kai-shek's policies meant only that the opium trade would change hands. Now it would be run by the Chiang regime itself, with "more addicts than ever" (314). "All these years," Philip tells Christopher, "you've thought of me as a despicable creature. Perhaps I am, but it's what this world does to you. I never meant to be like this. I meant to do good in this world" (314).

"To do good in this world": while these words could be easily dismissed as Philip's attempt to justify himself, they echo both Diana's countering "our company's actions" at whatever price and Christopher Banks's decision to abandon Sarah Hemmings in pursuit of his parents. Hence, *When We Were Orphans* investigates Hannah Arendt's observation that humans engage in actions without knowing their outcome and with the certainty that they will have effects that cannot be undone. The only "remedies" for the unpredictable outcome of our actions, Arendt claims, are the faculties of making and keeping promises and the faculty of forgiving.[18] There is, in fact, little Banks can say to dismiss Philip when he insists on his *initial* intention to do good. Once Philip's life becomes literally inseparable from certain decisions he has made, especially his choice to collaborate with the warlord, there is no way for him to reverse what follows. Similarly, when Diana opts for action in the face of what she finds to be endlessly disgraceful—the opium trade—she cannot foresee that her acts will lead to the dissolution of her family and to her own enslavement. It remains solely up to Christopher Banks to consider the possibility of forgiving. While he remains understandably firm in his quiet contempt for Philip, Banks also comes to understand his mother's position. As the novel draws to a close, he begins to grasp her need to do *just something* when confronted by the fact of the opium trade.

What eventually helps Banks absolve his mother from responsibility for his orphan fate is his discovery of the unintended outcome of her actions: before agreeing to the terms of her enslavement, Diana Banks negotiated for him to receive a regular allowance from the warlord (313). Besides her enslavement, Diana's fight against the opium trade thus also led, unintentionally, to Banks's ability to expose the mechanisms of the opium trade and present them in the form of a first-person narrative. The narration of *When We Were Orphans* is his way to "bear his sorrows in a story," to bear testimony to colonialism and its ghastly legacies.

At the end of the novel, Banks does not arrive at complete knowledge of what led to the catastrophe of his childhood. However, his pursuit of knowledge and his ability to move outside his professional and social confines do bring him the least one could hope for: a life whose course he has significantly affected, though in unintended ways. Concluding his story in 1958, after managing to see his mother one last time, Banks knows that although she is still alive, this fact does not change his orphan fate. Orphanhood in this novel signals a universal condition that cannot simply be overturned by individual action. Nothing can reverse the fortune of the woman, who—traumatized in the most severe manner—now lives completely oblivious of her past, unable even to recognize her own son (327–28). No reunion can undo the fate of the many who suffered and died because of the opium trade and colonial rule. Yet having told her story, having crafted the narrative that exposed what led to her dreadful fate—a fate shared by numerous, anonymous others across colonized Asia—Banks at least did *something*: and perhaps he reduced the possibility of a similar kind of imperial exploitation from reoccurring. By exposing in his first-person narrative (his testimony, one may say) the brutality of past cases of colonial manipulation, the violence it does to both the colonized and the colonizer, Banks may have made it a bit more difficult for others to follow a path similar to that of the British in Asia. Thus, although Banks knows that he might have been able to do more for his mother and that he "should have done a lot more" for Jennifer (331), he can still live with "a certain contentment" (336).

This reserved state of mind is highly reminiscent of Sebald's view of melancholy: Banks is the quintessential reflective, skeptical, modern human who has lived through the political upheaval of our time and—although never quite able to determine the course of events—was nevertheless capable of expressing his own "form of resistance," to use Sebald's expression. Indeed, his depiction of calamity—the narrative he offers us in the form of the novel—encompasses "*the possibility* of its overcoming"[19] as it relates a variety of "improbable" acts. Without achieving any redemptive resolution of the dark riddles of his childhood, without evading the catastrophes of the world war and of the political realities that emerged from British colonial rule in Asia (Chinese Communism included), Banks, like his mother, defies what seemed to be unalterable realities.

A Tale of Inaction: Ian McEwan, Atonement

Ian McEwan's 2001 *Atonement* tells a story that underlines the role of choice in our lives. The protagonist and narrator, Briony Tallis, has known for most of her life what she needs to do to redress the dreadful consequences of her past actions. She, however, opts to do nothing at all. Her narrative displays how this inaction ultimately deprives the passive individual of the chance to express natality.

Set against the backdrop of Britain in the mid-1930s and the Second World War, *Atonement* encompasses two distinctive narratives that are both presented by the same narrator: the first, a third-person narrative, stretches from parts I through III and the second is told in the first person and is titled "London, 1999." *Atonement*'s first narrative begins with the portrayal of a single hot summer day during 1935 in the life of an upper-class British family at their country estate in Surrey. At center stage we find the feverishly imaginative Briony Tallis—a thirteen-year-old who spends her time as an aspiring writer daydreaming and composing amateur plays.

On that day, Briony believes she has become a part of a dramatic story herself: through a series of childish misinterpretations, she comes to view her sister Cecilia's lover, Robbie Turner—the gifted son of the Tallis's housekeeper—as a driven "maniac."[20] Fascinated by the power of this attribute, Briony will identify that young man later in the day as a sexual offender after her cousin, Lola, is molested by an unknown man in the dark. Briony believes she saw Robbie Turner: "Everything connected. It was her discovery. It was her story, the one that was writing itself around her" (156). Discarding Lola's quiet doubts—"I couldn't say for sure"—Briony is ready to finger Robbie as the culprit: "Well I can. And I will" (157).

Briony's incriminating testimony will place her at the center of a world she actually creates with the power of her words. The innocent young Robbie is sent to prison; her story becomes his fate—a fate that, fitting with McEwan's metanarrative, will entangle Briony herself and her entire family.

Part II of *Atonement* tracks the consequences of Briony's moralist zeal. Here we reencounter Robbie, who has secured an early release from jail by becoming a soldier in His Majesty's army, as he joins the scores of British soldiers escaping the advancing German troops on their way to Dunkirk. McEwan's memorable evocation of the battle of Dunkirk mirrors the social decay that is implicit in part I of the novel, an era shadowed by the feeling that a "whole civilization" (190) is about to fall. Against this momentous backdrop, Briony's childish deed is juxtaposed with Robbie's heroism in a situation that displays the war's ravaging of "any remaining sense of individual responsibility" (237). Anxious, frantic soldiers stranded in Dunkirk descend here on an RAF pilot, accusing him of deserting them on the shores of France. Robbie, however, appears at this juncture as an attentive individual willing to act. Disregarding danger to himself—"It was madness to go to the man's defense, it was loathsome not to" (237)—Robbie and a few others do the improbable, clearly putting themselves at risk as they rescue the helpless victim from the "mob" (239).

As the drama of Robbie's life reaches its zenith with the Dunkirk war scenes, *Atonement* vividly explores action by imagining what Briony should and could have done. After much hesitation, Briony finally approaches her sister and Robbie (returned from the war) and admits that she has come to realize her mistake—that it had been, in fact, a family friend, Paul Marshal, and not Robbie Turner who molested Lola (309). Initially irritated by her plea for forgiveness, Robbie Turner "softly" outlines to her what she would need to do in order to reverse some of the damage she wreaked as a thirteen-year-old (329). "She knew what was required of her," concludes the narrator of *Atonement*'s first narrative: she should try to nullify, as Briony herself says, "the terrible thing that I did" (323) and, to address the fact that for years thereafter she "did nothing" (322), give a new testimony and put the facts "in much greater detail" (326) into a written account that she is to submit to Robbie. Briony knows that for once she should "just do all the things" Robbie and Celia (Cecilia) now demand of her (329). She also recognizes the meaning of these demands, the significance of this doing: what she must accomplish is "not simply a letter, but a new draft, an atonement, and she was ready to begin" (330).

To begin, to do, I argued above, is the signature of the most significant element of what Hannah Arendt terms *vita activa*. Had Ian McEwan concluded *Atonement* at this point, we might have been able to assume that Briony had finally chosen to reverse "her crime" (146) by uttering the words that would undo the circumstances she created. Her action would have constituted a new beginning in Arendt's sense for Robbie Turner, for Cecilia, and for Briony herself. The chronology established in this psychological romance would have underlined a succession from transgression and its consequences to repentance and forgiveness. Yet because this narrative of *Atonement* (part I through part III) is signed "BT, London, 1999," we must turn our attention at this point to the entire framework of McEwan's novel. The narrative we just concluded was, after all, only one of several "drafts" (349), one narrative of the many that document Briony's fantasies and hopes. Taken together, the narrative and its climactic end with repentance were only the promise of action, not action itself. Indeed, Briony reveals now, in the concluding section of the novel, that her story was but the last version of half a dozen narratives she has written in the course of the sixty-four years since that hot summer day of 1935 (349). She admits that she was not capable of turning what the draft outlines as a promise, as a plan, into action after all. The "cowardly Briony" (350), she admits, never made good on the act she wanted to perform, that is, exonerating Robbie; he, in fact, never reunited with his beloved, instead dying of septicemia in Bray Dunes on June 1, 1940, only a few months before Cecilia herself was killed at the Balham underground station during the German Blitz (350).

Yet Briony's self-castigation does not deliver the final judgment on her writing—*Atonement*'s first narrative. McEwan clearly shuns this kind of melodramatic moralism.[21] In a final appeal to the reader, Briony explains why she has gone, like Austerlitz, "behind time," refusing to accept the finality of the past—why she turned her own effort to understand what it would take "to begin" (330) into a fictional account of her actions. Admitting that she consistently opted for inaction, Briony asks the reader how the truth about the tragic death of the lovers could "constitute an ending? What sense of hope or satisfaction could a reader draw from such an account?" (350). It is not the search for truth alone that leads us to take interest in the past. The truth, in other words—the factual portrayal of what was—has only limited *use*. A literary narrative, however, like *Atonement*'s first section, can be useful in its betrayal of the truth: as it engages a past no one can change, it is capable of conveying and perhaps even should convey a "sense of hope."[22] Indeed, Briony's imagined action at the end of *Atonement*'s first narrative is an indication that even after committing such an unforgivable crime as Briony has, one can still "begin."

The only remedy against the "irreversibility and unpredictability of the process started by acting," Hannah Arendt notes in *The Human Condition*, does not arise out of some other, possibly higher or godly faculty "but is one of the potentialities of action itself" (*HC*, 236). That remedy is the power of forgiveness. Though one may be unable to undo what was done, "though one did not, and could not, have known what he was doing," Arendt notes, we remain capable of "forgiving." Without being forgiven—that is, potentially released from the guilt or shame related to "the consequences of what we have done"—the human "capacity to act" would remain "confined to one single deed from which we could never recover; we would remain the victims of its consequences forever" (*HC*, 236–37). Only through forgiveness as the constant mutual release from what we have done can humans remain free agents, "only by constant willingness to change their minds and start again can they be trusted with so great a power as that to begin something new. . . . Forgiving, in other words, is the only reaction which does not merely react but acts anew" (*HC*, 240–41).

Briony cannot forgive herself in the narrative she writes, but her story can achieve something just as important: as a personal alternate history, it unsettles the notion of time's one-directional movement, of the past as the unfolding of the inevitable. By imagining what she could have done differently, the past emerges in her story as more than the summation of what has taken place: it is the medium through which we, her readers (i.e., the readers of McEwan's novel), reflect on our ability to act. As Briony puts it:

> The problem these fifty-nine years has been this: how can a novelist achieve atonement when, with her absolute power of deciding outcome, she is also God? There is no one, no entity or higher form that she can appeal to, or be reconciled with, or that can forgive her. There is nothing outside her. In her imagination she has set the limits and the terms. No atonement for God,

or novelists, even if they are atheists. It was always an impossible task, and that was precisely the point. The attempt was all.
(350–51)

Nothing can now change the course of events as they took place. No narrative can reverse Robbie's imprisonment and the abrupt end of what
was a promising life. In this sense, Briony, who was not able to come
clean during her victims' lifetimes, "knew what was required of her"—
not just a statement of the facts but rather a story that would itself indicate the ability "to begin," the significance of exercising one's freedom.
Knowing that "there's always a certain kind of reader who will be com-
pelled to ask, 'what *really* happened?' " (350, emphasis in original), Briony replies with a story of what she should have done—a tale capable of
generating a sense of hope by pointing to the existential human capacity
to do, even if doing appears impossible or inconceivably demanding.

McEwan's *Atonement* is hardly a conventional novel intended to promote a moral agenda. Briony is ironic when she notes in the second framing narrative that the answer to the question what *really* happened "is
simple: the lovers survive and flourish" (350). Like Christopher Banks,
she refuses to accept the finality of the past as determined. The story of
what she should have done is an expression of natality: presenting *inac*-
tion, it points at the possibility of what she could have done.[23]

Both *Atonement* and *When We Were Orphans*, like *Austerlitz* and
Black Dogs, point to their own, immediate historical horizon—to the
intellectual and political question of what "the future" or "hope" may
mean today, in the post-1989 era, after "the romance of world history"
has ended, when once-widespread utopian notions have receded or disappeared entirely. There is little in Briony's imaginative conversation
with those who are by now long gone (Robbie and Celia) that might suggest a diminished sense of historicity in Western contemporary culture.
Rather, as Brian Finney notes, *Atonement*'s metafictional structure, its
consideration of the act of writing, reflects "the complexity and horror
of life" in the second half of the twentieth century.[24] In writing from a
contemporary perspective ("London, 1999") on her individual mistakes
and on her incapacity to take action, Briony offers a sense of hope in
her consideration of what remains possible vis-à-vis circumstances that
present themselves as extraordinarily tasking, if not as excluding human
agency. Toying in her first narrative with the impossible, with the idea
that one could actually do something that would amend the course of
events even after the death of those involved, Briony (in parts I through
III) offers no catharsis, no reiteration of reason's ability to illuminate and

comfort, no *at-one-ment* in the theological dimension, yet she neverthe-less does provide a significant sense of hope. In telling us about the ac-tion she avoided, Briony also suggests that this possibility remains open to those she implicitly addresses in her work: the readers. While deeply skeptical of any eschatological desires or transhistorical trajectories that might point to a possible utopia, none of the novels I have discussed in this chapter deem the past to be insignificant. On the contrary, they re-veal that in the past we discover what humans are capable of: acts of in-credible malice but also of repentance and reconciliation and the chance for new beginnings. Briony did not reverse her initial crime with new testimony and never managed to express regret to those she had so deci-sively wronged. However, she has given the dead Robbie a voice and a memorable image, and, most significantly, she has written a work that examines what humans can and should do even if they opt, as she did, for inaction. There is, indeed, "no entity or higher form" to which Briony can appeal, nothing outside her, only her own ability to acknowledge whatever amount of freedom humans possess to move beyond given cir-cumstance, beyond punishment and revenge. In this respect, the char-acter of Briony is very close to Ishiguro's Christopher Banks. As Banks tries to find his parents in embattled Chapei, he finally understands that he cannot alter his life's tragedies or the fatal blows dealt by events such as the Sino-Japanese War, yet he displays the value of the attempt and of the choice to insert oneself into the world with word and deed. Ishiguro's Banks and McEwan's Briony Tallis and June Tremaine embody what is possible in circumstances that seem utterly hopeless. They resist the fac-ticity of a past that presents itself as a set of unalterable circumstances in our present. In other words, June Tremaine in her thrust of the knife into the black dog, Banks in his drive to enter Chapei, and Briony with her ongoing attempt to return the dead to life all reject the idea Austerlitz also disputes: that historical events simply unfold in time, forcing us to accept them as a given. Briony's question, "What sense of hope or satis-faction could a reader draw from such an account?" (350) is not simply a guilty individual's retrospective justification but also an indication of what literary writing, as "a kind" of expiation, may strive for.[25]

14 The Terror of the Unforeseen

What the Science of History Hides: Philip Roth, The Plot against America

On the sweltering Tuesday evening of September 15, 2009, an exuberant Quentin Tarantino stood on a stage in Tel Aviv, Israel, and asked a stirred audience, "Are you ready to kill some Nazis?" The enthusiastic response: "Yeah!"[1] The question concluded Tarantino's short introduction to his film *Inglourious Basterds* (2009). While Tarantino's words might simply have been an effort to whip up enthusiasm in the audience, they also can be understood, along with the film they introduced, as something more. The question Tarantino asks is, indeed, directed to the viewers of his film some sixty-five years after 1945. The filmmaker views his work as a chance to give up the distinction between here and there, then and now, reality and fiction, and, by so doing, to ask what his audience might be capable of. By similarly asking, "What if?" Philip Roth's 2004 *The Plot against America* and Alexander Kluge's 2006 *Tür an Tür mit einem anderen Leben* (Door by door with a different life) question the identification of natural with human history and examine the ways individuals and groups may act to shape their fates.

By altering aspects of the past as we know it, by reshuffling earlier events, alternate histories imagine what could have happened and thus shed new light on significant historical moments as they did, in fact, unfold.[2] Tarantino's narrative, for example, imagines a group of Jewish soldiers fighting for the US Army during the Second World War. No ordinary rank-and-file unit, these young Jewish men are charged to kill as many Nazis as possible, as exotically as possible, in order to spread terror among the German forces in occupied France. To maximize the horror, the soldiers scalp their victims as American frontiersmen and Native Americans did in the United States. Tarantino's blood-soaked story peaks in an operatic scene in which a Jewish woman hiding in Paris and the group of Jewish American soldiers wipe out the Nazi elite by turning a Parisian cinema into a flaming inferno. By fantasizing about what could have been done, Tarantino's baroque scenario implicitly raises the question of whether the Allies could indeed have done more to demoralize the German killing machine. Without directly judging the choices the Allies made, the narrative considers, for example, whether they could have recruited Jews into special fighting units and what the effect of such groups may have been. By allowing the Jewish soldiers to focus their vengeance on the Nazi elite, the film also asks if the Allies did everything they could to target the German leadership, and perhaps even stop the Holocaust. The question "Are you ready to kill some Nazis?" is thus a question for the Allies, an inquiry into their commitment to address the genocide while it was taking place. Furthermore, it is implicitly the more comprehensive question "Are you willing to admit your ability to act now, in your given circumstances?"

Employing the conditional "what if," films such as *Inglourious Basterds* and the novels discussed here underscore what traditional historiographic narratives and historical novels often undermine: the role of choice, action, and human agency. Following the allure of fatalist or Hegelian views of history, the historical novel in its various manifestations frequently echoes Tolstoy's argument in *War and Peace* that "every action of [great men], that seems to them an act of their own free will, is in the historical sense not free at all but is bound up with the whole course of history and preordained from all eternity."[3]

This view of human history, as a case of natural history, is not restricted to the historical novel of the nineteenth century. W. G. Sebald, for example, reflects on the scale of the devastation caused by air raids on German cities during the Second World War while musing on the possibility that this man-made disaster may have been an expression of a "natural history" of destruction.[4] Considering a historical phenomenon that was initiated and carried out by thousands of humans as be-

ing somehow related to natural history mirrors the temptation to relate unfathomable catastrophes to an impersonal agent—be it "God,"
"fate," "instrumental reason," "technological modernity," "bourgeois
capitalism," "power," "discourse," an abstract Schmittian "sovereign,"
or "evil." Besides allowing us to rethink our realities from the perspective of a fantasized past, as Karen Hellekson suggests, alternate histories
probe the conscious or unconscious tendency to collapse any distinction
between natural and human history.[5]

Revisiting American history of the 1940s, Phillip Roth's *The Plot
against America* considers how we are able to choose and to act. "Fear
presides over these memories, a perpetual fear," notes the narrator, Phil
Roth, at the onset of the novel: "Of course, no childhood is without its
terrors, yet I wonder if I would have been a less frightened boy if Lindbergh hadn't been president or if I hadn't been the offspring of Jews."[6]
By using the word "if" three times right at the beginning of the plot, the
novel sets the stage for the fantasy to follow: it both alludes to the following, imaginary plot and undermines any attempt to see the events of
the 1940s as inevitable.[7]

In Roth's alternate history, Charles Lindbergh—flight pioneer, popular idol, and Nazi sympathizer—defeats FDR in the presidential election on November 5, 1940. From this vantage point, the novel sets off
to answer the questions Phil Roth began with: Would he have become
the frightened person he was (and, perhaps still is) had Lindbergh not
become president? Was he always a frightened boy, and thus—as we will
soon see—bound for moral failure? Does Phil turn anxious after Lindbergh's election because he is a Jew? Or are Jews more likely to be fearful
in light of their history and the fictitious past we will soon read about?
Phil asks what course history would have taken had Lindbergh not become president. The novel itself thus raises the inverse question: what
course would history have taken had someone like Lindbergh indeed
become president? The factual election of FDR is highlighted as what
it was: the realization of one possible outcome, the result of numerous
choices, political actions, and contingencies. The repeated use of "if"
also raises the question of what similar choices we face today and what
may assure us (if anything) that those choices will turn out as well as the
choice to elect FDR as president did in 1940.

As the novel's plot unfolds, our image of the past is shaken, along
with the peculiar comfort that accompanies the belief that history simply
unfolds, that we can do very little to affect our realities. In Lindbergh's
America, Roth's novel suggests, the issue would have been how to avoid
complicity with the regime, how to face fear. Soon after Lindbergh's

election, the country's new leader translates the wave of populist patriotism that carried him to power into policies targeting the Jews. Unlike the Nazi model, his racism aims not at segregation and annihilation but rather at assimilation: Jews should simply disappear as a distinctive religious and cultural entity into the non-Jewish population. The regime follows this policy by creating the "Office of American Absorption" (OAA)—a Kafkaesque entity that launches a program for dispersing American Jewry across the country until this rather homogenized, geographically concentrated minority loses its distinctiveness.

This fantastic scenario unfolds through the figure of the complicit, sleek Rabbi Lionel Bengelsdorf—a highly educated opportunist who is married to Phil's aunt, Evelyn. In the face of what recently (and, in this case, factually) occurred in Europe—the November 1938 Reichskristallnacht and the march of German troops into Poland—Bengelsdorf remains firm in his commitment to peace: "This is not an American war," he announces to a crowd gathered in Madison Square Garden in the summer of 1940. This is "Europe's war" (38). Opposing Roosevelt's wish to intervene on the side of the Allies, the rabbi asks, "Tell me, Mr. President, what sort of America will the massive slaughter of innocent American boys leave in its wake?" (39). A recognized opponent of Roosevelt, Bengelsdorf's loyalty to Lindbergh brings him the postelection prize of appointment as head of the OAA in the state of New Jersey. Phil Roth's Aunt Evelyn becomes his personal assistant.

This turn in the story line marks a crucial junction in the novel, where the protagonists are presented with choices and are forced to act. At the center of it all we find young Phil Roth, who acts in a manner with fateful consequences.[8] He sees an opportunity in Aunt Evelyn's new position: without telling her that his defiant father, Herman Roth, declined the OAA's offer to resettle the family in Kentucky, Phil convinces Evelyn to send a "reassignment" letter to the Roths' neighbors, the Wishnows. His wish is to have his neighbors' son, Seldon Wishnow, move with his family to Kentucky. The two boys are true opposites: while Phil wants to be counted as a genuine American boy, Seldon looks and behaves like a fragile Jew. Despising Seldon for his Jewishness and balking at his attempts at friendship, Phil asks Aunt Evelyn to send the Wishnows away in the hope that Seldon might simply disappear. "What is Seldon's last name?" Aunt Evelyn asks Phil (218), and he replies "Wishnow," thus sealing with a single word Seldon's and his mother's fate: later in the book, after resettling in Kentucky, she will die in the course of anti-Semitic riots.

Ross Posnock noted that Roth's novel makes the political doctrine of isolationism the corollary of human selfishness and apathy.[9] This is especially apparent through the combination of alternate history and individual action: the (imaginary) role of the United States in the war and Phil's questionable act. Not confronting European Fascism in the 1940s (as the novel imagines) would have been the most extreme form of the selfishness Phil so clearly exemplifies in his action. Yet Phil's retrospective account—the confessional narrative we read—also underlines the role of will, choice, and action. This interest in choice and action is most apparent when the novel deals with anti-Semitism. When the Roths travel to Washington, DC, following Lindbergh's victory (44–82), Phil's father is attacked in a cafeteria after he reacts angrily to someone describing the Jewish journalist Walter Winchell as a "loudmouth Jew." Accompanying the Roths on their trip is Mr. Taylor, an all-American guy and an unemployed college history teacher from Indiana. When Herman Roth is assaulted, Mr. Taylor faces the choice between silently watching what unfolds in front of him or reacting. He opts for the latter, jumping to his feet to shout at the attacker, "that is enough!" (78). Reflecting on this and other similar moments of that era, the older Phil Roth notes,

> I'd watched my father fall apart, and I would never return to the same childhood. The mother at home was now away all day working for Hahne's, the brother on call was now off after school working for Lindbergh, and the father who'd defiantly serenaded all those callow cafeteria anti-Semites in Washington was crying aloud with his mouth wide open—crying like both a baby abandoned and a man being tortured—because he was powerless to stop the unforeseen. And as Lindbergh's election couldn't have made clearer to me, the unfolding of the unforeseen was everything. Turned wrong way around, the relentless unforeseen was what we schoolchildren studied as "History," harmless history, where everything unexpected in its own time is chronicled on the page as inevitable. The terror of the unforeseen is what the science of history hides, turning a disaster into an epic. (113–14)

The noun "unforeseen," which appears four times within a few sentences, marks the limitations of Herman's ability to do anything about the political conditions he faces. Yet even in situations such as the one the Roths confront in Washington, in which their ability to act was literally nonexistent, others could have acted. In fact, the realm of action that is blocked for Herman Roth and other Jews in Lindbergh's America is the realm open to action for those who can do something, "anything at all," about anti-Semitism. While not all Gentiles have the same power to stop what the Roths sense as the unforeseen, they are nevertheless forced to define themselves, to disclose who they are through action or inaction in their given political realities. The unforeseen delineates what some of the characters cannot affect, but also what others can. Later in the novel, when the Wishnows face the "unfolding of the unforeseen" in the form of rabid racial violence, it will be the Roths who are called upon to act, and they do, risking their lives to rescue Seldon Wishnow.

The unforeseen is hardly a diabolic deity that regulates the course of events externally. Rather, it marks the chaos that humans face in any political situation and their ability to address it through action. Roth's choice of words is revealing: "History" with a capital H is "harmless history," since it is the thoroughly manufactured story of allegedly inevitable events. Just as Austerlitz resents "time" as the river in which history unfolds—the narrative that "tells us" of occurrences—Phil Roth discards History in its role as manifestation of the inevitable, the unavoidable, that is, what lies outside the realm of human power.

And herein lies the "terror": once the past is deprived of its appearance as other-directed, once History is no longer the narrative that explains events with little attention to human agency, then the role of will, choice, and action becomes central. If someone in the past like Mr. Taylor was able to exercise his ability to act when confronted with a difficult situation, the narrative suggests, then we can consider our ability to act, as well. We have, more often than we admit, the capacity to insert ourselves into our given realities. Accounting for past events then becomes precarious, since it emphasizes our ability to decide, to intervene, and to take responsibility for our actions and inactions. In this way, Roth's alternate history both redescribes American politics of the early 1940s and unsettles the temptation to view history as an epic detached from the acts of ordinary individuals.

The Plot against America disturbs this latter notion by its treatment of humble characters such as Mr. Taylor and Phil's mother, Bess, as well as by means of the structure of the novel as a whole. We can best observe this in the author's decision to add a postscript. Intended as a reference for readers interested in tracking where, presumably, "historical fact ends and historical imagining begins" (364), Roth wishes to lay out "the facts" (364) as declared by political biographies of the different actors (Roosevelt [365–68], Lindbergh [369–72], etc.). Seen from the perspective of individual actors, history is hardly an epic in the classical sense, in which heroes struggle with their predetermined fate, but rather the mundane story of how individuals such as Fiorello H. La Guardia (372–74), for example, operate in contingent situations. Indeed, in Roth's short, quasi-historiographical accounts, the actions of historical figures are cast as the driving force of all major events: Roosevelt the man (not his administration) "proposes" (365), "recognizes" (366), seeks changes (367), and so on. "History" is nothing greater than the acts of individuals, be they Phil Roth or a politician by the name of Roosevelt. It is but the daily maneuvering between options and choices, decisions and actions, carried out in ignorance of their possible outcomes. "History" in this sense is the insertion of oneself into a world that is filled both with contingencies over which one has no control and, simultaneously, with possibilities that humans often tend to ignore.

Knowing they cannot always trounce "the unforeseen," those "outside intrusion[s]" of history (184), the characters of *The Plot against America* contemplate alternatives and act upon them without knowing the ultimate outcome. We see these choices everywhere, whether it is Rabbi Bengelsdorf's participation in a dinner at the White House in honor of Nazi Germany's foreign minister von Ribbentrop (184), the death of Walter Winchell, the defiant journalist turned presidential candidate who pays dearly for his views, or Herman Roth's death-defying journey to Kentucky to rescue Seldon Wishnow (328–36). Uncovering what the "science of history" tends to obscure means regaining a sense of what humans are doing in the face of circumstances seemingly beyond their control.

Reflecting on *The Plot against America*, Roth noted, "History claims everybody, whether they know it or not and whether they like it or not. In recent books, including this new one, I take that simple fact of life and magnify it through the lens of critical moments I've lived through as a 20th-century American."[10] What "history claims everybody" implies is that historical events such as the emergence of anti-Semitic Fascism in Europe force everybody to make choices and to act on them. Hence, Roth considers George W. Bush's presidency, for example, as reaffirming "the maxim" that informed the writing of all his recent novels "and that makes our lives as Americans as precarious as anyone else's: all the assurances are provisional, even here in a 200-year-old democracy. We are ambushed, even as free Americans in a powerful republic armed to the teeth, by the unpredictability that is history." Being ambushed by history or being claimed by it does not mean surrendering oneself to the current of World History or the natural history of destruction à la Sebald, and thus, for example, retreating into a glum private sphere. Rather, being ambushed by history means asking, "And what should I, should we, do now?" Tellingly, Roth concludes his reflections on writing *The Plot against America* by quoting his own sentences:

> "Turned wrong way round, the relentless unforeseen was what we schoolchildren studied as 'History,' harmless history, where everything unexpected in its own time is chronicled on the page as inevitable. The terror of the unforeseen is what the science of history hides, turning a disaster into an epic."
>
> In writing these books [his last novels] I've tried *to turn the epic back into the disaster as it was suffered* without foreknowledge, without preparation, by people whose American expectations, though neither innocent nor delusional, were for something very different from what they got.[11]

Note here Roth's emphasis on his literary act of turning the epic back into disaster, turning what appears to be the unfolding of fate or of suprapersonal forces such as "spirit," "class," or "power" into an account of "people" as they wrestle with their catastrophic contingencies. Roth's words about replacing "epic" with an account of humans as they face disaster and what they do about it point us squarely back to such characters as June Tremaine and Christopher Banks. One could feature their lives as the unfolding of the "epic" that is modern history. Yet McEwan and Ishiguro depict these figures as active individuals, dealing with the calamities of their time.

"Why it [anti-Semitic Fascism] didn't happen is another book," notes Roth on the counterfactual at the basis of *The Plot against America*—another book "about how lucky we Americans are." His point is not, he reveals, "that this can happen and will happen; rather, it's that at the moment when it should have happened, it did not happen. *The Plot against America* is an exercise in historical imagination. But history has the final say. And history did it otherwise."[12] For anyone reading the novel it is clear that "history" in Roth's view is hardly a suprapersonal entity to which humans are subjected but is, rather, the sum of the actions of all its actors, in their given contingencies: "It" could have happened in America, but it did not because there were enough humans who acted to prevent it from happening.

Acknowledging the Multivalence of Reality: Paul Auster, Man in the Dark, *and Alexander Kluge,* Door by Door with a Different Life

The extent to which we are subjects of our socioeconomic and political circumstances or, alternatively, agents of our fates, is especially visible in Paul Auster's 2008 *Man in the Dark* and Alexander Kluge's 2006 *Tür an Tür mit einem anderen Leben* (Door by door with a different life). The frame narrative of Auster's work presents the narrator, August Brill—a seventy-two-year-old book critic confined to his wheelchair and to his bed after a car accident. Brill's physical captivity is reflected in the fates of the loved ones who surround him in the Vermont home where the story takes place: his daughter, Miriam, whose husband has left her recently, and his grandchild, Katya, whose ex-boyfriend has been murdered in Iraq. Brill's bodily and mental confinement is further mirrored in the time of the narrative: Auster's 180-page story takes place in one insomnia-ridden, bleak night.

Brill's only refuge during this sleepless night is his imagination. He tells himself a story whose protagonist is the thirty-year-old magician Owen Brick, who lives a quiet life with his wife, Flora, in Jackson Heights in 2007. One night, Brick wakes up to find himself, like Kafka's Gregor Samsa, lying on his back in a deep hole: "escape is out of the question."[13] Brick's only way out of this cavity comes in the form of another character, Sergeant (Sarge) Serge Tobak, through whom Brick discovers that he has landed in a universe parallel to his own.

In this parallel world of 2007, America is not fighting a war in Iraq; rather, "America is fighting a war with America" (8). The United States of America has split into two entities following the Supreme Court's decision in 2000 not to conduct a recount of the Florida ballot (50–51, 62): the new, secessionist Independent States of America and George W. Bush's United States of America. The war between "The Federals" and the secessionists has left more than thirteen million people dead.

As if this were not enough, Owen Brick finds out that the only way out of his captivity, and the only way to escape the abyss of the bloody civil war, is to assassinate the one person responsible for the fighting: a seventy-two-year-old wheelchair-bound book critic living in Vermont with his daughter and grandchild (71). It is Brill, Brick discovers, who tells himself the story that entraps him and allows his country to be torn to pieces. In fact, Brill "invented the war" and Brick's existence in the parallel reality so he, Brick, would come to kill him, thus ending the misery that his life has become (70). If Brick refuses to fulfill this mission and eliminate Brill, Brick will be killed alongside his beloved wife, Flora.

While it may be easy for some critics to dismiss *Man in the Dark* as an antiquated, postmodern Borgesian-Cortázarian fable, Brill's own life story and his embedded alternate history is both moving and thought-provoking.[14] Owen Brick's dilemma is not only how to return to his adored Flora but, in addition, how not to become victim of his circumstances—how to live a life of choice, even if the realm of choices one has seems immeasurably small. Knowing the answer all along, Brick nevertheless asks his commanders in the alternate reality, "Do I have a choice?" (72). When he tries to convince Flora that he has to kill August Brill in order to return to her—"I'm not saying I want to do it. I just don't have any choice"—she tellingly replies, "Don't talk like that. Everyone has a choice" (94).

What August Brill invents through Brick and the alternate history is a fable akin to Kafka's "Eine kleine Fabel," with which we began this book: Brick is the mouse whose world is closing in on him. He faces a reality in which his only choice is between different kinds of death. Like Kafka, Brill ends the life of his invented figure violently: "a bullet goes straight through his [Brick's] right eye and out of his head" (118). Yet by inventing Brick in the first place and taking him through the dreary alternate history, Brill and the novel traverse the gloom of the sleepless night and begin a day that holds at least some sense of hope.

Brill's nightmarish alternate history of the split United States underlines that the events we actually experienced after 2000—the disasters of 9/11 and the wars in Afghanistan and Iraq—are not the only events that could have occurred.[15] The facticity of what transpired does not mean that history was bound to evolve the way it did. Just accepting that another reality would have been possible allows those who feel entrapped in the hopelessness of post-2000, post-9/11 realities to maintain a sense of hope. Naturally, Brill never states that other courses would have been better. He does not say whether it may have been preferable to reject the decision of the Supreme Court and thus the presidency of George W. Bush, if necessary by force. What Brill's fictional experiment does indicate, however, is the elasticity of our given individual and political realities and the role of choice and action even in such extreme conditions as those Brill embodies, that is, even if our very physical ability to move is taken away from us.

If we consider the past as an actuality that did not necessarily have to take place, as Alexander Kluge similarly suggests in his 2006 *Door by Door with a Different Life*, we also acknowledge our contemporary conditions as open to change.[16] Kluge introduces this thought before presenting some 350 prose miniatures: "A reality that extinguishes people is 'actual' [*wirklich*]." However, Kluge goes on to say, people will deny a reality that presents itself as inhuman, although "this is 'actual' [*wirklich*] just the same." "So we live," he then concludes, "in parallel worlds: *DOOR BY DOOR WITH A DIFFERENT LIFE*" (7; capital letters in original).

Using the multivalence of the German adjective *wirklich*, which means "actual" as well as "real" and "objective," Kluge underlines the point in a key short prose piece that, significantly, shares the book's title. In it, he presents a story that displays how what is a factual, objective circumstance is not to be mistaken as necessary. An unrealized "reality" can be considered as always existing alongside what has, in fact, materialized. Kluge follows here a Parisian student who lives both her "actual" life and the "many other possible lives that still await her" (51). In this latter mode, she enters the King George V Hotel on the Champs-Elysées one fine day and enjoys the Wellness Center using the name of a guest of her age she has somehow learned. For the next four hours, she lives "in a parallel life" (52). She lives, as it were, as another person. Yet as Kluge notes, the student is not a con artist (51; *keine Hochstaplering*). Inhabiting another, possible life yields her a glimpse of freedom, the possibility of reality as open, even if only for a brief moment. Every step in the sequence that Kluge unfolds can lead in more than one direction. In any given moment, the student lives in her "actual" life but also, potentially, in the many other lives she could inhabit by making them her own, just as she did upon entering the lobby of the King George V.

Not all the stories in Kluge's volume are so buoyant in considering the manifold manifestations of "the real." In "Kurzfristige Terminverlegung" (Brief postponement), for example, he retells the story of the Wannsee Conference, which sealed the fate of millions of Jews during the Holocaust, by considering the fact that this fateful gathering of Nazi functionaries was delayed from December 1941 to January 20, 1942 (145). Asking, "What if the conference had not been deferred after all?" is significant, since in December 1941, the United States had not yet entered the war. It is thus not inconceivable that Nazi Germany would have sought a separate peace accord with the United States and that the Holocaust (at least as we know it) would thus not have taken place. "This," concludes the speaker in this prose piece—an evolutionary biologist and historian who studies "the history of species of Evil"—"translates into hope" (152). In other words, here an expert on natural history underlines the distinctiveness of human history, the fact that humans, unlike creatures of the natural world, might entertain "hope": even in the face of what occurred in the factual, unchangeable past, such as the Wannsee

Conference, one may still discover what could have taken place. "Evil plans will not be realized," the narrative considers, "as long as horizons of hope remain open" (151). We may continue to entertain hopes for the future as long as we acknowledge that we are not externally conditioned by "evil plans" or by anything else. "What does 'in reality' mean retrospectively?" Kluge asks while introducing another section of the book (193). He then answers with another question: "In which reality do we actually live if we consider that it always touches the unreal?" (193). "Reality," in other words, is much more than factual circumstance. It includes all other possibilities that humans once had, those that they have now, and those that they might pursue in the future.

Kluge's notion of the real thus differs substantially from the concept of "the real" in the critical thought of Alain Badiou and Slavoj Žižek, both philosophers who also consider the hopeful potential of radical breaks from accepted reality. "The real" for Badiou is not what presents itself as unchangeable fact in our given material or symbolically mediated reality but rather what exists *outside* and *beyond* the given. Significantly, Badiou in his lecture series "The Century" discusses the twentieth century as driven by "the passion of the real" (*la passion du réel*): by ideological zeal and political action motivated by the desire to bring about what reality obscures and prevents from becoming. In other words, "the passion of the real" is the thrust to unmask the given and to establish a completely different, utopian reality. According to Badiou, it is this "passion of the real" that led to Leninism, Maoism, and the Cultural Revolution—movements toward which Badiou takes a conciliatory approach.[17]

Unlike both Badiou and Žižek, who seek a sense of a possible future (what I am calling "futurity") through a return to the revolutionary traditions of the nineteenth and twentieth centuries, Kluge's futurity is located in the concrete and mundane demand to keep open the *possibility* of choice, the prospect of a less inhuman reality. For Kluge, the important thing is to recognize that both any given inhuman condition and its negation—the possibility of eliminating this very condition—are "real." In other words, a possible, more civilized humanity always exists simultaneously alongside the factual, often inhuman one we confront.

If utopian literature disrupts the forcefulness of given circumstances by imagining possible worlds, as Fredric Jameson recently suggested,[18] alternate histories like those of Roth and Auster turn to the past with the force of their imagination to disrupt what seems inalterable. There they discover that any circumstance is open to human agency and thus that any contemporary condition remains open to change. They offer the perspective of a future that might be better than the present by acknowledging the transience of *some* aspects of the given. They are hardly interested in celebrating the idea of unrestricted human freedom, but they indicate how we bear responsibility toward the worlds we inhabit and toward other human beings.[19] These responsibilities, as we have seen in the actions of such characters as Mr. Taylor, are not of the grand scale of revolutionary scenarios but rather of such humble scope as defending minorities when their rights are threatened or listening to the recollections of those who can hardly bear their pains.

15 On This Road: The Improbable Future

The Dead Child, or the Looming End of Natality

Numerous films and novels of recent years, works of both "high" and "popular" culture, imagine a world in which children are in grave danger or die before bringing their own offspring into the world.[1] Recasting our present as the horrendous past, Steven Spielberg's 2005 *The War of the Worlds* returns to H. G. Wells's tale of a bloodthirsty Martian invasion to focus on a father's Sisyphean attempt to rescue his children in the face of inexplicable brutality.[2] In Francis Lawrence's 2007 adaptation of Richard Matheson's *I Am Legend*, virologist Robert Neville is separated from his children and believes himself the sole human survivor of a ferocious, artificial virus.[3] Alfonso Cuarón's 2006 film of P. D. James's *The Children of Men* presents a not-too-distant future in which humanity is plagued by pandemic infertility and in which the protagonist must rescue a woman who carries the first child conceived in two decades.

These bleak cinematic scenarios find their counterparts in an entire array of recent novels. Kazuo Ishiguro's 2005 *Never Let Me Go* imagines a world similar to ours in which cloned children are raised for the sole purpose of harvesting their organs for transplants.[4] In Orhan

Pamuk's *Snow*, Turkish schoolgirls commit suicide when forced to remove their head scarves.[5] John Updike's *Terrorist* presents Ahmad, an American youth who sees no future for himself other than to become a suicide bomber.[6] *Incendiary*, by Chris Cleave, features a mother writing a letter to Osama Bin Laden as she mourns her son, who was killed in a horrific terrorist attack on a London stadium.[7] A world in danger of losing its sanity similarly haunts Ian McEwan's *Saturday*, in which a small-time crook invades the domestic sphere of the protagonist and orders the victim's pregnant daughter to take off her clothes.[8] Consuming fears about one's children equally haunts Don DeLillo's *Falling Man*. Here, a man who barely survived 9/11 is unsure how to carry on in a world in which his anxious nine-year-old son spends his days scouting New York's sky in search of the next planes that might hit the city.[9] These and other visions of a planet defined by threatened or dead children all display a deep anxiety about the future. The vulnerable child is a figure of our fears about the prospects of natality in our time. It is a cipher for pervasive concerns about contemporary political realities and a symbol of deep uncertainty about the prospects of humankind's survival.

The literary theme of the end—the end of civilization, the destruction of the human habitat, and so forth—is as old as the Mesopotamian cosmology and the story of Noah's ark. In modern times, the demise of human civilization has been the topic of a vast array of apocalyptic tales and science fiction dating back at least as early as Mary Shelley's 1826 *The Last Man*.[10] Between the end of the Second World War and 1989, many of these End of Days fantasies were born out of the anxiety of an impending nuclear disaster that would dwarf the bombing of Hiroshima and Nagasaki.[11] Simultaneously, there was also a flurry of what Brian Aldiss called "cozy catastrophes": science fiction stories about the day after civilization is destroyed and how a handful of survivors proceeded to create a new human polity.[12]

What distinguishes the depictions of the End of Days that focus on endangered children is the slippery nature of the looming catastrophe and the erratic nature of the danger. As in McCarthy's *The Road*, for example, many works imagine the apocalypse as originating not from a reckonable global power such as the Soviet Union but rather from "godspoke men." If immediately after 1989, many in the West celebrated the dawn of a fearless age, 9/11, the wars in Afghanistan and Iraq, and the looming fear of terrorist acts turned the exuberance into doubt regarding what lies ahead. In the short introduction to his 2003 *Die Lücke, die der Teufel läßt* (*The Devil's Blind Spot*), Alexander Kluge writes that immediately following the disintegration of "the Russian empire" he had the feeling that the new century would "take the bitter experience of the 20th century and turn it around into something hopeful." Yet now we seem to face "a relapse" into the era of the Thirty Years' War.[13] Echoing Kluge, Martin Amis noted recently: "history is accelerating; and so the future becomes more and more unknowable." After the next "untraceable mass-destructive strike," Amis asks, "what political system would ever know itself again?"[14] "Our generation is characterized by two major world-historical events," similarly remarks Haruki Murakami: "the fall of the Berlin Wall in 1989, which led to great optimism and the collapse of the Twin Towers in New York 2001, which was followed by a deep crisis to our sense of meaning [*eine tiefe Sinnkrise*]. People are looking for a way out of the chaos in which they live."[15]

The figure of the threatened child reveals a sense that the catastrophes of the twentieth century will reemerge in the twenty-first century with a yet-unknown destructive thrust. Simultaneously, the trope of the endangered child encodes the possibility of salvaging a future through political and ethical action. In Hannah Arendt's terminology, these works suggest that the only hope for averting the end of natality is to embrace natality itself: to accept the human capacity, inscribed at birth, to live the *vita activa*. The novels and films here hardly advocate the view that our present is defined by a "wholesale liquidation of futurity" and thus we must return to the "lost causes" of the radical-utopian tradition, as Slavoj Žižek and others suggest.[16] Rather, they contemplate the more or less mundane actions that may ensure the survival of humanity.

Crucial for this is the recognition of what threatens natality and the future: the deeming of "others" of all sorts to be mere substance, a means for economic, scientific, social, religious, or political goals. As Niall Ferguson has noted, when H. G. Wells's *War of the Worlds* was first published in 1898, blood-sucking aliens signaled the coming of a century that was marked by humans willing to deem other humans unworthy of the designation.[17] In contemporary apocalyptic scenarios, the future seems in question because humans turn their fellow humans into disposable stuff. The only way to counter this, these works suggest, is to expose the process for what it is and to acknowledge our ability as individuals and groups to counter it through our actions. What drives these horrific scenarios is not solely the terror of what is to come. Rather, the scenarios are "counterfactuals of the future" that promote "creative thinking," to borrow Steven Weber's idiom: they do not present what is bound to come but only what might, and thus they provide an opportunity to consider what actions might ensure the future of a civilized global polity.[18]

The End of Mankind: Paul Auster, Oracle Night

Paul Auster's 2003 noir novel *Oracle Night* connects the degradation of humans in the twentieth century with twenty-first century events such as 9/11 and the prospect of future disasters via the figure of the dead child.[19] At the center of one of Auster's many narratives is the story of Ed Victory. An American veteran of the Second World War, Victory was among the first to liberate Dachau, where he was a witness to "thirty thousand breathing skeletons" (92) and to the pleas of a woman begging him for some milk for the dead child she held in her hands. These pictures, he notes, "don't tell you what it was like. You have to go there and smell it for yourself. . . . Human beings did it to human beings, and they did it with a clear conscience. That was the end of mankind" (92).

The narrator of *Oracle Night*, the fragile Brooklyn writer Sydney Orr, recalls how he integrated Ed Victory's story into a novel he was working on in September 1982, a day after discovering a newspaper item about a drugged prostitute. According to this report, the woman, unaware she was pregnant, delivered her soon-to-be-dead child into a toilet bowl (113–15). Noticing the newborn only twenty minutes later, the woman then wrapped her in a towel and "dropped her in a garbage bin" (115). This, notes Orr, was for him "a story about the end of mankind" (115).[20] The room where the event took place became the "precise spot on earth where human life had lost its meaning" (115).

The narratives that feature these two dead children are symbolically entangled with the story of Sydney Orr himself. Set in the New York of 2002, *Oracle Night* recounts, against the backdrop of the shock following 9/11, the events that led to the brutal killing of Orr's unborn child in September 1982 (235–37). The child who did not survive Dachau, the newborn who perished because of her mother's drug addiction, and the death of Orr's unborn child from the blows of an addict are all related to each other by a logic analogous to what made the attacks of 9/11 possible—by a radical devaluation of human life. As Maurice Blanchot points out in *The Writing of the Disaster*, the death of a child marks the liminal point that "destroys time." At this moment, the succession of generations of humans, for whom alone time has meaning, is suspended.[21] The killing of children indicates the effacement of the civilizatory command established by the biblical story of the binding of Isaac: no belief, no principle, no devotion, and certainly no personal desire can justify the sacrifice of children or, by extension, the religiously based sacrificing of humans.

While *Oracle Night* refrains from a direct reference to the events of 9/11, the narrative is framed by its origin in the immediate aftermath of the World Trade Center attacks.[22] The metaphor of the dead children distills the reality that Ed Victory confronted in Dachau and that Orr confronted in the newspaper item, a reality in which humans become mere matter: the stuff of political or racial fantasies about a "perfect" social order (Dachau), the disposable by-product of a brutal, profit-driven drug industry (the prostitute), or faceless bodies needed to create the startling impact for a terrorist attack (9/11). What *ended*—as in "the end of mankind"—in Dachau, in the prostitute's Bronx apartment, and in New York on September 11, 2001, is what makes humans distinct: the civilizatory tradition that no desire, belief, ideology, interest, or policy indiscriminately trumps life. "Mankind" can indeed end more than once: the end occurs every single time that humans become the victims of a craving, conviction, idea, or blind economic exploit.

Reclaiming the Victims of the Crushing Effect

In *Homo Sacer: Sovereign Power and Bare Life*, the Italian philosopher Giorgio Agamben elaborates on the Roman judicial category of *homo sacer* as delineating sacrifice and homicide: to the sovereign, all men are potentially *homines sacri*, reducible to "bare life"—subject to killing with no need for further judicial justification.[23] *Homo sacer* for Agamben is thus the human stripped of her or his juridical rights and hence of humanity.[24] In *Remnants of Auschwitz: The Witness and the Archive*, Agamben interprets the figure of the Muselmann of the Nazi concentration camp—the inmate, who, starved and humiliated to exhaustion, loses his drive to survive—both as the incarnation of the Nazi state's power to reign over life and death and as the elemental figure of any human in the Western political tradition. According to Agamben, all subjects of the modern Western state are potentially deprived of any legal status: they are "bare life" de facto or in waiting.[25] As Leland de la Durantaye fittingly notes, "Agamben's *homo sacer* is a figure from the remote past who brings into focus a disturbing element in our political present—and points to a *possible* future."[26]

The proliferation of the dead child in contemporary literature and film points to a more general circumstance that encompasses both the idea of *homo sacer* and the perpetrators of 9/11: the reduction of humans to mere means.[27] In a short post-9/11 prose piece, "The Crushing Effect," Alexander Kluge, for example, wonders why no "cavities with

survivors" were found at Ground Zero, "no intact corpses." His answer:
flying airplanes into buildings meant turning thousands of humans into
plain substance, "dry as powder and completely pulverized."[28] The attacks were the outcome of the planners' ideology and the related view
that those who will be hurt have no rights. The violence that was carried out both eliminated life from the bodies and reduced them almost
instantaneously into matter—not even a corpse left to mourn. Katharina
Hacker's 2006 *Die Habenichtse* depicts the parents of a young German
lawyer killed in the Twin Towers insisting on having a coffin for their
son's funeral, "against any form of reason," since there is no corpse.[29]

The shock resulting from the right that terrorists claim to devalue
the lives of others similarly reverberates through Jonathan Safran Foer's
Extremely Loud and Incredibly Close, in which the nine-year-old Oskar
Schell mourns the death of his father at the World Trade Center. A dop-
pelgänger of Günter Grass's Oskar Matzerath, Oskar's quest to make
sense of his immense loss brings him to recall other historical events in
which humans were used to convey a message of shock and awe: the
firebombing of Dresden and the detonation of an atomic bomb over Hiroshima.[30] As in Auster's *Oracle Night*, Safran Foer's novel does not
equate Dresden and Hiroshima with 9/11. Rather, Oskar's minimalist
recitation of the images constantly displayed in the media underlines
how all three historical moments are characterized by the transformation of humans into "bodies," utterly reified entities:

> Planes going into buildings.
> Bodies falling.
> People waving shirts out of high windows.
> Planes going into buildings.
> Bodies falling.
> Planes going into buildings.
> People covered in gray dust.
> Bodies falling.
> Buildings falling.[31]

Philosophy and cultural criticism in the wake of 9/11 have remained
primarily focused on the dangers to civil liberties posed by institutional
political reactions to terrorism and on the ways the attacks were used
for the promotion of a conservative political agenda. Kluge, Safran Foer,
Katharina Hacker, and others, however, remain attentive to the significance of the "fabrication of corpses," in Arendt's idiom, in recent acts of
political terrorism: the indiscriminate mass killings of civilians in New

York, London, Madrid, Mumbai, Bali, Baghdad, and elsewhere.[32] There
can be no equating of the murders in the Nazi camps and the blind, mass
killings we witness in present-day terrorism. Yet in one crucial respect
a significant similarity between the systematic incarceration and later
elimination of humans in the camps and the blind targeting of humans
in contemporary terrorism can be suggested: in both cases, humans are
deemed utterly expendable, exterminated to ensure the wanted outcome—the terror of the beholder.

Of What Could Not Be Put Back: Cormac McCarthy, The Road

Hardly anywhere is the devaluation of human life due to ideological fantasies more radically explored than in Cormac McCarthy's *The Road*.
As a father and his son make their way through the scorched cities,
melted highways, and burnt forests of a devastated, dystopian United
States, McCarthy's tale portrays a time in our near future in which the
surviving few have all become like *Muselmänner*: "Wearing masks and
goggles, sitting in their rags by the side of the road like ruined avia-
tors," they look infinitely lost, like "something out of a deathcamp."[33]
Humans have been turned into "something," and the end of humanity has come about, McCarthy suggests, in the course of a holy war
in which raging prophets used modern technology to bring about the
End of Days: "On this road," thinks the man, "there are no godspoke
men. They are gone and I am left and they have taken with them the
world" (32).[34] It was, the narrator suggests, the same scientifically and
technologically driven universe that introduced modern time, with its
omnipresent clocks and measuring devices, that enabled the "godspoke
men" to produce the apocalypse that swept away most living things from
the face of the earth: "The clocks stopped at 1:17. A long shear of light
and then a series of low concussions" (52).

In McCarthy's world, Austerlitz's despised clocks no longer pose any
threat. They have become obsolete, remnants of an era obsessed with
time. Not only clocks but also the entire notion of a past no longer matter. Before this futureless world the past served as a source of insights,
identity, or comfort, but now that the present is empty and tomorrow
utterly meaningless, the past is useless. It has become the realm of hollow
nostalgia, "the perfect day" (13) of a childhood not only irretrievably
gone but also devoid of meaning for any future living being. Nothing
from the time before the godspoke men usurped the world forever will
be possible again: not a walk along the shore, the beauty of silent trees,
or the dream of a child. Indeed, *The Road*'s child knows that "ever is a

long time," yet for him, in this world deprived of any future, "ever is no time at all" (28). The eschatological hope of the godspoke men to overcome the limitations of time, to bring about a messianic tomorrow, was pursued at the price of creating a reality in which all plants have died "to the root" (21), animals are as good as gone, and words such as "ever" no longer mean anything. Indeed, if the biblical story of the binding of Isaac signaled the leap away from human sacrifice, *The Road*'s premise is a return to that primordial stage: besides the father and his son, groups of survivors are on the road, looking for anything they can consume, especially human prey. Making their way to what they hope will be the warmer south, the two discover remnants of "a charred human infant headless and gutted and blackening on the spit" (198).

What remains, then, in a world in which the bearers of natality, the offspring that ensure the capacity of humans to begin, become mere consumable flesh? From this pit of despair, the only reasonable option may be that chosen by this family's mother: to exit the world voluntarily and thus avoid becoming its victim. While the mother's "only hope" was to vanish into "eternal nothingness" (57), the father remains firm in holding on to life. In their struggle to survive and their mutual assurance that they carry "the fire"—and that "good guys" exist just as "bad guys" do—the father and his son are occupied for most of the narrative with simply surviving in the face of abyssal evil and utter void.[35] Constantly seeking reassurance from each other with the rudimentary language of a world reduced to its primal elements—"is it okay?" or simply "okay?"—they grapple with the most mundane questions and try to maintain their humanity.[36]

Despite being frightened, famished, and worn out, the child proves to be the character who, through minor, seemingly meaningless acts, affirms whatever limited futurity this bleakest of worlds might offer. As they come across an old man who, like them, is on his way south, the father will not stop for him. The son, however, insists that they offer the man some food (162–63). When a thief steals their humble possessions, it is again the son who pleads for sparing his life when they finally catch him (256–57). Gradually, his unadorned, humane stance brings to the fore the absurd idea that even in these utterly desolate circumstances, there may indeed be some prospective viewpoint, some hope. There is little redemption in suggesting that "the fire" or "goodness" might endure in a world plainly deprived of a future. Indeed, as the old man whom the father and son encounter on the road notes, "Where man can't live gods fare no better" (172). And yet, McCarthy's apocalyptic tale reveals through the child how end-time scenarios retain a futural dimension, shocking us into a consideration of how such horrors may not become a reality after all.[37]

McCarthy's tale is not about a future that is bound to materialize but rather about what the present holds as a dreadful possibility. From the perspective of a tomorrow in which the past and the future have ceased to hold any significance, the narrator concludes *The Road* with a clear redescription of our present as a point at which one might still be able to avert the course of events that will lead to the catastrophe:

> Once there were brook trout in the streams in the mountains. You could see them standing in the amber current where the white edges of their fins wimpled softly in the flow. They smelled of moss in your hand. Polished and muscular and torsional. On their backs were vermiculate patterns that were maps of the world in its becoming. Maps and mazes. Of a thing which could not be put back. Not be made right again. In the deep glens where they lived all things were older than man and they hummed of mystery. (287)

By using the past tense, *The Road*'s final paragraph recasts our present as the already bygone moment wherein a future "in which men would eat your children in front of your eyes" (181) could still be averted. Thus, this past (i.e., our present) gains a deeply troubling "practical" dimension, in Michael Oakeshott's conception. The issue is not what an object, utterance, or circumstance meant in the fictional past (i.e., our present) but rather what "use," in Oakeshott's term, what "meaning," it has "in a current present-future of practical engagement."[38] If, from the perspective of an ominous future, today's brook trout or the smell of moss will be gone, we can contemplate what action might ensure their continued existence. It is in this sense that McCarthy's bleak universe maintains a futural dimension and encompasses hope.[39]

From the perspective of what *can still* be put back in place, *The Road* points to W. G. Sebald's modern "we," asking where "we" come from and where "we" may be going. Reflecting, through the child, on good and evil, the wish to help, and the initiative for action, the novel alludes to what—regardless of the given situation—remains possible: giving food to the old man or sparing a thief, who, in spite of his deeds, never lost the distinctive features of a human being. In the face of "the end of mankind," *The Road* suggests that the child's insistence on maintaining an ethical stance might undo, even if only for the briefest moment, the devaluation of human life brought about by the "godspoke men." It is in this sense that the child might be seen as a "god," as the father at one point submits (172)—yet only as a human divinity: the bearer of natality who reiterates the fundamental right of his fellow humans to be treated as dignified human beings.

Of the Possibility of Making Things Happen in the Future

I Am Legend, Children of Men, The Road, and other dystopian narratives are interested in the reversal of natality's end through the human capacity to alter circumstances through distinctively ethical and political actions. What convinces John Updike's Ahmad in *Terrorist,* for example, not to obliterate the Lincoln Tunnel is, in the end, the two African American children he discovers sitting in the vehicle in front of his explosives-laden truck.[40] "Lovingly dressed and groomed by their parents" (307), they gaze through the rear window, trying to "achieve" Ahmad's "recognition" (301). This human gaze brings about their "rescue" (307). It is their humanity and the promise made present in the child that finally prevents Ahmad from producing mass death. As he finds himself forced to recognize their smiling faces with a hand wave, he opts for action of a specific kind: not setting off the bomb.

And as Paul Auster's *Oracle Night* displays, if the distant or more recent past can teach us anything at all, the human ability both to bring about "the end of mankind" and to find ways out of such man-made catastrophes often exceeds our expectations. In the face of a hopeless future, there remain only two choices: to exit the world, like the mother of the family in *The Road,* or to opt for the implausible—the reversal, by whatever means, of the genealogical breach. Having seen the "breathing skeletons" in Dachau, Ed Victory of *Oracle Night* understands that he "was going to have to do something" (93). He thus establishes a one-man operation called The Bureau of Historical Preservation: an underground warehouse in which he collects a great number of American and international telephone books. Among these most obsolete of all artifacts of our technological age, he safeguards a Warsaw phone directory from 1937–38.

Doing means for Ed Victory depriving the past of its pastness, bringing the telephone books into his warehouse, and creating a room that can "contain . . . the world . . . or at least a part of it. The names of the living and of the dead. The Bureau of Historical Preservation is a house of memory, but it's also a shrine to the present. By bringing those two things together in one place, I prove to myself that mankind isn't finished" (91). Bringing the two together means in this case literally creat-

11 40 44 Orlean Ch., Karmelicka 29
12 20 51 Orlean Josef, m., Muranowska 36
12 08 51 Orlean Josek, m., Św. Jerska 9
2 37 68 Orlean Mieczysław, m., Chłodna 22
12 07 94 Orlean Ruta, m., Gęsia 29
6 18 99 Orleańska Paulina, Złota 8
2 06 98 Orleański D., m., Moniuszki 8
8 83 21 Orleńska O., artystka teatr. miejsk., m., Marszałkowska 1

12 61 33 Orlewicz Stanisław, dr., płk., Pogonowskiego 42
12 69 99 Orlewicz Stefan, m., Pogonowskiego 40
11 91 94 „Orle", Zjedn. Polsk. Młodzieży Prac., okr. Stoł., Leszno 24

2 14 24 Orlicki Stanisław, adwokat, Orla 6
11 77 10 Orlik Józefa, m., Babice, parc. 165
10 06 84 Orlikowscy B-cia, handel win, wódek i tow. kolonj., Ząbkowska 22

6 24 38 Orlikowska Janina, m., Alberta 2
9 28 26 Orlikowski Antoni, lek. dent., pl. 3-ch Krzyży 8
10 12 19 Orlikowski Jan, skł. towarów kolonjalnych, Targowa 54

10 26 02 Orlikowski Jan, m., Targowa 19
12 73 03 Orlikowski Stanisław, m., Zajączka 24
4 22 70★ Orliński Bolesław, m., Racławicka 94
5 85 97 Orliński Maks, dr. med., chor. nerw., Wielka 14
8 11 10 Orliński Tadeusz, dziennik., Jerozolimska 31
9 96 24 Oriot Leroch Rudolf, mjr., Koszykowa 79a

„Ortorog", daw. Orłowski L., Rogowicz J. i S-ka, Sp. z o. o., fabr. izol. kork., bud. wodochr., bituminy, asfaltów
9 81 23 — wydz. techn., pl. 3-ch Krzyży 13
— „ — — (dod.) gab. inż. J. Rogowicza
— „ — — (dod.) biuro i buchalterja
5 05 59 — fabryka, Bema 53
8 07 66 Orłow Grzegorz, m., Mokotowska 7
7 01 69 Orłów Ludwik, przeds. rob. budowl., Buska 9
11 52 63 Orłow P. A., sprzed. lamp i przyb. gazowych, Zamenhofa 26

4 19 01★ Orłowscy Janina i Stefan, m., Wejnerta 19
8 80 57 Orłowska Halina, m., Polna 72
3 16 29 Orłowska Lilla, Kopernika 12
4 28 36★ Orłowska Marja, kawiarnia, Rakowiecka 9
12 52 54 Orłowska Marja, m., Cegłowska 14
9 27 63 Orłowska-Czerwińska Sława, artystka Opery, Wspólna 37

3 19 47 Orłowska Stefanja, mag. kapeluszy damsk., Chmielna 4

9 40 41 Orłowska-Świostek Zofja, lek. dent., Wspólna 63
8 61 75 Orłowska Zofja, m., Al. 3 Maja 5
6 88 98 Orłowski Adam, inspektor skarb., Chłodna 52
8 16 66 Orłowski Edward, dr. med., Hoża 15
2 47 59 Orłowski Feliks, szofer, Elektryczna 1
11 06 01 Orłowski Izrael, m., Gęsia 20
8 53 04 Orłowski Jan, m., 6-go Sierpnia 18
5 98 63 Orłowski Juljan, Sienna 24
2 57 24 Orłowski M., handel win i tow. kolonj., Marjensztat 7
5 24 65 Orłowski Maksymiljan, dr. med., rentgenolog, Graniczna 6

11 69 91 ...
12 61 62 Orth Anna, ... Orthwein, Karasi...
5 01 58 — dyrektor,
— „ — — (dod.) m...
2 63 45 Ortman Stefa...
2 10 21 „Ortopedja",
11 56 93 „Ortozan", ...
8 75 14 Urtwein Edw...
2 22 30 „Orwil", Sp...
5 86 86 ...
9 39 69 „Oryginalna...
9 55 89 Orynowski W...
8 14 23 Orynżyna Jan...
7 10 92 Orzażewski E...
10 17 29 Orzażewski R...
8 16 19 Orzażewski R...
11 69 79 Orzech J. B.,
9 98 19 Orzech L., d...
2 16 01 Orzech M.,
5 33 43 Orzech Maur...
12 13 01 Orzech Moric...
5 38 00 Orzech Paweł...
11 84 29 Orzech Pinku...
6 59 39 Orzech Szym...
2 16 01 Orzechowa N...
6 44 22 ...
9 42 28 Orzechowska
2 63 15 Orzechowska
9 71 24 Orzechowska
8 32 16 Orzechowska
10 17 31 Orzechowska
8 93 81 Orzechowska
4 08 59★ Orzechowska
8 84 02 Orzechowski
6 50 92 Orzechowski
5 36 59 Orzechowski
12 74 22 Orzechowski
6 35 30 Orzechowski
5 83 80 Orzechowski
5 04 72 Orzechowski
5 30 09 Orzechowski
9 66 51 Orzechowski
4 35 24★ Orzechowski
12 52 55 Orzechowski
4 32 85★ Orzechowski
5 83 22 Orzechowski
12 58 23 Orzechowski
2 76 02 Orzechowski
2 04 23 Orzechowski
11 41 31 Orzelski Marj...
6 77 66 „Orzeł", zob.

FIGURE 8 A page from the Warsaw phone book (1937). From Paul Auster's *Oracle Night* (New York: Henry Holt, 2003).

ing a physical space in which the past and the present coexist, effecting a reversal of what had taken place in the death camps, a reversal achieved by what Arendt would call an "improbable" act. What Ed Victory does is to symbolically nullify the genealogical breach: the names of the murdered Jews of Warsaw who were erased by their brutal deaths are reconnected with the names of the living in one space. Ed Victory's Bureau of Historical Preservation is not a tomb for the dead but rather a site in which the murdered are still present for the sake of the future. In this space, he reestablishes the genealogical chain, at least as an idea. His hope is to thus save humanity from the extinction it might experience should it ever again condone what led to the vanishing of the Jewish names from Warsaw's telephone books—the conversion of humans into matter. "He can imagine a hundred other ways to translate the experience of the death camp into an enduring lifelong action" (93), another character notes about Ed Victory's strange endeavor, "but who is he to judge another man's passion?" (93).

Writing in the months following 9/11, Sydney Orr (and thus Paul Auster) uses the facsimile of the telephone book to bring the dead of the past together with the dead of those recent events. Orr writes so there will, indeed, be a future not overshadowed by dead children. We find some indication for this in another of *Oracle Night*'s many embedded narratives: the story of a promising young French author who, two months after publishing a book-length poem about the drowning of a little girl, loses his own five-year-old daughter to the water of Normandy (220). Upon his loss, the writer decides never to write again, discovering that "words could kill . . . could alter reality, and [are] therefore . . . too dangerous to be entrusted to a man who loved them above all else" (221). While Sydney Orr concedes that he initially rejected this notion using a "bland, commonsense argument, a defense of pragmatism and science over the darkness of primitive, magical thinking" (221), he finally became sympathetic to it: "Thoughts are real. . . . Words are real. Everything human is real, and sometimes we know things before they happen, even if we aren't aware of it. We live in the present, but the future is inside us at every moment. Maybe that's what writing is all about. . . . Not recording events from the past, but making things happen in the future" (222).

Stories about the end of humankind that bring together the names of the dead, the living, and those who might be born are—with all their oddity and fascination with gloom—decisive examples of making things happen. Summoning the ashes of both Dachau and New York, the result of two moments when humans fell prey to fantasies about an eschatological tomorrow, these narratives disturb the seemingly orderly flow of time from a known past to an expected future. To put it somewhat differently, through Arendt's reading of Kafka's "HE": they *deflect* the thrust of the past. The genealogical metaphors, the inclusion of the visual image of the telephone book, and the labyrinthine plot that brings together historical fact, artifact, and fiction are all *inserted* between the given past and the feared future, thus allowing us to reflect on what may bring about a new trajectory.[41]

In this respect, labyrinthine parables about the relationship of the past, the present, and the future such as Auster's *Oracle Night* and scenarios such as McCarthy's *The Road* are just as real as the most mundane stories we might tell. They overcome "the power of time"—the idea that we simply swim in a river that carries us against our will—because they allow us to weigh our options in light of paths not yet taken. The disturbing image of dead children prompts us to consider what would allow them to live on.

Reflecting on "end-time thinking"—the belief in a world that will be purified by the flames of a cleansing, raging, heavenly fire such as the one that brought down the Twin Towers—Ian McEwan thus asks in an essay if we have "reached a stage in public affairs when it really is no longer too obvious to say that all the evidence of the past and all the promptings of our precious rationality suggest that our future is not fixed?" We have no reason to believe, McEwan concludes,

> that there are dates inscribed in heaven or hell. We may yet destroy ourselves; we might scrape through. Confronting that uncertainty is the obligation of our maturity and our only spur to wise action. The believers should know in their hearts by now that, even if they are right and there actually is a benign and watchful personal God, he is, as all the daily tragedies, all the dead children attest, a reluctant intervener. The rest of us, in the absence of any evidence to the contrary, know that it is highly improbable that there is anyone up there at all. Either way, in this case it hardly matters who is wrong—there will be no one to save us but ourselves.[42]

Coda: Toward a Hermeneutic of Futurity

It is hard to resist walking into the mystifying forest of two thousand seven hundred and eleven concrete stelae set on Ebert Straße in Berlin's center—Peter Eisenman's Memorial to the Murdered Jews of Europe. This crisscross of geometrically ordered gray stones seems at first glance like an ominous giants' cemetery. This should come as no surprise. Erected near the remains of the bunkers that sheltered Nazi Germany's political elite and on ground that was, after the Second World War, part of Berlin's no-man's-land, the memorial evokes modernity's catastrophic history, with all its darkness.

Yet on entering the grounds, one soon notices that many of the visitors are blithely wandering the endless possible paths they may create for themselves. Children play hide-and-seek. Italian high school students on a Berlin discovery tour take part in a loud game of catch. Lovers use the scenery as a background for a Berlin photo op.

Peter Eisenman's memorial is thus not a symbolic tombstone for the millions of Jews murdered during the Nazi era. Rather, commemorating the dead, it is an artistic creation that invites its visitors to relate the past to their immediate present in imaginative ways: visitors enter and leave the ground in endless manners. Lying on top of the stelae, some indulge in slumber or in silent contemplation. Others wander through the halls of the underground

FIGURE 9 Peter Eisenman's Memorial to the Murdered Jews of Europe (detail). Photograph by Amir Eshel, 2009.

information center to learn about the Holocaust. It is there, in the lobby, that they encounter a prominently displayed quotation from Primo Levi's *The Drowned and the Saved*: "Es ist geschehen, und folglich kann es wieder geschehen: darin liegt der Kern dessen, was wir zu sagen haben" (It happened, therefore it can happen again: this is the core of what we have to say).[1]

The visitors' meandering, playing, conversations, and thoughts are essential elements of the memorial itself. Viewed from above, the area seems like an enormous grid in motion. Composed of both silent stones and the humans who variously engage them, the site is a constantly evolving creation shaped by the experiences visitors bring to bear on it. Eisenman himself has stated how he hopes to tie the past to the present—how he wants the visitors to "be in the present" and have an "experience they had never had before."[2] While it is impossible to be certain exactly how these experiences affect visitors, it is possible that as they wander among the silent colossi, they link the increasingly distant moment that is the Holocaust to their own lifeworld—to the range of practices and attitudes defining who they are, as well as to all possible forms of thought, behavior, and action that will shape who they will become.[3] In Eisenman's words, here "there is only the living memory of the individual experience. Here, we can only know the past through its manifestation in the present."[4] One of the most distinctive aspects of the creation of the memorial was the public debate surrounding its construction. For years, German politicians, public intellectuals, artists, writers, and citizens from all walks of life debated all aspects related to the memorial. They wondered if Germany needed such a memorial and, if so, what it should look like. They argued over its proper location, the size of the arena, and the kinds of experiences visitors to the site should have. The lively dissensus that originated in the proposal to create the Berlin Holocaust Memorial is, one can argue, an implicit facet of Eisenman's artwork itself, a demonstration of how the past manifests itself in the present.[5]

About four hours' flight from Berlin's Holocaust Memorial, a much more modest artwork also harks back to the persecution of Jews in Europe, prompting reflection on the past as it touches the present and a possible future. Yigal Shtayim's *Tmunot archiyon* (Archival photographs) is composed of a set of paintings made by projecting enlarged photographs on to two deserted Palestinian houses, their doors cemented shut, in Haifa's Wadi Nissnas neighborhood.

FIGURE 10 Peter Eisenman's Memorial to the Murdered Jews of Europe (detail). Photograph by Amir Eshel, 2009.

FIGURE 11 Yigal Shtayim, *Archival Photographs*. Photograph by Amir Eshel, 2009.

Shtayim found the main image he used for his artwork in Haifa's municipal archive. It dates from 1937 and depicts a group of Jewish men, immigrants to Mandate-era Palestine. Like others who arrived in Haifa at that time, they managed to escape from Fascist Europe. In the backdrop, behind the immigrants with their dark suits, we recognize local Palestinian workers in summer clothes. This juxtaposition of the detached newcomers and the land's inhabitants is enhanced by the other photograph that makes up *Archival Photographs*: an image of a woman who appears to stand at the window.

Originally, Yigal Shtayim intended to include only the image of the Jewish refugees and the Palestinian workers in his artwork. His aim was to depict the "historical fact," as he puts it, of a building the original Palestinian inhabitants left when new inhabitants came to occupy it.[6] The topic of exile was central to him, because his own family escaped from Berlin in the course of Nazism. While Shtayim was painting the image of the Jewish refugees on the building's exterior, however, some of the current Palestinian residents of Wadi Nissnas, whom he befriended, wondered about the image, noting that the men in the dark suits had not originally lived in the building on which their image was now projected. Shtayim told them that this was exactly his theme: how people are forced

to leave their homes behind while others come to inhabit them. At this
point, his unexpected audience brought him a photo of the Palestinian
woman who actually lived in that house until 1948. Shtayim then decided to insert her image into his artwork, creating, in fact, a new work
of art.

Now Shtayim's evolving *Archival Photographs* became composed of
images that relate to various, multidirectional memories. While the men
in dark suits stand for the fate of European Jewry as it touches the history of Israel/Palestine, the Palestinian woman we gaze at in the window invokes the moment in which she, like many other Palestinians,
escaped from the city out of fear of what the Jewish victors might do
to her.[7] Whereas the image of the Jewish refugees alludes to the pain of
exile caused by fervent European racism, the projected photograph of
the woman evokes the suffering that many Palestinians endured during

FIGURE 12 Yigal Shtayim, *Archival Photographs* (detail). Photograph by Amir Eshel,
2009.

FIGURE 13 Yigal Shtayim, *Archival Photographs* (detail). Photograph by Amir Eshel, 2009.

and after the war of 1948. In Shtayim's artwork, these memories do not efface each other in a zero-sum game. Rather, the installation displays the proximity of multiple, conflicting memories that haunt contemporary Haifa. It also demonstrates how these divergent memories are bound to continue to exist in the future, very near to each other, expressing the fates of both Israelis and Palestinians.

Moreover, Yigal Shtayim's *Archival Photographs* actually ties the past to the present and to a possible future in several ways. To begin with, it changes the very lay of the land. It turns a deserted house whose inhabitants' history was known only locally into a disturbing presence for all to see and into a metaphor for the lingering memory of those exiled from their land. The painted house is no mausoleum but rather a space that challenges viewers, be they Israeli Jews, Palestinian citizens of Israel, or others, to consider their national tragedies—the Holocaust and al-Nakba—as other than mutually exclusive frameworks of reference imparting special rights or an uncontested position in Israel/Palestine. *Archival Photographs* prompts them instead to mull over their position vis-à-vis the convergence of these two tragedies. It encourages them to ask how they can move from where they are to where they may want to be.

The projection of the former inhabitant's image on to the cemented windows ties the past to a possible future in another manner: following Shtayim's artistic move to fill with a human image what has been for decades a blank slate, the *re*shaped house allows the beholder to contemplate what may bring physical life back to this and similar haunted houses. Viewers are wordlessly asked to dwell on what it would take to revive this and numerous other empty dwellings in Haifa and elsewhere in Israel.

The ability of *Archival Photographs* to change the given vocabulary, to propel thought, and even action, is seen in the decision—prompted

FIGURE 14 Yigal Shtayim, *Archival Photographs* (detail). Photograph by Amir Eshel, 2009.

FIGURE 15 Yigal Shtayim, *Archival Photographs* (detail). Photograph by Amir Eshel, 2009.

by the images now painted on the walls—of Haifa's municipal authority to reverse its plan to demolish the cemented house.[8] The work itself has also continued to evolve: a year after Shtayim completed his original artwork, he returned to the same street in Wadi Nissnas to add another set of paintings to his installation on an adjacent empty house. What originally began with the single image and one painting has now become a growing web of images and human interactions that include uncovering the unnoticed (the photograph that Shtayim originally used), artistic imagination, conversation, reckoning with the unsaid, and ultimately the emergence of new artistic creations. In a nutshell, *Archival Photographs* displays the capacity of art to offer new ways to experience past circumstances, to reshape a given, seemingly determined environment (in this case, the street in Wadi Nissnas), and, most significantly, to push "us"— artists, viewers, citizens, and municipal authorities—beyond where we find ourselves in the given moment.

By encouraging visitors to the Berlin memorial to participate in shaping the artwork with their movements through the space, and by provoking reflection and even action through photographic projections, Eisenman's and Shtayim's creations define what I have described throughout this book as *futurity*. In the three parts of this study, I have drawn attention to contemporary literature as it addresses the sentiment Franz Kafka expressed in his "Eine kleine Fabel" ("A Little Fable"). Grappling with modernist events such as the world wars, genocide, or mass flight

and expulsion, the works I have discussed present metaphors, characters, and stories to combat the feeling that Kafka's mouse embodies—
that our modern world threatens to close in on us because of the pain we
inflict on each other as a result of our racial, social, or national fantasies.
I have traced how a variety of post-1945 literary works spanning several
languages and cultures allow us to reshape the reservoir of words, images, and ideas we draw on as we *re*-create ourselves. These works thus
effectively keep the world "unfrozen," as David Grossman puts it.[9]

I do not want to rehash my arguments here, but rather, through my
brief consideration of Eisenman and Shtayim, I want to point to the hermeneutic opportunities my discussion offers beyond the study of literature. To begin with, observing these two artworks, we see that many of
the concepts used earlier in this book—"imaginative redescription," a
"practical past," and the creation of "dissensus"—help us make sense of
the visual arts as they turn to modernity's catastrophes. Thus, my brief
discussion of Eisenman and Shtayim underlines futurity as a broad hermeneutic perspective, as an interpretive point of view that includes readers and viewers of films and the visual arts, as well as critics—in short,
as a way of addressing contemporary culture that places an emphasis on
the latent futural dimension of the relevant object. The hermeneutic of
futurity emerging from the pages of this book is the critical-analytical
counterpart to David Grossman's suggestion that contemporary literature not only acknowledges the realities of the modern world as it threatens to close in on us but also allows us to see possibilities for shaping the

FIGURE 16 Yigal Shtayim, *Archival Photographs*. Photograph by Amir Eshel, 2009.

future: to recognize what allows hope, the prospects of human advancement. Eisenman's memorial and Shtayim's work offer us a glimpse into modernity's abyss but also tie together that past, the present, and a possible future. A hermeneutic that underlines these works' retrospective and prospective dimensions acknowledges their power not just to confront that abyss but to point to ways of overcoming it.

Recognizing futurity in these works is dependent on the viewer's or critic's willingness to pay attention to the interplay of retrospection and prospection. As with all other critical approaches, a hermeneutic that ponders an artwork's prospective qualities is the result of a set of choices. It involves opting to combine a reading of a work's display of trauma with its possible gestures toward new beginnings. It implies complementing the delights of a distant, analytical stance vis-à-vis the artwork—the joys of the detective-like uncovering of its commitments to prevalent discourses, for example—with exploring how it adds to our view of the given and of what may come. It is, after all, the choice of the critic to read Günter Grass's Sigismund Markus as merely the expression of anti-Semitic stereotypes or as the result of a prevalent bigoted iconography and a young German author's attempt to imagine a Jewish person in pain. A hermeneutic of futurity means indulging less in the pleasures of indicting art that evokes modernity's horrors for what it fails to achieve and focusing instead on how it may potentially bring about what David Grossman calls *tikkun*: an active engagement with ethical and political challenges of the present.[10]

My notion of a hermeneutic of futurity draws on Walter Benjamin and Hannah Arendt's view of what constitutes meaningful criticism. The critic, Benjamin contends, should not only comment on the work's "subject matter"—say, its historical context or place in discourse—but also uncover its "truth content," what allows it to attain an "afterlife."[11] While the critic who remains solely focused on commenting on the work's subject matter becomes, in fact, a chemist analyzing the wood and the ashes of a funeral pyre, meaningful criticism, Benjamin states, "inquires about the truth whose living flame goes on burning over the heavy logs of the past and the light ashes of life gone by."[12] Adopting Benjamin's simile, Arendt sees the critic as an alchemist "practicing the obscure art of transmuting the futile elements of the real into shining, enduring gold of truth or rather watching and interpreting the historical process that brings about such magical transfiguration."[13] Emphasizing the critic's role in unfolding the artwork's capacity to transfigure, to have a substantive "afterlife," Benjamin and Arendt harken back to the philosophical heritage of Kant and German Romanticism. Yet this critical tradition with its stress on futurity continues well into our own days. I find it echoed, for example, in a recently published conversation, "Kritik: Aus Nächster Nähe" (Critique: In close proximity), conducted between Joseph Vogl and Alexander Kluge.[14] *Kritik*, the two agree, has little to do with criticizing a book or an author. Kluge asks rhetorically, "Why would one want to waste time with writing about bad literature anyway?" (12–13). Rather, he notes, *Kritik* in its classical sense, that of the Romantic age—Kant's *Kritik der Reinen Vernunft*, for example— was not about finding fault, but rather it was a highly developed application of "the positive ability to distinguish . . . to state what is new" (12). If we think of *Kritik* as an act, adds Vogl, then it means to hesitate, to be indecisive (10). The essence of *Kritik*, Kluge sums up, "is always to marvel, to be astonished" (20). In other words, *Kritik*, for Vogl and Kluge, has little to do with faulting the work of art for what the critic sees as lacking—failures to pay tribute to other works, for example—and everything to do with experiential sensing (*zögern* and *zaudern*), with discovering and unfolding what is new about the work. *Kritik* is concerned with exploring what is different, remarkable, and puzzling about artistic phenomena. It has to do with taking in innovative creations and unexpected experiences and describing their newness. It means considering how a novel, a photograph, a film *changes* what we see, know, or think—how it can alter the ways in which we make sense of the world and of ourselves.

As I have emphasized throughout this book, a hermeneutic of futurity hardly means a literal *tracing* out of any given artwork's role in propagating a promise of a better future. Rather, a hermeneutic perspective that emphasizes futurity in the artworks of Shtayim or Eisenman, for example, highlights these creations' turn to issues of present and future responsibility, their attentiveness to the pains of others, *and* their ability to suggest to the beholder the possibility of addressing both of these things through action. Futurity as a hermeneutic perspective in Shtayim's case means accepting that the woman with the piercing eyes at the window is not just a marker of the past's persistent pains but also a concrete challenge to the viewer: How do you deal with my condition? With the pain of my children? And with the suffering of their children? The beholder has the choice of reading her gaze as a sign of her anguish—as merely an expression of the demand to be recognized for her past suffering—or of engaging the image practically, as a force for "a current present-future of practical engagement."[15]

We can further deepen our grasp of futurity as a hermeneutic perspective by juxtaposing two responses to the modernist events of our time:

Walter Benjamin's ubiquitous angel of history from "On the Concept of History" and Hannah Arendt's imaginative reading of Kafka's character Er (He). Famously, Benjamin drafted his "On the Concept of History" on the verge of the Holocaust and shortly before he would take his own life. In this work, Benjamin attempts to come to terms with his immediate, bleak historical moment by means of the rich philosophical tradition of *Geschichtsphilosophie*, the philosophy of history discussed often in this book. Benjamin adopts a point of view that both embraces and ironically questions Marxian "historical materialism."[16] As he struggles with "the concern of history" (390), "the sky of history" (390), "the open air of history" (395), "the continuum of history" (395, 396), "the structure of history" (402), and so forth, using the vocabulary of a historical materialist, Benjamin also dryly admits that "the true image of the past flits by. The past can be seized only as an image that flashes up at the moment of its recognizability, and is never seen again" (390). Although the past exists only as an "image," Benjamin offers a figure of thought to help us envision this ephemeral entity. He does so by alluding to Paul Klee's drawing *Angelus Novus* (1920), which he possessed at the time:

> There is a picture by Klee called *Angelus Novus*. It shows an angel who seems about to move away from something he stares at. His eyes are wide, his mouth is open, his wings are spread. This is how the angel of history must look. His face is turned toward the past. Where a chain of events appears before *us*, *he* sees one single catastrophe, which keeps piling wreckage upon wreckage and hurls it at his feet. The angel would like to stay, awaken the dead, and make whole what has been smashed. But a storm is blowing from Paradise and has got caught in his wings; it is so strong that the angel can no longer close them. This storm drives him irresistibly into the future, to which his back is turned, while the pile of debris before him grows toward the sky. What we call progress is this storm. (392, emphasis in original)

Note here Benjamin's description of the angel as unveiling to "us," who regard the past as "a chain of events," the past's true nature "one single catastrophe." Note also Benjamin's view of the passage of time as bringing nothing new: the pile of wreckage that is human history just keeps growing from day to day, from one millennium to the next. Furthermore, Benjamin's angel is deprived of any agency. His wish, his dream to mend the world ("make whole"), is meaningless in light of immense, cosmic forces, a heavenly storm that inexorably drives him forward in time. The future here is only the next point in time, a point where the pile of catastrophes will become even bigger. It is essentially an empty future in which neither the angel nor any human will be able to do anything to affect its determinist trajectory. Tellingly, in this melancholic allegory, the storm is blowing "from Paradise" and is equated with "progress." In other words, what is called "progress" has nothing to do with merely human intervention, with what individual actors or groups may do concretely as they encounter new catastrophes.

Visiting the Berlin site of Eisenman's memorial or the houses that Shtayim has chosen for his artwork, one may be tempted to adopt a hermeneutic perspective that follows Benjamin's melancholic gaze. The Berlin memorial's cobbled surface, after all, covers the very earth that housed the bunkers of the murderers. Close to Eisenman's work, one finds many historical remnants that—taken together—seem to suggest that what his work captures is the sense that the past is indeed "wreckage *upon* wreckage." Shtayim's Haifa artwork, likewise, could be seen as merely painting over the material remnants of the suffering and pain that Palestinians endured during and after 1948. The artwork can be interpreted as testifying to the storm that swept Europe and then Palestine, uprooting whole generations in its disastrous thrust and leaving us today with the piles of debris. Given modernity's destructions in the past, present, and possibly the future, there can be no question in our minds that Benjamin's angel of history offers an apt metaphoric constellation for understanding, a rubric to interpret artworks that contemplate the abyss of the twentieth century and imagine what may transpire with even greater force in the twenty-first.

Yet this is not enough. This is a surrender to a delectation of melancholy and to a relentless focus on modernity's horrors. We, as viewers and critics of Eisenman's and Shtayim's works, can choose instead to turn to another figure of thought that emerged following modernity's recent catastrophes: Hannah Arendt's free interpretation of Kafka's "HE." As mentioned earlier, Arendt contends that Kafka's He battles both the past that pushes him forward and the fear of his uncertain future.[17] Unlike Benjamin, Arendt views the past not as "one single catastrophe" or, as she puts it, as "a burden man has to shoulder and of whose dead weight the living can or even must get rid in their march into the future." Rather, she sees Benjamin's ever-growing pile of wreckage as a "force" that "presses forward," or, in my words, as a resource in which we may discover potentialities. Arendt thus highlights He's ability to fight—to hold his own "against past and future." She in effect rewrites Kafka's short text into an Arendtian story in which He is "inserted into time":

"It is this insertion—the beginning of beginning, to put it in Augustinian terms—which splits up the time continuum."[18]

Futurity as a hermeneutic outlook prompts us to consider works such as the Berlin Holocaust Memorial, with its abstract stelae and documentation center, both as accounting for the wreckage of the Holocaust and as what one may call, with Arendt, a *mode of human insertion*. A hermeneutic of futurity underlines the ways this work is battling the past and the future. By reshaping Berlin's urban space it faces up to a past the weight of which often threatens to crush us and to an uncertain future that may appear empty—just more wreckage. Eisenman's and Shtayim's works allow us, such a perspective suggests, to view our past and thus our given conditions as not merely the outcome of supernatural "storms" but rather the result of human action. Futurity as a hermeneutic outlook gives us the possibility of engaging the work of art as an insertion in space and time and of responding to the ways it prompts us to converse with others and to consider how we might insert ourselves into our own stormy circumstances. Such a perspective underscores the Berlin Holocaust Memorial's ability to encourage visitors to consider what Arendt tellingly calls new beginnings, or simply human agency. Observing Shtayim's work from this point of view means placing the emphasis on how the images suggest the possibility of a new beginning in Arendt's sense, specifically, the possibility of ethical or political action that would help bring life back to the haunted dwelling.

The hermeneutic of futurity traces how these works' insertion into space and thus into our mental realities can cause the forces of past and future to "deflect, however lightly, from their original direction."[19] It allows us to view Kafka's mouse from "A Little Fable" not as the depiction of a given, unchangeable state of things but rather as a warning, as a disruption to our way of thinking and acting. Viewed as the victim of "storms" to which it is passively subjected, Kafka's mouse, like all of us, may indeed be destined to exist at a point where no change of direction is possible. But we need not succumb to the idea of human history as a recurring set of storms.

It is not that we readers, visitors to memorials, or beholders of works of art need to decide between Benjamin and Arendt, between acknowledging the unredeemable "single catastrophe" that modernity often appears to be and the past as a "force" that is both terrible and possibly redemptive.[20] Rather, a hermeneutic of futurity calls on us to keep both the retrospective and prospective viewpoints intact—to take interest not only in measuring the depth of the abyss as works of art present it but also in what they suggest it would take to avert "the end of mankind,"

as Paul Auster emblematically calls it in *Oracle Night*. After several decades of scholarship and writing in which considerable emphasis has
been placed on the past as a burden we can hardly sustain, futurity allows us, I believe, to venture in a new direction. For Benjamin, who
wrote his "On the Concept of History" during one of the most hopeless moments of the modern era, "the future" seemed available only by
means of a revolutionary "real state of emergency" (392). Benjamin
drew inspiration from what he took to be the Jewish messianic tradition in which "the Jews were prohibited from inquiring into the future:
the Torah and the prayers instructed them in remembrance" (397). The
disenchanted future, Benjamin maintained, remained nevertheless a viable horizon, since "every second was the small gateway in time through
which the Messiah might enter" (397). For the literature and the art this
book presents, having a future means no longer waiting for the coming
of a Messiah or waiting for a "real state of emergency" of the kind witnessed by the twentieth and twenty-first centuries in order to change our
world. Rather, this literature and the interpretive philosophy this book
promotes seek to maintain the idea of the future as a viable aspect of everyday human life, one that we need to pursue actively if we are to have
a future at all. What artists of our age deserve are interpreters who acknowledge the futural elements of their work, who can thus help them
help us avert the fate of Kafka's mouse.

Notes

ACKNOWLEDGMENTS

1. Zali Gurevitch, *Sicha* [Conversation] (Tel-Aviv: Babel, 2011), 43–44, my translation.

INTRODUCTION

1. Franz Kafka, "A Little Fable," in *The Complete Stories*, ed. Nahum N. Glatzer, trans. Willa Muir and Edwin Muir (New York: Schocken Books, 1971), 445. On the genealogy of "A Little Fable," see Richard T. Gray et al., *A Franz Kafka Encyclopedia* (Westport, CT: Greenwood Press, 2005), 162.

2. Hayden White, "The Modernist Event," in his *Figural Realism: Studies in the Mimesis Effect* (Baltimore, MD: Johns Hopkins University Press, 1999), 66–86. The historian Dan Diner famously coined the term *Zivilisationsbruch* (breach of civilization) to underline the sense that the Holocaust forces us to rethink the very notion of civilization. Dan Diner, ed., *Zivilisationsbruch: Denken nach Auschwitz* (Frankfurt am Main: Fischer, 1988).

3. White, "Modernist Event," 69.

4. David Grossman, *Writing in the Dark: Essays on Literature and Politics* (New York: Farrar, Straus and Giroux, 2008), 59. Hereafter, page references to this work will be given parenthetically in the text.

5. *Tikkun* (or *tiqqun*) is a noun based on the root *t q n*. This root's semantic field includes the notions of "to set straight," "to put in order," and "to mend." In the Mishnah, the idea of *tikkun* appears as the proper ordering of the world, that is, *tikkun olam* (the mending of the world), to justify the role of rabbinic

ordinance in improving social and legal arrangements. In Lurianic Kabbalah (the tradition to which Grossman refers), the term points to the mystical process of mending the primordial disaster of the "breaking of the vessels" by which the devastated world of chaos becomes redeemed through human practice. See R. J. Zwi Werblowsky and Geoffrey Wigoder, eds., *The Oxford Dictionary of the Jewish Religion* (New York: Oxford University Press, 1997), s.v. "Tiqqun 'Olam," 693.

6. For a compelling alternative and comparative perspective on the "unprecedented" nature of modern-era violence, see Steven Pinker, *The Better Angels of Our Nature: Why Violence Has Declined* (New York: Penguin Books, 2011). In contrast to Pinker, I see in such modern, technologically enabled man-made catastrophes as Auschwitz and Hiroshima the introduction of a new kind of violence that provokes fears of complete annihilation (of an entire people or of the human race). Although human violence as such has declined, as Pinker forcefully shows, modern technology nonetheless gives rise to the justifiable concern that in the future we will witness even worse eruptions of technologically enabled violence than those of the last century.

7. Svetlana Boym, *The Future of Nostalgia* (New York: Basic Books, 2001), xvi.

8. The term Kindertransport refers to the transfer of Jewish children to Great Britain and elsewhere after the so-called Reichskristallnacht. In the course of the operation, which was organized by Jewish groups, Jewish children were sent from Germany, Austria, and Czechoslovakia to Great Britain. The first transport arrived on December 2, 1938, in the East Anglian port of Harwich—some sixty miles from Norwich, where Sebald taught at the University of East Anglia. The Kindertransport operation was ended at the beginning of the war on September 1, 1939. Approximately ten thousand children came to Great Britain.

9. Aristotle, *Poetics*, ed. and trans. Stephen Halliwell (Cambridge, MA: Harvard University Press, 1995), 59.

10. Ibid., 59, note b.

11. Ibid., 59, 61.

12. Percy Bysshe Shelley, "A Defence of Poetry," in *Shelley's Poetry and Prose*, 2nd ed., ed. Donald H. Reiman and Neil Fraistat (New York: W. W. Norton, 2002), 535.

13. Nicholas M. Gaskill, "Experience and Signs: Towards a Pragmatist Literary Criticism," *New Literary History* 39 (2008): 165–83; Günter Leypoldt, "Uses of Metaphor: Richard Rorty's Literary Criticism and the Poetics of World-Making," *New Literary History* 39 (2008): 145–63.

14. John Dewey, *Experience and Nature* (1925; New York: Dover, 1958), 378, 381–82 (emphasis in original), quoted in Leypoldt, "Uses of Metaphor," 148.

15. John Dewey, *Art as Experience* (1934), in *The Later Works, 1925–1953*, vol. 10, ed. Jo Ann Boydston (Carbondale: Southern Illinois University Press, 1981), 9. I am quoting here using Gaskill, "Experience and Signs."

16. See Dewey, *Art as Experience*, 245; and Gaskill, "Experience and Signs," 171.

17. The term "lifeworld" follows Edmund Husserl's concept of *Lebenswelt*. In its original meaning, notes Hans Ulrich Gumbrecht, "'life-world' compre-

hends the totality of possible forms of behavior that we—or, more precisely, the traditions of Western culture—attribute to human beings." Hans Ulrich Gumbrecht, *In 1926* (Cambridge, MA: Harvard University Press, 1997), 418. According to Gumbrecht, each particular culture selects from the range of possibilities contained in the lifeworld. To distinguish the resulting practices that make up a certain culture or milieu from the lifeworld that encompasses actions and behaviors that can never become reality (e.g., "eternity"), Gumbrecht calls the former the "everyday-world." Somewhat paradoxically, Gumbrecht notes, "the life-world includes the human capacity to imagine actions and forms of behavior which it explicitly excludes from the range of human possibilities" (418).

18. Richard Rorty, "Grandeur, Profundity, and Finitude," in Richard Rorty, *Philosophy as Cultural Politics*, vol. 4 of *Philosophical Papers* (Cambridge: Cambridge University Press, 2007), 84. Rorty quotes here Isaiah Berlin, *The Roots of Romanticism* (Princeton, NJ: Princeton University Press, 2001), 87. Rorty referred on many occasions to his debt to the Romantic tradition. See, e.g., his essay "Pragmatism as Romantic Polytheism," in *The Revival of Pragmatism: New Essays on Social Thought, Law, Culture*, ed. Morris Dickstein (Durham, NC: Duke University Press, 1998), 21–36.

19. Richard Rorty, "Pragmatism and Romanticism," in Rorty, *Philosophy as Cultural Politics*, 115.

20. Ibid., 118.

21. Ibid.

22. Richard Rorty, *Contingency, Irony and Solidarity* (Cambridge: Cambridge University Press, 1989), 41. Rorty makes it clear on several occasions that he uses the term "poetry" in an extended sense—prose writers and also thinkers who created entire, new vocabularies (Newton, Marx, Darwin, Freud) are all "strong poets" in Harold Bloom's sense: innovative makers of a new language that is capable of altering our perceptions about our circumstances in ways that allow us to live fuller, richer individual and social lives. See, e.g., Rorty's very concise remarks in "The Fire of Life," *Poetry Magazine*, November 2007, available online at http://www.poetryfoundation.org/journal/feature .html?id=180185 (accessed July 20, 2010).

23. Richard Rorty and Edward Ragg, "Worlds or Words Apart? The Consequences of Pragmatism for Literary Studies" (interview), in Richard Rorty, *Take Care of Freedom and Truth Will Take Care of Itself*, ed. Eduardo Mendieta (Stanford, CA: Stanford University Press, 2006), 132.

24. Richard Rorty, "Unfamiliar Noises: Hesse and Davidson on Metaphor," in *Objectivity, Relativism and Truth*, vol. 1 of *Philosophical Papers* (Cambridge: Cambridge University Press, 1991), 163 (emphasis in original). On Rorty's reading of Davidson and on Davidson's own view of the goals of literary criticism, see Bryan Vescio, "Donald Davidson, Pragmatism, and Literary Theory," *Philosophy and Literature* 22, no. 1 (1998): 200–211, esp. 207–9.

25. Rorty, *Contingency, Irony and Solidarity*, 82.

26. Hayden White, "The Metaphysics of Narrativity: Time and Symbol in Ricoeur's Philosophy of History," in Hayden White, *The Content of the Form: Narrative Discourse and Historical Representation* (Baltimore, MD: Johns Hopkins University Press, 1987), 172–73. White expands on "emplotment" as

describing the capacity of fictional narrative (and thus larger plot sequences, as they are embedded in novels) to present us with new views of historical events such as the Holocaust in "Historical Emplotment and the Problem of Truth in Historical Representation," in his *Figural Realism: Studies in the Mimesis Effect* (Baltimore, MD: Johns Hopkins University Press, 1999), 27–42, esp. 30–32. For a full account of Ricoeur's notion of emplotment in fictional narratives, see his classic discussion of "Mimesis2" in *Time and Narrative*, vol. 1, trans. K. McLaughlin and D. Pellauer (Chicago: University of Chicago Press, 1984), 64–70. See also Peter Brooks, *Reading for the Plot: Design and Intention in Narrative* (Cambridge, MA: Harvard University Press, 1992).

27. Hayden White, "The Question of Narrative in Contemporary Historical Theory," in White, *The Content of the Form*, 52–53.

28. I follow in this judgment Leypoldt, "Uses of Metaphor," 145. On the critique of Rorty's notion of literature, see, e.g., Leypoldt's discussion of Christoph Demmerling, 147.

29. Ibid., 145.

30. S. Yizhar finished writing the novellas *Sipur Khirbet Khizah* and *Hashavui* (The captive) in November 1948. They were published in 1949 in a volume entitled *Sipur Khirbet Khizah* (Merhavyah: Sifriyat Poalim, 1949). Quoting from the story, however, I will use the English translation, *Khirbet Khizeh*, trans. Nicholas de Lange and Yaacob Dweck (Jerusalem: Ibis Editions, 2008), and thus will follow the translators' decision to call the village Khizeh and not Khizah.

31. Richard Rorty, "Der Roman als Mittel zur Erlösung aus der Selbstbezogenheit," trans. Andrew James Johnston, in *Dimensionen ästhetischer Erfahrung*, ed. Joachim Küpper and Christoph Menke (Frankfurt am Main: Suhrkamp, 2003), 49–66. Hereafter, page references to this work will be given parenthetically in the text. My English quotations from this text are based on its unpublished English version, "Redemption from Egotism: James and Proust as Spiritual Exercises," which Rorty kindly sent me after a conversation at Stanford.

32. Rorty uses the German term *Reflexion* ("Der Roman," 55), which I interpret, in the philosophical tradition, as indicating self-examination, unguided thought, and debate. On literary criticism that follows de Man's search for "nothingness at the heart of everything" as impoverishment, see Rorty and Ragg, "Worlds or Words Apart?," 137.

33. See Rorty, *Contingency, Irony and Solidarity*, 41–42; and Richard Rorty, "Persuasion Is a Good Thing" (an interview with Wolfgang Ullrich and Helmut Mayert), in Rorty, *Take Care of Freedom and Truth Will Take Care of Itself*, 70–72.

34. Revisiting modernist and postmodern American fiction, Timothy Parrish similarly points out that writers such as William Faulkner in *Absalom, Absalom!* (1936) and Cormac McCarthy in *Blood Meridian* (1985) are not simply critiquing a certain version of the past but are actually "practicing history by writing, or making, it themselves." These writers, Parrish goes on to say, "*write history as a form of fiction.*" Timothy Parrish, *From the Civil War to the Apocalypse: Postmodern History and American Fiction* (Amherst: University of Massachusetts Press, 2008), 2 (emphasis in original).

35. Michael Oakeshott, "Present, Future and Past," in his *On History and Other Essays* (Indianapolis: Liberty Fund, 1999), 39, 40.

36. Ibid., 40.

37. Ibid., 41.

38. In my previous publications, I have examined the work of German Jewish writers, occasionally comparing the work of German and German Jewish authors. See, e.g., Amir Eshel, "Die Grammatik des Verlusts: Verlorene Kinder, verlorene Zeit in Barbara Honigmanns *Soharas Reise* und in Hans-Ulrich Treichels *Der Verlorene*," in *Deutsch-jüdische Literatur der neunziger Jahre: Die Generation nach der Shoah*, ed. Hartmut Steinecke and Sander Gilman, Beiheft zur Zeitschrift für deutsche Philologie (Berlin: Erich Schmidt, 2002), 59–74.

39. Some recent studies have begun outlining the parameters of a comparative examination. See, e.g., Gil Z. Hochberg, *In Spite of Partition: Jews, Arabs, and the Limits of Separatist Imagination* (Princeton, NJ: Princeton University Press, 2007), esp. 1–19 and 116–38. Furthermore, Michael Rothberg has insightfully suggested in his recent *Multidirectional Memory: Remembering the Holocaust in the Age of Decolonization* (Stanford, CA: Stanford University Press, 2009) that group memories (or national remembrance) do not necessarily compete with or exclude the memories of "others" in a "zero-sum struggle for preeminence" (3). Rather, memory is, as Rothberg shows, "multidirectional," the result of an ongoing process by which different actors and agents negotiate their memories with those of others and by so doing evolve. I will return to Rothberg's contribution to this study below.

40. Alain Badiou, *The Century*, trans. Alberto Toscano (Cambridge: Polity, 2007), 105.

41. See, e.g., Georg Lukács, *The Historical Novel*, trans. Hannah Mitchell and Stanley Mitchell (London: Merlin, 1962), 88–98, 123–32, 136–52; Georg Lukács, *Realism in Our Time: Literature and the Class Struggle*, trans. John Mander and Necke Mander (New York: Harper, 1964), 17–23, 44–56, 75–96; and Fredric Jameson, *The Political Unconscious: Narrative as a Socially Symbolic Act* (Ithaca, NY: Cornell University Press, 1981), 17–35, 105–31.

42. In considering contemporary literature's prospective capacity, I also build on studies such as Amy Elias's *Sublime Desire: History and Post-1960 Fiction* (Baltimore, MD: Johns Hopkins University Press, 2001), specifically on Elias's claim that novels such as Thomas Pynchon's *Gravity's Rainbow* (1973) and D. M. Thomas's *The White Hotel* (1981) articulate a post–Second World War sensibility of the limits of epistemological certainty and a focus on the uses and abuses of the past for the construction of identity and nationhood (xxvi). Elias shows how self-conscious historical fiction (what she terms the "metahistorical romance") turns away from history and toward romance because, "like the postmodernist historiography and postmodernist philosophy of its own time" (xi), it can no longer hold on to empirical certainty: "For the postmodern, post-traumatic, metahistorical imagination, history is not a knowledge we learn and 'own,'. . . rather postmodern arts and sciences posit that history is something we . . . can only desire" (xviii). Elias claims, furthermore, that by turning away from the desire to depict the past realistically, works such as Art Spiegelman's graphic novel *Maus* (1986) are able to confront the "terrifying" (42) nature of watershed events such as the Second World War. As they challenge their readers to acknowledge the horror of what remains incomprehensible, such novels also enable "contemplation and enactment of ethical action" (42).

43. Rothberg, *Multidirectional Memory*, 4.

44. Ibid., 11.

45. Ibid., 5.

46. I wish to confine my discussion to a consideration of literature written in the languages I know well: Hebrew, German, and English. Naturally, a full assessment of the literary engagement of the past in contemporary literature should include literatures written outside the confined and protected borders of the First World.

47. See, e.g., the interview with Alain Badiou, "'We Need a Popular Discipline': Contemporary Politics and the Crisis of the Negative," *Critical Inquiry* 34, no. 4 (Summer 2008): 645–59; and Slavoj Žižek, *The Parallax View* (Cambridge, MA: MIT Press), 317–28.

48. Richard Rorty, "The End of Leninism and History as Comic Frame," in *History and the Idea of Progress*, ed. Arthur M. Melzer, Jerry Weinberger, and M. Richard Zinman (Ithaca, NY: Cornell University Press, 1995), 211–26. Rorty regards the insight that the "romance of world history" has lost its sway as the main argument behind Fukuyama's thesis. For a somewhat different version of this essay, see also Richard Rorty, "The End of Leninism, Havel, and Social Hope," in Richard Rorty, *Truth and Progress: Philosophical Papers*, vol. 3 (Cambridge: Cambridge University Press, 1998), 228–46.

49. Rorty, "The End of Leninism and History as Comic Frame," 212.

50. Ibid., 213–14.

51. Jay Winter, *Dreams of Peace and Freedom: Utopian Moments in the Twentieth Century* (New Haven, CT: Yale University Press, 2006), 1, 4. Winter goes on to discuss what he calls "minor utopias": the effort to imagine a "radically better world" (1), "liberation usually on a smaller scale, without the grandiose pretensions or the almost unimaginable hubris and cruelties of the 'major' utopian projects" (5).

52. Ibid., 1.

53. Mark Lilla, "A New, Political St. Paul?" *New York Review of Books*, October 23, 2008, 69–70. Lilla goes on to outline how essentially capitalist, liberal ideas and practices have spread in Europe and elsewhere since the collapse of the Soviet Union and how Marxist-leaning thought has turned, implausibly, to Saint Paul in the hope of reenergizing the leftist, utopian tradition.

54. John N. Gray, *Black Mass: Apocalyptic Religion and the Death of Utopia* (New York: Farrar, Straus and Giroux, 2007), 1–35. Beginning in the 1980s, and even more so after 1989, we have witnessed the rise of religious utopianism, to be sure, or rather the rise of eschatology in the form of such ideologies as those propagated by Al Qaeda. Yet these are substantially different from the utopias to which Gray and others are referring, since they involve "redemption," a new, dominant role available only to a part of humanity—the followers of the creed.

55. Amy Hungerford, "On the Period Formerly Known as Contemporary," *American Literary History* 20, nos. 1–2 (Spring–Summer 2008): 410–19.

56. Russell Jacoby, *Picture Imperfect: Utopian Thought for an Anti-utopian Age* (New York: Columbia University Press, 2005), 5. Jacoby's book is, as the title suggests, a staunch defense of the tradition of utopian thought and literature.

57. Fredric Jameson, *Archaeologies of the Future: The Desire Called Utopia and Other Science Fictions* (London: Verso, 2005).

58. Francis Fukuyama, *The End of History and the Last Man* (New York: Free Press, 1992). As Ernst Breisach, among many others, observed, Fukuyama's book was only the most recent expression of a line of thought that goes back to Hegel and Alexander Kojève and that is centered on the idea that history as we have known it might indeed approach its conclusion. See Ernst Breisach, *On the Future of History: The Postmodernist Challenge and Its Aftermath* (Chicago: University of Chicago Press, 2003), 49–54. On the "end of history" discourse, see also Lutz Niethammer, *Posthistoire: Has History Come to an End?*, trans. Patrick Camiller (London: Verso, 1994). For a critique of Fukuyama's "triumphalism," see Jacques Derrida's emblematic discussion in *Specters of Marx: The State of the Debt, the Work of Mourning, and the New International*, trans. Peggy Kamuf (New York: Routledge, 1994), 56–75.

59. Rorty, "The End of Leninism and History as Comic Frame." Rorty is certainly not alone in taking a more balanced approach to Fukuyama's *The End of History and the Last Man*. Peter Sloterdjik, for example, dedicates large sections of *Zorn und Zeit: Politisch-psychologischer Versuch* (Frankfurt am Main: Suhrkamp, 2006) to reconsidering this work in light of the political realities of the era following 9/11.

60. Badiou, *The Century*, 105 (my emphasis).

61. Ibid.

62. Fredric Jameson, "The End of Temporality," *Critical Inquiry* 29, no. 4 (Summer 2003): 704.

63. I refer here to Fredric Jameson's claim that "it is still difficult to see how future Utopias could ever be imagined in any absolute dissociation from socialism in its larger sense of anti-capitalism; dissociated, that is to say, from the values of social and economic equality and the universal right to food, lodging, medicine, education and work" (*Archaeologies of the Future*, 196–97). Significantly, although we now know so much about the fundamental abuses of all these rights in previous experiments with socialist utopias such as the Soviet Union, for Jameson the existence of the Soviet Union can still be seen as having produced "a new kind of ideological object, positive and negative all at once" (197).

64. Giorgio Agamben, *Homo Sacer: Sovereign Power and Bare Life*, trans. Daniel Heller-Roazen (Stanford, CA: Stanford University Press, 1998). On Agamben's debt to Arendt, see Rothberg, *Multidirectional Memory*, 44–46.

65. Rothberg, *Multidirectional Memory*, 33–65. Rothberg also points in his discussions to Arendt's shortcomings in recognizing the impact of colonial practices and of colonial discourse in her writing.

66. Hannah Arendt, *Men in Dark Times* (San Diego: Harcourt, Brace, 1968), ix (my emphasis).

67. Hannah Arendt, *The Life of the Mind*, 1-vol. ed. (New York: Harcourt Brace Jovanovich, 1978), 102–3, 226n67.

68. Hannah Arendt, *Denktagebuch: 1950–1973*, ed. Ursula Ludz and Ingeborg Nordmann, 2 vols. (Munich: Piper Verlag, 2002), 1:46.

69. Ibid., 48.

70. Hannah Arendt, *The Origins of Totalitarianism* (New York: Harcourt, Brace, 1979), 478–79. Arendt refers to the "crisis of our time" on 478.

71. Hannah Arendt, "No Longer and Not Yet," in Hannah Arendt, *Essays in Understanding, 1930–1954,* ed. Jerome Kohn (New York: Harcourt, Brace, 1994), 159–60. On Arendt's thought regarding the locus of literature in the tension field of past and future, see Barbara Hahn, "Vom Ort der Literatur zwischen Vergangenheit und Zukunft: Über Hannah Arendt," in *Im Nachvollzug des Geschriebenen: Theorie der Literatur nach 1945,* ed. Barbara Hahn (Würzburg: Königshausen und Neumann, 2007), 87–98.

72. Hannah Arendt, *Between Past and Future: Eight Exercises in Political Thought* (New York: Penguin, 1977). Hereafter, page references to this work will be given parenthetically in the text, preceded by *BPF.* Arendt returned to Kafka's parable in *Life of the Mind,* 202–10. On Arendt's reading of this parable as "a figure of thought describing modern man," see Vivian Liska's insightful reading in *When Kafka Says We: Uncommon Communities in German-Jewish Literature* (Bloomington: Indiana University Press, 2009), 210–12. More recently, Svetlana Boym has offered an inspiring interpretation of Arendt's reading of Kafka's "HE" as both offering "a perfect metaphor for the activity of thought" (229) and pointing to human freedom. See Svetlana Boym, *Another Freedom: The Alternative History of an Idea* (Chicago: University of Chicago Press, 2010).

73. Since my point here relates to Arendt, and not to Kafka, I quote here from the version that Arendt gives in *Between Past and Future,* 7. For this version Arendt relies mostly on Willa Muir and Edwin Muir's translation in *The Great Wall of China* (New York: Schocken Books, 1946). In a footnote, Arendt acknowledges that she "slightly" adapted the Muirs' translation. She also gives the German original in a separate footnote (*Between Past and Future,* 283). It is interesting to note that the entire section of the German text that she supplies was erased by Kafka, yet reinserted by Max Brod. Since Arendt refers to the entire text as it appeared in *The Great Wall of China* and thus as she knew it, I am leaving it in this form in the quotation. On Kafka's erasure and Brod's insertion, see Liska, *When Kafka Says We,* 224n4.

74. When Arendt interprets Kafka's parable in her *Life of the Mind,* she writes, "Man lives in this in-between, and what he calls the present is a life-long fight against the dead weight of the past, driving him forward with hope, and a fear of a future (whose only certainty is death), driving him backward toward 'the quiet of the past' with nostalgia for and remembrance of the only reality he can be sure of" (205).

75. See Peg Birmingham's insightful discussion of Arendt's interpretation of Kafka's parable in Peg Birmingham, *Hannah Arendt and Human Rights: The Predicament of Common Responsibility* (Bloomington: Indiana University Press, 2006), 17–23.

76. Hannah Arendt, *The Human Condition* (Chicago: University of Chicago Press, 1958), 5. Hereafter, page references to this work will be given parenthetically in the text, preceded by *HC.* On Hannah Arendt's concept of "natality," see Patricia Bowen-Moore, *Hannah Arendt's Philosophy of Natality* (London: Macmillan, 1989). On the role of natality in the overall structure of Arendt's

thought, see Seyla Benhabib, *The Reluctant Modernism of Hannah Arendt* (Lanham, MD: Rowman and Littlefield, 2000), 102–22, esp. 108–9. Referring to Arendt's concept of natality, Benhabib aptly speaks of "anthropological universalism." See Seyla Benhabib, "Arendt's Eichmann in Jerusalem," in *The Cambridge Companion to Hannah Arendt*, ed. Dana Villa (Cambridge: Cambridge University Press, 2000), 80. On Arendt's concept of natality, see also the detailed discussion in Birmingham: *Hannah Arendt and Human Rights*, 6–34.

77. Arendt, *Denktagebuch*, 1:208. This note was written in May 1952, that is, before the publication of *The Human Condition*.

78. Arendt, *Denktagebuch*, 1:292.

79. Hannah Arendt, "Franz Kafka: A Revaluation on the Occasion of the Twentieth Anniversary of His Death," in *Essays in Understanding*, 71.

80. Ibid., 73 (my emphasis).

81. In what amounts to a little history of the novel, Arendt notes: "The basis for the classical novel was an acceptance of society as such, a submission to life as it happens, a conviction that greatness of destiny is beyond human virtues and human vice. It presupposed the decline of the citizen, who, during the days of the French Revolution, had attempted to govern the world with human laws. It pictured the growth of the bourgeois individual for whom life and the world had become a place of events and who desired more and more happenings than the usually narrow and secure framework of his own life could offer him. *Today* these novels which were always in competition (even if imitating reality) with reality itself have been supplanted by the documentary novel. *In our world* real events, real destinies, have long surpassed the wildest imagination of novelists" (ibid., 79, my emphasis). What makes Kafka so modern among his contemporaries is that "he refused to submit to any happenings. . . . He wanted to build a world in accordance with human needs and human dignities, a world where man's actions are determined by himself and which is ruled by his laws and not by mysterious forces emanating from above or from below" (80).

82. Arendt then repeats this reference in her essay "Truth and Politics," in *Between Past and Future*, 262. On Arendt's reference to Dinesen's remarks, see Lynn R. Wilkinson, "Hannah Arendt on Isak Dinesen: Between Storytelling and Theory," *Comparative Literature* 56, no. 1 (Winter 2004): 77–98. Wilkinson also discusses in detail Arendt's view on narratives as revealing the meaning of human action (80–81, 90).

83. Arendt, *Men in Dark Times*, 112.

84. Hannah Arendt, "The Achievement of Hermann Broch," in Hannah Arendt, *Reflections of Literature and Culture*, ed. Susannah Young-ah Gottlieb (Stanford, CA: Stanford University Press, 2007), 148.

85. Paul Rabinow, *Marking Time: On the Anthropology of the Contemporary* (Princeton, NJ: Princeton University Press, 2008), 1–2 (emphasis in original).

86. For Post·45, see http://post45.research.yale.edu/?page_id=31 (accessed April 23, 2010).

87. On the Holocaust as the "paragon" of all crimes of the twentieth century and as the event at the century's heart, see Badiou, *The Century*, 2. On the Holocaust as the "paradigmatic" "modernist event," see White, "Modernist Event," 69.

CHAPTER ONE

1. Günter Grass, *Beim Häuten der Zwiebel* (Göttingen: Steidl, 2006). The English version appeared in 2007 as *Peeling the Onion*, trans. Michael Henry Heim (New York: Harcourt, 2007). In the following, I will quote from and cite pages in the English translation. The initial interview with Grass made it to the headline of page 1 of Germany's leading daily, the *Frankfurter allgemeine Zeitung*, on August 12, 2006: "Günter Grass: Ich war Mitglied der Waffen-SS."

2. Martin Kölbel, ed., *Ein Buch, Ein Bekenntnis: Die Debatte um Günter Grass's "Beim Häuten der Zwiebel"* (Göttingen: Steidl, 2007), 141–42. Here and elsewhere, unless otherwise noted, translations are mine. The article first appeared as Eva Menasse and Michael Kumpfmüller, "Wider die intellektuelle Gernotokratie: Ein Plädoyer für weniger Grass und mehr Nahost in der Debatte," *Süddeutsche Zeitung*, August 17, 2006.

3. The scholarly work on postwar German culture as it deals with Nazism is a vast "moving target," as Chloe Paver recently noted: every week new novels, films, TV programs, and public debates surrounding that past demand our attention. Chloe Paver, *Refractions of the Third Reich in German and Austrian Fiction and Film* (Oxford: Oxford University Press, 2007), 1. Under the rubric of the "Psychoanalytical Turn," Paver discusses the immense impact of Alexander Mitscherlich and Margarete Mitscherlich's *The Inability to Mourn: Principles of Collective Behavior* (New York: Grove Press, 1975) on such central studies as Eric Santner's *Stranded Objects: Mourning, Memory and Film in Postwar Germany* (Ithaca, NY: Cornell University Press, 1990); Ernestine Schlant's *The Language of Silence: West German Literature and the Holocaust* (New York: Routledge, 1999); and Helmut Schmitz's *On Their Own Terms: The Legacy of National Socialism in Post-1990 German Fiction* (Edgbaston/Birmingham, UK: University of Birmingham Press, 2004). The question in Paver's analysis, however, remains the ability of literature to account, retrospectively, for what occurred. Similarly, in his concise account of the matter, Robert C. Holub offers an overview of the quest for the past that focuses on modes of confronting the historical. Holub notes at the outset: "From 1945 until at least reunification in 1989 German intellectual and cultural life, including philosophy and literature, was dominated by the endeavor to come to terms with the past." Robert C. Holub, "Coming to Terms with the Past in Postwar Literature and Philosophy," in *Philosophy and German Literature, 1700–1990*, ed. Nicholas Saul (Cambridge: Cambridge University Press, 2002), 245. Paver rightly classifies previous studies on the matter along the lines of ethical and psychological considerations. Judith Ryan's significant study *The Uncompleted Past: Postwar German Novels and the Third Reich* (Detroit: Wayne State University Press, 1983) underlines the ability of fiction to promote a conscious and critical approach to history (18). Elisabeth Snyder Hook discusses the ability of characters in the novels she studies to convey the author's moral trajectory. For a comprehensive analysis of postwar German literature's engagement with National Socialism, see volumes 10 and 11 of Rolf Grimminger, general ed., *Hanser Sozialgeschichte der deutschen Literatur vom 16. Jahrhundert bis zur Gegenwart*. Volume 10 is dedicated to the period from 1945 to 1967, and volume 11 covers the period from 1968 to what was then the present, 1992. See Ludwig Fischer, ed., *Hanser Sozialgeschichte*

der deutschen Literatur vom 16. Jahrhundert bis zur Gegenwart, vol. 10, *Literatur in der Bundesrepublik Deutschland bis 1967* (Munich: Carl Hanser Verlag, 1986); and Klaus Briegleb and Sigrid Weigel, eds., *Hanser Sozialgeschichte der deutschen Literatur vom 16. Jahrhundert bis zur Gegenwart*, vol. 11, *Gegenwartsliteratur seit 1968* (Munich: Carl Hanser Verlag, 1992). A more recent overview is offered in Wilfried Barner, ed., *Geschichte der deutschen Literatur von 1945 bis zur Gegenwart*, 2nd ed. (Munich: C. H. Beck, 2006).

4. Schlant, *Language of Silence*, 1. Hereafter, page references to this work will be given parenthetically in the text.

5. Unlike Schlant, who cites the diagnosis offered by the Mitscherlichs with affirmation, Frank Trommler offers a more critical assessment. Trommler views the notion that the (West) Germans are simply incapable of meaningful mourning more as a signal of a future shift in addressing National Socialism than as a description of a current social mental condition. I fully agree with Trommler on this issue. Frank Trommler, "What Should Remain: Exploring the Literary Contribution to Postwar German History," in *Beyond 1989: Re-reading German Literary History since 1945*, ed. Keith Bullivant (Providence, RI: Berghahn, 1997), 171–72.

6. Schlant seems to substantiate her argument at this point by referring (*Language of Silence*, 246n31) also to Günter Butzer, *Fehlende Trauer: Verfahren epischen Erinnerns in der deutschsprachigen Gegenwartsliteratur* (Munich: Wilhelm Fink Verlag, 1998).

7. See Helmut Schmitz, *On Their Own Terms: The Legacy of National Socialism in Post-1990 German Fiction* (Birmingham, UK: University of Birmingham Press, 2004). Schmitz's learned analysis of a variety of literary works of the period following the collapse of the Berlin Wall follows to a large extent the Mitscherlichs' framework, which is presented in his study as a central paradigm (11). Accordingly, Schmitz's periodization of the postwar era is established along the lines of the following matrix: 1945–70 was a period of "Repression and Confrontation," 1970–83 occurred under the sign of "Melancholia," and 1983–92 was a period of "Historisation." The years 1992–2001 were a time of "Integration," and the years after 2001 constitute a period of "Decentralisation" (see 25). What is "decentralized" is the crime, the Holocaust. In her astute reflections on the discourse regarding "the past" in *The Turkish Turn in Contemporary German Literature: Toward a New Critical Grammar of Migration* (New York: Palgrave Macmillan, 2005), Leslie A. Adelson notes that *Vergangenheitsbewältigung* was rarely delineated "as a discrete structure, entity, or even as a problem" (91). Adelson refers especially to the discourse of *Vergangenheitsbewältigung* in West Germany of the 1950s and the 1960s and to its literature. She mentions two prominently discussed novels of that era—Günter Grass's *The Tin Drum* and Heinrich Böll's *Billiards at Half-Past Nine*—as examples of how West German literature "muddied the referential waters approaching and retreating from a past that somehow encompasses the Holocaust as well as the Third Reich and World War II" (91). Unlike Adelson, whose critique in this regard I greatly respect, I choose to follow in this matter the historian Gavriel D. Rosenfeld, who, in referring to the widespread question of whether "the Germans" failed or succeeded in dealing with the Nazi past, points to the epistemological difficulty of determining

what a "mastered past" might actually look like. Introducing his study of the ways in which different actors in postwar Munich dealt with the heritage of National Socialism, he notes that rather than asking if the Germans have come to terms with the past, "it is better to examine how they have attempted to do so." Gavriel D. Rosenfeld, *Munich and Memory: Architecture, Monuments, and the Legacy of the Third Reich* (Berkeley and Los Angeles: University of California Press, 2000), 3–4.

8. Kölbel, *Ein Buch, Ein Bekenntnis*, 141–42; and http://www.signandsight .com/features/899.html (accessed July 10, 2010). Writing against what he understood as the "surfeit of memory" in the study of the past in recent decades, the historian Charles Maier had already indicated in 1992 the limitations of an emphasized focus on remembrance as retrospection—that is, on stressing the need to keep the memory of the past alive for memory's sake. Maier sees in such an attitude an indication of retreat from a transformative politics. Thus, at the conclusion of his essay, he expresses the hope that the future of memory might not be "too bright." Charles S. Maier, "A Surfeit of Memory? Reflections on History, Melancholy, and Denial," *History and Memory* 5, no. 2 (Winter 1993): 150–51. Although I do not share the view that literature is at its most significant when committed to a transformative politics, in my study I echo Maier's concern by stressing the futurity of significant works of literature, that is, their ability to allow a consideration of the future. On the future of memory as a central concern in the study of literature's (and cinema's) engagement with the past, see also Susan Rubin Suleiman, *Crises of Memory and the Second World War* (Cambridge, MA: Harvard University Press, 2006), esp. 5.

9. Paramount for developing the notion of *Erinnerungskultur* is the work of Jan Assmann and Aleida Assmann. See Jan Assmann, "Collective Memory and Cultural Memory," *New German Critique* 65 (1995): 132; Jan Assmann, *Das kulturelle Gedächtnis: Schrift, Erinnerung und politische Identität in frühen Hochkulturen* (Munich: C. H. Beck, 1992), 30–34; and Aleida Assmann, *Der lange Schatten der Vergangenheit: Erinnerungskultur und Geschichtspolitik* (Munich: C. H. Beck, 2006). For a discussion of the cultural turn to the past in Germany of the 1980s and after, see Aleida Assmann and Ute Frevert, *Geschichtsvergessenheit/Geschichtsversessenheit: Vom Umgang mit deutschen Vergangenheiten nach 1945* (Stuttgart: Deutsche Verlags-Anstalt, 1999), 144–47; and Wulf Kansteiner, *In Pursuit of German Memory: History, Television, and Politics after Auschwitz* (Athens: Ohio University Press, 2006), 248.

10. On the global fascination with memory and public remembrance as an indication of the economic, social, and cultural conditions of late modernity or postmodernity, see Andreas Huyssen, *Twilight Memories: Marking Time in a Culture of Amnesia* (New York: Routledge, 1995), 5; and Andreas Huyssen, *Present Pasts: Urban Palimpsests and the Politics of Memory* (Stanford, CA: Stanford University Press, 2003), esp. 1–29.

11. Huyssen, *Present Pasts*, 18.

12. Daniel Levy and Natan Sznaider, *The Holocaust and Memory in the Global Age*, trans. Assenka Oksiloff (Philadelphia: Temple University Press, 2005).

13. In his speech, von Weizsäcker emphasized that the Germans' catastrophic plight of flight, expulsion, and deprivation of freedom resulted not from military

defeat but rather from the Fascist tyranny that brought about the war in the first place. The sociologist Jeffrey K. Olick sees von Weizsäcker's speech as "perhaps the most noted of all speeches on the past in the forty years of West German history." Jeffrey K. Olick, *The Politics of Regret: On Collective Memory and Historical Responsibility* (New York: Routledge, 2007), 75. On the role of historical remembrance, especially of the Holocaust in West Germany, see Jan-Werner Müller, *Another Country: German Intellectuals, Unification, and National Identity* (New Haven, CT: Yale University Press, 2000). For a discussion of the period before 1989, see esp. 20–63. Frank Trommler notes the "tremendous reaction, especially among younger people," following the screening of *Holocaust*. Frank Trommler, "Stalingrad, Hiroshima, Auschwitz: The Fading of the Therapeutic Approach," in *Catastrophe and Meaning: The Holocaust and the Twentieth Century*, ed. Moishe Postone and Eric Santner (Chicago: University of Chicago Press, 2003), 142–43. Peter Reichel notes that the screening of *Holocaust* was not the turning point in addressing the Holocaust as a central facet of National Socialism and in directly accounting for the suffering of Jews but rather the acme of the first efforts to deal with it—a phenomenon that should be seen not least as a result of generational succession. Peter Reichel, *Vergangenheitsbewältigung in Deutschland: Die Auseinandersetzung mit der NS-Diktatur von 1945 bis heute* (Munich: C. H. Beck, 2001), 205.

14. Wulf Kansteiner notes that the memory of National Socialism was a facet of West German cultural and political discourse during the 1950s, but as "internalized" memory—that is, as a past remembered personally or through familial relations (one was a soldier during the war; one had parents who lived through the period). In the 1980s, the memory of the same era was reshaped through the integration of "external" memories of a time and events that one did not experience personally—most crucially, memories of the Holocaust. See Kansteiner, *In Pursuit of German Memory*, 249–50.

15. See Stephen Brockmann, *Literature and German Reunification* (Cambridge: Cambridge University Press, 1999), 13. Brockmann also points to another significant public discussion: the one surrounding the November 10, 1988, speech by Phillip Jenninger, the president of the German parliament, to commemorate the fiftieth anniversary of the infamous Reichskristallnacht. As Jeffrey K. Olick has noted, Jenninger's speech avoided the ubiquitous ceremonial language and the expected gestures of atonement that are used to address National Socialism and the Holocaust (*Politics of Regret*, 49–50). The public outcry that followed that speech in fact led to Jenninger's fall. On the mostly routine reactions to Jenninger's speech, see Klaus Briegleb, *Unmittelbar zur Epoche des NS-Faschismus: Arbeiten zur politischen Philologie, 1978–1988* (Frankfurt am Main: Suhrkamp, 1989), 11–12n1.

16. See Brockmann, *Literature and German Reunification*, 46. On Jürgen Habermas's worry that the process of rapid German unification might devalue the West German constitution and promote a new form of nationalism, see Müller, *Another Country*, 102. On Grass's substantial criticism of reunification, see Müller, *Another Country*, 64–89.

17. The most explicit expression of new German nationalism in the post-wall era was the publication of a volume of collected essays by publicists, historians,

and cultural figures such as (most prominently) the writer Botho Strauß, which, taken together, expressed the need to overcome suspicions vis-à-vis German nationalism in the wake of Nazism and the Holocaust and reestablish a new, "normal," and assertive German nationalism. On Strauß's key essay, "Anschwellender Bockgesang" (Goat song crescendo), see Brockmann, *Literature and German Reunification*, 131–36. The essay that was originally published in the weekly *Der Spiegel* in 1993 is reprinted in Heimo Schwilk and Ulrich Schacht, eds., *Die selbstbewußte Nation: "Anschwellender Bocksgesang" und weitere Beiträge zu einer deutschen Debatte*, 3rd ed. (Berlin: Ullstein, 1995).

18. The issue of the post-wall tendency to emphasize German victimhood is discussed at length in Bill Niven, ed., *Germans as Victims: Remembering the Past in Contemporary Germany* (New York: Palgrave Macmillan, 2006); and, in recent literature, in Helmut Schmitz, "Representations of the Nazi Past, II: German Wartime Suffering," in *Contemporary German Fiction: Writing in the Berlin Republic*, ed. Stuart Taberner (Cambridge: Cambridge University Press, 2007), 142–58. The significant scale of actual German suffering is outlined by Robert Moeller, who reminds us that the bombing of German cities left six hundred thousand civilians dead and nine hundred thousand wounded, and that some five hundred thousand ethnic Germans died in the course of the trek westward that was undertaken by twelve million Germans. Robert Moeller, "The Politics of the Past in the 1950s: Rhetorics of Victimisation in East and West Germany," in Niven, *Germans as Victims*, 27.

19. See Michael Geyer, "The Long Good-Bye: German Culture Wars in the Nineties," in *The Power of Intellectuals in Contemporary Germany*, ed. Michael Geyer (Chicago: University of Chicago Press, 2001), 368–72; and Konrad H. Jarausch, *After Hitler: Recivilizing Germans, 1945–1995* (Oxford: Oxford University Press, 2006), 229.

20. A clear indication of the magnitude and sincerity that characterized these debates is the thirteen-hundred-page volume that contains the most significant documents in the debate surrounding the building of the Berlin Holocaust memorial: Ute Heimrod, Günter Schlusche, and Horst Seferens, eds., *Der Denkmalstreit—das Denkmal? Die Debatte um das "Denkmal für die ermordeten Juden Europas": Eine Dokumentation* (Berlin: Philo Verlagsgesellschaft, 1999). On the controversy over the Wehrmacht crimes exhibition, see Hamburger Institut für Sozialforschung, ed., *Eine Ausstellung und ihre Folgen: Zur Rezeption der Ausstellung Vernichtungskrieg; Verbrechen der Wehrmacht, 1941 bis 1944* (Hamburg: Hamburger Edition, 1999). A lucid overview of the major debates regarding the future of "the German past" is offered by Bill Niven in *Facing the Nazi Past: United Germany and the Legacy of the Third Reich* (London: Routledge, 2002).

21. On the impact of the philosophical "linguistic turn" on historiography, see Elizabeth A. Clark, *History, Theory, Text: Historians and the Linguistic Turn* (Cambridge, MA: Harvard University Press, 2004); and Ernst Breisach, *On the Future of History: The Postmodernist Challenge and Its Aftermath* (Chicago: University of Chicago Press, 2003). In referring to the impact of the "linguistic turn" on First World literature that engages with history, I draw on Linda Hutcheon's *Poetics of Postmodernism: History, Theory, Fiction* (New York:

Routledge, 1988); and Amy Elias's *Sublime Desire: History and Post-1960 Fiction* (Baltimore, MD: Johns Hopkins University Press, 2001).

22. Hayden White, "The Modernist Event," in Hayden White, *Figural Realism: Studies in the Mimesis Effect* (Baltimore, MD: Johns Hopkins University Press, 1999), 69.

23. Ibid., 70. White identifies in the literature and the arts of our post-catastrophic era a tendency to dissolve "the trinity of event, character, and plot" that was a staple both of the nineteenth-century realist novel and of historiography (69, 66).

24. Richard Rorty, "Unfamiliar Noises: Hesse and Davidson on Metaphor," in Richard Rorty, *Objectivity, Relativism and Truth*, vol. 1 of *Philosophical Papers* (Cambridge: Cambridge University Press, 1991), 163.

25. Ibid.

26. Wendy Brown, *Politics Out of History* (Princeton, NJ: Princeton University Press, 2001), 23.

27. The German noun *Schuld* exceeds the semantics of the English "guilt" because it echoes economic discourse as well: *Schuld* is related to *Schulden* (debt, liability). As Sigrid Weigel has observed in her analysis of the discussion of guilt in postwar German literature, the rhetoric of *Schuld* was often coupled with the hope that West Germany's reparations (*Wiedergutmachung*) would yield forgiveness (by "the Jews") and the relegation of recent German history to the realm of the past. See Sigrid Weigel, "Shylocks Wiederkehr: Die Verwandlung von Schuld in Schulden oder; Zum symbolischen Tausch der Wiedergutmachung," in *50 Jahre danach: Zur Nachgeschichte des Nationalsozialismus*, ed. Sigrid Weigel and Birgit R. Erdle (Zurich: Hochschulverlag AG an der ETH Zürich, 1995), 165–92. Interestingly, major non-German authors were much more nuanced in their reading of Grass's autobiography and their response to what the book has to offer. Across Germany's border, the Polish Nobel laureate Wisława Szymborska signed an open letter in which she and other authors lauded Grass's "demonstration of courage" and pointed to "the great tragedy of a person who admits that he has always perceived his guilt as a shameful thing." (The letter, also signed by Stefan Chwin and Paweł Huelle, was published in the Polish newspaper *Rzeczpospolita* on August 21, 2006.) For an attuned, well-balanced assessment of Grass's autobiography in the context of his previous writing and the 2006 Grass affair, see Timothy Garton Ash, "The Road from Danzig," *New York Review of Books* 54, no. 13 (August 16, 2007).

28. Claus Leggewie, "'Kommunikatives Beschweigen'" (interview with Daniel Haufler), *Tageszeitung*, August 16, 2006, http://www.taz.de/index.php?id=archivseite&dig=2006/08/16/a0170 (accessed October 28, 2008).

29. See Karl Heinz Bohrer, "Kulturschutzgebiet DDR?" *Merkur* 500 (October–November 1990): 1015–18; Karl Heinz Bohrer, "Die Ästhetik am Ausgang ihrer Unmündigkeit," *Merkur* 500 (October–November 1990): 851–65; and Karl Heinz Bohrer, "Das Ethische am Ästhetischen," *Merkur* 620 (December 2000): 1149–62. For a detailed presentation of Bohrer's positions on aesthetics and politics with emphasis on his criticism of postwar German culture as "provincial" and guided by moralism or the conflation of aesthetics and ethics, see Müller, *Another Country*, 177–98; and Frank Finlay, "Literary Debates and

the Literary Market since Unification," in Taberner, *Contemporary German Fiction*, 21–24.

30. In coining the term *Gesinnungsästhetik*, Bohrer played on Max Weber's famous distinction between *Gesinnungsethik* (the ethics of conviction) and *Verantwortungsethik* (the ethics of responsibility). Other critics echoed Bohrer's positions in different ways. See, for example, the polemic of Ulrich Greiner, the literary editor of the weekly *Die Zeit*, "Die deutsche Gesinnungsästhetik," *Die Zeit* (November 2, 1990): 59; and Frank Schirrmacher, "Abschied von der Literatur der Bundesrepublik: Neue Pässe, neue Identitäten, neue Lebensläufe; Über die Kündigung einiger Mythen des westdeutschen Bewußtseins," *Frankfurter allgemeine Zeitung*, October 2, 1990. These and other essays became central contributions to what soon came to be known as the *Literaturstreit*—the public discussion among writers and critics in which intellectuals such as Bohrer, Greiner, and Schirrmacher attacked the GDR writer Christa Wolf (for failing to speak up against the totalitarian state and claiming to have belonged to the opposition after the wall came down) yet at the same time pleaded for an end to the socially engaged and historically conscious literature and criticism that characterized the literary association Group 47 in the Federal Republic and the work of such writers as Heinrich Böll and Günter Grass. As many critics have noted, this critique amounted to a call for abandoning the critical and historically aware discourse that was so instrumental in creating a denationalized, democratic public sphere in the postwar Federal Republic. See, e.g., Brockmann, *Literature and German Reunification*, 64–79.

31. Mitscherlich and Mitscherlich, *Inability to Mourn*. The book was originally published as *Die Unfähigkeit zu trauern: Grundlagen kollektiven Verhaltens* (Munich: R. Piper, 1967). On the impact of the book, see, e.g., Tony Judt, *Postwar* (New York: Penguin, 2005), 416.

32. Eric Santner, *Stranded Objects: Mourning, Memory, and Film in Postwar Germany* (Ithaca, NY: Cornell University Press, 1990).

33. Dominick LaCapra, *Representing the Holocaust: History, Theory, Trauma* (Ithaca, NY: Cornell University Press, 1994), 205. See also Dominick LaCapra, *Writing History, Writing Trauma* (Baltimore, MD: Johns Hopkins University Press, 2001), esp. 141–53.

34. Michael S. Roth traces how Freud developed "a science of interpretation that made meaning out of memory in the service of the present." See Michael S. Roth, "Freud's Use and Abuse of the Past," in Michael S. Roth, *The Ironist's Cage: Memory, Trauma, and the Construction of History* (New York: Columbia University Press, 1995), 186–200. Roth underlines "practical" threads within Freud's thought that point to the possibility of redescription as a way to gain "freedom from the past" (188)—that is, to see mourning as "the process through which one disconnects from a painful loss in the recent past" (188). "Freedom" from the past does not, to be sure, assume the avoidance of what happened during a taxing moment of history. Rather, as Roth states, Freud assumes the need to address that moment and to mourn the pain. However—and here, I believe, lies the crux—this engagement with the past is in the service of gaining a different quality of life *in the present*, with the hope of acting differently in the future. Much of the psychoanalytically informed discussion of postwar German litera-

ture and culture is colored by investigating how the literary imagination grapples, not with finding livable narratives for the present and the future, but rather with what is seen as a gaping lack of engagement with Nazism.

35. Schlant, *Language of Silence*, 14.

36. See ibid., 56. Schlant's discussion of Alexander Kluge—an author whom I will discuss later—is exemplary in this regard. The phenomenon of symptomatic reading is not restricted, however, to literary criticism. The historian Elizabeth Domansky, for example, sees in the immense scholarly production on National Socialism and the Holocaust as of the late 1970s and attendance at museums and public commemorative events no indication of less repression—of a "real," "knowing," or "genuine" "historical consciousness." Yet she does not indicate clearly what, in her opinion, might qualify as "real" and "genuine." See Elizabeth Domansky, "A Lost War: World War II in Postwar German Memory," in *Thinking about the Holocaust after Half a Century*, ed. Alvin Rosenfeld (Bloomington: Indiana University Press, 1997), 238–39.

37. Alon Confino, *Germany as a Culture of Remembrance: Promises and Limits of Writing History* (Chapel Hill: University of North Carolina Press, 2006), 235–43. On the "myth of repression," see 236.

38. There are, to be sure, different variants of this approach. In his thought-provoking *Mißachtung und Tabu: Eine Streitschrift zur Frage "Wie antisemitisch war die Gruppe 47?"* (Berlin: Philo Verlagsgesellschaft, 2002), Klaus Briegleb explores how authors of Group 47 failed to overcome anti-Semitic impulses. At times, he follows psychoanalytical models, with the result that he expresses judgments not only about the ways in which a work participates in a discourse of evasion and chauvinistic exclusion but about how it fails to convince as a meaningful literary work. Briegleb's account thus adds to our broad view of the group by demonstrating how it was not only breaking away from past ideological convictions—a profound critique of Nazism and of the role large segments of the German population played in the regime—but also sustaining a certain form of prejudice and guilt avoidance (see 12, 21, 37). Ernestine Schlant, however, is less self-reflective. In regard to the commonplace that the Federal Republic during the first decades simply "suppressed" the Nazi past, I share Jeffrey K. Olick's unease: a democratic system, by most measures, that adopted and then defended the Basic Law (Grundgesetz) while helping many survivors to regain some normalcy through reparations can hardly be seen as merely engaged in a consistent politics of forgetting. Olick, *Politics of Regret*, 141. As Olick admits, however, there were, to be sure, elements of avoidance and self-victimization, as well as attempts all too quickly to define West Germany as completely "normal." It was in the course of the late 1960s that these moves were sharply criticized and a new degree of engagement with history and a new sense of democratic culture began to emerge. Again, the role of literature in this process was unquestionable.

39. Trommler, "Stalingrad, Hiroshima, Auschwitz," 136.

40. On memory as exceeding the realm of pain and endurance, see Huyssen, *Present Pasts*, 8.

41. Due to the same limitations on what this study can encompass, my discussion will not involve, for example, such important issues as the engagement with Germany's past in works that place the body at the center of their symbolic

worlds or in the writing of German Turkish writers—two issues thoroughly discussed in the incisive books of Leslie A. Adelson: *Making Bodies, Making History: Feminism and German Identity* (Lincoln: University of Nebraska Press, 1993); and *The Turkish Turn in Contemporary German Literature*, esp. 79–122. I will not discuss here the postwar work of German Jewish writers. One of my aims in parts I and II of this book is, after all, to reflect on how writers who belong to a nation that grapples with a difficult modern history redescribe *their own* troubling national pasts. Furthermore, I will only allude to significant differentiations such as that between the literature of the Federal Republic and that of the former GDR.

42. On the role of literature in this process, see, e.g., Jarausch, *After Hitler*, 143–44; and Brockmann, *Literature and German Reunification*, 2. On the role of writers in shaping the political discourse of the GDR, see David Bathrick, "Crossing Borders: The End of the Cold War Intellectual?," *German Politics and Society* 27 (1992): 77–87. To be sure, literature was only one catalyst in this process. For a view of other elements, see, e.g., the work of the political scientist Helmut König, *Die Zukunft der Vergangenheit: Der Nationalsozialismus im politischen Bewusstsein der Bundesrepublik* (Frankfurt am Main: S. Fischer, 2003). In referring to the role of regret, I am indebted to Jeffrey K. Olick and his *Politics of Regret*. See especially his discussion of the notion in the context of postwar German politics and culture (121–51). In *The Politics of the Nazi Past in Germany and Austria* (Cambridge: Cambridge University Press, 2006), David Art offers a thorough discussion of the political arena from the 1950s on with special attention to the 1980s and thus with emphasis on the evolving language of public debates (49–100).

43. On the engagement with National Socialism as an indication of individual responsibility, see, e.g., Ryan, *Uncompleted Past,* esp. her introductory remarks, 14.

44. Derek Attridge identifies the formal devices of J. M. Coetzee's modernist writing as enabling reflection on ethical issues. He notes that "the literary use of language involves the performing of meanings and feelings, and that what has traditionally been called form is central to this performance. The literary work is an event (though an event that cannot be distinguished from an act) for both its creator and its reader, and it is the reader—not as free-floating subject but as the nexus of a number of specific histories and contextual formations—who brings the work into being, differently each time, in a singular performance of the work not so much as written but as writing. The meaning of a literary work, then, can be understood as a verb rather than a noun: not something carried away when we have finished reading it, but something that happens as we read or recall it." Derek Attridge, *J. M. Coetzee and the Ethics of Reading: Literature in the Event* (Chicago: University of Chicago Press, 2005), 9.

CHAPTER TWO

1. Günter Grass, *The Tin Drum*, trans. Breon Mitchell (Boston: Houghton Mifflin Harcourt, 2009), 3. Hereafter, page references to this work will be given

parenthetically in the text. The novel was first published as *Die Blechtrommel* by Luchterhand in 1959. The first English edition appeared in 1961.

2. On Oskar as an unreliable narrator, see Peter Demetz, *After the Fires: Recent Writing in the Germanies, Austria, and Switzerland* (New York: Harcourt Brace Jovanovich, 1986), 369–73.

3. Patrick O'Neill, "The Exploratory Fictions of Günter Grass," in *The Cambridge Companion to Günter Grass*, ed. Stuart Taberner (Cambridge: Cambridge University Press, 2009), 42.

4. On Oskar as a picaresque figure who signals observation and detachment from his surrounding social world, see John Reddick's classic reading in *The "Danzig Trilogy" of Günter Grass: A Study of "The Tin Drum," "Cat and Mouse" and "Dog Years"* (New York: Harcourt Brace Jovanovich, 1974), 58–63.

5. On the realist and laconic poetics of the *Trümmer-* and *Kahlschlagliteratur*, see Ralf Schnell, *Geschichte der deutschsprachigen Literatur seit 1945* (Stuttgart: Metzler, 1993), 88.

6. A major achievement in charting that silence during the first years of the Federal Republic is Norbert Frei's *Adenauer's Germany and the Nazi Past: The Politics of Amnesty and Integration* (New York: Columbia University Press, 2002).

7. Robert G. Moeller, *War Stories: The Search for a Usable Past in the Federal Republic of Germany* (Berkeley and Los Angeles: University of California Press, 2001)

8. See Frank Trommler, "Der zögernde Nachwuchs: Entwicklungsprobleme der Nachkriegsliteratur in Ost und West," in *Tendenzen der deutschen Literatur*, 2nd ed., ed. Thomas Koebner (Stuttgart: Alfred Kröner Verlag, 1984), 10. On the 1950s as a period characterized by the rhetoric of "crimes" that were committed "in the name of the German people" and "unspeakable crimes," see Jeffrey Herf, *Divided Memory: The Nazi Past in the Two Germanies* (Cambridge, MA: Harvard University Press, 1997), 282–83; Frei, *Adenauer's Germany and the Nazi Past*, 307, 311; and Wulf Kansteiner, *In Pursuit of German Memory: History, Television, and Politics after Auschwitz* (Athens: Ohio University Press, 2006), 7. Referring to a broad array of sources, including political discussions, cinematic renditions of the recent past, and historiography, Robert Moeller concludes that Germans of that period "represented a Germany doubly victimized, first by a Nazi regime run amok, then by communists, and they allowed all West Germans to order the past in mutually exclusive categories in which perpetrators and victims were never the same people." Robert G. Moeller, *War Stories: The Search for a Usable Past in the Federal Republic of Germany* (Berkeley and Los Angeles: University of California Press, 2001), 173.

9. On the budding sense of guilt in the immediate postwar years and its resonance in culture and literature, see Schnell, *Geschichte der deutschsprachigen Literatur seit 1945*, 68. Schnell mentions the 1946 publication of Karl Jaspers's *Die Schuldfrage* as a significant moment in the history of the discourse of guilt in West Germany's postwar culture. On the rhetoric of the "dark past" (*finstere Vergangenheit*), see Ludwig Fischer, "Literarische Kultur im sozialen Gefüge,"

in Fischer, *Hanser Sozialgeschichte der deutschen Literatur vom 16. Jahrhundert bis zur Gegenwart*, 10:142.

10. On Grass's employment of myth, fairy-tale tropes (in the tradition of German Romanticism), and magical realism, see Peter Arnds, "Günter Grass and Magical Realism," in *The Cambridge Companion to Günter Grass*, ed. Stuart Taberner (Cambridge: Cambridge University Press, 2009), 52–66.

11. In an often-cited critique, Ruth (Angress) Klüger claims that Grass's Sigismund Markus is "like the typical Jew of the Nazi press, [is] unattractive as a man, though he lusts after an Aryan woman, and ludicrous as an individual. For he acts and looks like a dog. He is a harmless parasite, a Jew without a Jewish community or a family, without a background, or religious affiliation, but with business acumen of sorts. . . . He has no conviction, has just converted, a pathetic gesture from which he vainly expects to benefit, and seems to have no emotions about the German victory, which he predicts, except that it might help him elope with Agnes to England" (quoted in Schlant, *Language of Silence*, 70, 250n26). Ernestine Schlant notes that Klüger's judgment "weighs heavily" (71) because among postwar German writers Grass was in his public pronouncements the most explicit in his condemnation of the Nazi genocide. Schlant goes on to state, following Klüger, that in Grass's creative writing "there is an ingrained obtuseness and insensitivity to those who suffered and died, evident in a language where silence is veiled in verbal dexterity and a creative exuberance rooted in pre-Holocaust aesthetics" (71). While I understand why for a survivor of the Holocaust such as Klüger Grass's fictional character appears to resemble racist representations of Jews in modern German literature, I do not share her view, nor do I share Schlant's assessment.

12. On the conservative, often oblivious political culture of postwar Germany in the first decade after the Second World War, see Heinrich August Winkler, *Germany: The Long Road West, 1933–1990* (Oxford: Oxford University Press, 2007), 154–71; and Herf, *Divided Memory*, 267–333.

13. On Grass's "The Onion Cellar" as an acute metaphor for Adenauer's Germany, see Steve Crawshaw, *Easier Fatherland: Germany and the Twenty-First Century* (New York: Continuum, 2004), 31–32.

14. Mitscherlich and Mitscherlich, *Inability to Mourn*. In his panoramic overview of major literary works of the decade following the end of the Second World War, Jochen Vogt notes of Oskar Matzerath that, unlike others in his environment, he proves to be "capable of mourning [*zur Trauer fähig*]" and that he is rejected by the surrounding society precisely for this reason. See Jochen Vogt, "Nonkonformismus in der Erzählliteratur der Adenauerzeit," in Fischer, *Hanser Sozialgeschichte der deutschen Literatur vom 16. Jahrhundert bis zur Gegenwart*, 10:293.

15. Judith Ryan highlights *The Tin Drum*'s ability to mobilize "the reader's critical faculties" in *Uncompleted Past*, 67. On the *The Tin Drum* as a cultural-political polemic, see Manfred Durzak, "Die zweite Phase des westdeutschen Nachkriegsromans," in *Geschichte der deutschen Literatur von 1945 bis zur Gegenwart*, 2nd ed., ed. Wilfried Barner (Munich: C. H. Beck, 2006), 379–80.

16. Günter Grass, *Dog Years*, trans. Ralph Manheim (New York: Harcourt, Brace and World, 1965), 295–96. Hereafter, page references to this work will be

given parenthetically in the text. The novel was originally published as *Hunde-jahre* by Luchterhand in 1963.

17. On the Persil certificate in the context of Grass's literature during that period, see, e.g., Ian Buruma, "War and Remembrance: Shrouded by the Günter Grass Controversy Is an Extraordinary New Memoir," *New Yorker*, September 18, 2006, available online at http://www.newyorker.com/archive/2006/09/18/060918crat_atlarge (accessed July 12, 2010).

18. On the transformative role of Grass (especially in *The Tin Drum*) and other writers and intellectuals in West Germany of the 1950s and early 1960s, see Müller, *Another Country*, 37–45. In his reading of *The Tin Drum*, Gordon Craig attributes to Grass's novel the achievement (which also marks the work of other writers of Group 47) of resolving the "nimbus of mystery and fate" surrounding Nazism that prevailed in such major literary works as Thomas Mann's *Doctor Faustus* (1947) and in the writings of less central figures such as Elisabeth Langgässer and Hermann Kasack. Indeed, according to Craig, Grass's prose participated in "cleansing" the German language of the corrupting influence of bureaucrats, soldiers, and philosophers, thus becoming a factor in the democratic discourse of the new German state. See Gordon Craig, "1958: Günter Grass Wins the Group 47 Prize for Two Chapters from His Novel in Progress, *Die Blechtrommel*," in *A New History of German Literature*, ed. David E. Wellbery et al. (Cambridge, MA: Harvard University Press, 2004), 873.

19. Theodor Adorno noted famously in 1959 that "'coming to terms with the past' does not imply a serious working through of that past, the breaking of the spell through an act of clear consciousness." Reflecting specifically on the German cultural and political discourse of the 1950s, Adorno observed a broad discursive attempt to "turn the page," to wipe the crimes of the Nazi regime "from memory." Theodor W. Adorno, "What Does Coming to Terms with the Past Mean?" in *Bitburg in Moral and Political Perspective*, ed. Geoffrey H. Hartmann (Bloomington: Indiana University Press, 1986), 115. Adorno juxtaposed West German discourse with Freud's *Durcharbeiten*—the final of the three stages of a successful confrontation with traumatic moments of the past ("Erinnern-Wiederholen-Durcharbeiten"). Contrary to undertaking the necessary confrontation with the past through continuous, conscious effort, West Germany is defined by the desire simply to move on. Sigmund Freud, "Erinnern, Wiederholen und Durcharbeiten," in *Gesammelte Werke*, ed. Anna Freud et al. (Frankfurt am Main: Fischer, 1999), 10:126–36. On the history of the notion *Vergangenheitsbewältigung*, see Charles S. Maier, *The Unmasterable Past: History, Holocaust, and German National Identity* (Cambridge, MA: Harvard University Press, 1988); and Peter Reichel, *Vergangenheitsbewältigung in Deutschland* (Munich: Beck, 2001). Regarding the implied notion of "mastering" in the noun *Bewältigung*, see the opening remarks in Wilhelm Heinrich Pott, "Die Philosophie der Nachkriegsliteratur," in *Hanser Sozialgeschichte der deutschen Literatur vom 16. Jahrhundert bis zur Gegenwart*, 10:263.

20. On the reaction triggered by *The Tin Drum*, see Michael Jürgs, *Bürger Grass: Biographie eines deutschen Dichters* (Munich: C. Bertelsmann 2002), 147–50; Schnell, *Geschichte der deutschsprachigen Literatur seit 1945*, 303–4;

and Siegfried Mews, *Günter Grass and His Critics* (Rochester, NY: Camden House, 2008), 16–19.

21. Richard Rorty, *Contingency, Irony and Solidarity* (Cambridge: Cambridge University Press, 1989), 16; Donald Davidson, "What Metaphors Mean," in his *Inquiries into Truth and Interpretation* (Oxford: Oxford University Press, 1984), 262.

22. Rorty, *Contingency, Irony and Solidarity*, 16; Mary Hesse, *Revolution and Reconstructions in the Philosophy of Science* (Bloomington: Indiana University Press, 1980), 111.

23. See Müller, *Another Country*, 81.

24. Günter Grass, *Schreiben nach Auschwitz: Frankfurter Poetik-Vorlesung* (Frankfurt: Luchterhand, 1990), 42. I follow here for the most part Stephen Brockmann's translation in *Literature and German Reunification*, 57.

25. Müller, *Another Country*, 80–81.

26. Günter Grass, *My Century*, trans. Michael Henry Heim (Orlando, FL: Harcourt, 1999); Günter Grass, *Crabwalk*, trans. Krishna Winston (Orlando, FL: Harcourt, 2002).

27. Katharina Hall even regards *Crabwalk* as a further element of the *Danzig Trilogy*. Besides *The Tin Drum* (1959), *Cat and Mouse* (1961), and *Dog Years* (1963), she argues that both *Local Anaesthetic* (1969) and *Crabwalk* (2002) belong to the same literary framework. Katharina Hall, "Günter Grass's 'Danzig Quintet,'" in Taberner, *Cambridge Companion to Günter Grass*, 67–80.

28. Helmut Schmitz underlines, I believe correctly, how Grass's plot is "sober" and "reflective" of the contemporary uses and abuses of German suffering during the war. Schmitz, "Representations of the Nazi Past, II," 150. The historian Gilad Margalit expresses a much less favorable view of *Crabwalk*. Gilad Margalit, *Ashma, sevel vezikaron: Germaniya zocheret et meyteha bemilchemet haolam hashniya* [Guilt, suffering, and memory: Germany remembers its dead of the Second World War] (Haifa: University of Haifa Press, 2005). He sees Günter Grass as "bewailing" (170) that the sinking of the *Wilhelm Gustloff* was forgotten and examines the book in the context of what he sees as a broad tendency in recent years to emphasize German suffering during and after the Second World War and thus as a new chapter in the history of numerous attempts during the postwar era to ignore Nazi Germany's crimes or to balance them against the pain inflicted on Germans during and after the war (another issue to which I will return later). To contextualize his analysis of *Crabwalk*, Margalit points to W. G. Sebald's 1998 claim that the suffering of the German civil population during the massive air raids has been a "taboo" subject for German postwar literature (156). While Margalit does not equate Grass (or Sebald) with figures on Germany's Far Right, he maintains that many Germans who did not read these writers' literary work absorbed their public statements as a critique of the "taboo" regarding public references to German suffering during the war. To be sure, Margalit's claims address a viable concern regarding postwar and contemporary, post-wall tendencies to ignore the historical path that led to the suffering of the German civil population or to use it to wash oneself clean of historical responsibility. However, he does not pay attention to the fact that literary works are *not*

discursive claims but rather artistic, imaginary expositions whose meanings and effects (as we have discussed above) exceed the author's intentions.

29. Grass, *Crabwalk*, 175. Hereafter, page references to Winston's translation will be given parenthetically in the text. The novel was first published as *Im Krebsgang* by Steidl in 2002.

30. In a recent essay, Gary Baker presents a different, more favorable view of the novella, claiming that "it expands—through discrete intermediary means—the otherwise limited binary of perpetrator and victim." Baker does not refer, however, to the scenes I mention in my analysis. Gary Baker "The Middle Voice in Günter Grass' *Im Krebsgang*," *German Quarterly* 83, no. 2 (Spring 2010): 231.

31. On April 4, 2012, Grass published a poem titled "Was gesagt werden muss" (What must be said) in the daily *Süddeutsche Zeitung*, in which he declares, in the first-person singular, that he can no longer remain silent—that he needs to speak out what "must be spoken" ("sage ich, was gesagt werden muß"). Speaking out means in this poem to warn the world of the possibility that Israel may attack Iran. What makes this otherwise aesthetically debatable poem fascinating is Grass's *poetic* move to reframe "silence" in relation to himself, the writer Günter Grass: whereas since the 2006 Grass affair readers and critics around the world have discussed Grass in relation to his silence about his role in the Waffen-SS, the poem attempts to present Grass as a writer who in the past was forced to be silent about Israel's presumably belligerent intentions yet was finally able to speak out freely. The repetitious reference to "silence" in the poem makes it difficult to avoid the impression that Grass is hoping that his muteness about his time in the Waffen-SS may somehow be replaced by a recognition of his ability to end the alleged silence in regard to Israel's intentions and actions. What the poem plainly displays, however, is the attempt of an aging poet, transfixed by a sense of guilt, to preempt possible future accusations of remaining silent. Directly and implicitly Grass ties the fact that he remained silent about his time in the Waffen-SS to his ability now to "speak out." Grass's emphasis on his German *Herkunft* (origin, descent) as a burden of guilt (about the past) and responsibility (for the future) reflects his efforts from the early 1960s onward to take on the role of his country's conscience and, upon receiving the Nobel Prize in 1999, to assume the role of the world's conscience. Both efforts must be seen, just as the poem "Was gesagt werden muss" itself, as "rather pathetic," Tom Segev aptly notes. On the poem, the 2012 Grass affair, and Tom Segev's assessment, see Luke Harding and Harriet Sherwood, "Günter Grass's Israel Poem Provokes Outrage," *Guardian*, April 5, 2012, http://www.guardian.co.uk/books/2012/apr/05/gunter-grass-israel-poem-iran?INTCMP=SRCH (accessed April 11, 2012).

32. On the "phenomenal success" enjoyed by "princes in an enlightened" aristocracy such as Habermas, Grass, and the historian Hans-Ulrich Wehler, that is, on the unique role these intellectuals and writers played in addressing Germany's Nazi past and creating an enlightened public sphere, see Michael Geyer, "The Long Good-Bye: German Culture Wars in the Nineties," in *The Power of Intellectuals in Contemporary Germany*, ed. Michael Geyer (Chicago: University of Chicago Press, 2001), 370–72.

33. Günter Grass, *Peeling the Onion*, trans. Michael Henry Heim (New York: Harcourt, 2007), 3. Hereafter, page references to this work will be given parenthetically in the text.

34. Günter Grass, "Warum ich nach sechzig Jahren mein Schweigen breche" (interview with Frank Schirrmacher and Hubert Spiegel), *Frankfurter allgemeine Zeitung*, August 12, 2006.

35. Interestingly, among the more cogent and balanced reactions to Grass's autobiography and the Grass affair were those written by critics from outside Germany and its bustling *Literaturbetrieb*—the often-overbearing public sphere of German letters that is composed of newspaper and university critics, public intellectuals, and writers involved in the political arena. These reactions include Timothy Garton Ash's review essay "The Road from Danzig," *New York Review of Books* 54, no. 13 (August 16, 2007); and Buruma's "War and Remembrance." Similarly, observing from outside the almost daily occurrences in Germany's ongoing debate over the past's future, Nadine Gordimer noted in an interview with the *Independent* (May 25, 2007, available at http://arts .independent.co.uk/books/features/article2579393.ece) that she finds the controversy symptomatic of a culture "addicted to scandal but lacking context." She asks: "why did he keep quiet about it [his role in the Waffen-SS]? Well, he didn't keep quiet. . . . If you read his books, the wonderful knowledge of what happened to people—he never would have had it if he hadn't gone through that experience." In the same vein, Polish Nobel laureate Wisława Szymborska signed an open letter in which she and other authors lauded Grass's "demonstration of courage" and pointed out "the great tragedy of a person who admits that he has always perceived his guilt as a shameful thing." Letter from Wisława Szymborska, Stefan Chwin, and Paweł Huelle published in the Polish newspaper *Rzeczpospolita*, August 21, 2006.

36. For a different view of that matter, see, e.g., Klaus Briegleb, *Mißachtung und Tabu; Eine Streitschrift über die Frage: "Wie antisemitisch war die Gruppe 47?"* (Berlin: Philo Verlagsgesellschaft, 2002).

CHAPTER THREE

1. Alexander Kluge, *Chronik der Gefühle*, 2 vols. (Frankfurt am Main: Suhrkamp, 2000), 1:7 (my italics, but Kluge writes "orientation" and "chronicle" with capital letters). Hereafter, volume and page references to this work will be given parenthetically in the text. The translations are mine.

2. Kluge's term *Basisgeschichten* also implies the notion of basic histories, while *Lebensläufe* implies biographies. The English translation of Kluge's early volume *Lebensläufe* opted for "case histories": Alexander Kluge, *Case Histories* (New York: Holmes and Meier, 1988).

3. This collection was in fact prompted by the events of 1989, a historical moment Kluge saw as the reopening of what he called a "horizon of hope," allowing for what he viewed as at least the fantasy of a "completely new world." Alexander Kluge, "Der große Sammler der Wahrheit" (interview), *Süddeutsche Zeitung*, November 11, 2000. In another interview, he says, "More dramatically new events occurred between 1900 and 2000 than even after the upheaval

of 1945." Alexander Kluge, "'Ich liebe das Lakonische,'" *Der Spiegel* 45 (2000): 336.

4. Michael Oakeshott, *On History and Other Essays* (Indianapolis: Liberty Fund, 1999), 40, my emphasis.

5. Referring to Kluge's previous volumes, Stefanie Carp calls Kluge's historical narratives a "work project" (*Arbeitsprojekt*) aimed at German history. Stefanie Carp, *Kriegsgeschichten: Zum Werk Alexander Kluges* (Munich: Wilhelm Fink, 1987), 11. Harro Müller observes, similarly, that "Kluge's combining of different texts and materials . . . aims at his readers' developing a relation to history. Kluge does not obtain hereby a clear ideological or critical position that presumes to know and understand everything but is actually reductive and ignorant." Harro Müller, "'In solche Not kann nicht die Natur bringen': Stichworte zu Alexander Kluges *Schlachtbeschreibung*," *Merkur* 36, no. 9 (September 1982): 891. The translation is mine.

6. "Der Luftangriff auf Halberstadt am 8. April 1945" first appeared in Alexander Kluge, *Unheimlichkeit der Zeit: Neue Geschichten Hefte 1–18* (Frankfurt am Main: Suhrkamp Verlag, 1977). In what follows, I will quote from the reprint in *Chronik der Gefühle*, 2:27–82.

7. Johannes von Moltke, *No Place Like Home: Locations of Heimat in German Cinema* (Berkeley and Los Angeles: University of California Press, 2005), 56–57.

8. Ibid., 57–58.

9. I follow here Bernhard Malkmus, "Intermediality and the Topography of Memory in Alexander Kluge," *New German Critique* 36 (2009): 231–52. Malkmus convincingly analyzes Kluge's text-image constellations. Malkmus notes that in "Kluge's more recent text-image compositions . . . he [Kluge] moves from using images to illustrate, interrupt, and undermine the narrative to a more integral interrelation, which emphasizes *mutual* illustration, interruption, and deconstruction" (251). He goes on to note (correctly in my view) that "Kluge's patchwork of texts and images creates a nonnarrative arena of competing discourses grouped around certain shifting centers of metaphorical or thematic gravity. Kluge opens up a textual-visual space that allows an individual encounter with the political and collective unconscious" (251). On Kluge's employment of montage as an aesthetic procedure, see Christoph Zeller, *Aesthetik des Authentischen: Literatur und Kunst um 1970* (Berlin: De Gruyter, 2010), 112–21.

10. Thomas von Steinaecker rightly reads this scene and Frau Schrader's reaction as "grotesque." See von Steinaecker's insightful discussion of "The Air Raid on Halberstadt" in *Literarische Foto-Texte: Zur Funktion der Fotographien in den Texten Rolf Dieter Brinkmanns, Alexander Kluges und W. G. Sebalds* (Bielefeld: transcript Verlag, 2007), 204.

11. Theodor W. Adorno and Max Horkheimer, *Dialectic of Enlightenment: Philosophical Fragments*, ed. Gunzelin Schmid Noerr, trans. Edmund Jephcott (Stanford, CA: Stanford University Press, 2002).

12. On Kluge's work in the context of Adorno's and Horkheimer's critique of instrumental reason, see Ulrike Bosse, *Alexander Kluge — Formen literarischer Darstellung von Geschichte* (Frankfurt am Main: Peter Lang, 1989), 54–55.

13. See Alexander Kluge, Christian Schulte, and Rainer Stollmann, *Verdeckte*

Ermittlung: Ein Gespräch mit Christian Schulte und Rainer Stollmann (Berlin: Merve Verlag, 2001), 61–62.

14. On Kluge's amalgamation of fact and fiction in this work, see Richard Langston, *Visions of Violence: German Avant-Gardes after Fascism* (Evanston, IL: Northwestern University Press, 2008), 226.

15. Kluge notes in an interview given shortly after the publication of the volume: "Feelings interest me a lot, those that one does not immediately recognize as feeling, that are thus built into institutions, that only first make an appearance in the case of emergency through self-abandonment [*Selbstvergessenheit*], thus in *Einsatz*, as one says." Kluge, Schulte, and Stollmann, *Verdeckte Ermittlung*, 43. Significantly, Kluge uses two Heideggerian terms here in a nonpejorative manner to illustrate his poetic interest.

16. On Kluge's understanding of literature as a *Baustelle*, see Miriam Hansen, introduction to "Alexander Kluge," special issue, *New German Critique* 49 (Winter 1990): 4; and Andreas Huyssen, *Twilight Memories: Marking Time in a Culture of Amnesia* (New York: Routledge, 1995), 146. The notion of writing and reading as a process that never comes to a halt is crucial to Kluge's work. Decades after publishing his 1964 *Schlachtbeschreibung* (The Battle)—the volume dedicated to the battle of Stalingrad—Kluge continued adding and cutting material from the text. Almost thirty years after the book appeared in print, Kluge added some eighty pages to the last version of the book (*Schlachtbeschreibung: Neue Geschichten*, vols. 20–27, *"Vater Krieg"* [Frankfurt am Main: Suhrkamp, 1983]) and included it in the 2000 *Chronik der Gefühle*.

17. *Chronik*, 1:46. On Kluge's critique of Habermas's notion of rationality, see von Steinaecker, *Literarische Foto-Texte*, 178.

18. Kluge, Schulte, and Stollmann, *Verdeckte Ermittlung*, 49. On Kluge's avoidance of moral categories, see Jörg Drews, "Der Mensch, nach Dr. Kluge: Stehaufmaennchen und Phoenix," *Merkur* 697 (May 2007): 448. Andreas Huyssen also notes that Kluge's aesthetics differs in this matter considerably from that of the "documentarism" that swept German literature in the 1960s, for which literature and the theatrical stage were vehicles of a progressive political enlightenment; see Huyssen, *Twilight Memories*, 150.

19. I follow here Linda Hutcheon's consideration of irony in *Irony's Edge: The Theory and Politics of Irony* (London: Routledge, 1994), 39.

20. J. Hillis Miller, *Fiction and Repetition: Seven English Novels* (Cambridge, MA: Harvard University Press, 1982), 106; and J. Hillis Miller, *Others* (Princeton, NJ: Princeton University Press, 2001), 12.

21. Alexander Kluge, "Der große Sammler der Wahrheit" (interview), *Süddeutsche Zeitung*, November 11, 2000.

22. Pointing to the emergence of a new "focus on futurity" in German and transnational migration literature, Leslie Adelson indicates significant futural elements in Kluge's work. As Adelson reveals through her analysis of a futuristic fantasy first published in 1973 and reprinted in *Chronik der Gefühle*, Kluge's creations often display the interplay between past and future. Leslie A. Adelson, "Experiment Mars: Contemporary German Literature, Imaginative Ethnoscapes, and the New Futurism," in *Über Gegenwartsliteratur: Interpretationen und Interventionen*, ed. Mark W. Rectanus (Bielefeld: Aisthesis, 2008), 29–33. Tara Forrest similarly highlights that for Kluge the past's "possibilities for the future"

may be unearthed by developing "non-linear historical narratives." Tara Forrest, *The Politics of Imagination: Benjamin, Kracauer, Kluge* (Bielefeld: transcript Verlag, 2007), 140.

23. In an attempt to explain the relation between narration and possible emancipation, Kluge notes, "It is not completely true that I write these stories out of a passion for enlightenment [*Aufklärungselan*]. I do consider if they are useful for emancipation, but ultimately I say: That's what I saw, that's what I love, and that's why I write it." Kluge, Schulte, and Stollmann, *Verdeckte Ermittlung*, 50.

24. Alexander Kluge and Romain Leick, "Der Konjunktiv des Krieges" (interview), *Der Spiegel*, February 2012, 122–23. The translations are mine. On Alexander Kluge's notion of the *Auswege*, see Stefanie Harris's splendid essay "Kluge's *Auswege*," *Germanic Review* 85, no. 4 (2010): 294–317.

CHAPTER FOUR

1. On Walser's position regarding German unity prior to reunification, see Keith Bullivant, *The Future of German Literature* (Oxford: Berg, 1994), 107–8; and Stuart Taberner, "'Deutsche Geschichte darf auch einmal gutgehen': Martin Walser, Auschwitz and the 'German Question' from *Ehen in Philippsburg* to *Ein springender Brunnen*," in *German Culture and the Uncomfortable Past: Representations of National Socialism in Contemporary Germanic Literature*, ed. Helmut Schmitz (Aldershot, UK: Ashgate, 2001), 45–64.

2. Martin Walser, *Ein springender Brunnen* (Frankfurt am Main: Suhrkamp, 1998). Page references to this work will be given parenthetically in the text. The translations are mine. The laudatory reviews of Walser's novel include Joachim Kaiser, "Es war einmal am Bodensee," *Süddeutsche Zeitung*, July 28, 1998. See also Jost Nolte, "Wörterbäume eines frühreifen Bengels," *Die Welt*, July 29, 1998; Friedemann Berger, "Nachruf auf die Literatur des 20. Jahrhunderts," *Dresdner Neueste Nachrichten*, July 29, 1998; Martin Ebel, "Lehrjahre der Sprache," *Rheinischer Merkur*, July 29, 1998; and Jörg Magenau, "Abschied von der Einmischung," *Tageszeitung*, July 25–26, 1998. On the reception of Walser's novel, see also Amir Eshel, "Vom eigenen Gewissen: Die Walser-Bubis Debatte und der Ort des Nationalsozialismus im Selbstbild der Bundesrepublik," in *Deutsche Vierteljahresschrift für Literaturwissenschaft und Geistesgeschichte* 2 (June 2000): 333–60.

3. On how closely *Ein springender Brunnen* follows Walser's actual life, see Jörg Magenau, *Martin Walser: Eine Biographie* (Reinbek bei Hamburg: Rowohlt, 2005), 21–46.

4. Hans Ulrich Gumbrecht, *Production of Presence: What Meaning Cannot Convey* (Stanford, CA: Stanford University Press, 2004), 51–90.

5. I follow here Stuart Taberner, "'Deutsche Geschichte darf auch einmal gutgehen,'" 61.

6. On Martin Walser's unique mode of historical thinking, see Dieter Langewiesche, "'Erzählen, wie es war, ist ein Traumhausbau': Zum Geschichtsdenken Martin Walsers," in *Die Kunst der Geschichte: Historiographie, Ästethetik, Erzählung*, ed. Martin Baumeister, Moritz Föllmer, and Philipp Müller (Göttingen: Vandenhoeck und Ruprecht, 2009), 63–73.

7. See Volker Hage, "Königssohn von Wasserburg," *Der Spiegel* 31 (1998): 149.

8. On the significance of dealing with guilt and shame in the context of postwar German literature (including in the work of Martin Walser), see Sigrid Weigel, "Zur nationalen Funktion des Geschlechterdiskurses im Gedächtnis des Nationalsozialismus—Alfred Andersch 'Die Rote,'" in *Zwischen Traum und Trauma—die Nation: Transatlantische Perspektiven zur Geschichte eines Problems*, ed. Claudia Mayer-Iswandy (Tübingen: Stauffenburg, 1994), 28–29.

9. Without gliding into a moralist reading or a simplistic identification of the author with the narrator, it is interesting to note that Walser describes his mother, who, unlike the fictive mother of *Ein springender Brunnen*, joined the party before 1933, as "Thomas Aquinas of the twentieth century, without having heard of him." See Martin Walser and Rudolf Augstein, "Erinnerung kann man nicht befehlen: Martin Walser und Rudolf Augstein über ihre deutsche Vergangenheit," *Der Spiegel* 45 (1998), http://www.spiegel.de/spiegel/print/d-8027905 .html (accessed April 7, 2010), in which he describes his mother's crucial role in saving his family's inn during the financial hardships of the early 1930s.

10. Magenau, *Martin Walser*, 478–79.

11. Paul Ricoeur, *Memory, History, Forgetting*, trans. Kathleen Blamey and David Pellauer (Chicago: University of Chicago Press, 2004), 320. Hereafter, page references to this work will be given parenthetically in the text.

12. Mark Osiel, *Mass Atrocity, Collective Memory, and the Law* (New Brunswick, NJ: Transaction Publishers, 1999).

13. Rorty, "Grandeur, Profundity, and Finitude," 84.

14. Martin Walser, "Auschwitz und kein Ende," in Martin Walser, *Werke in zwölf Bänden*, ed. Helmuth Kiesel (Frankfurt am Main: Suhrkamp, 1997), 11:631–36. My citations are from Martin Walser's speech and are based on Thomas A. Kovach and Martin Walser, *The Burden of the Past: Martin Walser on Modern German Identity; Texts, Contexts, Commentary* (Rochester, NY: Camden House, 2008), 25–29. Page references to *Burden of the Past* will be given parenthetically in the text.

15. Rorty, *Contingency, Irony and Solidarity*, 16.

16. Matthias N. Lorenz, *"Auschwitz drängte uns auf einen Fleck": Judendarstellung und Auschwitzdiskurs bei Martin Walser* (Stuttgart: Metzler, 2005). In his acerbic study of Walser's representation of Jews and his evolving understanding of Auschwitz as the epitome of Nazism and thus postwar Germany's greatest test, Lorenz comes to the conclusion that Walser constructed negative, clichéd figures of Jews (483). Lorenz underlines that Walser did not intend to dispense hatred of Jews but rather to overcome the stigmatized perception of Germans in the postwar era as *"Tätervolk* [nation of perpetrators]" (483). In other words, Walser uses figures of Jews (consciously or not) as a way to reestablish a positive German nationalism—one that is to a large extent free of "Auschwitz." While Lorenz convincingly shows that Walser's pre- and post-wall work (especially the novel *Tod eines Kritikers* [Death of a critic], which I will discuss below) "reproduces anti-Semitic stereotypes," undermines the differences between victims of National Socialism and the regime's perpetrators, and "personifies bad conscience" (see 79–220, 257–353; my translation), he fails to develop a con-

vincing model to explain the fact that Walser's work in many respects also offers an important encounter with recent German history and with the challenges of imagining a Jewish figure in German. Indeed, Lorenz overlooks the fact that Walser, in his wish to escape Auschwitz (again, especially as of the late 1980s), also indicated the impossibility of fulfillment of this wish *and* (perhaps unwillingly) helped propel several vital discussions of this very issue. Reading Lorenz's immensely detailed and well-researched book, one learns a lot about the difficulties of being a young German author in the postwar era, who is necessarily someone who cannot write about his life *without* addressing the immediate past. Walser's moral "failings" as meticulously unfolded in Lorenz's work strike me as a mere indication of Walser's ability to take on *poetically* the impossibility of writing in that era: turning the taxing biographical circumstance into literature. His work remains an indication of the painful process by which imagination becomes   admittedly not always laudably—self-creation and communal creation. I use "creation" in the sense of presenting debatable images, offering metaphoric constellations for consideration, and so on.

17. Jacques Rancière, "The Aesthetic Dimension: Aesthetics, Politics, Knowledge," *Critical Inquiry* 36, no 1 (Autumn 2009): 9.

18. Ibid., 11. See also Jacques Rancière, *Dissensus: On Politics and Aesthetics*, trans. and ed. Steven Corcoran (London: Continuum, 2010), where Rancière explains dissensus as "a conflict between a sensory presentation and a way of making sense of it, or between several sensory regimes and/or 'bodies.' This is the way in which dissensus can be said to reside at the heart of politics, since at the bottom the latter itself consists in the activity that redraws the frame within which common objects are determined. Politics breaks with the sensory self-evidence of the 'natural' order that destines specific individuals and groups to occupy positions of rule or of being ruled, assigning them to private or public lives, pinning them down to a certain time and space, to specific 'bodies,' that is to specific ways of being, seeing and saying" (139; see also 37–38).

19. Rancière, *Dissensus*, 140.

20. See Ignatz Bubis, Salomon Korn, Frank Schirrmacher, and Martin Walser, "Wir brauchen eine neue Sprache für die Erinnerung," in *Die Walser-Bubis Debatte: Eine Dokumentation*, ed. Frank Schirrmacher (Frankfurt am Main: Suhrkamp, 1999), 442.

21. The director of the Hamburger Institute for Social Research (Hamburger Institute für Sozialforschung), Jan Philipp Reemtsma, offers a careful assessment of the novel that concludes that Walser expresses "anti-Semitic affectation." Jan Philipp Reemtsma, "Ein antisemitischer Affektstrum," *Frankfurter allgemeine Zeitung*, June 27, 2002. On this matter, see also Bill Niven, "Martin Walser's *Tod eines Kritikers* and the Issue of Anti-Semitism," *German Life and Letters* 56, no. 3 (2003): 299.

CHAPTER FIVE

1. Marcel Beyer, "Kommentar; Holocaust: Sprechen," in *Nonfiction* (Cologne: DuMont, 2003), 257. Beyer's questions are echoed in his own literary work, especially his novel *Flughunde* (1995; available in English as *The Karnau*

Tapes), in which he focused on language and speech through the portrayal of Hermann Karnau, a sound engineer who in 1945 was ordered to preserve the sound of the führer's voice during his last days in the Berlin bunker and to tend to the five young children of Joseph Goebbels. On the sonic qualities of Beyer's evocation of Nazism, see Leslie Morris, "The Sound of Memory," in "Sites of Memory," special issue, *German Quarterly* 74, no. 4 (Fall 2001): 374–76; and the detailed analysis of the novel in the context of contemporary German literature's engagement with Nazism in Helmut Schmitz, "Soundscapes of the Third Reich—Marcel Beyer's *Flughunde*," in Schmitz, *German Culture and the Uncomfortable Past*, 119–41.

2. On the "phenomenal success" of such "interventionist intellectuals" as Heinrich Böll, Grass, and others in promoting an "enlightened" public sphere, see Geyer, "Long Good-Bye," 369–70.

3. Norbert Gstrein, *Fakten, Fiktionen und Kitsch beim Schreiben über ein historisches Thema* (Frankfurt am Main: Suhrkamp, 2003), 12.

4. Hirsch, *Family Frames*, 22.

5. On conservative postwar German literary criticism, see Volker Hage, "To Write or Remain Silent? The Portrayal of the Air War in German Literature," in *Victims and Perpetrators, 1933–1945: (Re)Presenting the Past in Post-unification Culture*, ed. Laurel Cohen-Pfister and Dagmar Wienroeder-Skinner (Berlin: Walter de Gruyter, 2006), here 95; and Bullivant, *Future of German Literature*, 19.

6. On the theme of German suffering in contemporary German literature, see Stuart Taberner, "Representations of German Wartime Suffering in Recent Fiction," in *Germans as Victims*, 164–80; and Anne Fuchs, *Phantoms of War in Contemporary German Literature, Films and Discourse* (New York: Palgrave Macmillan, 2008), 11. Until the 1990s, most of postwar German literature dealing with the issue of expulsion concentrated on German self-victimhood. See Frank-Lothar Kroll, ed., *Flucht und Vertreibung in der Literatur nach 1945* (Berlin: Mann, 1997). While the 1980s were characterized by a new attentiveness to the memory of the Holocaust, the decades following the collapse of the Berlin Wall were marked by a growing awareness of the pain experienced by Germans. At times, this interest reflected the wish to balance pains inflicted by Nazi Germany with those caused to Germans, as some critics observed. To be sure, some representations of air raids on German cities, such as Jörg Friedrich's journalistic book *Der Brand: Deutschland im Bombenkrieg, 1940–1945* (Munich: Dropyläen Verlag, 2002), seem defined by a language that brings pain inflicted by Germans and pain inflicted on them into disturbing proximity. However, other publications, such as the testimonial by Marta Hillers, *Eine Frau in Berlin: Tagebuchaufzeichnungen vom 20. April bis 22. Juni 1945* (Frankfurt/Main: Eichborn Verlag, 2003), published in English as *A Woman in Berlin: Eight Weeks in the Conquered City; A Diary* (New York: Metropolitan Books, 2005), which documented the frequent rapes to which German women were subjected toward the end of the war, offered an opportunity to better understand the era and not necessarily to shift the attention from Nazi crimes. At times, artistic historical representations have shed new, controversial light on what we know concerning historical circumstances and have underlined the absurdity of such

historical chapters as Hitler's last days in his Berlin bunker. I mean here Oliver Hirschbiegel's movie *Der Untergang* (2004; Downfall), which portrayed this historical moment by interpreting Joachim C. Fest's historiographic sketch *Der Untergang: Hitler und das Ende des Dritten Reiches* (Berlin: Alexander-Fest Verlag, 2002), published in English as *Inside Hitler's Bunker: The Last Days of the Third Reich* (New York: Picador, 2004), and the testimonial of Hitler's secretary Traudl Junge in Melissa Müller, *Bis zur letzten Stunde: Hitlers Sekretärin erzählt ihr Leben* (Berlin: Ullstein, 2004), published in English as *Until the Final Hour: Hitler's Last Secretary* (New York: Arcade Publishing, 2004).

7. On contemporary German literature as it deals with partition and the fall of the Berlin Wall, see Elke Brüns, *Nach dem Mauerfall: Eine Literaturgeschichte der Entgrenzung* (Munich: Fink, 2006). Brüns also considers the role of Nazism in the literary engagement with partition (150–54).

8. Briegleb uses the term "Neue Schreibweisen des Erinnerns" when he discusses the work of Gert Hofmann (1931–93) and Birgit Pausch (b. 1942), among others. See Klaus Briegleb and Sigrid Weigel, eds., *Hanser Sozialgeschichte der deutschen Literatur, Gegenwartsliteratur seit 1968* (Munich: Hanser, 1992), 133–40. Earlier in this volume, Briegleb analyzes different expressions of engagement with the events that are often referred to through the metonymy "Auschwitz" and what he views as other writers' convincing engagement—for example, the work of Ingeborg Bachman (74–78), Uwe Johnson, and Peter Weiss (106–13)—and varied avoidance maneuvers. He traces common thematic threads, such as attempts to confront the fathers' generation (so-called *Väterliteratur*, "father literature") and thus the generation of those who actively perpetrated the crimes (89–95). Briegleb remains rather critical in his assessment of mainstream postwar German culture and literature in its ability to address National Socialism consciously. He is especially suspicious of attempts to propagate a "German-Jewish" symbiosis in the postwar era (117–20). Similar to Eric Santner and Ernestine Schlant, Briegleb views much of the related rhetoric as an expression of repression (*Verdrängung*) in the Freudian sense. According to this analysis, instead of undertaking a painful accounting for German guilt and a serious attempt to conduct the "labor of mourning," many Germans—be they individuals or authors in their literary creations—opted for a more or less well-articulated cover-up of the historical circumstances of German culpability and guilt.

9. Marcel Mauss, *The Gift: The Form and Reason for Exchange in Archaic Societies*, trans. W. D. Halls (London: Routledge, 1990). See esp. 83, where Mauss reflects on the implications of his study in considering modern societies.

10. Jacques Derrida, *Given Time: 1. Counterfeit Money*, trans. Peggy Kamuf (Chicago: University of Chicago Press, 1992), 30.

11. Hans-Ulrich Treichel, *Der Verlorene* (Frankfurt am Main: Suhrkamp, 1998), available in English as *Lost*, trans. Carol Brown Janeway (New York: Vintage, 1999); and Hans-Ulrich Treichel, *Menschenflug* (Frankfurt am Main: Suhrkamp, 2005). Page references to *Lost* and *Menschenflug* will be given parenthetically in the text. In January 1945, Treichel's parents took their sixteen-month-old firstborn, Günter, and fled East Prussia and the advancing Red Army. The trek was extremely dangerous, and their lives, as Treichel's father later testified, were constantly threatened. In a moment of dire threat, they were forced to

abandon all their belongings and their child, who was in a carriage at the time, in order not to be shot at. Hans-Ulrich Treichel was born 1952 in Versmold, East Westphalia. He never found out what happened to his brother Günter. Nor did he ever speak with his parents about this incident. In the 1950s, his parents tried to locate their lost son through the Red Cross. What they found was a child marked Number 2037. All tests to determine the child's relation to the Treichels failed to produce a clear identification. Jan Brandt, "Bruder, wo bist du?," *Frankfurter allgemeine Sonntagszeitung*, July 17, 2005. On the relation between the Treichel family's fate and *Lost*, see Stuart Taberner, "Hans-Ulrich Treichel's *Der Verlorene* and the 'Problem' of German Wartime Suffering," *Modern Language Review* 97 (2002): 123–34; and Elena Agazzi: "Die Erfindung des Autobiographischen und die Geographie des Sehnens: Das Werk Hans-Ulrich Treichels," in *Erinnerte und rekonstruierte Geschichte: Drei Generationen deutscher Schriftsteller und die Fragen der Vergangenheit* (Göttingen: Vandenhoeck und Ruprecht, 2005), 92–109.

12. Treichel's painful, yet often hilarious, account of Stephan's struggle to tell the story of his childhood in light of received family and collective history reflects the "transgenerational" trauma of flight, expulsion, and the miseries of forced displacement. See Rhys W. Williams, "'Lesererfahrungen sind Lebenserfahrungen': Gespräch mit Hans-Ulrich Treichel," in *Hans Ulrich Treichel*, ed. David Basker (Cardiff: University of Wales Press, 2004), 22.

13. Michael Rothberg, *Multidirectional Memory: Remembering the Holocaust in the Age of Decolonization* (Stanford, CA: Stanford University Press, 2009), 4.

14. Ibid., 5.

15. In fact, Stephan does not meet his brother in person to tell him about himself and the "truth" he believes he has found because his sisters demand that he not do so. Because discussing the family's intricacies would divert at this point from my argument, I leave these circumstances to be discussed elsewhere.

16. On the phrase "No more past" as signaling the end of an obsessive relation to his and to the German past, see Martina Olke, "'Flucht und Vertreibung' in Hans-Ulrich Treichel's *Der Verlorene* und *Menschenflug* und in Günter Grass' *Im Krebsgang*," *Seminar: A Journal of Germanic Studies* 43, no. 2 (May 2007): 130.

17. Freud's essay was published in 1914 as "Erinnern, Wiederholen und Durcharbeiten" (Remembering, repeating, and working through).

18. Gstrein was born in the Austrian Tyrol in 1961, and his early years were characterized by the region's Catholic conservatism and by the widespread perception of Jews as "stingy" and as responsible for Christ's crucifixion. See Gstrein, *Fakten, Fiktionen und Kitsch*, 19–20. Growing up during the socialist Bruno Kreisky's reign as chancellor of Austria, Gstrein first viewed National Socialism as a "German," not an Austrian, matter. After all, according to the ubiquitous Austrian postwar myth, Austria had been Nazi Germany's first victim. On the myth of Austria as "Hitler's first victim," see Tony Judt, *Postwar: A History of Europe since 1945* (New York: Penguin, 2005), 2, 52, 813; and Judith Beniston, "'Hitler's First Victim'?—Memory and Representation in Postwar Austria," *Austrian Studies* 11, no. 1 (September 1, 2003): 1–13.

19. Norbert Gstrein, *The English Years*, trans. Anthea Bell (London: Harvill Press, 2002), 284. The book was originally published as *Die englischen Jahre* (Frankfurt am Main: Suhrkamp, 1999). In the following, I will quote from the English edition, giving the page numbers parenthetically in the text. See also Sigrid Weigel, "Norbert Gstreins hohe Kunst der Perspektive: Fiktion auf dem Schauplatz von Recherchen," *manuskripte* 162 (2003): 108.

20. Gstrein refers to ritualized remembrance in the contemporary German-speaking world in an interview in which he also underlines the need to overcome habitual acts of memory and to ensure, through self-conscious writing, the vibrancy (*Lebendigkeit*) and relevance of the ethical and political questions the past raises. See Axel Helbig and Norbert Gstrein, "Der obszöne Blick: Zwischen Fakten und Fiktion," in *Norbert Gstrein: Dossier*, ed. Kurt Bartsch, Gerhard Fuchs (Graz: Droschl, 2006), 16.

21. On the stormy controversy regarding the literary qualities of *The Reader*, see Hans-Jachim Hahn, *Repräsentationen des Holocaust: Zur westdeutschen Erinnerungskultur seit 1979* (Heidelberg: Universitätsverlag Winter, 2003), 215. An overview of the reception of *The Reader* in Germany and abroad is offered in Juliane Köster, *Bernhard Schlink, "Der Vorleser"* (Munich: Oldenbourg Schulbuchverlag, 2000); and in William Collins Donahue, "Illusions of Subtlety: Bernhard Schlink's *Der Vorleser* and the Moral Limits of Holocaust Fiction," *German Life and Letters* 54, no. 1 (January 2001): 60–81.

22. Bernhard Schlink, *The Reader* (New York: Random House, 1997). The book was originally published as *Der Vorleser* (Zurich: Heinemann, 1995). In the following, I will quote from the English edition, giving the page numbers in the text. In 2008 the novel was turned into a popular film directed by Stephen Daldry.

23. After the war, this survivor described in a memoir how she and many other women were placed in a church during the evacuation of the camp toward the end of the war and how the place of worship turned into an inferno when it took a hit from an Allied bomb. Because the inmates did not try to open the doors of the church and escape, believing that the doors were locked, almost all of them burned to death (107). One of the interesting questions in Schlink's plot, whether or not Hanna claimed that she did not have the key to the doors of the church, remains undecided to the end (108–10).

24. On the discussion surrounding Hanna's illiteracy, see Chloe Paver, *Refractions of the Third Reich*, 40. Schlink's *The Reader* is indeed one of the most controversial novels to appear in recent decades regarding the question of appropriately addressing Germany's past. While some critics, such as the historian Omer Bartov, see in the novel a literary attempt to exonerate the perpetrators and to view—through the figure of Hanna—Germany itself as a victim, others, such as Bill Niven, follow Michael as he vacillates between feelings of love for Hanna and his deep sense of guilt and are thus able to acknowledge the complexities of this novel as a troubling yet valuable work of art. See Omer Bartov, "Germany as Victim," *New German Critique* 80 (2000): 29–40; Bill Niven, "Representations of the Nazi Past, I: Perpetrators," in *Contemporary German Fiction*, 136–39, 141n13, where he lists some of the dismissive and, I would say, moralistic readings of the novel. On Michael's presumed "inability to mourn," see Schmitz, *On Their Own Terms*, 63–68.

25. In his comprehensive study of *The Reader*, including its role in German and American cultural life and its reception and manifold manifestations (including the 2008 movie), *Holocaust as Fiction: Bernhard Schlink's "Nazi" Novels and Films* (New York: Palgrave Macmillan, 2010), William Collins Donahue views it as a case of "Holocaust Lite"—a popularized, well-marketed, ultimately exonerating and relieving fictional Holocaust narrative. Donahue evaluates the novel's international success as reflecting the questionable need to relegate the Holocaust to the past, to treat it as mastered. Impressive in scope and well argued, Donahue's reading of the novel is based, however, in what I call in this book symptomatic reading: he studies its characters, metaphors, themes, as well as its entire plot, as indicating a psychological, moral, and cultural-political condition. While I see such an approach as legitimate in its own right, I choose to follow here, as throughout this book, a different path. For me, *The Reader* is ultimately an attentive writer's serious exploration of questions of guilt and responsibility in the postwar era. Schlink's numerous essays and interview statements in the decade and a half after the publication of *The Reader* are, in my view, a clear indication that he is not merely expressing a broader discursive desire in Germany or in Western consumer societies to relegate the Holocaust to pastness or to trivialize it altogether. Rather, I see Schlink as an author and an essayist who struggles to define the place of the genocide in the lives and psyches of those Germans who were born after the war. In recent years, Schlink broadened his treatment of the subject by examining, for example, the concept of responsibility. See Bernhard Schlink, "Die Zukuft der Verantwortung," *Merkur* 738 (November 2010): 1047–58.

26. The German term *Wiedergutmachung* was used after the Second World War to refer to the reparations that the German government agreed to pay. To *wiedergutmachen* means literally "to make well again" or to compensate. *Wiedergutmachungsgeld* means "*Wiedergutmachung* money." See Hans Günter Hockerts, "Wiedergutmachung: Ein umstrittener Begriff und ein weites Feld," in *Nach der Verfolgung: Wiedergutmachung nationalsozialistischen Unrechts in Deutschland*, ed. Hans Günter Hockerts and Christiane Kuller, Dachauer Symposien (Göttingen: Wallstein Verlag, 2003), 7–33.

27. Schlant, *Language of Silence*, 216.

28. Schlink describes this banality in *Guilt about the Past*, 26. Hereafter, page references to this work will be given parenthetically in the text.

29. Katharina Hacker, *Eine Art Liebe* (Frankfurt am Main: Surkamp, 2003). Hereafter, page references to this work will be given parenthetically in the text.

30. Amy Elias, *Sublime Desire: History and Post-1960 Fiction* (Baltimore, MD: Johns Hopkins University Press, 2001).

31. Saul Friedländer, *When Memory Comes*, trans. Helen R. Lane (New York: Farrar, Straus, Giroux, 1978).

32. W. G. Sebald, *Austerlitz*, trans. Anthea Bell (New York: Random House, 2001). Hereafter, page references to this work will be given parenthetically in the text.

33. Gumbrecht, *Production of Presence*, 102–3.

34. Eric Santner, *On Creaturely Life: Rilke, Benjamin, Kafka* (Chicago: University of Chicago Press, 2006), 12.

35. Ibid., 140–41.

36. Avishai Margalit, *The Ethics of Memory* (Cambridge, MA: Harvard University Press, 2002), 82.

37. Kluge, *Chronik der Gefühle*, 2:82.

38. A scholar of German literature I hold in highest regard expressed the view that Katharina Hacker takes on the role of the victim by appropriating Saul Friedländer's biography—by putting her words into his mouth. It is precisely this kind of paralyzing moralism that I hope this chapter helps to overcome.

39. Paul Ricoeur defines the "hermeneutics of faith" as a hermeneutics based on recovering what has become forgotten or obscured, and the "hermeneutics of suspicion" as a hermeneutics that tends to seek an essential reality, requiring one to penetrate beneath the surface of the sign and thus seek to tear away what the sign masks, what consciousness obscures. See Paul Ricoeur, *De l'interprétation: Essai sur Freud* (Paris: Seuil, 1965), 40–44.

40. Derek Attridge, *J. M. Coetzee and the Ethics of Reading: Literature in the Event* (Chicago: University of Chicago Press, 2005), 9.

41. I share the view of the historian Konrad H. Jarausch that "the extent of German profession of contrition over the Holocaust seems almost exemplary" when compared with what has occurred in Japan, Italy, or Austria. Jarausch, *After Hitler*, 279–80. On the emergence of a German "culture of civility," see ibid., 98. In their reconsideration of modern German history, Jarausch and Michael Geyer also note: "In plain speech, the Germans got themselves into a murderous past and they got themselves out of it, not all by their own doing, but surely also a [*sic*] result of their thought and action. It is the history of a disastrous and wanton miscarriage of civility, of unprecedented destruction of bonds of human solidarity, of unspeakable collective acts that were thought impossible in a modern age. At the same time, it is also a record of the desperate effort to learn from the self-inflicted disaster and reconstruct a better polity based on a more equitable social order and the pursuit of a more peaceful foreign policy." Konrad H. Jarausch and Michael Geyer, *Shattered Past: Reconstructing German Histories* (Princeton, NJ: Princeton University Press, 2003), 13.

42. Timothy Garton Ash, "The Stasi on Our Minds," *New York Review of Books* 54, no. 9 (May 31, 2007), 8. Writing two decades after German reunification, Ruth Wittlinger and Steffi Boothroyd further strengthen Garton Ash's observation by pointing to the fact that the German past in recent decades has indeed become "usable." In their view, which I share, the unambiguous acknowledgment of the German national culpability "no longer provides an obstacle to a positive identification with the German nation." Ruth Wittlinger and Steffi Boothroyd, "A 'Usable' Past at Last? The Politics of the Past in United Germany," *German Studies Review* 33, no. 3 (October 2010): 489–502.

43. Rorty, "Grandeur, Profundity, and Finitude," 84.

CHAPTER SIX

1. Reinhart Koselleck, *Zeitschichten: Studien zur Historik* (Frankfurt am Main: Suhrkamp, 2000).

2. W. J. T. Mitchell, "Imperial Landscape," in *Landscape and Power*, 2nd ed., ed. W. J. T. Mitchell (Chicago: University of Chicago Press, 2002), 5.

3. On Israel's landscape in relation to colonialism, see W. J. T. Mitchell, "Holy Landscape: Israel, Palestine, and the American Wilderness," in Mitchell, *Landscape and Power*, 270, 271. Yet as S. Ilan Troen remarks, the most crucial characteristic of imperialism—the desire to occupy, dominate, and colonize a territory outside the "mother country"—was not a dominant characteristic of Zionism prior to the 1967 Six-Day War. S. Ilan Troen, *Imagining Zion: Dreams, Designs, and Realities in a Century of Jewish Settlement* (New Haven, CT: Yale University Press, 2003), xiv. After the 1967 Six-Day War, colonial fantasies became, nevertheless, an element in the spectrum of Zionist ideologies and political practices. On Israeli landscape as the result of "orientalist" projections, see Edward W. Said, "Invention, Memory, and Place," in *Landscape and Power*, 241–59. On Zionist orientalism and its birth from European Romanticism, see Ariel Hirschfeld, "Locus and Language: Hebrew Culture in Israel, 1890–1990," in *Cultures of the Jews: A New History*, ed. David Biale (New York: Schocken Books, 2002), 1012–13.

4. See Lila Abu-Lughod and Ahmad H. Sa'di, "Introduction: The Claims of Memory," in *Nakba: Palestine, 1948, and the Claims of Memory*, ed. Lila Abu-Lughod and Ahmad H. Sa'di (New York: Columbia University Press, 2007), 1–24.

5. I borrow the idiom "the war to begin all wars" from the title of a review essay by Gershom Gorenberg, *New York Review of Books*, May 28, 2009, 38–41, in which he discusses recent historiographic works on "1948," including Benny Morris's *1948: A History of the First Arab-Israeli War* (New Haven, CT: Yale University Press, 2008).

6. So-called post-Zionist historiography sees the Palestinian exodus as the result of a clear colonial trajectory within Zionism. On "post-Zionist" discourse, see, for example, the supportive overview offered in Laurence J. Silberstein, *The Postzionism Debates: Knowledge and Power in Israeli Culture* (New York: Routledge, 1999), 89–126. The critique of such approaches is representatively summarized in Anita Shapira, "The Past Is Not a Foreign Country: The Failure of Israel's 'New Historians' to Explain War and Peace," *New Republic*, November 29, 1999; and Gadi Taub, "Postzionut—hakesher hazarfati-amerikai-yisraeli" [Post-Zionism—the French-American-Israeli connection], in *Tshuva leamit postzioni* (An Answer to a Post-Zionist Colleague), ed. Tuvia Friling (Tel Aviv: Yediot Ahronot/Hemed, 2003), 224–42.

7. Citing Hebrew books and articles in an English scholarly work is a challenging task due to the lack of a practical system of transcribing their titles. My solution is to give a standardized transliteration of the Hebrew title upon the first mention of each novel. Readers who are proficient in Hebrew will have no trouble recognizing the original titles. For the same reason, when mentioning secondary literature written in Hebrew, I will give the Hebrew title first, followed by the translation of the title. In the notes, in cases where the title of a book or essay is not translated in the book or essay itself, I offer a translation, in square brackets, following the title of the Hebrew original. When an English title is supplied in the published Hebrew work (often opposite the Hebrew title page), that title is given in parentheses. For example, Gadi Taub, "Postzionut—hakesher hazarfati-amerikai-yisraeli" [Post-Zionism—the French-American-Israeli connection], in

Tshuva leamit postzioni (*An Answer to a Post-Zionist Colleague*), ed. Tuvia Friling (Tel Aviv: Yediot Ahronot/Hemed, 2003). Here, the translation of the essay title is my own, but the English title of the book appears in the book itself.

8. Yael Zerubavel, *Recovered Roots: Collective Memory and the Making of Israeli National Tradition* (Chicago: University of Chicago Press, 1995).

9. In her detailed analysis of contemporary Israeli Arab and Israeli Jewish literature, especially in its relation to the Israeli-Palestinian conflict, Rachel Feldhay Brenner sees a direct relation between the discourse of *shlilat hagolah*, the ideologically driven negation of Jewish culture in the Diaspora, and the emergence of the Israeli-Palestinian conflict. In viewing Diaspora Jewry as the modern reincarnation of biblical Israelites wandering through the desert and Palestine of the nineteenth century as the Promised Land—just like the biblical Canaan, only empty—the foundation was established for what would later become blindness to the fact that Palestinians lived in Palestine for centuries before Zionism's rise. The Zionists arriving in Palestine viewed themselves as redeeming the promised "empty" land and leading the first generation of modern Jewish redemption. See Rachel Feldhay Brenner, *Inextricably Bonded: Israeli Arab and Jewish Writers Re-Visioning Culture* (Madison: University of Wisconsin Press, 2003), 6, 19.

10. See Yigal Schwartz, *Hayadata et haaretz sham halimon poreach: Ilandasat hamerchav umachshevet hamerchav basifrut haivrit hachadasha* (*Do You Know the Land Where the Lemon Blooms? Human Engineering and Landscape Conceptualization in Hebrew Literature*) (Or Yehuda: Kinneret, Zmora-Bitan, Dvir, 2007), 9–24, esp. 14. In his discussion of the Zionist metanarrative, Schwartz focuses on spatial metaphors and symbolic arrangements that emphasize space. On Hebrew literature's participation in the creation of this metanarrative, see Gershon Shaked, "Hasiporet vesiper haal hazioni: Hasiporet haivrit behitmodedut dialectit im metziut mishtanah" [The literature and the Zionist metanarrative: Hebrew literature and its dialectic engagement with a changing reality], in *Atzmaut: 50 hashanim harishonot* (*Independence: The First Fifty Years*), ed. Anita Shapira (Jerusalem: Zalman Shazar Center, 1998), 488; and Hannan Hever, "Mapping Literary Spaces: Territory and Violence in Israeli Literature," in *Mapping Jewish Identities*, ed. Laurence J. Silberstein (New York: New York University Press, 2000), 203.

11. Michael Gluzman, *Haguf hazioni: Leumiyut, migdar uminiyut basifrut haivrit hachadasha* (*The Zionist Body: Nationalism, Gender, and Sexuality in Modern Hebrew Literature*) (Tel Aviv: Hakkibutz Hameuchad, 2007), esp. 11–33.

12. See, on this period, Hirschfeld, "Locus and Language," 1018.

13. Yochai Oppenheimer, *Meever lagader: Yizug haaravim basiporet haivrit vehayisraelit 1906–2005* (*Barriers: The Representation of the Arab in Hebrew and Israeli Fiction, 1906–2005*) (Tel Aviv: Am Oved, 2008), 142–48.

14. The Israeli historian Yoav Gelber underlines the simultaneity of *komemiyut* and al-Nakba in his comprehensive study *Komemiyut venakbah: Yisrael, hafalastinim humedinot arav, 1948* (*Independence versus Nakba*) (Or Yehuda: Dvir, 2004). Backed by historical documentation and self-reflective analysis, Gelber's account of 1948 is written, however, from a distinctive Israeli-Zionist perspective. One can find a more critical view of the events in studies such as Morris, *1948*; Benny Morris, *The Birth of the Palestinian Refugee Problem*

Revisited (Cambridge: Cambridge University Press, 2004); Ilan Pappé, *A History of Modern Palestine: One Land, Two Peoples* (New York: Cambridge University Press, 2006); and Ilan Pappé, *The Ethnic Cleansing of Palestine* (Oxford: Oneworld, 2006). See also the rather polemical Nur Masalha, *Expulsion of the Palestinians: The Concept of "Transfer" in Zionist Political Thought, 1882–1948* (Washington, DC: Institute for Palestine Studies, 1992). The historiographical literature on 1948 and on the Israeli-Palestinian conflict is vast and would demand a careful study of its own. Hence, I refrain from giving here further bibliographical references.

15. On Hebrew poetry as it turns to the Israeli-Palestinian conflict and to the plight of Palestinians during and after 1948, see Hannan Hever, ed., *Al tagidu begat: Hanakba hafalastinit bashira haivrit 1948–1958* [Tell it not in Gath: The Palestinian Nakba in Hebrew poetry, 1948–1958] (Tel Aviv: Sedek, 2010); and Haggai Rogani, *Mul hakefar sheharav: Hashirah haivrit vehasikhsukh hayehudi-arvi, 1929–1967 (Facing the Ruined Village: Hebrew Poetry and the Jewish Arab Conflict, 1929–1967)* (Haifa: Pardes, 2006). On the literary representation of "the Arab," see Gilead Morahg, "New Images of Arabs in Israeli Fiction," *Prooftexts* 6, no. 2 (1986): 147–62; and Menakhem Perry, "The Israeli-Palestinian Conflict: A Metaphor in Recent Israeli Fiction," *Poetics Today* 7, no. 4 (1986): 603–19. A more comprehensive discussion is offered in Gila Ramras-Rauch, *The Arab in Israeli Literature* (Bloomington: Indiana University Press, 1989). Recently, Gil Z. Hochberg notes in *In Spite of Partition: Jews, Arabs, and the Limits of Separatist Imagination* (Princeton, NJ: Princeton University Press, 2007) how some Israeli and Palestinian writers undercut what she calls "the Zionist orientalist imagination" in its attempt to "set apart the Jew and the Arab" (8). Hochberg is interested in literature as it potentially or actually moves beyond such stable markers as "Arab" and "Jew," that is, beyond "fully separable, if not radically opposed, identities" (16).

16. On the reluctance of Israeli political discourse to address al-Nakba, if not to repress it altogether, see, e.g., Anita Shapira, "Hirbet Hizah: Between Remembrance and Forgetting," *Jewish Social Studies* 7, no. 1 (2000): 1–62, esp. 23–25 and 31–41. See also Yfaat Weiss, *Wadi Salib: Hanocheach vehanifkad (Wadi Salib: A Confiscated Memory)* (Jerusalem: Van Leer Jerusalem Institute and Hakibbutz Hameuchad, 2007), 42–57; and David N. Myers, *Between Jew and Arab: The Lost Voice of Simon Rawidowicz* (Waltham, MA: Brandeis University Press, 2008), 1–19, 70–87.

17. Michael Oakeshott, *On History and Other Essays* (Indianapolis: Liberty Fund, 1999), 40.

18. On the tensions between nationalist and universalistic tendencies in Zionist discourse as echoed and thematized in Hebrew literature, see Gershon Shaked, *Sifrut az, kan veachshav (Literature Then, Here, and Now)* (Tel Aviv: Zmora-Bitan, 1993), 29–32. On the tension between universal and national humanism in Zionist discourse and modern Hebrew literature, see Nurith Gertz, *Myths in Israeli Culture: Captives of a Dream* (London: Vallentine Mitchell, 2000), 35.

19. Hannah Arendt, *Denktagebuch: 1950–1973*, ed. Ursula Ludz and Ingeborg Nordmann, 2 vols. (Munich: Piper Verlag, 2002), 1:354. Heidegger himself uses the term "unsaid" in relation to "saying" (*sagen*). Like seeing (*sehen*),

which means "to let see, to show," *sagen* (unlike *aussagen*, "to assert, to state")
indicates something in contrast to making a proposition or speaking: "Someone
can speak [*sprechen*] . . . without saying anything. Conversely, someone is silent, he does not speak and can say a lot in his not speaking. . . . 'Saying' means:
to show, to let appear, to let be seen and heard." Martin Heidegger, *Unterwegs
zur Sprache*, 9th ed. (Pfullingen: Neske, 1990), 252; translated as *On the Way
to Language*, trans. P. D. Hertz (New York: Harper and Row, 1982), 122. Interpreting Kant, Heidegger points out that "what is put before our eyes is still
unsaid [*Ungesagtes*] by what is said." Martin Heidegger, *Kant und das Problem
der Metaphysik*, 5th ed. (Frankfurt am Main: Klostermann, 1991), 201; in translation, *Kant and the Problem of Metaphysics*, trans. R. Taft (Bloomington: Indiana University Press, 1997), 137.

20. "Von hier aus rückverwandelt sich das Werk aus dem Resultathaft-tot-
Gedruckten in eine lebendige Rede, auf die Widerrede möglich ist. Es ergibt sich
ein Zwiegespräch bei dem der Leser nicht mehr von aussen kommt, sondern mit-
tendrin mitbeteiligt ist" (Arendt, *Denktagebuch*, 1:354).

21. *Mul hayearot* was first published in the literary journal *Keshet* 5, no. 3
(Spring 1963): 18–45. Later, it was included in Yehoshua's second collection of
stories, *Mul hayearot* (Tel Aviv: Hakibbutz Hameuchad, 1968).

22. Richard Rorty, "Unfamiliar Noises: Hesse and Davidson on Metaphor,"
in *Objectivity, Relativism and Truth*, vol. 1 of *Philosophical Papers* (Cambridge:
Cambridge University Press, 1991), 163.

23. Yitzhak Laor, *Anu kotvim otach moledet* (*Narratives with No Natives*)
(Tel Aviv: Hakibbutz Hameuchad, 1995), 130, 145. In a series of later essays,
Laor went on to intensify his polemical attack on what he views as "the myth"
of the liberal Zionism of such writers as Amos Oz, A. B. Yehoshua, and David
Grossman. See Yitzhak Laor, *The Myths of Liberal Zionism* (London: Verso,
2009).

24. Yochai Oppenheimer, *Meever lagader: Yizug haaravim basiporet haivrit
vehayisraelit 1906–2005* (*Barriers: The Representation of the Arab in Hebrew
and Israeli Fiction, 1906–2005*) (Tel Aviv: Am Oved, 2008), 9, 10, 19.

25. Interestingly, this sweeping claim is relativized in Oppenheimer's actual
analysis. Here it becomes clear that what used to be an overwhelmingly patroniz-
ing, racialized perspective on Arabs in Hebrew prose gradually evolved over the
decades into a nuanced approach to Arabs and a more thoughtful consideration
of Palestinian suffering. Crucial in this process has been the writing of Mizrahi
authors—writers who arrived in Israel in the course of the 1950s from the Arab
world (ibid., 264–310)—and the growing resistance in Israeli cultural discourse
to the occupation of the West Bank and the Gaza Strip as of the 1980s.

26. Hannan Hever, "Lo techat gam mipnei 'Al tagidu begat' ": Hanakba hafalastinit bashira haivrit 1948–1958" [Do not be afraid even in the face of 'tell it
not in Gath': The Palestinian Nakba in Hebrew poetry, 1948–1958], in Hever,
Al tagidu begat, 13.

27. While it is impossible to assess the exact impact of authors and intellectuals on Israel's political leaders, there are many indications that the latter—from
Ben-Gurion to Benjamin Netanyahu—were at least interested in listening to the
views of the former. Before delivering his so-called Bar-Ilan speech in 2009, for

example, in which he accepted the vision of a two-state solution for the Israeli-Palestinian conflict, Netanyahu met for an informal, initially unpublicized meeting with writers David Grossman and Eyal Megged. According to some reports, Grossman and Megged even suggested to Netanyahu some phrases to include in his speech. Although according to Megged, Netanyahu chose not to adopt any of their suggestions for his Bar-Ilan speech, it is not implausible that these writers' views may, in fact, have had some impact on him. See Dan Ephron, "The Unlikely Peacemaker: Netanyahu Says He'll 'Surprise the Critics and Skeptics.' Really?," *Time Magazine*, September 6, 2010, 32–33.

28. Rogani, *Mul hakefar sheharav*, 41. Rogani's discussion of poets such as Nathan Alterman, Avot Yeshurun, and Yehuda Amichai offers a powerful enhancement of my argument: Hebrew narrative prose written by Jewish Israeli writers did not simply reflect (or, worse, serve) the oblivious political discourse regarding 1948. Rather, Hebrew literature played a central role in bringing the fate of Palestinians and the responsibility of Israelis to address that fate to national awareness and into the center of the cultural-political discourse.

29. Alon Hilu, *The House of Rajani* (New York: Vintage Books, 2011).

30. Yoram Kaniuk, *Tashach (1948)* (Tel Aviv: Miskal/Yedioth Aharonoth/Chemed, 2010). Kaniuk's memoir, alongside the reactions to his book, is a prime example of the way in which Hebrew literature has brought the unsaid of 1948 into the Israeli public sphere with increasing urgency and clarity. In this deeply unsettling first-person testimony that focuses on Kaniuk's service in the Palmach (see chap. 7, n. 2, below), the writer redescribes what we came to call the 1948 "war" as a set of chaotic circumstances, a war of all against all, in which no side could claim the moral high ground. Dedicated to his friends and fellow soldiers, Kaniuk defines Tashach (1948 in the Jewish calendar), the synecdoche for the war, as "gehenom hatevach"—the massacre's hell (5). He depicts the desperation of the Zionist population over what to do with the numerous Holocaust refugees arriving in Palestine in the hope of finally finding a homeland. Kaniuk also delivers a deeply distressing account of the immeasurable pain of the Palestinian population in the course of the war. Crucial for the ethical questions that the book raises is Kaniuk's report of an incident in which he shot a little boy in order to prevent a soldier from killing both the child and his mother (115–20). This scene is among the most disturbing I encountered in depictions of 1948. Since I focus in this book on fictional prose, I will not discuss Kaniuk's memoir in the following pages. However, for a historical perspective on the book and to find out more about the reactions Kaniuk's memoir engendered, see Motti Golani, "Fugat hamavet: Tashach meet Yoram Kaniuk" [The death fugue: *Tashach* by Yoram Kaniuk], *Haaretz*, July 9, 2010, available online at http://www.haaretz .co.il/hasite/spages/1177969.html#yoram (accessed August 2, 2010).

31. See Or Kashti, "Larishona: Sefer limud latichonim mazig et taanat ha-falastinim le'tihur etni' be'48" [For the first time a schoolbook for Israeli high schools presents the Palestinian claim regarding 'ethnic cleansing' in 1948], *Haaretz*, September 9, 2009, http://www.haaretz.co.il/hasite/spages/1116059. html (accessed July 28, 2010). See also Or Kashti, "Education Minister under Fire for 'Nakba' textbook," *Haaretz*, July 23, 2007, http://www.haaretz.com /print-edition/news/education-minister-under-fire-for-nakba-textbook-1.226074

(accessed November 8, 2010). On the proliferation of publications surrounding al-Nakba, see, e.g., the journal *Sedek: Ktav et lanakba shekan* [Sedek: A journal on the ever-present Nakba], http://www.zochrot.org/images/sedek_small_english.pdf (accessed July 28, 2010); and Ariella Azoulay, *Alimut mechonenet 1947–1950: Genealogia chazutit shel mishtar vehafichat haason le'ason minkudat mabatam'* (*Constituent Violence, 1947–1950: A Genealogy of a Regime and 'A Catastrophe from Their Point of View'*) (Tel Aviv: Resling, 2009). *Sedek* and Azoulay's book were supported by Zochrot, a Jewish Israeli group dedicated to promoting awareness of al-Nakba. The evolving and, I would argue, growing recognition of al-Nakba as a historical event with which Israelis must reckon is also reflected in the 2008 exhibition *Batei habeer: Haarmonot haneelamim shel yafo* [Well houses: Disappearing palaces of Jaffa] that was sponsored by the Israeli Ministry of Science, Culture, and Sports, the municipality of Tel Aviv, and Tel Aviv University. See http://www.bateibeer.com/index.html and the catalog at http://www.bateibeer.com/Binder.pdf (both accessed July 28, 2010).

32. In May 2009, a ministers' committee of the newly elected Israeli government under Benjamin Netanyahu decided to support the draft of a law that would outlaw the commemoration of al-Nakba on Israel's Independence Day. See *Haaretz*, May 24, 2009, http://www.haaretz.com/hasite/spages/1087791.html (in Hebrew) (accessed July 28, 2010).

33. While some translate the idiom *hatsofe leveit Yisrael* as "the watchman of the house of Israel," I follow here and throughout the book the translation of *The New Oxford Annotated Bible with the Apocryphal/Deuterocanonical Books*, new rev. standard version, ed. Bruce M. Metzger and Roland E. Murphy (New York: Oxford University Press, 1991).

34. Zeev Goldberg, "Mendele Mocher Sfarim veharaayon hatsiyoni" [Mendele Mocher Sforim and the Zionist idea], *Hatsiyonut* 20 (1996): 31. Quoted from Todd Hasak-Lowy, *Here and Now: History, Nationalism, and Realism in Modern Hebrew Fiction* (Syracuse, NY: Syracuse University Press, 2008), xxvii. See also Dan Miron, "Hirhurim beidan shel proza" [Reflections in an age of prose/a prosaic age], in *Shloshim shanah, shloshim sipurim* (*Thirty Years, Thirty Stories: An Anthology of Hebrew Stories from the '60s to the '90s*), ed. Zisi Stavi (Tel Aviv: Yediot Ahronot, 1993), 397–427.

35. Hasak-Lowy, *Here and Now*, xxviii.

36. On this role, see Brenner, *Inextricably Bonded*, 96–97.

37. Grossman, *Writing in the Dark*, 65.

CHAPTER SEVEN

1. S. Yizhar finished writing these novellas in November 1948. They were published in 1949 with the title *Sipur Khirbet Khizah* (Merhavyah: Sifriyat Poalim, 1949). Quoting from the story, I will use, however, the English translation, *Khirbet Khizeh*, trans. Nicholas de Lange and Yaacob Dweck (Jerusalem: Ibis Editions, 2008), and thus will follow the translators' decision to call the village Khizeh, not Khizah. Page references to the English translation will be given parenthetically in the text.

2. Palmach is an acronym for Plugot Machatz, or "strike force." It was the

fighting force of the Haganah, the Jewish paramilitary organization during the period of the British Mandate in Palestine.

3. I follow here Gidi Nevo's brilliant study of S. Yizhar's work in which he shows in what ways Yizhar's poetics diverged from realism in favor of what Nevo views as the attempt to get closer, with poetic means, to what is by now a lost reality, rather than to represent it. See Gidi Nevo, *Shiva yamim banegev: Al Yemei Ziklag le S. Yizhar* (*Seven Days in the Negev: On "Days of Ziklag" by S. Yizhar*) (Tel Aviv and Beer-Sheva: Hakibbutz Hameuchad and Ben-Gurion Research Institute, 2005), esp. 184–230. For more on this generation of writers in a larger context, see Gershon Shaked, *Modern Hebrew Fiction*, ed. Emily Miller Budick, trans. Yael Lotan (Bloomington: Indiana University Press, 2000), 139–59; and Gershon Shaked, *Hasiporet haivrit, 1880–1980* (*Hebrew Narrative Fiction, 1880–1980*), 5 vols. (Jerusalem: Keter, 1977), 3:181–261.

4. On the trope of the fallen soldier as related to the birth of the nation, see George L. Mosse, *Fallen Soldiers: Reshaping the Memory of the World Wars* (Oxford: Oxford University Press, 1990).

5. See Oppenheimer, *Barriers*, 173.

6. On Yizhar's figurative choice to present the order in this abbreviated form as generating ethical reflection, see Adia Mendelson-Maoz, *Hasifrut kemaabadah musarit: Keriah bemivhar yetsirot baprozah haivrit shel hameah haesrim* (*Literature as a Moral Laboratory: Reading Selected Twentieth-Century Hebrew Prose*) (Ramat-Gan: University of Bar-Ilan Press, 2009), 100–102.

7. Menachem Brinker, "Teud veomanutiyut basifrut" [Documentation and artistic quality in literature], in Menachem Brinker, *Sovev sifrut: Maamarim al gvul haphilosophia vetorat hasifrut vehaomanut* (*About Literature: Essays on the Borderline of the Philosophy of Art and Literary* Theory) (Jerusalem: Hebrew University Magnes Press, 2000), 293–97.

8. Ibid., 295.

9. Yfaat Weiss documents the chain of events that began in 1930s Europe in Yfaat Weiss, *Wadi Salib: Hanocheach vehanifkad* (*Wadi Salib: A Confiscated Memory*) (Jerusalem: Van Leer Jerusalem Institute and Hakibbutz Hameuchad, 2007), 43, 56.

10. The idiom was apparently first used in relation to the Holocaust by the Polish-born poet and activist Abba Kovner, who in 1941 wrote a pamphlet distributed in the Vilna ghetto calling on the Jewish ghetto prisoners not to go to their deaths "like lambs to the slaughter." As Tom Segev notes, Kovner probably borrowed the expression from the book of Isaiah (53:7) (or from Psalms 44:23). Segev observes that the phrase came to express "a national trauma," setting Zionist activist heroism in Palestine against the weakness of Jewish Diaspora. See Tom Segev, *The Seventh Million: The Israelis and the Holocaust*, trans. Haim Watzman (New York: Henry Holt, 1991), 110.

11. David N. Myers, "Victory and Sorrow," review of S. Yizhar, *The Story of Khirbet Khizeh*, *New Republic*, October 22, 2008, http://www.sscnet.ucla.edu /history/myers/CV/Victory_Sorrow_K.%20Khizeh.pdf (accessed July 30, 2010).

12. S. Yizhar and Hayim Nagid (interview), "Katavti et 'Hirbet Hizah' lo kiyehudi mul aravi, ela keadam shenifga" [I wrote 'Khirbet Khizeh' not as a Jew facing an Arab but rather as a human who was hurt], *Maariv*, February 10, 1978. Quoted from Shapira, "Hirbet Hizah," 9.

13. Zionist culture has made widespread use of biblical imagery in producing a Jewish national narrative for those arriving in old-new Zion and those soon to be born there. See Yael Zerubavel, *Recovered Roots: Collective Memory and the Making of Israeli National Tradition* (Chicago: University of Chicago Press, 1995).

14. In this episode of 1 Kings, God instructs the prophet to confront Ahab when the latter brutally takes possession of Naboth's vineyard (after Jezebel, the queen, orchestrates the innocent man's murder). The charge God desires Elijah to deliver, "Have you killed and also taken possession?" (*haratzachta vegam yarashta*), has become idiomatic, representing a grievous trespass against a fellow human being.

15. On Yizhar's allusion to the story of Sodom, see Nurit Gertz, *Khirbet Khizah vehaboker shelemaharat* (*Generational Shift in Literary History: Hebrew Narrative Fiction in the Sixties*) (Tel Aviv: Hakibbutz Hameuchad, 1983), 77; and Hever, *Producing the Modern Hebrew Canon*, 114.

16. Yizhar's letter to Hanegbi and the introduction were discovered and published by Uri S. Cohen in "Al hitnatzluto hamaashima shel S. Yizhar" [On the accusatory apology of S. Yizhar], *Haaretz*, September 18, 2009, http://www.haaretz.co.il/hasite/pages/ShArt.jhtml?itemNo=1115389&contrassID=1&subContrassID=18&sbSubContrassID=0 (accessed July 30, 2010).

17. Shapira, "Hirbet Hizah," 31–32.

18. Ibid., 38.

19. Nahum Barnea, *Yorim uvochim* (*They Shoot and They Cry*) (Tel Aviv: Zemorah, Bitan, Modan, 1981). On this issue, see also Ruth Linn, *Conscience at War: The Israeli Soldier as a Moral Critic* (Albany: State University of New York Press, 1996), 149–50.

20. Hannan Hever, "Mapping Literary Spaces: Territory and Violence in Israeli Literature," in *Mapping Jewish Identities*, ed. Laurence J. Silberstein (New York: New York University Press, 2000), 206–7; and Hannan Hever, *Hasipur vehaleom: Kriot bikortiyot bekanon hasiporet haivrit* (*Narrative and the Nation: Critical Readings in the Canon of Hebrew Fiction*) (Tel Aviv: Resling, 2007), 219. Yerach Gover argues similarly that the narrator of *Hashavui* (the other novella published by Yizhar immediately after 1948, also dealing with the moral dilemmas of warfare) ignores the significance of violating principles in the course of exercising force. Had the narrator not ignored this, he would have been "unable to continue inflicting pain." Thus, Yizhar's story illustrates "the sentimentality and hollowness of hermetic reflection." Yerach Gover, *Zionism: The Limits of Moral Discourse in Israeli Hebrew Fiction* (Minneapolis: University of Minnesota Press, 1994), 11. Oz Almog claims reasonably that Yizhar's narratives invoke the ways in which Israeli soldiers viewed the clay houses in Arab villages—permeated with odor, filth, ants, fleas, and lice that swarm in the houses and yards—as elements of a culture and landscape that they, the young, unquestioning Zionists, needed to "clean" and thus "redeem." According to Almog, Yizhar's description of the Sabra in *Hashavui* became controversial in Israel because it presented the soldiers as self-assured conquerors. Oz Almog, *The Sabra: The Creation of the New Jew* (Berkeley and Los Angeles: University of California Press, 2000), 232.

21. Shapira, "Hirbet Hizah," 1–62.

22. Raja Shehadeh, "Echoes of the Present: S. Yizhar's *Khirbet Khizeh* and Israel Today," *Journal of Palestine Studies* 38, no. 1 (Autumn 2008): 82.

23. In a 1993 interview, S. Yizhar said, "The War of Independence was the positive end of an age; but from the moral point of view, it also spelled the negative end of an era. Up to that point, we had always known that some things could never be done, and most certainly never by Jews. My tale 'Khirbet Khizah,' a story that has angered everyone now for almost fifty years, is about things that before the War of Liberation I believed we Jews don't do." Interview with Shmuel Hupert, "Gam haleluyah vegam rekviem" [A hallelujah and a requiem], *Yediot Ahronot*, December 10, 1993. In another interview, Yizhar added, "In the War of Independence, people lived in a myth. There was only one solution. When the war began, the naïve faith of those young men got its first slap in the face. People seized and plundered. Arabs were ousted. And we had after all believed that Jews could never be capable of expelling others." Interview with Yotam Reuveni, "Shiur moledet" [A homeland lesson], *Yediot Ahronot*, April 26, 1985, as quoted in Shapira, "Hirbet Hizah," 9.

24. See Lily Rattok, *Hasipur haliri haivri (The Hebrew Lyrical Narrative)* (Tel Aviv: Massada, 1990), 104.

25. S. Yizhar, "Sipur shelo hitchil" [A story that did not yet begin], in *Sipurei mishor (Stories of the Plain)* (Tel Aviv: Hakkibutz Hameuchad, 1963), 146, 147. The section "Shtikat hakfarim" is printed on 145–64. Hereafter, page references to this work will be given parenthetically in the text. The translations are mine.

26. Oppenheimer, *Barriers*, 196–97.

27. S. Yizhar's short biographical essay "Ma anu mashivim" [What we reply] quoted here was first published in the daily *Hadashot* on the eve of Israel's Independence Day in 1992. I use here the version reproduced in Hannan Hever, *Hasipur vehaleom: Kriot bikortiyot bekanon hasiporet haivrit (Narrative and the Nation: Critical Readings in the Canon of Hebrew Fiction)* (Tel Aviv: Resling, 2007), 217.

CHAPTER EIGHT

1. As I noted in chapter 6, *Facing the Forests* was first published in *Keshet* 5, no. 3 (Spring 1963): 18–45, and was included in Yehoshua's second collection of stories, *Mul hayearot* (Tel Aviv: Hakibbutz Hameuchad, 1968). Citations here are to Miriam Arad's translation as it appears in A. B. Yehoshua, *The Continuing Silence of a Poet: Collected Stories* (London: Halban, 1988), 203–36, with the translation modified where necessary using A. B. Yehoshua, *Kol hasipuirim (The Stories)* (Tel Aviv: Hakibbutz Hameuchad, 1993), 99–128. Page references to this work will be given parenthetically in the text. All deviations from Arad's translation are noted as such.

2. Gershon Shaked rightly regards *Facing the Forests* as a narrative that takes an "antithetical" position toward what Shaked himself defined as the Zionist metanarrative. See Shaked, *Hasiporet haivrit, 1880–1980*, 5:92–93. Roughly speaking, the fiction of Dor Hamedinah tended toward depictions of individual psyches embroiled in politics and national ideology and reflected a more ambivalent attitude toward the rhetorical form, if not toward the political substance, of

Zionism. In his recent extensive study of the modern history of Hebrew literature, Yigal Schwartz names *Facing the Forests* among the "foundational works" of Dor Hamedinah. See Schwartz, *Do You Know the Land Where the Lemon Blooms?*, 368. On the generational transition from Dor Hapalmach to Dor Hamedinah, see Gershon Shaked, *Modern Hebrew Fiction*, trans. Yael Lotan, ed. Emily Miller Budick (Bloomington: Indiana University Press, 2000), 139–41, 187–89; and Shaked, *Hasiporet haivrit, 1880–1980*, 5:19–21. On A. B. Yehoshua's *Facing the Forests* in the larger context of this generation of writers, see also Hever, *Producing the Modern Hebrew Canon*, 140.

3. Hever, *Producing the Modern Hebrew Canon*, 143.

4. See Mitchell, "Israel, Palestine, and the American Wilderness."

5. On the trope of the Crusaders in Hebrew literature and in A. B. Yehoshua's *Facing the Forests*, see Oppenheimer, *Barriers*, 231–33, 478n43.

6. The historian David Ohana aptly names this sentiment "the crusader anxiety." See Ohana's extensive discussion in *Lo knaanim, lo tsalbanim: Mekorot hamitologia hayisraelit (Neither Canaanites nor Crusaders: The Origins of Israeli Mythology)* (Jerusalem: Shalom Hartman Institute; Ramat Gan: Keter, 2008), 291–348; translated as *The Origins of Israeli Mythology: Neither Canaanites nor Crusaders*, trans. David Maisel (Cambridge: Cambridge University Press, 2011).

7. In this reading I follow Shaked, *Hasiporet haivrit, 1880–1980*, 5:224.

8. On the idiom *Shoah utkuma*, see Dan Michman's review essay "She'erit Hapletah, 1944–1948: Rehabilitation and Political Struggle," *Holocaust and Genocide Studies* 7, no. 1 (Spring 1993): 107–16. On the combination *Shoah vegvurah* in Israeli cultural-political discourse of the 1950s, of which the Warsaw ghetto uprising is perhaps the most obvious example, see Anita Shapira, "Lean halcha 'shelilat hagalut'?" [Where did 'the negation of the Diaspora' disappear?], *Alpayim* 25 (2003): 36; and Gulie Ne'eman Arad, "Israel and the Shoah: A Tale of Multifarious Taboos," *New German Critique* 90 (Fall 2003): 8–10.

9. See Idith Zertal, *Hauma vehamavet: Historia, zikaron, politika (Death and the Nation: History, Memory, Politics)* (Or-Yehuda: Dvir, 2002), 137–78.

10. Surprisingly, Miriam Arad's English translation leaves this rich metaphor of the world between sleep and sleep untranslated. The missing line appears in A. B. Yehoshua, *Kol hasipuirim (The Stories)* (Tel Aviv: Hakibbutz Hameuchad, 1993), 112. In a conversation about the novella, Robert Alter suggested that observation from outside, from afar, seems to be the underlying condition of many protagonists in Yehoshua's early fiction, for example, in his story "Hamifkad haaharon."

11. Hever suggests that the map, a prevalent symbol in Hebrew literature of the 1960s, points to the "narcissism" of those who wish to escape their responsibility as a majority in a sovereign state by "adopting the perspective of the [Palestinian] minority." Hever, *Narrative and the Nation*, 232.

12. In the traditional Jewish context, a person's name is identical with his or her reputation, as in the idiom "tov shem mishemen tov" (Ecclesiastes 7:1): "A good name is better than precious ointment."

13. As Gilead Morahg has shown, this "dark matter" might be considered, from a narratological standpoint, the reason for the protagonist's elusiveness—

for his inability to "confront truths" that he is "determined to deny." Gilead Morahg, "Shading the Truth: A. B. Yehoshua's 'Facing the Forests,'" in *History and Literature: New Readings of Jewish Texts in Honor of Arnold J. Band*, ed. William Cutter and David C. Jacobson (Providence, RI: Brown Judaic Studies, 2002), 417.

14. Naomi Sokoloff argues that the novella continues the discursive intervention Yehoshua began in his 1980 volume *Bizchut hanormaliut* (translated into English as *Between Right and Right* [Garden City, NY: Doubleday, 1981]), a narrative that rejects the stereotypical image of the enemy and that signals a more complex understanding of the figure of the Arab in Israeli literature but that still is hardly a truly complex account of the challenges of the conflict. Naomi B. Sokoloff, "Bemaavak im hastereotipiut: Dmut ha'aravi be'mul hayearot' le'A.B. Yehoshua 'aharei 25 shana' " (Combatting the Stereotype: The Image of the Arab in A. B. Yehoshua's *Facing the Forests*), *Hadoar*, May 22, 1987, 14–17.

15. R. J. Zwi Werblowsky and Geoffrey Wigoder, eds., *The Oxford Dictionary of the Jewish Religion* (New York: Oxford University Press, 1997), s.v. "Yom Kippur."

16. Hever, *Producing the Modern Hebrew Canon*, 144–45. On *Facing the Forests* as "criticizing" Israel's dispossession and "unjust treatment" of Palestinians, see also Brenner, *Inextricably Bonded*, 88.

17. On this claim, see Ehud Ben-Ezer, "Portsim unetsurim" [Besieged conquerors], *Keshet* 4 (Summer 1968): 149; and Gertz, *Generational Shift in Literary History*, 102.

18. On Yehoshua's protagonist as a transformed character, capable of at least some form of caring for the Palestinian girl, see Brenner, *Inextricably Bonded*, 188.

19. On the ongoing discussion surrounding *Facing the Forests* as a story with a political resonance, see Shaked, *Hasiporet haivrit, 1880–1980*, 5:165–66, 519n57.

20. Hever, *Producing the Modern Hebrew Canon*, 184–85; and Gil Z. Hochberg, *In Spite of Partition: Jews, Arabs, and the Limits of Separatist Imagination* (Princeton, NJ: Princeton University Press, 2007), 75–76.

21. I do not address *Arabeskot* in detail in this book given my focus on futurity in the work of Jewish Israeli writers. For a thorough discussion of this important work, see Hochberg, *In Spite of Partition*, 73–93; and Hever, *Producing the Modern Hebrew Canon*, 175–204.

22. Amir Gutfreund, "Yaaran," in *Achuzot hachof (Shoreline Mansions)* (Tel Aviv: Zmora-Bitan, 2002), 140–50. Hereafter, page references to this work will be given parenthetically in the text. The translations are mine.

23. In an interview with Tsur Ehrlich, Gutfreund notes that "when you look at Israel's history since 1967 . . . you see that Israelis hardly have two weeks for carefully thinking about what may be the right thing to do. We [Israelis] are always attempting to defend ourselves [*bematsav shel hitgonenut*], always reacting to events. We are living with the feeling that we are constantly burning." *Makor Rishon*, June 15, 2007, http://tsurehrlich.blogspot.com/2010/01/blog-post_6339.html (accessed August 1, 2010). In an interview with Meirav Yudelovitch, Gutfreund likewise and emblematically notes, "I often ask myself what I am do-

ing here [in Israel]. For long periods of time, I do not feel that I belong." What nonetheless keeps him in the country, he continues, is the language: "Hebrew is the only language I can swim in while not using a flotation belt." Meirav Yudelovitch, "Mi shechalam" [The one who dreamed], *Ynet*, September 16, 2005, http://www.ynet.co.il/articles/0,7340,L-3142718,00.html (accessed August 1, 2010).

CHAPTER NINE

1. On the Eichmann trial as a watershed moment in Israeli consciousness, see Shapira, "Lean halcha 'shelilat hagalut'?," 31. Gershon Shaked sees in the Eichmann trial one of the most significant moments in the process by which the rhetoric of creating a "new Hebrew" in the "empty land" was weakened. See his *Hasiporet haivrit, 1880–1980,* 5:23.

2. Yariv Ben Aharon (the son of the Israeli labor leader Yitzhak Ben Aharon), who fought in the Six-Day War, said of the waiting period before the beginning of hostilities in June 1967: "We believed that annihilation [of Israeli Jews] would take place were we to lose. The Holocaust gave us this term ["the Jewish fate," "the Jewish tragedy"], or we inherited it. This is a very viable term for anyone who grew up in Israel, even if he did not survive the Holocaust himself but only heard of it or read about it." Quoted in Shapira, "Lean halcha 'shelilat hagalut'?," 39.

3. On the effects of the Yom Kippur War on Israeli society and Hebrew literature, see Miron, "Reflections in an Age of Prose/Prosaic Age," 418. On the impact of the Yom Kippur War on Israeli society and culture, see also Glenda Abramson, *Drama and Ideology in Modern Israel* (Cambridge: Cambridge University Press, 1998), 57; and Gertz, *Myths in Israeli Culture,* 121.

4. Gush Emunim is a movement formed in March 1974 to promote the ideology of Eretz Yisrael hashlemah, "the Land of Israel whole and complete." On the ideologies and practices of the settler movement, see, e.g., Robert I. Friedman, *Zealots for Zion: Inside Israel's West Bank Settlement Movement* (New Brunswick, NJ: Rutgers University Press, 1994).

5. See Dan Miron, *Im lo tihyeh Yerushalayim: Masot al hasifrut haivrit beheksher tarbuti-politi* (*If There Is No Jerusalem: Essays on Hebrew Literature in a Cultural-Political Context*) (Tel Aviv: Hakibbutz Hameuchad, 1987), 233–35. While Miron claims that Hebrew literature widely ignored the reality that the 1967 war created, Yochai Oppenheimer presents a more nuanced judgment. He acknowledges differences between Hebrew poetry, which displayed a clear awareness of the political and moral impact of the war, and Hebrew prose, which widely ignored these issues. However, Openheimer states, this initial obliviousness ended around 1977, and even more so after the 1982 Lebanon War. See Oppenheimer, *Barriers,* 234–35.

6. David Schütz, *Shoshan lavan, shoshan adom* (*White Rose, Red Rose*) (Jerusalem and Tel Aviv: Keter, 1988). Page references to this work will be given parenthetically in the text. The translations are mine.

7. Yehoshua Kenaz, *Hitganvut yehidim* (Tel Aviv: Am Oved, 1986), translated as *Infiltration,* trans. Dalya Bilu (South Royalton, VT: Zoland Books,

2003). Page references to the translation will be given parenthetically in the text.

8. On Kenaz's novel in relation to Yizhar's *Yemei Ziklag*, see also Shaked, who notes that while Yizhar's characters are a synecdoche of Israel's "noble" self, Kenaz's characters see the country from the viewpoint of "Sparta's discarded children." Shaked, *Hasiporet haivrit, 1880–1980*, 5:290.

9. On *Infiltration* as a "social novel" that observes through its "polyphonic" structure Israeli society of the 1950s, see Shaked, *Hasiporet haivrit, 1880–1980*, 5:289–90.

10. Michael Gluzman, *Haguf hazioni: Leumiyut, migdar uminiyut basifrut haivrit hachadasha* (*The Zionist Body: Nationalism, Gender, and Sexuality in Modern Hebrew Literature*) (Tel Aviv: Hakibbutz Hameuchad, 2007), 221.

11. I owe this insight to Nir Evron. In a recent interview, Kenaz defined himself as "non-Zionist": "A Zionist is someone who believes that a Jewish state will solve the problem of anti-Semitism, and I don't think so. But this does not mean that one should dismantle the [Jewish] state. The Zionists should reach a good, comfortable agreement [*Havana tova venocha*] with the Palestinians. If both sides do not want to go insane [*meshugaim*], they can reach it." Shiri Lev-Ari, "Hitganvit yechimdim" (interview with Yehoshua Kenaz), *Haaretz*, September 19, 2008, http://www.mouse.co.il/CM.articles_item,1050,209,28004,.aspx (accessed January 25, 2010).

12. David Grossman, *Writing in the Dark*, 43–44. *Chiyuch hagdi* appeared in Hebrew in 1983. It has been translated into English as *The Smile of the Lamb*, trans. Betsy Rosenberg (New York: Farrar, Straus, Giroux, 1990). On the novel as expressing a critical position regarding Israel's occupation of the West Bank, see, e.g., Gershon Shaked, "Hayeled hatamim-mefukach: Al yetzirato shel David Grossman" [The innocent-sober child: On David Grossman's work], in Gershon Shaked, *Tmunah kvutzatit: Hebetim besifrut yisrael uvetarbuta* (*A Group Portrayal: Aspects of Israeli Literature and Culture*) (Or Yehuda: Kinneret, Zmora-Bitan, Dvir, 2009), 210–11.

13. Grossman, *Writing in the Dark*, 44.

14. Ibid., 23.

15. David Grossman, *Ayen erech ahava* (Tel Aviv: Keter, 1986), translated as *See Under: Love*, trans. Betsy Rosenberg (New York: Farrar, Straus, and Giroux, 1989). Page references to the translation will be given parenthetically in the text.

16. For Dan Miron, *See Under: Love* follows the long trajectory in Hebrew prose of works that, in developing personal, realistic-psychological plots, also offer a metonymy for the national, collective condition. Miron relates this trajectory to the notion *hatsofe leveit Yisrael*, "the sentinel for the house of Israel" (Ezekiel 3:17, 33:7), which I mentioned in chapter 6. This tradition of the writer as national guardian goes back to the beginnings of modern Hebrew literature in the European Enlightenment and to what became in the course of the late nineteenth century and in the first decades of the twentieth century Hebrew literature's self-understanding as possessing the role of the guardian and observer of the Jewish national house—that is, the role of prophet and critic. See Miron's

remarks in "Hirhurim beidan shel prosa," in Stavi, *Shloshim shana, shloshim sipurim,* 424.

17. See Hanna Yablonka, "The Formation of Holocaust Consciousness in the State of Israel: The Early Years," in *Breaking Crystal: Writing and Memory after Auschwitz,* ed. Efraim Sicher (Urbana: University of Illinois Press, 1998), 119–36. On Grossman's fantastic idiom, see Gilead Morahg, "Breaking Silence: Israel's Fantastic Fiction of the Holocaust," in *The Boom in Contemporary Israeli Fiction,* ed. Alan Mintz (Hanover, NH: University Press of New England, 1997), 141–83.

18. On Grossman's use of the metaphor "the Nazi Beast" as a contemporary challenge that Momik faces and finally confronts and overpowers, see Gershon Shaked's sensible reading in "Hayeled hatamim-mefukach," 216–20.

19. On the Holocaust as a motive behind Israel's striving to become a nuclear power, see, e.g., Segev, *Seventh Million,* 367. On the role of the Holocaust in informing Grossman's writing, see, e.g., Leon I. Yudkin, "Holocaust Trauma in the Second Generation: The Hebrew Fiction of David Grossman and Savyon Liebrecht," in Sicher, *Breaking Crystal,* 170–81.

20. As Avraham Even-Shoshan's *New Dictionary* of modern Hebrew notes, the noun *kivshan* may have its origin in the word for lamb, *keves,* and is thus related to the act of ritual sacrifice in which the animal is completely burnt. Avraham Aven-Shoshan, *Hamilon hechadash (The New Dictionary in Four Volumes)* (Jerusalem: Kiryat Sefer, 1991), 2:523. It is interesting to note that both the English and the German translations of the book omit the following line completely: "and the name of the first Israeli nuclear reactor will be 'Kivshan,' which is an acronym standing for, as its director explained, Reactor–Swimming Pool–Nahal Rubin" (cf. the Hebrew original, 63).

21. Benny Morris, *The Birth of the Palestinian Refugee Problem Revisited* (Cambridge: Cambridge University Press, 2004), 436.

22. References to the 1980s are interspersed throughout the novel. See, e.g., *See Under: Love,* 120.

23. Quoted after Segev, *Seventh Million,* 399. Segev describes how the Holocaust was politicized before 1982 and then increasingly so in the course of the Lebanon War (399, 411–13). On Begin's rhetoric as amalgamating Holocaust anxieties with post-1967 discourse and politics, see Gertz, *Myths in Israeli Culture,* 59–89; on the use of the Holocaust in Israeli public discourse and nationalist rhetoric, see Hannah Yablonka, "The Commander of the Yizkor Order: Begin, Herut and the Holocaust," in *Israel: The First Decades of Independence,* ed. Ilan S. Troen and Noah Lucas (Albany, NY: SUNY Press, 1995), 211–31.

24. Quoted in Segev, *Seventh Million,* 399.

25. Ibid. On September 16 and 17, 1982, the Lebanese Christian Phalangist militia caused a horrific bloodbath in the Palestinian refugee camps of Sabra and Shatila. When Israeli soldiers finally entered the camps to stop the killing, they found hundreds of Palestinian bodies (estimates vary from 460 to 800), including numerous women and children. The victims of the camps were either Palestinians who experienced al-Nakba firsthand or their descendants. The shock many Israelis felt at these events resulted from the fact that some Israeli Defense

Force commanders knew about the massacre—even if not about its horrific dimensions—and did little or nothing at all to stop it while it was taking place. This shocking recognition was later graphically represented by Ari Folman in his 2008 animated documentary on the horrors of the 1982 Lebanon War, *Waltz with Bashir*. Folman's narrative explores the ways in which an Israeli soldier fighting in Lebanon (who is also the child of Holocaust survivors) experiences and reacts to the massacres in Sabra and Shatila. Folman's work also displays how the images of murdered Palestinians were disturbingly reminiscent of those of victims of the Holocaust.

26. Segev, *Seventh Million*, 400.

27. David Grossman, "The Art of Fiction" (interview with Jonathan Shainin), *Paris Review* 194, no. 182 (Fall 2007), http://www.theparisreview.org /interviews/5794/the-art-of-fiction-no-194-david-grossman (accessed November 9, 2010).

28. Grossman, *Writing in the Dark*, 77 (my emphasis).

29. David Grossman first published his traveling notes in the weekly *Koteret rashit* in 1988. The translation I am referring to here is David Grossman, *The Yellow Wind*, trans. Haim Watzman (New York: Noonday, 1998).

30. Grossman, *Yellow Wind*, 6.

31. "Israel Wrestles with Nazi Insults," BBC News, published on May 24, 2004, http://news.bbc.co.uk/go/pr/fr/-/2/hi/middle_east/3742365.stm (accessed November 29, 2010).

32. David Grossman, *Sleeping on a Wire: Conversations with Palestinians in Israel*, trans. Haim Watzman (New York: Farrar, Straus, and Giroux, 1993), 324. Hereafter page references to this work will be given parenthetically in the text.

33. David Grossman, "Looking at Ourselves," trans. Haim Watzman, *New York Review of Books*, January 11, 2007, 4.

34. Dan Pagis, *Kol hashirim; "Aba" Pirke proza (Collected Poems and "Father" [Prose Passages])* (Tel Aviv: Hakibbutz Hameuchad; Jerusalem: Mosad Byalik, 1991), 211, my translation.

35. Grossman, "Looking at Ourselves," 4.

36. Ibid., 6.

CHAPTER TEN

1. Although the question at the heart of this part of our discussion—the expulsion of Palestinians from their homeland in 1948—is also at the center of the historiographic post-Zionism debate, the literature generated by this debate has grown too extensive to account for here in detail. A supporting presentation of post-Zionism is offered in Laurence J. Silberstein, *The Postzionism Debates: Knowledge and Power in Israeli Culture* (New York: Routledge, 1999); and in Uri Ram, "Postnationalist Past: The Case of Israel," in *States of Memory: Continuities, Conflicts, and Transformations in National Retrospection*, ed. Jeffrey K. Olick (Durham, NC: Duke University Press, 2003), 227–58. For a critique of post-Zionist discourse, see, e.g., Shapira, "The Past Is Not a Foreign Country"; and Taub, "Post-Zionism—The French-American-Israeli Connection." On the

relationship between representations of Palestinian flight and expulsion and contemporary Israeli political debates, see Nissim Kalderon, "Post-zionut al reka ribuy tarbuyot beyisrael" [Post-Zionism on the background of multiculturalism in Israel]," in Friling, *An Answer to a Postzionist Colleague*, 173–223.

2. Amos Oz, *How to Cure a Fanatic* (Princeton, NJ: Princeton University Press, 2006), 6.

3. Amos Oz, *A Tale of Love and Darkness*, trans. Nicholas de Lange (Orlando, FL: Harvest, 2005). Page references to this work will be given parenthetically in the text. Amos Oz, *Tmunot michayey kfar* (*Scenes from Village Life*) (Jerusalem: Keter, 2009).

4. On the "orientalist" gaze of Oz's early work, see, e.g., Oppenheimer, *Barriers*, 200–213; and Hever, *Producing the Modern Hebrew Canon*, 148–53.

5. Elsewhere, Oz views himself as a child and "a brainwashed little fanatic all the way. Self-righteous, chauvinistic, deaf and blind to any view that differed from the powerful Jewish, Zionist narrative of the time, a Jewish Intifada kid." Oz, *How to Cure a Fanatic*, 43.

6. Amos Oz, "Hayehudi hasored" [The surviving Jew] (interview with Ari Shavit), in *Beetzem yesh kan shtey milchamot* (*But These Are Two Different Wars*) (Jerusalem: Keter, 2002), 134. The capacity of Oz's novel to address the complexities of 1948 successfully, including Israeli responsibility toward the Palestinians, is well reflected, I believe, in the translation of *A Tale of Love and Darkness* into Arabic. As the *New York Times* reported on March 7, 2010, it was thanks to the efforts of Elias Khoury, whose twenty-year-old son, George, was killed in a Palestinian terrorist attack (because the assassins believed he was a Jew) that Oz's novel was translated into Arabic. In an article on the translation of Oz's novel into Arabic, Ethan Bronner notes, "Sari Nusseibeh, a Palestinian philosopher who wrote his own powerful autobiography of growing up in Jerusalem in the same era, *Once Upon a Country*, said in that book's opening that it was upon reading Mr. Oz's volume that he was struck by the parallel existences of Jews and Palestinian Arabs of the time. 'Weren't both sides of the conflict totally immersed in their own tragedies, each one oblivious to, or even antagonistic toward, the narrative of the other?' he wrote. 'Isn't this inability to imagine the lives of the "other" at the heart of the Israeli-Palestinian conflict?'" Ethan Bronner, "Palestinian Sees Lesson Translating an Israeli's Work," *New York Times*, March 6, 2010, http://www.nytimes.com/2010/03/07/world/middleeast/07khoury.html (accessed May 6, 2010).

7. On criticism of Oz and his work as expressions of the "myth" of liberal Zionism, see, e.g., Laor, *The Myth of Liberal Zionism*, 72–126. Although Laor spends some fifty pages on a thorough, one could say merciless, deconstruction of Oz's *A Tale of Love and Darkness* (he calls it, for example, "a cunning work of flattery of both the Hebrew reader and the reader in the West"; 77), he tellingly ignores such scenes as the story of the al Silwanis.

8. Yitzchak Laor, *Hineh adam* (Tel Aviv: Hakibbutz Hameuchad, 2002). Page references to this work will be given parenthetically in the text. The translations are mine.

9. Tel Aviv University was indeed partially constructed on the lands of the Palestinian village of Sheikh Muwanis. The university makes no mention of the

fate of the villagers who left in March 1948. The only remaining trace of the village, the so-called Green House, serves as the university clubhouse. On this matter, see, e.g., http://www.nakbainhebrew.org/index.php?id=143 (accessed July 19, 2010).

10. Daniella Carmi, *Leshachrer pil: Massa bricha mizichronot yaldut mefukpakim* [To free an elephant: An escape journey from doubtful childhood memories] (Tel Aviv: Am Oved, 2001). Page references to this work will be given parenthetically in the text. The translations are mine.

11. Morris, *The Birth of the Palestinian Refugee Problem Revisited*, 237–40.

12. Eshkol Nevo, *Arbaa batim vegaagua* (Lod: Kinneret, Zmora-Bitan, Dvir, 2004); translated as *Homesick*, trans. Sondra Silverston (London: Chatto and Windus, 2008). Page references to the translation will be given parenthetically in the text.

13. Meron Rapoport, "Seeing Ghosts," *Haaretz*, April 5, 2008, http://www.haaretz.com/seeing-ghosts-1.243316 (accessed July 20, 2010).

14. Although an English translation is now available from Vintage Books, the translations in the text are my own, from the Hebrew original: *Achuzat Dajani* (Tel Aviv: Yediot Aharonot, 2008).

15. On *The House of Rajani*'s allusions to Hamlet, see Shira Stav, "Hakol omed al mekomo beshalom" [All stands in place], *Haaretz sfarim* [Haaretz books, the literary supplement of the Israeli daily *Haaretz*], August 4, 2008, http://www.haaretz.co.il/hasite/spages/962721.html (accessed April 21, 2009).

16. Kalvaryski, the historical figure, is the subject of strongly divergent views. See, e.g., Anita Shapira, *Land and Power: The Zionist Resort to Force, 1881–1948*, trans. William Templer (Stanford, CA: Stanford University Press, 1999), 171–72; and Abigail Jacobson, "Alternative Voices in Late Ottoman Palestine: A Historical Note," *Jerusalem Quarterly* 7, no. 1 (2004): 41–48; and Abigail Jacobson, "'Nishalti harbe aravim meadmatam veavoda zo einena min hadvarim hakalim'" ["I banished many Arabs from their land and this task is not an easy one"], *Haaretz*, December 25, 2009, http://www.haaretz.co.il/hasite/pages/ShArt.jhtml?itemNo=1137419 (accessed February 8, 2010).

17. Abigail Jacobson, "The Dispossessor's Dilemma," *Haaretz*, January 7, 2010, http://www.haaretz.com/the-dispossessor-s-dilemma-1.978 (accessed July 20, 2010).

18. Rona Kuperboim, "Sofer leachor" [Counting backward] (interview with Alon Hilu), *Ynet*, March 2, 2008, http://www.ynet.co.il/Ext/Comp/Article Layout/CdaArticlePrintPreview/1,2506,L-3513208,00.html (accessed April 22, 2009).

19. Grossman, *Writing in the Dark*, 62–63.

20. See, e.g., Howard Schneider and Samuel Sockol, "Israeli Author's Zionist Novel Creates Controversy," *Washington Post*, July 15, 2009, http://www.washingtonpost.com/wp-dyn/content/article/2009/07/14/AR2009071403322.html (accessed February 8, 2010).

21. Alon Hilu, e-mail to Amir Eshel, April 12, 2012.

22. Oren Kakun, "Kitsch shedarko mitmarek hamatzpun" [Kitsch to cleanse one's conscience], *Haaretz*, May 30, 2008, http://www.haaretz.co.il/hasite/pages/ShArtPE.jhtml?itemNo=988348&contrassID=2&subContrassID=5&sb

SubContrassID=0 (accessed April 28, 2009). Kakun's polemical review has itself been the center of a heated dispute among critics and readers. See, e.g., Elie Eshed's blog, http://www.notes.co.il/eshed/44561.asp (accessed April 28, 2009).

23. Aharon Meged and Alon Hilu, "Beyn emet livdaya" (correspondence), *Ynet*, May 29, 2008, http://www.ynet.co.il/articles/0,7340,L-3549051,00.html (accessed April 22, 2009). On the public reactions to Hilu's novel and the debate between Megged and Hilu, see also the reportage of the Israeli TV channel Arutz 10 (first aired on June 3, 2008), http://www.haaretz.com/hasen/spages/989813.html (accessed April 28, 2009).

24. In a short statement to the website *Portal Jafo* (Jaffa portal), Hilu cites this biographical fact as "the trigger" for writing the novel *Achuzat Dajani* in the first place. See http://www.yaffo.co.il/article_k.asp?id=3118, (accessed April 12, 2012).

25. Joel Greenberg, "In Israeli City, a Tribute to a Palestinian Doctor," *Washington Post*, February 27, 2012, http://www.washingtonpost.com/world/middle_east/in-israeli-city-tribute-to-a-palestinian-doctor/2012/02/27/gIQAJ weJeR_print.html (accessed April 12, 2012).

26. Dan Miron, *Im lo tihyeh Yerushalayim: masot al hasifrut haivrit behek-sher tarbuti-politi* (*If There Is No Jerusalem: Essays on Hebrew Literature in a Cultural-Political Context*) (Tel Aviv: Hakibbutz Hameuchad, 1987), 235. In a similar manner, Hannan Hever observes a clear avoidance of mention of the occupation of the territories in contemporary Hebrew literature. See Hannan Hever, "Sifrut Yisraelit megiva al milhemet 1967" [Israeli literature reacts to the 1967 Six-Day War], in *Chamishim learbaim ushmone: Momentim bikortiyim betoldot Medinat Yisrael* (*Fifty to Forty-Eight: Critical Moments in the History of the State of Israel*), ed. Adi Ophir (Tel Aviv: Hakibbutz Hameuchad, 1999), 181.

27. Michal Govrin, *Hevzekim* (Tel Aviv: Am Oved, 2002); translated as *Snapshots*, trans. Barbara Harshav (New York: Riverhead, 2007). Page references to the translation will be given parenthetically in the text.

28. Ilana Zuriel's "snapshots" are organized sequentially by the novel's narrator, Tirza Weintraub. A professor of narratology at the Sorbonne, Weintraub puts together Zuriel's notes, photographs, and sketches (reminiscent of W. G. Sebald's *Austerlitz*) after Zuriel has been killed in a car accident. On *Snapshots* as a poetic reflection on the tension between space and place as defined in Michel de Certeau's work, see the insightful analysis in Shlomith Rimmon-Kenan, "Place, Space, and Michal Govrin's *Snapshots*," *Narrative* 17, no. 2 (May 2009): 220–34.

29. Some of the notes that make up *Snapshots* are taken, in fact, from the writings of Michal Govrin's father, Pinhas Govrin, who arrived in Palestine during the third Aliya. In 2005, Pinhas Govrin published his work as Pinhas Govrin, *Hayinu kecholmim: Megilat mishpacha* (*We Were as Dreamers*), ed. Michal Govrin (Jerusalem: Carmel, 2005). Michal Govrin herself addresses the reader before the actual narrative begins and acknowledges having made use of her father's autobiography.

30. Rimmon-Kenan, "Place, Space, and Michal Govrin's *Snapshots*," 227.

31. According to the concept of *shmita*, whatever grows on the land is designated as ownerless in the seventh year, and all enjoy equal rights to it. Every fifty

years, after seven *shmita* cycles of seven years each, comes the *yovel* year. Both the forty-ninth and fiftieth year are holy. During this period, one should abstain from agricultural work, free the slaves, and let purchased properties return to their original tribal owners. See R. J. Zwi Werblowsky and Geoffrey Wigoder, eds., *The Oxford Dictionary of the Jewish Religion* (New York: Oxford University Press, 1997), s.v. "Shemittah."

32. In the Jewish tradition, the sukkah is a booth or tabernacle to be dwelt in for seven days "in order that your generations may know that I caused the children of Israel to dwell in tabernacles when I brought them out of Egypt" (Leviticus 23:42–43). According to Kabbalistic tradition, it is customary to welcome *ushpizin*, or guests, in the sukkah. Hence, the days of dwelling in the sukkah during the holiday of Sukkot are days of hospitality. See s.v. "Sukkot," in *Oxford Dictionary of the Jewish Religion*. On the difference between Govrin's fantasy of an Israeli-Palestinian relationship and those of Amos Oz in "Nomads and Viper" and A. B. Yehoshua in *The Lover* (1977), see Yohai Openheimer's review of Michal Govrin's *Snapshots*, "Hachaim hakfulim shel hautopia" [The double life of the utopia], *Haaretz*, June 5, 2002, http://www.haaretz.co.il/hasite/pages /ShArtPE.jhtml?itemNo=172951&contrassID=2&subContrassID=6&sbSubCo ntrassID=0 (accessed July 20, 2010).

33. Arendt, *Between Past and Future*, 11.

34. This conflict led more than once to incidents between Jewish and Arab children, including the murder of Moran Amit on February 8, 2002. See Nadav Shragai, "Midu kiyum lenikur verichuk" [From coexistence to alienation and distance], *Haaretz*, February 10, 2002, http://www.haaretz.co.il/hasite/pages /ShArt.jhtml?itemNo=128089&contrassID=1 (accessed May 5, 2009). More recently, there have been clashes over plans to build Jewish homes near the Palestinian neighborhood of Jabel Mukaber, once again in the vicinity of this site.

35. Govrin reflects on the possible significance of adopting an approach to the land that is based on "letting go" of the knife in an essay she published during the al-Aqsa intifada: Michal Govrin, "Martyrs or Survivors? Thoughts on the Mythical Dimension of the Story War," trans. Barbara Harshav, *Partisan Review* 3 (2003): 274–97. In it, she focuses on the figure of the Palestinian martyr (the suicide bomber) as she discusses the importance of moving from martyrdom to religious devotion based on symbolic acts. She points to the biblical story of the Binding of Isaac as the moment in which the "principle of exchange" (the ram for the human) led to the end of human sacrifice (286) and the fact that both Judaism and Islam, in rejecting sacrifice, adopted that very "principle" (287).

36. Dalia Karpel and Michal Govrin (interview), "Oh My Love, Comely as Jerusalem," *Haaretz Magazine*, April 19, 2002, http://www.haaretz.com/oh-my-love-comely-as-jerusalem-1.47474 (accessed July 20, 2010).

37. Jameson, *Archaeologies of the Future*, 232.

38. Victoria Comella and Michal Govrin (interview), "A Conversation with Michal Govrin, Author of *Snapshots*," www.michalgovrin.com/snapshots/ SNAPSHOTS (accessed May 25, 2009).

39. Richard Rorty, "Der Roman als Mittel zur Erlösung aus der Selbstbezogenheit," trans. Andrew James Johnston, in *Dimensionen ästhetischer Erfah-*

rung, ed. Joachim Küpper and Christoph Menke (Frankfurt am Main: Suhrkamp, 2003), 56.

CHAPTER ELEVEN

1. W. G. Sebald, *Austerlitz,* trans. Anthea Bell (New York: Random House, 2001), 100. Hereafter, page references to this work will be given parenthetically in the text. Since I also read the novel in the context of intellectual debates following the collapse of European Communism around 1989, it is interesting to note that *Austerlitz* first appeared in print in German in 2001. The novel also gives clear indications as to its temporal setting. In the case of the conversation between Austerlitz and the narrator in Greenwich, one can easily deduce that it took place in 1996.

2. See Richard Rorty, "The End of Leninism and History as Comic Frame," 215. Rorty is certainly not alone in taking a favorable approach to Francis Fukuyama's *The End of History and the Last Man* (New York: Free Press, 1992). Fukuyama saw in the events of 1989 the end of a decades-long clash: "the end of history" in the sense of the vanishing of a substantial struggle between capitalist liberal democracy and its leftist rivals. Peter Sloterdijk, for example, dedicates large sections of *Zorn und Zeit: Politisch-psychologischer Versuch* (Frankfurt am Main: Suhrkamp, 2006) to reconsidering Fukuyama's claims in light of the political realities of the era following 9/11.

3. Amy Hungerford, "On the Period Formerly Known as Contemporary," *American Literary History* 20, nos. 1–2 (2008): 410.

4. Jay Winter, *Dreams of Peace and Freedom: Utopian Moments in the 20th Century* (New Haven, CT: Yale University Press, 2006).

5. Interview with Alec Ash, in *The Browser,* http://thebrowser.com /interviews/ian-mcewan-on-five-books-have-influenced-my-novels?page=full, first published on April 22, 2011 (accessed October 3, 2011).

6. Interview with Lynn Wells, in Lynn Wells, *Ian McEwan* (Houndmills, UK: Palgrave Macmillan, 2010), 135. Hereafter, page references to this work will be given parenthetically in the text.

7. McEwan alludes here to the Stalin-era proverb "You can't make an omelet without breaking eggs," which was apparently used to justify the mass starvations in Ukraine in the name of the bigger cause—the creation of a modernized Communist society. I will return to this proverb below while discussing Arendt and McEwan's *Black Dogs.*

8. See http://www.youtube.com/watch?v=IxeorO6mB68 (accessed May 24, 2010).

9. Jonathan Lear, "Ethical Thought and the Problem of Communication: A Strategy for Reading *Diary of a Bad Year,*" in *J. M. Coetzee and Ethics: Philosophical Perspectives on Literature,* ed. Anton Leist and Peter Singer (New York: Columbia University Press, 2010), 66.

10. Alain Badiou and Slavoj Žižek, *Philosophy in the Present,* trans. Peter Thomas and Alberto Toscano (Cambridge: Polity, 2009), 96. On Žižek's projection of the end of "global capitalism," see Slavoj Žižek, *Living in the End of Times* (London: Verso, 2010), 1–53.

11. On the demise of history as the decline of the "mise-en-scène of modernity," see also Huyssen, *Present Pasts*, 1.

12. Hannah Arendt, "The Ex-Communists," in *Essays in Understanding, 1930–1954* (New York: Schocken Books, 1994), 397.

13. Thus, Arendt remarked in August 1950: "The Western way out of the impossibility of politics within the framework of the Western creation myth is the transformation or the substitution of politics with history. Through the notion of world history, the multiplicity of men is fused together into an individual man [*Menschenindividuum*] that can also be named humankind. The monstrous and inhuman character of history [*das Monströse und Unmenschliche der Geschichte*] that originates from this notion only prevails at its very end so fully and brutally in politics itself." I thank Lilla Balint for her help with this translation. Hannah Arendt, *Denktagebuch: 1950–1973*, ed. Ursula Ludz and Ingeborg Nordmann (Munich: Piper Verlag, 2002), 1:17.

14. Ibid., 341.

15. Arendt, *Human Condition*, 178. Hereafter, page references to this work will be given parenthetically in the text, preceded by *HC*.

16. Arendt goes on to stress that "nothing in fact indicates more clearly the political nature of history—its being a story of action and deeds rather than of trends and forces or ideas—than the introduction of an invisible actor behind the scenes whom we find in all philosophies of history, which for this reason alone can be recognized as political philosophies in disguise" (*HC*, 185–86).

17. On narrative in its ability to display action, see Benhabib, *The Reluctant Modernism of Hannah Arendt*, 125–27, 129–30.

18. In thinking about literary, cinematic, or other types of narratives as a mode of "insertion" in Arendt's sense, I draw, for example, on Agnes Heller's contention that Arendt's *The Human Condition* is "political intervention": the "intervention," Heller remarks, follows "*the story* of the glory of political action . . . a story told to the contemporary active human, who might reflect on the glory of political action *and* begin as well." Agnes Heller, "Al masoret vehatchalot chadashot" [On tradition and new beginnings], in *Hannah Arendt in Jerusalem*, ed. Steven Aschheim (Jerusalem: Richard Koebner Minerva Center for German History, Hebrew University of Jerusalem, by Hebrew University Magnes Press, 2007), 35, emphasis in original. In fact, Heller regards the narrative of *The Human Condition* as a means for political intervention: "The object of Arendt's intervention is not only to tell the reader a philosophical narrative *on* political action in antiquity, but also to tell him that action is always possible" (33).

19. Huyssen, *Present Pasts*, 15. Hereafter, page references to this work will be given parenthetically in the text.

20. Jonathan C. D. Clark, *Our Shadowed Present: Modernism, Postmodernism, and History* (Stanford, CA: Stanford University Press, 2004), 2, 5.

21. Harry D. Harootunian, "Remembering the Historical Present," *Critical Inquiry* 33 (Spring 2007): 472.

22. Ibid., 473–74.

23. Alain Badiou, *Polemics*, trans. Steve Corcoran (London: Verso, 2006), 38.

24. Alain Badiou, *The Century*, trans. Alberto Toscano (Cambridge: Polity, 2007), 105. See also Slavoj Žižek's discussion of the lecture "The Caesura of Ni-

hilism" that Badiou delivered at the University of Essex on September 10, 2003, in which he claimed, as Žižek approvingly puts it, that "our time is devoid of world": since capitalism is now "global, encompassing all worlds," it deprives "the great majority of people of *any* meaningful 'cognitive mapping.'" Slavoj Žižek, *The Parallax View* (Cambridge, MA: MIT Press, 2006), 318, 422n73, emphasis in original.

25. Badiou, *The Century*, 32; Slavoj Žižek, *In Defense of Lost Causes* (London: Verso, 2008), 421. See also Žižek's sharp criticism of Fukuyama's notion of the "end of history" (420–23). Elsewhere, Badiou diagnoses that in our time the very idea of "community" has become impossible, since "reasonable management, capital and general equilibria are the only things that *exist*." Alain Badiou, *Conditions* (London: Continuum, 2008), 149, emphasis in original.

26. Jameson, *Postmodernism*, 16, 25. On the Marxist criticism of postmodernism, see also Ernst Breisach, *On the Future of History: The Postmodernist Challenge and Its Aftermath* (Chicago: University of Chicago Press, 2003), 169.

27. Terry Eagleton, *After Theory* (New York: Basic Books, 2003), 6–7, 16, 50–51.

28. Fredric Jameson, "The End of Temporality," *Critical Inquiry* 29, no. 4 (Summer 2003): 704.

29. Ibid., 704, 708. In an optimistic twist, however, toward the end of this essay, Jameson notes that the tendency of late capitalism to reduce our lived experience to the realm of the present and the body remains "in any case unrealizable" and that human beings cannot, after all, "revert to the immediacy of the animal kingdom" (717).

30. Walter Benn Michaels, *The Shape of the Signifier: 1967 to the End of History* (Princeton, NJ: Princeton University Press, 2004), 19. Hereafter, page references to this work will be given parenthetically in the text. According to Michaels, instead of debating the issues of class division and workers' exploitation (17) and thus alternatives to the given socioeconomic and political order, we find ourselves debating (or celebrating) individual and group identities, be they national, ethnic, racial, or sexual. Instead of consciously disagreeing "about what we want," we just emphasize that we "want different things" (31). Rather than grasping that we are the incarnation of the momentary (and thus the subject of constant change), we mark "differences" that are ostensibly outside history (32).

31. I quote here Slavoj Žižek's *Welcome to the Desert of the Real!* from Michaels, *Shape of the Signifier*, 156.

32. Similarly, Toni Morrison's *Beloved* is "historicist" in that the novel, while setting out to remember "the disremembered," "redescribes something we have never known as something we have forgotten and thus makes the historical past a part of our own experience" (Michaels, *Shape of the Signifier*, 137). According to Michaels, films that engage with the past through the employment of formal devices that disrupt the past-present divide such as Claude Lanzmann's *Shoah* are, likewise, less about transmitting knowledge or a new analytical perspective and more about reenacting emotions first unleashed during the past, ultimately in the service of fostering a present identity (141–45).

33. In *The Holocaust of Texts: Genocide, Literature, and Personification* (Chicago: University of Chicago Press, 2003), Amy Hungerford argues similarly

that the tendency of some contemporary literature on the Holocaust to personify texts and to efface the difference between the historical victims of Nazism or the pains inflicted by the Nazis and those who only encounter those horrors second-hand is related to the cultural-political discourse of the 1960s and, more recently, to post–Cold War political and cultural dynamics—the emergence of multicul-turalism (1–13). Emblematic of this tendency in Hungerford's account is Spiegel-man's *Maus* (85–96) but also the employment of trauma theory in literary and cultural studies by critics such as Shoshana Felman and Cathy Caruth (103–15).

34. See Terry Eagleton, "Capitalism, Modernism and Postmodernism," *New Left Review* 152 (July–August 1985): 61, 68; and Fredric Jameson, "Postmod-ernism, or, The Cultural Logic of Late Capitalism," *New Left Review* 146 (July–August 1984): 67.

35. Hutcheon, *A Poetics of Postmodernism*, 19. Similarly, Ursula Heise has pointed out that because the postmodern novel deals with the contingency of the future by projecting indecisiveness into the narrative present and past, it provides a "basis for reflecting on the interplay of determinism and indeterminacy, or causality and contingency in our temporal experience." Ursula Heise, *Chrono-schisms: Time, Narrative, and Postmodernism* (Cambridge: Cambridge University Press, 1997), 68. While Heise is less confident than Hutcheon about postmod-ern literature's ability to generate a futural perspective, she does contend that its multiple alternative temporalities upset the ontological stability of the present (74).

36. Hans Ulrich Gumbrecht, "Presence Achieved in Language (with Special Attention Given to the Presence of the Past)," in "Forum on Presence," special is-sue, *History and Theory* 45 (October 2006): 319, 323; Hans Ulrich Gumbrecht, *Production of Presence*, 21–90. See also his earlier formulation of this position in *In 1926*, ix–xv, 411–36.

37. Eelco Runia, "Spots of Time," in "Forum on Presence," special issue, *History and Theory* 45 (October 2006): 305, emphasis in original.

38. Eelco Runia, "Burying the Dead, Creating the Past," *History and Theory* 46 (October 2007): 325. Runia relates this claim to the act of burial: to "bury the dead" in Runia's view is an expression of the "creative," "inventive" human faculty to externalize.

39. Grossman, *Writing in the Dark*, 64.

40. Elias, *Sublime Desire*. Elias specifically mentions *Maus* and *Beloved* as problematizing memory and resisting "closure" (52). It is indeed hard to see how, in their fragmented form and avoidance of realistic representation, these two works *primarily* suggest the establishment or enhancement of group identity as Walter Benn Michaels argues.

41. On Elias's discussion of Morrison's *Beloved* and Spiegelman's *Maus*, see *Sublime Desire*, 48, 52.

42. Elias, *Sublime Desire*, 52. See also Elias's more recent "Metahistorical Romance, the Historical Sublime, and Dialogic History," in *Rethinking History* 9, nos. 2–3 (June–September 2005): 161. Significantly, Elias also restricts her analysis to literature of the so-called First World.

43. Elias, *Sublime Desire*, 42.

44. Toni Morrison's *Beloved* was first published in 1987 by Knopf. I quote here from the Vintage International edition (2004), 322.

45. Timothy Parrish, *From the Civil War to the Apocalypse: Postmodern History and American Fiction* (Amherst: University of Massachusetts Press, 2008), 131.

46. J. M. Coetzee, *Disgrace* (London: Penguin, 1999).

47. Ibid., 198.

48. Ibid., 205.

CHAPTER TWELVE

1. On Sebald's writing as marking the Second World War as the end of history, see Peter Fritzsche's perceptive "W. G. Sebald's Twentieth Century Histories," in *W. G. Sebald: History, Memory, Trauma*, ed. Scott Denham and Mark McCulloh (Berlin: Walter de Gruyter, 2006), 291–300, esp. 298.

2. In at least two prominent scenes, hearing or conversing with the dead plays a prominent role. See W. G. Sebald, *Austerlitz*, trans. Anthea Bell (New York: Random House, 2001), 128–32, 200. Hereafter, page references to this work will be given parenthetically in the text.

3. I discuss Sebald's place within his generation of writers in Amir Eshel, "Against the Power of Time: The Poetics of Suspension in W. G. Sebald's *Austerlitz*," *New German Critique* 88 (Winter 2003): 71–96. For the literature of Sebald's generation, see such representative, albeit varying, works as Peter Schneider's *Lenz: Eine Erzählung* (Berlin: Rotbuch, 1973) and *Vati: Erzählung* (Darmstadt: Luchterhand, 1987), Wolfgang Hilbig's *Ich* (Frankfurt am Main: S. Fischer, 1993), Peter Handke's *Mein Jahr in der Niemandsbucht: Ein Märchen aus den neuen Zeiten* (Frankfurt am Main: Suhrkamp, 1994), and Bernhard Schlink's *The Reader* (New York: Random House, 1995). *The Reader* was originally published as *Der Vorleser* (Zurich: Heinemann, 1995).

4. On the Kindertransport in *Austerlitz*, see my discussion in chapter 5.

5. On the symbolism of Penelope Peacefull's name, see the insightful discussion of Yahya Elsaghe, "Das Kreuzwortraetsel der Penelope: Zu W. G. Sebalds *Austerlitz*," in *Gegenwartsliteratur: A German Studies Yearbook 6* (Theme Issue: W. G. Sebald) (Tübingen: Staufenberg Verlag, 2007), 164–84.

6. On the returning dead, see, e.g., the narrator's comment in "Dr. Henry Selwyn," the first story of W. G. Sebald's *The Emigrants*: "And so they are ever returning to us, the dead. At times they come back from the ice more than seven decades later and are found at the edge of the moraine, a few polished bones and a pair of hobnailed boots." W. G. Sebald, *The Emigrants*, trans. Michael Hulse (New York: New Directions, 1996), 23. See also Stephanie Harris, "The Return of the Dead: Memory and Photography in Sebald's *Die Ausgewanderten*," *German Quarterly* 74, no. 4 (2001): 379–91.

7. On the traumatic quality of Austerlitz's experience and the role of trauma in the novel as a whole, see Katja Garloff, "Moments of Symbolic Investiture in W. G. Sebald's *Austerlitz*," in Denham and McCulloh, *W. G. Sebald*, 157–69; and Carolin Duttlinger's discussion of the relationship of photographic images

and trauma in "Traumatic Photographs: Remembrance and the Technical Media in W. G. Sebald's *Austerlitz*," in *W. G. Sebald—a Critical Companion*, ed. J. J. Long and Anne Whitehead (Seattle: University of Washington Press, 2004), 155–71.

8. See Derek Howse, *Greenwich Time and the Discovery of the Longitude* (Oxford: Oxford University Press, 1980), 87.

9. Elizabeth Deeds Ermarth, *Sequel to History: Postmodernism and the Crisis of Representational Time* (Princeton, NJ: Princeton University Press, 1992), 22.

10. Ludwig Wittgenstein is invoked directly or implicitly throughout the novel. A section of one of his most famous photos appears, for example, on page 5. On Wittgenstein's concept of "family resemblances," see Ludwig Wittgenstein, *Philosophical Investigations*, rev. trans., 3rd ed., trans. G. E. M. Anscombe (Oxford: Blackwell, 2001), 27. While Sebald specifically and in an unquestionable reference to Wittgenstein uses the term *Familienähnlichkeiten* (see *Austerlitz* [Munich: Hanser, 2001], 48), the English translation "family likeness" rather than "family resemblances" (33) misses the reference to *Philosophical Investigations*.

11. On railway transportation as a metaphor for "the human condition" in modernity, see Deane Blackler, *Reading W. G. Sebald: Adventure and Disobedience* (Rochester, NY: Camden House, 2007), 198–204.

12. On Sebald's Benjaminian "*kulturkritische*" metaphysics, see his telling commentary on Walter Benjamin's allegorical angel of history in *Luftkrieg und Literatur* (Munich: Hanser, 1999), 79–80. In a late interview with the *New Yorker* Sebald noted, "I've always thought it very regrettable, and, in a sense, also foolish, that the philosophers decided somewhere in the nineteenth century that metaphysics wasn't a respectable discipline and had to be thrown overboard, and reduced themselves to becoming logisticians and statisticians. . . . So metaphysics, I think, shows a legitimate concern." Originally published as Joseph Cuomo, "The Meaning of Coincidence—an Interview with the Writer W. G. Sebald," *New Yorker*, September 3, 2001. Quoted here from Joseph Cuomo, "A Conversation with W. G. Sebald," in *The Emergence of Memory: Conversations with W. G. Sebald*, ed. Lynne Sharon Schwartz (New York: Seven Stories Press, 2007), 115.

13. Andreas Huyssen, "On Rewritings and New Beginnings: W. G. Sebald and the Literature about the *Luftkrieg*," *Lili-Zeitschrift für Literaturwissenschaft und Linguistik* 124 (2001): 89. On Sebald's implied philosophy of history, see also Michael Rutschky, "Das geschenkte Vergessen: W. G. Sebald's *Austerlitz* und die Epik der schwarzen Geschichtsphilosophie," *Frankfurter Rundschau* 21 (March 2001), http://www.lyrikwelt.de/rezensionen/austerlitz-r.htm (accessed August 20, 2010).

14. See "Wie kriegen die Deutschen das auf die Reihe?" (interview), *Wochenpost*, June 17, 1993.

15. Ibid.

16. On Sebald's deep affinity with Benjamin's thought and with Frankfurt school critical theory, see Karin Bauer, "The Dystopian Entwinement of Histories and Identities in W. G. Sebald's *Austerlitz*," in Denham and McCulloh, *W. G. Sebald*, 233–49.

17. "Wie kriegen die Deutschen das auf die Reihe?" *Wochenpost*, June 17, 1993.

18. Uwe Pralle, "Mit einem kleinen Strandspaten Abschied von Deutschland nehmen" (interview with Sebald), *Süddeutsche Zeitung* 22–23 (December 2001).

19. Ibid. On the tension between "nature" and "history" as a constitutive element of Sebald's work, see also Fritzsche, "W. G. Sebald's Twentieth Century Histories," 292. Fritzsche is right to note that this tension remains "unresolved." However, in many instances such as those just mentioned, one can clearly trace the temptation Sebald faced to resort to viewing human history as a mere "case" of natural history, thus refraining from endowing his characters with significant agency.

20. J. J. Long, *W. G. Sebald—Image, Archive, Modernity* (New York: Columbia University Press, 2007), 3, 168–74; Mark Anderson, "The Edge of Darkness: On W. G. Sebald," *October* 106 (2003): 102–21.

21. Sebald uses the term *historisches Paradigma* in his interview with Martin Doerry and Volker Hage, "Ich fürchte das Melodramatische," *Der Spiegel*, March 12, 2001, 230.

22. In an unpublished manuscript of the 1949 lecture that was later to be known as *The Question concerning Technology*, Heidegger famously stated: "Agriculture is now motorized food industry—in essence the same as the manufacturing of corpses in gas chambers and extermination camps, the same as blockading and starving of nations, the same as the manufacture of hydrogen bombs." This remark was dropped from the final version of the manuscript. See Richard Bernstein, *The New Constellation: The Ethical-Political Horizons of Modernity/Postmodernity* (Cambridge, MA: MIT Press, 1992), 130.

23. See Frank Kermode, *The Sense of an Ending: Studies in the Theory of Fiction* (Oxford: Oxford University Press, 1967), 46–47.

24. I am borrowing the term "time effects" from Malcolm Bowie's study of Proust, *Proust among the Stars* (New York: Columbia University Press, 1998), 35.

25. Sebald's photographic images are "genuine images" in Walter Benjamin's sense, devices that relate the reader to what is and will remain absent—the events and the protagonists of the past. Christian Scholz, "Aber das Geschriebene ist ja kein wahres Dokument" (interview with W. G. Sebald), *Neue Zürcher Zeitung*, February 26–27, 2000. Sebald's photographs are indeed Benjaminian images, "dialectics at a standstill" or, in Benjamin's words, "what comes together in the flash with the now to form a constellation"; Walter Benjamin, *The Arcades Project*, trans. Howard Eiland and Kevin McLaughlin (Cambridge, MA: Belknap Press of Harvard University Press, 1999), 462. I agree with Stephanie Harris that Sebald's diagrams and photographs serve as a form of narration—a facet in an entirety composed of text and image. See Stephanie Harris, "The Return of the Dead: Memory and Photography in W. G. Sebald's *Die Ausgewanderten*," *German Quarterly* 74, no. 4 (Fall 2001): 379–91; and Karen Remmler's discussion in "The Shape of Remembering: W. G. Sebald's *Die Ringe des Saturn* and *Austerlitz*," in *Gegenwartsliteratur: A German Studies Yearbook*, 152–54. The issue of Sebald's unique poetics of commingling text and image has received abundant attention in recent years. See J. J. Long's detailed discussion in *W. G. Sebald*,

esp. 46–70; and John Sears, "Photographs, Image, and the Space of Literature in Sebald's Prose," in *Searching for Sebald: Photography after W. G. Sebald*, ed. Lise Patt and Christel Dillbohner (Los Angeles: Institute of Cultural Inquiry, 2007), 204–25.

26. Interview with W. G. Sebald, first broadcast on CBC Radio's *Writers and Company* on April 18, 1998. I quote from the version printed in Eleanor Wachtel, "Ghost Hunter," in Schwartz, *Emergence of Memory*, 37–62. There is, however, another sense in which the photographs arrest time. As Todd Presner claimed in his attentive reading of *Austerlitz*, while photographs "appear to arrest the fugitive and the contingent, their intelligibility and materiality remain time bound, finite, and fleeting." "Far from evoking permanence or transcendence," Presner continues as he refers to Roland Barthes's *Camera Lucida*, the photograph is marked by "finitude and transience." Todd Samuel Presner, *Mobile Modernity: Germans, Jews, Trains* (New York: Columbia University Press, 2007), 271.

27. Martin Doerry and Volker Hage, "Ich fürchte das Melodramatische" (interview with W. G. Sebald), *Der Spiegel*, March 12, 2001, 234.

28. W. G. Sebald, *Die Beschreibung des Unglücks: Zur österreichischen Literatur von Stifter bis Handke* (Salzburg: Residenz, 1985), 12 (my emphasis).

CHAPTER THIRTEEN

1. One could also talk of Anglophone literature here. John J. Su, for example, uses the term "contemporary Anglophone literature" in *Ethics and Nostalgia in the Contemporary Novel* (Cambridge: Cambridge University Press, 2005), 15, to introduce his discussion of a variety of ethnic American, Caribbean, British, and African authors of the period following the Second World War. My approach in this chapter follows Su's terminology as he describes it there: "my study adopts with reservations the term contemporary Anglophone literature. This selection recognizes the concerns expressed by critics about broadly inclusive labels, but it also recognizes that trying to avoid terms altogether would be too awkward and disingenuous" (15).

2. See "Interview with Ian McEwan," in *Ian McEwan: The Essential Guide*, ed. Margaret Reynolds and Jonathan Noakes (London: Vintage, 2002), 20–21. Paul Crosthwaite points to an interview with McEwan in which McEwan refers to the war as dominating his childhood as well as his generation of writers. Paul Crosthwaite, "Speed, War, and Traumatic Affect: Reading Ian McEwan's *Atonement*," in *Cultural Politics* 3, no. 1 (2007): 52.

3. McEwan refers to *Black Dogs* as a "novel of ideas." He wished to write "something which has life and energy at the level of the plot's intricacy and the characters' emotions at the same time as indulging in intellectual preoccupation." Jon Cook, Sebastian Groes, and Victor Sage, "Journeys without Maps: An Interview with Ian McEwan," in *Ian McEwan: Contemporary Critical Perspectives*, ed. Sebastian Groes (London: Continuum, 2009), 127.

4. Ian McEwan, *Black Dogs* (London: J. Cape, 1992), 5. Hereafter, page references to this work will be given parenthetically in the text.

5. In an interview with Helen Whitney for *Frontline* following the attacks

of 9/11, Ian McEwan (referring to Isaiah Berlin) expressed much doubt about utopian visions that promise to deliver "the blessed kingdom" or "Utopia." He relates the desire for a "simple solution that will take us to paradise or Utopia or the blessed kingdom" to human nature and expresses his own inclination toward skepticism and doubt. See http://www.pbs.org/wgbh/pages/frontline /shows/faith/interviews/mcewan.html (accessed August 23, 2010). Dominic Head observes in McEwan's work as a whole a "keen anxiety" about the absence of "foundational beliefs." See Dominic Head, *Ian McEwan* (Manchester: Manchester University Press, 2007), 15. McEwan's characters thus often explore possible orientations by pondering their options for taking action. In a world lacking a metaphysical sovereign, humans can rely only on themselves as they seek to solve their personal and social dilemmas.

6. On the relationship between evil and oblivion as captured in the metaphor of the black dogs, see Dominic Head's discussion of the novel in *Ian McEwan*, 108–9. Lars Heiler also points to the "metaphorical quality" of June's and Jeremy's narrative regarding the black dogs. See Lars Heiler, "Unleashing the Black Dogs: Cathartic Horror and Political Commitment in *The Innocent* and *Black Dogs*," in *Ian McEwan: Art and Politics*, ed. Pascal Nicklas (Heidelberg: Universitätsverlag Winter, 2009), 111.

7. J. M. Coetzee, *Diary of a Bad Year* (New York: Viking, 2007). Page references to this work will be given parenthetically in the text.

8. Lear, "Ethical Thought and the Problem of Communication," 67.

9. Ibid., 68.

10. Lear characterizes the novel as "ethical thinking in action" (ibid., 69).

11. François Gallix and Kazuo Ishiguro, "Kazuo Ishiguro: The Sorbonne Lecture," in *Conversations with Kazuo Ishiguro*, ed. Brian W. Shaffer and Cynthia F. Wong (Jackson: University Press of Mississippi, 2008), 139, 141. Interestingly, the Second World War was not a major theme of British literature in the immediate postwar era. In her review of *Atonement*, Michiko Kakutani, in fact, notes that it was "the great ignored, unignorable subject for a generation of English novelists" ("And When She Was Bad She Was . . .," *New York Times*, March 7, 2002). Brian W. Schaffer, on the other hand, names a variety of British novels of the postwar era, such as Malcolm Lawry's 1947 *Under the Volcano* and Orwell's 1949 dystopian *1984*, that "respond" to the "Crisis of Civilization" of the mid-twentieth century. Brian W. Schaffer, *Reading the Novel in English, 1950–2000* (Malden, MA: Blackwell, 2006), 11. Most of the novels he mentions, however, are of the period following 1955. This relative avoidance seems to have come to an end, however, in the course of the 1990s, as Nick Bentley remarks: Nick Bentley, "Mapping the Millennium: Themes and Trends in Contemporary British Fiction," in *British Fiction of the 1990s*, ed. Nick Bentley (London: Routledge, 2005), 11–13.

12. According to Pascal Zinck, the figuration of trauma in *When We Were Orphans* defines the center of the narrative in a manner similar to other contemporary narratives and reflects the "obsession with memory" of our fin de siècle. See Pascal Zinck, "The Palimpsest of Memory in Kazuo Ishiguro's *When We Were Orphans*," *Études britanniques contemporaines* 29 (December 2005): 157.

13. Ishiguro himself, one should note, regards the orphan metaphor of *When We Were Orphans* as signaling the universal condition of emerging from what he calls the protected "bubble" of childhood. See, e.g., "An Interview with Kazuo Ishiguro," 168. I would caution against accepting this rather restricted perspective for two reasons, however. To begin with, as Ishiguro readily admits, Banks believes that solving the case of his parents' disappearance will help avert the impending Second World War (ibid., 164). Reversing his orphan fate would thus mean preventing nothing less than the political catastrophe whose shadow one senses clearly throughout the novel. Second, Ishiguro seems to be reluctant to relate his literature (and literature as such) to specific historical realities. In several interviews, he stresses that historical settings are for him merely the set for the plot. In a 1989 interview with Suanne Kelman, he also mentions that he does not particularly enjoy talking about his books in Germany, because they seem to be read not "as fiction" but rather as contributions "to some debate," specifically, as expressions of literary reflection on Fascism, be it in Japan or in Germany. See Suanne Kelman and Kazuo Ishiguro, "Ishiguro in Toronto," in Shaffer and Wong, *Conversations with Kazuo Ishiguro*, 49.

14. In fact, Tobias Döring views Ishiguro's *When We Were Orphans* as a "postmortem of the English detective's telling power." See Tobias Döring, "Sherlock Holmes—He Dead: Disenchanting the English Detective in Kazuo Ishiguro's 'When We Were Orphans,'" in *Postcolonial Postmortems: Crime Fiction from a Transcultural Perspective*, ed. Christine Matzke and Susanne Mühleisen (Amsterdam: Rodopi, 2006), 85.

15. Kazuo Ishiguro, *When We Were Orphans* (New York: Knopf, 2000), 138, 228. Hereafter, page references to this work will be given parenthetically in the text.

16. See, for example, his conversation with Sarah Hemmings in which he expresses the view that the British society of Shanghai actually expects him to help them avert what seems by now the imminent collapse of their world (226–27).

17. On Christopher Banks's time in Shanghai as a point at which the novel "deviates" from "the norms of realism," see Barry Lewis, *Kazuo Ishiguro* (Manchester: Manchester University Press, 2000), 149. Ishiguro himself describes Banks as remaining "arrested" in childhood. See Ron Hogan, "Kazuo Ishiguro," in Shaffer and Wong, *Conversations with Kazuo Ishiguro*, 158. In her interpretation of Banks's arrested development, Cynthia F. Wong emphasizes this condition as a psychological symptom. Cynthia F. Wong, *Kazuo Ishiguro*, 2nd ed. (Tavistock: Northcote [British Council], 2005), 89. What remains absent in such a psychological approach is the structural affinity between the actions of Banks and of his mother—a relation that is at the heart of the ethical and political issues the novel raises: colonialism, the opium trade, and the ability of individuals to address their historical and social contingencies in a moment of universal havoc such as those of the Sino-Japanese War and the Second World War.

18. Arendt, *Human Condition*, 237. Hereafter, page references to this work will be given parenthetically in the text preceded by *HC*.

19. Sebald, *Die Beschreibung des Unglücks*, 12.

20. Ian McEwan, *Atonement* (New York: Nan A. Talese Doubleday, 2001), 112. Hereafter, page references to this work will be given parenthetically in the text.

21. I fully agree in this regard with Alistair Cormack's reading of *Atonement* in "Postmodernism and the Ethics of Fiction in *Atonement*," in Groes, *Ian McEwan: Contemporary Critical Perspectives*, 70–82.

22. Maria Margaronis suggests (and I agree) that *Atonement*'s betrayal of the truth is, in fact, a hallmark of modernist writing. See her "The Anxiety of Authenticity: Writing Historical Fiction at the End of the Twentieth Century," *History Workshop Journal* 56, no. 1 (Spring 2008): 148.

23. I agree with John Mullan, who in the fourth installment of his discussion of *Atonement* for the *Guardian* notes that the novel is not a case of playful, postmodern metafiction. Rather than retaining the ironic stance of many postmodern novels of the 1980s, "McEwan wants you to identify with characters, to succumb to narrative illusion. For Briony to undertake her 'atonement,' her work of fiction must make up for, and confess, the wrong that she has done. In a novel, she can make the world better than it truly is. She can make Cecilia and Robbie survive and meet again. And we must be allowed to believe it." John Mullan, "Beyond Fiction," *Guardian*, March 29, 2003, http://books.guardian.co.uk/review/story/0,12084,923904,00.html (accessed August 23, 2010).

24. Brian Finney, "Briony's Stand against Oblivion: The Making of Fiction in Ian McEwan's *Atonement*," *Journal of Modern Literature* 27, no. 3 (2004): 68–69, 81.

25. On writing as "a kind" of atonement, see Elke D'hoker, "Confession and Atonement in Contemporary Fiction: J. M. Coetzee, John Banville, and Ian McEwan," *Critique: Studies in Contemporary Fiction* 48, no. 1 (2006): 31–43.

CHAPTER FOURTEEN

1. See http://www.youtube.com/watch?v=ldu78AXlu4k. See also http://www.youtube.com/watch?v=3EQI_jj6I7U&feature=related. (Both accessed August 24, 2010.)

2. I use the term "alternate histories" following Karen Hellekson's comprehensive study of this genre: *The Alternate History: Refiguring Historical Time* (Kent, OH: Kent State University Press, 2001).

3. I quote here Tolstoy's words as cited by Amy Elias, *Sublime Desire*, 6–7, who correctly notes that according to this line of thought, history works as an expression of "natural law" in the tradition of Newtonian physics (7).

4. W. G. Sebald, *Luftkrieg und Literatur: Mit einem Essay zu Alfred Andersch* (Munich: Hanser, 1999), 41. The English translation, which includes two additional essays, is even titled *On the Natural History of Destruction*, trans. Anthea Bell (New York: Random House, 2003).

5. Hellekson, *Alternate History*, 5.

6. Philip Roth, *The Plot against America* (New York: Houghton Mifflin, 2004), 1. Hereafter, page references to this work will be given parenthetically in the text.

7. As Michael Rothberg has noted, the Holocaust did not play a major role in Roth's work until *The Plot against America*. It is plausible that the events of 9/11 and the ensuing debate regarding the Iraq War triggered Roth's *Plot*. See Michael Rothberg, "Roth and the Holocaust," in *The Cambridge Companion to Philip Roth*, ed. Timothy Parrish (Cambridge: Cambridge University Press, 2007), 63.

8. Indeed, Roth and McEwan seem to share the sense that "history," as Phil's father, Herman Roth, puts it, "is everything that happens everywhere . . . even what happens in his house to an ordinary man—that'll be history too someday" (180).

9. Ross Posnock, *Philip Roth's Rude Truth: The Art of Immaturity* (Princeton, NJ: Princeton University Press, 2006), 27.

10. "The Story behind *The Plot against America*," *New York Times*, September 19, 2004, http://www.nytimes.com/2004/09/19/books/review/19ROTHL.html?pagewanted=print (accessed August 25, 2010).

11. Ibid., emphasis added.

12. Ibid.

13. Paul Auster, *Man in the Dark* (New York: Henry Holt, 2008), 5. Hereafter, page references to this work will be given parenthetically in the text.

14. This possibility is well articulated in Michael Dirda's review essay of Paul Auster's recent works: "Spellbound," *New York Review of Books*, September 4, 2008, http://www.nybooks.com/articles/archives/2008/dec/04/spellbound (accessed August 25, 2010).

15. In an interview with Gil Tamary, Auster entertains as a possibility that 9/11 may not have occurred had the outcome of the 2000 elections been different. Auster goes on to state that the decision of the Supreme Court was, in fact, a legal coup d'état. Ever since the 2000 elections, Auster says, he has had the eerie sense that "we've been living in a parallel world": in the "real world" Al Gore is finishing his second term, and "the shadow world" is the world in which we actually have been living since 2000. See http://www.youtube.com/watch?v=XRbgYecGmr8&feature=PlayList&p=49A2EBC693398D91&playnext=1&index=8 (accessed August 25, 2010).

16. Alexander Kluge, *Tür am Tür mit einem anderen Leben* (Frankfurt am Main: Suhrkamp, 2006), 7. Hereafter, page references to this work will be given parenthetically in the text. The translations are mine.

17. The notion of "the real"/"the Real" in the thinking of Badiou and Žižek is one of the intrinsic concepts in the vocabulary of contemporary thought. Žižek views the attacks of 9/11 as an expression of what Badiou views as "the passion of the real." Slavoj Žižek, *Welcome to the Desert of the Real: Five Essays on September 11 and Related Dates* (London: Verso, 2002), 5. Later, in *In Defense of Lost Causes* (London: Verso, 2008), Žižek explores the redeemable elements of Jacobinism, Stalinism, and even Heidegger's flirtation with Nazism as expressions of the same thrust. While rejecting revolutionary terror, Žižek still sees in these cases modes of commitment to the need for revolutionary change. On Žižek's reading of Badiou's "the Real," see, e.g., Slavoj Žižek, "From Purification to Subtraction: Alain Badiou and the Real," in *Think Again: Alain Badiou and the Future of Philosophy*, ed. Peter Hallward (London: Continuum, 2004), 165–81.

18. Jameson, *Archaeologies of the Future*, 270.

19. See David Gray Shaw, "Happy in our Chains? Agency and Language in the Postmodern Age," in "Agency after Postmodernism," special issue, *History and Theory* 40, no. 4 (December 2001): 1. In his introduction to the special issue, Shaw gives several illuminating examples of the tendency to depict human

action as the outcome of the gods' will or mood or, as in the Torah, as the result of God's rage. In regard to the notion of human agency as a chimera, Shaw refers to how the humanities and the social sciences deploy language in the wake of the twentieth century's "linguistic turn" and offers the telling example of Pierre Bourdieu's famous claim that "the history of the individual is never anything other than a certain specification of the collective history of his group or class" (5). Bourdieu's claim appears in his *Outline of a Theory of Practice*, trans. Richard Nice (Cambridge: Cambridge University Press, 1977), 86.

CHAPTER FIFTEEN

1. It would be almost impossible to discuss here the onslaught of post-catastrophic narratives published in recent years, many of which clearly allude to 9/11 or to looming ecological dangers. To name only two: Jim Crace's *The Pesthouse* (London: Picador, 2007) and Jeanette Winterson's *The Stone Gods* (Orlando, FL: Harcourt, 2008).

2. Kenneth Turan, for example, concludes his review of the movie by stating, "By showing us how fragile our world is, how imperiled we might well be from without and within, he [Steven Spielberg] raises almost against his will a most provocative question: is the ultimate fantasy an invasion from outer space, or is it the survival of the human race?" Kenneth Turan, "'War of the Worlds': Steven Spielberg's Latest Is Sci-Fi at Its Best—Riveting and Relevant," *Los Angeles Times*, June 29, 2005, http://www.calendarlive.com/movies/turan/cl-et-world-29jun29,0,1011790.story (accessed August 25, 2010).

3. In Terry Gilliam's 1995 *Twelve Monkeys*, human action is the cause of a similar catastrophe in which humans are forced underground to survive as a deadly virus wreaks havoc in the cities where they once lived.

4. Kazuo Ishiguro, *Never Let Me Go* (New York: Knopf, 2005).

5. Orhan Pamuk, *Snow*, trans. Maureen Freely (New York: Alfred A. Knopf, 2004).

6. John Updike, *Terrorist* (New York: Knopf, 2006).

7. Chris Cleave, *Incendiary* (New York: Knopf, 2005). In what was a morbid coincidence, this set-in-the-future, imagined-history book was launched a day before the July 7, 2005, attacks on London. See Brigitte Weeks's review of the novel, "Letter to Osama," *Washington Post*, July 31, 2005.

8. Ian McEwan, *Saturday* (New York: Doubleday, 2005), 211–48.

9. Don DeLillo, *Falling Man* (New York: Scribner, 2007). On Justin (the protagonist's son) and his reaction to 9/11, see, e.g., 65–66, 72–75, 100–102. A world in which parents bury their offspring similarly haunts Yasmina Khadra's *The Attack*, trans. John Cullen (New York: Doubleday, 2005), in which an Arab Israeli doctor tries to understand what brought his wife to blow herself up and kill nineteen people, eleven of them schoolchildren celebrating a birthday party (17–18). In the course of his quest, he will find out that the motive for this act was his wife's wish to bring about a homeland for Palestinian children: "No child is completely safe," she writes to her husband in her farewell note, "if it has no country" (69). Unsurprisingly, the dread of lost children also haunts recent Israeli fiction, such as A. B. Yehoshua's *A Woman in Jerusalem*, in which the

ageless Yulia Ragayev, who has been killed in a suicide bombing, is brought back to her mother in Russia so she can bid her daughter farewell. A. B. Yehoshua, *A Woman in Jerusalem*, trans. Hillel Halkin (Orlando, FL: Harcourt, 2006). The novel was first published as *Shlichuto shel ha-memune al mashabei enosh* [The mission of the human resource man] (Tel Aviv: Hakibbutz Hameuchad/Siman Kriah, 2004). Shifra Horn's *Ode to Joy* likewise follows a young mother in the Jerusalem of 2002 as she tries to find out who the little blonde girl was whom she saw in the back window of a bus shortly before it was blown to pieces by a suicide bomber. Shifra Horn, *Ode to Joy*, trans. Anthony Berris (London: Piatkus, 2005). The novel was first published as *Himnon la-simcha* (Tel Aviv: Am Oved, 2004).

10. For an overview of apocalyptic fiction, see W. Warren Wagar's classic study *Terminal Visions: The Literature of Last Things* (Bloomington: Indiana University Press, 1982).

11. Paul Brians, *Nuclear Holocausts: Atomic War in Fiction* (Kent, OH: Kent State University Press, 1987).

12. Brian Aldiss, *Billion Year Spree: The True History of Science Fiction* (Garden City, NY: Doubleday, 1973).

13. Alexander Kluge, *The Devil's Blind Spot: Tales from a New Century*, trans. Martin Chalmers and Michael Hulse (New York: New Directions, 2004), vii.

14. Martin Amis, "Terrorism's New Structure," *Wall Street Journal*, August 16, 2008, http://online.wsj.com/article/SB121883817312745575.html (accessed August 25, 2010).

15. "'Ich darf nicht schwach werden'" (interview with Haruki Murakami), *Focus* 43 (2010), http://www.focus.de/kultur/buecher/haruki-murakami-ich-darf-nicht-schwach-werden_aid_565426.html (accessed November 29, 2010).

16. Slavoj Žižek, *In Defense of Lost Causes* (London: Verso, 2008). See, for example, Žižek's claim that his book is "committed" to the "Messianic" "standpoint of the struggle for universal emancipation" (6). This "standpoint" includes, for example, revisiting Stalinism (211–63) and suggesting that the Stalinist terror of the 1930s was "a humanist terror," since it adhered to a "'humanist' core" (214). On the presumably pending end of global capitalism, see Slavoj Žižek, *Living in the End of Times* (London: Verso, 2010).

17. Niall Ferguson, *The War of the World: Twentieth-Century Conflict and the Descent of the West* (New London: Penguin, 2006), xxxiii–xxxiv.

18. Steven Weber, "Counterfactuals, Past and Future," in *Counterfactual Thought Experiments in World Politics: Logical, Methodological, and Psychological Perspectives*, ed. Philip E. Tetlock and Aaron Belkin (Princeton, NJ: Princeton University Press, 1996), 287, 279.

19. Paul Auster, *Oracle Night* (New York: Picador, 2004). Page references to this work will be given parenthetically in the text. The novel was first published in 2003 by Henry Holt and Company.

20. Auster lets Sydney Orr state in a footnote that while Ed Victory is a "fictional character" (112), the story about the mother and her dead child is based on fact. I take this to be a clear indication that the novel does not simply cannibalize history for the sake of indulging in exhilarating horror but rather seeks to

find in the past a resource to help Orr deal with the present condition—with a reality in which many became targets of blind political terror during the attacks of 9/11, a reality that hints at what might still come. It is interesting to note that besides the dead children mentioned above, the killer of Orr's unborn child, Jacob Trause—the drug-addicted son of Orr's writer friend, John—will be killed himself by drug dealers (242). He will never get to bring his own offspring into the world. Indeed, *Oracle Night*'s central metaphor is that of dead children.

21. Blanchot writes, "'A child is being killed.' Let us make no mistake about this present: it signifies that the deed cannot be done once and for all, that the operation is completed at no privileged moment in time—that, inoperable, it operates and that thus it tends to be none but the very time which destroys (effaces) time." Maurice Blanchot, *The Writing of the Disaster*, new ed., trans. Ann Smock (Lincoln: University of Nebraska Press, 1995), 71.

22. In his "Random Notes—September 11, 2001–4:00 PM," Auster displays the same dark aura that haunts *Oracle Night*. He ends these notes, which were written in the immediate aftermath of the attacks, stating, "And so the twenty-first century finally begins."

23. Giorgio Agamben, *Homo Sacer: Sovereign Power and Bare Life*, trans. Daniel Heller-Roazen (Stanford, CA: Stanford University Press, 1998), 8–9. On Agamben's reading of Arendt's *Human Condition*, see 3–4.

24. Agamben, *Homo Sacer*, 90.

25. See Giorgio Agamben, *Remnants of Auschwitz: The Witness and the Archive*, trans. Daniel Heller-Roazen (New York: Zone Books, 1999), 41–86. In *Homo Sacer*, Agamben states, "If today there is no longer any one clear figure of the sacred man, it is perhaps because we are all virtually *homines sacri*" (115).

26. Leland de la Durantaye, *Giorgio Agamben: A Critical Introduction* (Stanford, CA: Stanford University Press, 2009), 211.

27. Similarly, some apocalyptic scenarios, such as Alan Weisman's *The World without Us* (New York: Thomas Dunne Books/St. Martin's Press, 2007) and Francis Lawrence's film *I Am Legend*, focus on modernity's all-consuming, environmentally devastating practices.

28. Kluge, *Devil's Blind Spot*, 20.

29. Katharina Hacker, *Die Habenichtse* (Frankfurt am Main: Suhrkamp, 2006), 50.

30. Jonathan Safran Foer, *Extremely Loud and Incredibly Close* (Boston: Houghton Mifflin, 2005), 187–89.

31. Ibid., 230–33.

32. As Todd Presner has shown, Arendt's idiom refers to the indiscriminate, senseless killing of an entire population with the means of modern technology during the Holocaust. Todd Samuel Presner, "'The Fabrication of Corpses': Heidegger, Arendt, and the Modernity of Mass Death," *Telos* 135 (Summer 2006): 84–108.

33. Cormac McCarthy, *The Road* (New York: Random House, 2006), 28, 117. Hereafter, page references to this work will be given parenthetically in the text.

34. On the possibility that a holy war was the cause of the disaster, see William Kennedy's review, "Left Behind," *New York Times*, October 8, 2006. On

The Road in the context of the literary reflection on 9/11, see James Wood, "Getting to the End," review of Cormac McCarthy, *The Road, New Republic,* May 17, 2007, http://www.powells.com/review/2007_05_17.html (accessed August 26, 2010).

35. Naturally, the pervasive discussion between the father and his son about the good and the bad should be read in the broader context of McCarthy's interest in the question of evil. Central to any detailed evaluation of *The Road,* evil is only peripheral to my perspective on the novel. On McCarthy's notion of evil, see William C. Spencer, "Cormac McCarthy's Unholy Trinity: Biblical Parody in *Outer Dark,*" in *Sacred Violence: A Reader's Companion to Cormac McCarthy,* ed. Wade Hall and Rick Wallach (El Paso: University of Texas Press, 1995), 69–76.

36. In his review of *The Road,* Michael Chabon suggests that the fragmented structure and splintered sentences of the novel remain, in spite of the utter destruction they allude to, "an affirmation." See Michael Chabon, "After the Apocalypse," a review of Cormac McCarthy's *The Road, New York Review of Books* 54, no. 2 (February 15, 2007), http://www.nybooks.com/articles/19856 (accessed August 26, 2010).

37. Rorty, "Grandeur, Profundity, and Finitude," 84.

38. Michael Oakeshott, *On History and Other Essays* (Indianapolis: Liberty Fund, 1999), 40.

39. In her discussion of *The Road* in the context of contemporary literature's turn to religious authority "as a renewable resource for literature," Amy Hungerford reads the novel's last paragraph as indicating that it is not "the light" carried by the son and the father but rather "the words" that "hold out hope— that put the speckled trout back into the river and the river back into the valley and make things right again even as the words say these things cannot be done." Amy Hungerford, *Postmodern Belief: American Literature and Religion since 1960* (Princeton, NJ: Princeton University Press, 2010), 136. I agree with Hungerford, yet wish to stress the temporal dimension of these words: how they tie— from the perspective of an imagined *possible* future—our factual past, present, and ominous future together.

40. Updike, *Terrorist,* 299. Hereafter, page references to this work will be given parenthetically in the text.

41. See Auster, *Oracle Night,* 112n8, in which the writer, Orr, or the author, Auster, reassures the reader of the facticity of the Warsaw telephone book and of the Dachau story that Ed Victory tells. For Arendt's discussion of Kafka's parable "HE," see her *Between Past and Future: Eight Exercises in Political Thought* (New York: Penguin, 1977), 7–14.

42. Ian McEwan, "The Day of Judgment," *Guardian,* May 31, 2008, http://www.guardian.co.uk/books/2008/may/31/fiction.philosophy (accessed December 3, 2010).

CODA

1. Primo Levi, *Die Untergegangenen und die Geretteten,* trans. Moshe Kahn (Munich: Hanser, 1990), 205. The English translation appears in *The Drowned*

and the Saved, trans. Raymond Rosenthal (New York: Random House, 1988), 199.

2. Peter Eisenman, "How Long Does One Feel Guilty?" (interview with *Der Spiegel*), http://www.spiegel.de/international/0,1518,355252,00.html (accessed August 26, 2010).

3. Giorgio Agamben, for example, noted that the visitors walking their own pathways between the stones "enter a different dimension of remembrance," that each visitor to the site "flips through the pages of a different book." Giorgio Agamben, "Die zwei Gedaechtnisse," *Die Zeit*, no. 19 (May 4, 2005), http://www.zeit.de/2005/19/Mahnmal_2f_Agamben (accessed August 26, 2010).

4. Peter Eisenman, "Memorial to the Murdered Jews of Europe," in *Barfuß auf weiß glühenden Mauern*, ed. Peter Noever (Ostfildern-Ruit: Hatje Cantz, 2004), 159.

5. On the dissensus generated by the proposal to create the Berlin memorial, see Ute Heimrod, Günter Schlusche, and Horst Seferens, eds., *Der Denkmalstreit—das Denkmal? Die Debatte um das "Denkmal für die ermordeten Juden Europas": Eine Dokumentation* (Berlin: Philo Verlagsgesellschaft, 1999). On the controversy over the Wehrmacht crimes exhibition, see Hamburger Institut für Sozialforschung, ed., *Eine Ausstellung und ihre Folgen: Zur Rezeption der Ausstellung Vernichtungskrieg; Verbrechen der Wehrmacht 1941 bis 1944* (Hamburg: Hamburger Edition, 1999). A lucid overview of the major debates regarding the future of "the German past" is offered by Bill Niven in *Facing the Nazi Past: United Germany and the Legacy of the Third Reich* (London: Routledge, 2002).

6. I am indebted for the details regarding this original project, *Archival Photographs*, to Yigal Shtayim and an e-mail to me dated August 19, 2008.

7. On the intricate circumstances surrounding the departure of most of Haifa's Palestinian population, see the detailed, nuanced account in Yfaat Weiss, *Wadi Salib: Hanocheach veha'nifkad* (*Wadi Salib: A Confiscated Memory*) (Jerusalem: Van Leer Jerusalem Institute and Hakibbutz Hameuchad, 2007).

8. Daniella Talmor, "Painting in the New Millennium," in *Focus on Painting*, ed. Daniella Talmor (Haifa: Haifa Museum of Art, 2002), 155. Published in conjunction with the exhibition *Focus on Painting* shown at the Haifa Museum of Art in 2002.

9. Grossman, *Writing in the Dark*, 64.

10. Ibid., 63.

11. I quote here from Hannah Arendt's "Introduction: Walter Benjamin: 1892–1940," in Walter Benjamin, *Illuminations*, trans. Harry Zohn (New York: Schocken Books, 1969), 4–5.

12. Ibid., 5.

13. Ibid.

14. Alexander Kluge and Joseph Vogl, *Soll und Haben: Fernsehgespräche* (Zurich: Diaphanes, 2009), 7–21. Hereafter, page references to this work will be given parenthetically in the text. The translations are mine.

15. Oakeshott, *On History and Other Essays*, 40.

16. Walter Benjamin, "On the Concept of History," in *Selected Writings*, vol. 4, *1938–1940*, ed. Howard Eiland and Michael W. Jennings, trans. Harry

Zohn (Cambridge, MA: Belknap Press of Harvard University Press, 2003), 389. Hereafter, page references to this work will be given parenthetically in the text.

17. In *The Life of the Mind*, Arendt writes, as she interprets Kafka's parable, "Man lives in this in-between, and what he calls the present is a life-long fight against the dead weight of the past, driving him forward with hope, and a fear of a future (whose only certainty is death), driving him backward toward 'the quiet of the past' with nostalgia for and remembrance of the only reality he can be sure of" (205).

18. Arendt, *Between Past and Future*, 10.

19. Ibid., 11.

20. Famously, it was Arendt who saved Benjamin's "Theses on the Philosophy of History," as she carried his manuscripts with her while escaping Europe in 1940. It was Arendt who first introduced this work, in the Benjamin collection she edited for Schocken Books, *Illuminations* (first published in 1968), to the English-speaking world. In her essay on Franz Kafka, Arendt mentions Benjamin's "angel of history," saying, "If progress is supposed to be an inevitable superhuman law which embraces all periods of history alike, in whose meshes humanity inescapably got caught, then progress indeed is best imagined and most exactly described in the following lines quoted from the last work of Walter Benjamin: 'The Angel of History'" (Arendt, *Essays in Understanding*, 74). Yet when Arendt comes close to outlining something like her own philosophy of history in *Between Past and Future* or in *The Life of the Mind*, it is Kafka's "HE" that guides her thought and not Benjamin. I am thus unsure if Arendt's thinking about past and future is "haunted" by Walter Benjamin and his angel of history as Svetlana Boym contends. I do agree with Boym, however, when she writes, quoting Arendt's *The Life of the Mind*, "Arendt questioned Benjamin's messianic and catastrophic idea of history with a capital H: 'we may reclaim our human dignity, win it back, as it were, from that pseudo-divinity named History of the modern age without denying its importance' [Arendt, *Life of the Mind*, 216]. Benjamin's 'Angel of History' turns into Arendt's angel of freedom. There is no humanoid representation of this figure, no embodiment, only a suggestive diagram with many textual folds." See Svetlana Boym, *Another Freedom: The Alternative History of an Idea* (Chicago: University of Chicago Press, 2010), 232. Boym also distinguishes between Benjamin and Arendt, claiming that "[un]like Benjamin, Arendt is not concerned with the messianic 'final judgment'" (330n97).

Index